ON THE EDGE

ON THE EDGE

LIFE ALONG THE RUSSIA-CHINA BORDER

Franck Billé and Caroline Humphrey

HARVARD UNIVERSITY PRESS
Cambridge, Massachusetts & London, England   2021

First printing

Library of Congress Cataloging-in-Publication Data

Names: Billé, Franck, author. | Humphrey, Caroline, author.
Title: On the edge : life along the Russia-China border / Franck Billé and
    Caroline Humphrey.
Description: Cambridge, Massachusetts : Harvard University Press, 2021. |
    Includes bibliographical references and index.
Identifiers: LCCN 2021017869 | ISBN 9780674979482 (cloth)
Subjects: LCSH: Borderlands—Russia (Federation) | Borderlands—China. |
    Boundaries—Anthropological aspects—Russia (Federation) | Boundaries—
    Anthropological aspects—China. | Russia (Federation)—Boundaries—China. |
    China—Boundaries—Russia (Federation)
Classification: LCC DK68.7.C6 B55 2021 | DDC 957/.7—dc23
LC record available at https://lccn.loc.gov/2021017869

To our families

CONTENTS

MAPS

NOTE ON LANGUAGE AND SPELLING

We use pinyin/simplified characters for all Chinese terms in the text, without tone marks. For Russian we follow a simplified version of the American Library Association and Library of Congress system. This system usually includes a number of diacritics as well as two-letter tie characters, such as "ĭ" and "i͡a" (for the letters "й" and "я," respectively), but for reasons of legibility we have decided to omit them. Thus "ya" is used to denote "я," and "yu" to denote "ю," while an apostrophe denotes both "ь" and "ъ."

For terms in Mongolian, Buryat, and other minority languages for which no standard system exists, we have followed the most common practices in anthropology. For the names of rivers and mountains, rarely the same in Russian and Chinese, we provide both names on first mention and then use the term that is most appropriate depending on the side of the border we discuss. Unless specified, all translations are our own.

Map 1. The border region

For thousands of miles, Russia and China are hard up against each other, on either side of a border that consists mainly of rivers. This long meandering borderline with Mongolia at one end and North Korea at the other, the location for our book, reveals much about the two countries and their actual relationship that is not obvious from their metropolitan capitals. Unlike the geopolitical setting of most historical empires and current world powers, such as the United States or the European Union, here there is no buffer zone, no intervening territory of client or hybrid states, and no ocean to soften the sovereign conjunction of Russia and China.

The economist Branko Milanovic has observed that capitalism comes in two variants: a democratic "liberal" form and a "political" or authoritarian one that encompasses both China and Russia.[1] This is a helpful broad framework, but our book questions the validity of the "political capitalism" category. Russia and China are utterly different from each other in the way systems are organized and things are done. This is not just a political matter, with the Chinese single-party-ruled, well-oiled bureaucratic system contrasting starkly with the personalized, irregular, and fitful way power operates in Russia. These two countries are unlike "all the way down" and to their very peripheries. Indeed, without wishing to venture into historical teleology, we suggest that it is no accident that China and Russia have come up with variants of the politics of capitalism that are poles apart. It is such "civilizational differences" (an idea that is current in both countries) that make the long border shared by the two countries in northeast Asia so interesting.

The world has been somewhat taken by surprise by the ways in which Russia and China have developed since the demise of Soviet socialism in 1991. Instead of a homogenous, default-mode capitalism, we find two contrasting, competing, yet to some extent mutually interdependent economic models in which the state and hierarchical structures are deeply involved. The interpretation of national interest in China radically diverges from the path adopted in Russia, and both are strange, even mystifying, in a Western political context. The interior organization of these two societies is also difficult to understand. One reason for this is that both governments are highly active in information management— from hopeful projections of the future through manipulation of the media to plain disinformation. This makes the facts on the ground difficult to discern, and not only for observers in the West. It also means that Moscow and Beijing can maintain their own skewed or paranoid ideas about what goes on in their own peripheries. Furthermore, it obscures each country to the other, and gives a never-never-land quality to their joint communiqués. The aim of this book, based on recent firsthand field research along the border, is to penetrate these gaps in understanding. We describe what is actually happening, record real-life events, and explain the experience of citizens of Russia and China as they deal with both the policy injunctions from above and their encounters with one another.

The last two decades have seen dramatic transformations in China, in directions that have not always been consonant with the changes occurring in Russia and that frequently have been starkly at odds with them. From the early 1990s, when the border with Russia reopened after decades of hostility, China showed much eagerness to expand beyond its borders and to trade—but to trade worldwide, not only with Russia. China is now putting every effort into increasing domestic consumption, private sector innovation, investment in emerging technologies, and infrastructure projects linked with global markets, all as a means of progressing beyond its earlier unbalanced cheap labor economy. In this context Siberia's empty spaces have suddenly acquired new value, not only for their resources of oil and gas but also for their potential incorporation into China's economic orbit to supply other essentials such as water and agricultural products that China will need. Yet Russia as a country appears to China as an unreliable partner with a too rigid and centralized economy, too dependent on its role as global energy provider.

These tectonic shifts have suddenly placed in the spotlight the region of northeast Asia, where the two giants share one of the world's longest international borders.[2] Yet surprisingly, in spite of its strategic significance, the Russia-China border remains one of the least studied borders in the world. Informed by a multi-disciplinary and multi-sited research project running at the University of Cambridge between 2012 and 2015 and by our own research in the region, *On the Edge* focuses on this zone of interaction as a way to supplement, as well as challenge, international-relations studies that have traditionally privileged top-down centrist views.[3] As a number of analysts have remarked, Russia and China can act as each other's buffer against the geopolitical might of America. However, their border, more than 2,600 miles long, has become a thin line of direct engagement, extraordinary contrast, and frequent tension. By looking at what is happening on the ground, this book suggests that the changes occurring in the region are harbingers of larger trends. The border, where people are embedded in dissimilar social systems on either side and mostly cannot speak each other's language, is where conflicting versions of history and attitudes to the future become starkly visible. Since each state exercises full sovereignty right up to their mutual border, there is no better place to compare the two remarkably dissimilar ways that economic development, the rule of law, citizens' rights, migration, and inequality are managed. As border scholar

Alessandro Rippa writes, "The borderlands are a particularly compelling place from which to observe the state. As junctures and points of friction, borderlands offer a particular perspective on the complexities of contemporary global development—one that arrives not from the centers nor necessarily from below, but rather from multiple edges and corners."[4]

For almost all of its length the northeastern border consists of great rivers: the Argun, the Amur, and the Ussuri. Yet, despite the distance spanned and the fact that large cities lie right on the banks, it is telling that at the time of writing there is no functioning road or rail bridge to connect the two countries. One of the stories we tell in this book is about the phantom bridges—projects planned, announced, and started countless times and yet to date not put into practical effect. We explore the complex mix of competing businesspeople, bureaucrats, and security agencies, who at times act in ways that seem to belie the repeated glowing announcements of thriving cross-border partnership. In addition, China's border with Russia lacks the huge wholesale bazaars and the vast, often illegal, commerce that one finds at its borders with Central Asia and Southeast Asia.[5] Without the presence of prosperous trader groups sympathetic to China or important mediator communities (such as the Chinese-speaking Dungans in the case of Kazakhstan), the chances of cultural misunderstandings are greater.[6] As a result, there is more of a break at the China-Russia border, with few dual-loyalty intermediaries and a relative absence of thriving economic cross-border activity on the ground.

All of this might seem to imply that the two peoples are turning their backs on each other. But there have to be interactions at the border. We argue that these are important and can tell us much about how the situation is changing in ways that are not (yet) perceptible in macro analyses. Many Russian and Chinese citizens are happy to develop relationships with one another. Local initiatives have encouraged Chinese investment in the Russian hinterland, whatever Moscow might say. And there are marriages, friendships, sexual encounters, small joint businesses, underground deals, and smuggling networks. As we describe in Chapter 3, some of the indigenous peoples of the borderlands (but not all) eagerly seek to "revive" supposed historical cross-border social groupings that are spread through northeast China, Mongolia, and south Siberia, and they organize religious events and popular festivals with tens of thousands of attendees. None of these interactions are straightforward. There is an added edge to these encounters that our book seeks to elucidate.

In writing the book we have drawn gratefully on recent studies of China's contemporary borderlands. These include perceptive travel accounts, monographs, and edited collections dealing with particular themes.[7] Among the latter, there are studies focusing on nationalism and its varieties in the region, the "agonistic intimacies" brought about by "neighboring" across borders, the intricacies of "border work" and the ways in which actors make borders "work" for them, trust and mistrust in cross-border trade and business relations, sovereignty and the territorial imagination, gender and identity, migrations and diasporas, and political loyalty and disloyalty.[8] In this book, however, rather than focus on a particular theme, we want to present a general picture of many interrelated phenomena. Although we are anthropologists, we do not intend to propose or defend an anthropological theory, or to see diverse material through the lens of a single encompassing idea, such as "neighboring" or "border work"—even though both of these are multifaceted and productive concepts. Instead, this book has a more straightforward descriptive aim, mainly based on field research carried out in person and in collaboration with colleagues.

These lived realities of the border tend to be obscured in official accounts and are in fact palpable only at the border, through extended investigations in the field spearheaded by researchers native to the region. These experiences are crucial if we are to understand the attitudes of the local populations, sentiments that in the end are likely to shape the trajectories of their respective countries, given that the "big picture" is actually made up of myriad local initiatives and the incremental results of decisions by ordinary people. These micro effects will to a great extent determine the future of the region. It is because these are not straightforward but rather involve different values (such as "face" and "honor"), each side's political scare stories, the pervasive agency of social media, dissimilar views of gender and family, and abiding cultural ways of doing things that there is a need for an account of actual practices on the ground. Here anthropology can play a crucial role in bringing to light internal structures and incipient trends that have not yet percolated into large-scale analyses.

THE GEOPOLITICAL CONTEXT

As we enter the second decade of the twentieth century, relations between Russia and China are the strongest they have been for a very long time, and China has become one of Russia's most important economic partners. Up 27.1 percent from the previous year, the value of trade between them reached $107 billion in 2018, and the two countries hope to double that number over the next five years, to $200 billion by 2024, by implementing joint projects in energy, industry, and agriculture. Chinese president Xi Jinping and Russian president Vladimir Putin reportedly enjoy excellent personal relations, with Xi even calling Putin his "best friend" during a state visit to Russia in 2019. With around thirty visits over six years, Russia has indeed been the state most visited by the Chinese president, and the two leaders are committed to developing a strategic cooperation and comprehensive partnership, as well as to strengthening global strategic stability.

This current state of affairs is, however, largely uncharacteristic of the relations between the two countries over the modern period. Save a brief interlude of warmth in the 1950s when, having adopted a socialist government in 1949, China modeled itself politically and culturally after the Soviet Union, relations between the two countries have been tense, if not downright bellicose.[9] Following Stalin's death in 1953, Khrushchev's de-Stalinization political reforms led to an ideological rift between the two countries. The Chinese accused the Soviet Union of emasculating, betraying, and revising Marxism-Leninism, while Khrushchev reviled Mao Zedong as an ultra-leftist, an ultra-dogmatist, and a left revisionist. With this ideological rift, lingering resentment about territorial disputes reemerged. The Chinese labeled the Soviet Union an imperialist power, just like the old Russian Empire that in the mid-nineteenth century had seized more than 580,000 square miles of Chinese territory through unequal treaties. Unwilling to give up land or compromise, the Soviet government denied that the treaties signed between the two countries were unequal, and all subsequent negotiations on border issues proved unproductive. Memories of traumatic events, such as the massacre of 5,000 Chinese citizens in Blagoveshchensk at the turn of the twentieth century, discussed in Chapter 5, also reemerged.[10]

The years 1964–1968, characterized by border skirmishes and military reinforcements on both sides, reached a climactic point on March 2, 1969, when Chinese troops ambushed Soviet border guards on Damansky Island (Ch: Zhenbao Island), a marshy islet of just 0.29 square miles in the Ussuri River.[11] Over the next few months, both sides suffered losses, and the battle threatened to erupt into a more generalized conflict between the two countries.[12] An informal meeting between Soviet premier Aleksei Kosygin and Chinese leader Zhou Enlai in September 1969 and their agreement to solve border problems through peaceful negotiations led to the end of the military confrontation, but relations between the two countries remained frosty.[13] Other islands subject to dual claims have also been points of extraordinary tension, way beyond the practical significance of these waterlogged patches of ground; in Chapter 2 we focus on the curious fate of another such island, Bolshoi Ussuriiskii/Heixiazi in the Amur River.

The border remained closed until the late 1980s, and only since the collapse of the Soviet Union have more cordial relations resumed.[14] The reopening of the border at a few crossing points led to an intense flurry of commercial activity—new market opportunities for the Chinese, and the chance for Russians to purchase items that were not, or were no longer, locally available. With bilateral relations continuing to improve—and relations with the United States continuing to deteriorate—in 2008 Russia announced a "pivot to the East" (*povorot na vostok*), the focus of which has essentially been China.

Of course, geography plays a significant role in this partnership, in that it is crucial to have good relations with a neighbor with whom you share a long border.[15] Russia's abundant natural resources, notably in natural gas, oil, and timber, and China's rapid economic development have ensured that the relationship is mutually beneficial. In the Arctic, Chinese investment has been essential to extract natural resources under the permafrost and monetize Russia's long Arctic coast.[16] China, in turn, needs Russia's cooperation if it is to gain a foothold in a fast-thawing natural environment and open up a new sea passage—what Beijing refers to as the "Polar Silk Road." With climate change, drought in parts of China, and restive millions still remaining in rural hinterlands, the empty swaths of the Russian Far East that are now becoming suitable for agriculture look, in principle, like an ever more inviting prospect, as we discuss in Chapter 3.[17]

However, this strategic partnership must also be seen in a global context of increasing friction with the West, especially after the sanctions imposed following Russia's annexation of Crimea in 2014 and the United States' current trade war with China. In many ways it is the very tension with the United States and the European Union that is bringing the two countries together.[18] Brought together through what Gilbert Rozman has called "parallel identities," Russia and China embrace the vision of a multipolar world free of American meddling.[19] It is by combining forces that China and Russia can outcompete the West and counter America's political and cultural dominance.[20] Their relations have therefore been largely contingent on a broader international context, a phenomenon historian Sergei Radchenko traces back to a much earlier period. The Sino-Soviet rapprochement of the early 1980s after two decades of hostility was, he writes, greatly aided by the fears and hopes both countries had for their relations with Washington.[21] In fact, Russia's foreign policy toward Asia has traditionally been subordinate to Western dynamics, with the country turning to Asia whenever it was stonewalled or stalemated in Europe.[22] These analyses are largely supported by our research at the border, where official statements of friendship and collaboration, while symbolically important, are rarely accompanied by genuine popular engagement.[23]

Russia and China's pragmatic approach has prompted foreign policy analyst Bobo Lo to call the partnership a "marriage of convenience," unlikely to survive tensions and divergences inherent in the relationship.[24] In a more recent publication, political scientist Yu Bin writes that bilateral ties are not as solid as officially articulated and that too many sociological and psychological hurdles remain for a genuine and healthy strategic partnership to flourish.[25] Even professor of international affairs Alexander Lukin, who is generally dismissive of the "marriage of convenience" analysis, concedes that Russians and Chinese know surprisingly little about each other, and the knowledge they do have tends to be filtered through imported negative Western biases.[26]

This is complicated by an inherent imbalance between the two partners. If for Russia, China is at the very top of the foreign policy agenda, for China, Russia is just one of many aspects of its foreign policy.[27] The population of China is roughly ten times that of Russia and continues to increase, whereas Russia faces a natural demographic decline (particularly marked in Siberia and the Far East) that is compensated for only by in-migration.[28] The disparity in wealth and trade between the two countries is also widening. In 2018, Russia's trade with China—both imports and exports—was greater than its trade with any other state; by contrast, Russia accounted for a tiny 1.9 percent of China's overall exports.[29] If *The Economist*'s comparison of the relationship to that of a rabbit and a boa constrictor is a bit of an exaggeration, Russia is nonetheless clearly the "weaker partner that needs China more than the other way around."[30] Optimistically, Alexander Lukin writes that Russia continues to outstrip China in terms of military might and that it is premature to "speak of China's overall superiority or of any broad asymmetry," but the economic disparities are certain to eventually chip away at Russia's remaining military and technological advantages, especially when one considers China's proficiency at reverse-engineering foreign products.[31]

Similarly, Russia's capacity to leverage its vast natural gas reserves (amounting to around a quarter of the world's proven reserves) will be limited in relation to China. Although Russia has been able to wield considerable power and influence as a dominant supplier of piped gas—notably in Central and Eastern Europe, the Caucasus, and Central Asia—a well-diversified importer such as China can be in a position of strength and play the politics of demand for gas even vis-à-vis a sizable exporting state such as Russia.[32] It is thus increasingly clear, political scientist Agnia Grigas writes, that "Beijing, not Moscow, will dictate the terms of the emerging Sino-Russian gas relationship."[33] As we discuss in Chapter 1, these issues are compounded by a wholly inadequate transport infrastructure, which prevents Russia from capitalizing on economic opportunities, particularly with its Asian partners. The dense railway and road network, including high-speed lines, that exists in the northeast of China is lacking in the Russian Far East, where there are only a few overburdened routes and more than 46,000 settlements are not connected to the broader transport system. Russia is therefore finding it challenging, if not impossible, to position its Far Eastern region as a logistics hub that will facilitate closer links to Asia and Europe.[34]

These geopolitical shifts are particularly evident in Central Asia, traditionally considered Russia's backyard, or "near abroad" (*blizhnee zarubezh'e*). This term, professor of government and international affairs Gerard Toal explains, simultaneously indexes a new arrangement of sovereignty and an old familiarity, a long-standing spatial entanglement, and a range of geopolitical emotions. It does not merely, as many in the West assume, indicate reluctance on the part of Russia to acknowledge the full sovereignty of the new post-Soviet states.[35] Central Asia is therefore a region where China treads carefully, while continuously extending its economic interests. Former Chinese ambassador to Russia Li Fenglin, addressing Russian concerns about China's growing role there, stated ambiguously that China had no intention of becoming a leader at either the regional or global level—at least for the immediate future: "China understands Russia's desire to preserve its traditional influence in Central Asia. . . . Central Asia is like Russia's backyard. . . . We understand that, but you have to take care of your backyard, water the flowers, so that it does not become overgrown with weeds."[36] Some changes in the dynamic have already been seen with Chinese investments in the China–Central Asia Gas Pipeline, which for the first time broke the effective control that Russian giant Gazprom enjoyed over export routes. Until 1990, professor in international relations Daniel Markey writes, Central Asia's energy pipelines (as well as transportation and communications networks) all ran to and through Russia, giving Moscow an overwhelming advantage in its negotiations with former Central Asian republics.[37] That looks set to change. China's place in the region is undeniably growing, and this role will increasingly spill beyond the purely economic.[38]

The same is true of the two countries at either end of the border. Mongolia, whose imbalanced economy based on herding and mining has been faltering, is now increasingly propped up by its economic dependence on China. Meanwhile, Russia's influence in North Korea is declining. Embroiled in confrontations with the West, Russia can no longer play an effective mediator role in North Korea's relations with the world and is unwilling to subsidize its economy.[39] Even if it is not directly evident at the border we studied, this growing competition over influence in Central Asia, Mongolia, North Korea, and the Arctic is a momentous development.[40] It offers a larger backdrop for the growing disparities between the two countries and the attendant geopolitical shift in the balance of power. The economic and demographic disparities have made collaborative development of the Russian Far East difficult. Thirty-eight million Chinese live in Heilongjiang province, which abuts the Russian border. By contrast, the entire Russian Far East region, an enormous landmass encompassing 2.3 million square miles—slightly over a third of the entire territory of the Russian Federation—has only 6 million residents. This demographic imbalance between China and Russia and their starkly divergent economic trajectories are exacerbated by China's hunger for natural resources such as timber, gas, minerals, water, and animal products—all found in significant quantities in the Russian Far East. Eager to trade, Russia is nonetheless anxious about becoming China's "natural resources appendage" and wary about becoming dependent on Chinese payment systems.[41] It is even more concerned about mass in-migration. These anxieties manifest themselves through the bottlenecks in the border-crossing infrastructure (notably a persistent absence of bridges across the river boundaries, as we discuss in Chapter 1, as well as the interdiction on crossing the border in personal vehicles). Russia's restrictive foreign migrant labor quota system has resulted in the majority of guest workers in the Russian Far East being ex-Soviets from Central Asia rather than people from the neighboring provinces of China, and in a comparative dearth of genuine collaborations overall.[42] Scholars agree that the partnership between Russia and China is dominated by lost opportunities—an analysis largely supported by our own research.[43] Furthermore, while the Kremlin may have a clear vision of Russia's close future relations with China, this vision is not shared throughout

Russian society. Indeed, as Viktor Larin, a leading Russian expert on China, has argued, "the lower you go, the worse it gets."[44]

As we discuss in Chapter 7, Russia has found it difficult to reconcile itself with the fact that it is being increasingly sidelined on the global chessboard, outranked status-wise by China. As China continues to grow, Daniel Markey writes, it threatens to leave Russia at the margins of international decision-making—an especially frightening prospect for a country like Russia, eager to assert its status on the world stage.[45] These anxieties are further fueled by unresolved historical issues, notably the unequal treaties signed by China with tsarist Russia in 1858–1860 and the enduring Chinese resentment at having thereby lost large swaths of territory. These territorial histories, compounded by the huge demographic disparities, create a climate of suspicion in Russia, where the presence of Chinese individuals is often interpreted as an attempt to colonize the vast and sparsely populated Russian Far East. The very term "Chinatown," for instance, evokes anxieties of ethnic, cultural, and geographical intrusions.[46] As political scientists Harvey Balzer and Maria Repnikova note, "Russians' preoccupation with an impending Chinese influx derives from a deeply held belief that demographic imbalance generates migration." And yet, in spite of a very long border, Russia has received less than 3 percent of post-1978 Chinese migration. Indeed, Chinese migrants prefer to go to other Asian countries, such as Singapore, where they can earn multiples of what they would earn in Russia. When they do go to Russia, they predominantly settle in the cities to the west rather than in the Far Eastern regions.[47] The media stories that depict the Chinese as migrants eager to move to the rich and underpopulated Russian Far East are thus not reflected on the ground. Not only is the number of Chinese residents in the region nowhere near the alarmist levels mentioned in the Russian media (there are in fact more Russian citizens living in China than the other way around), but as we describe in Chapter 3, the Chinese who do work in the Russian

Far East are there predominantly for short stints before returning home. They see the region's unforgiving climate and the challenging economic and political environment as reasons not to make it a permanent home—echoing, in fact, many of the local Russian population's own concerns.

Russian anxieties are in any case not assuaged by China's current geopolitical assertiveness, particularly its expansion in the South China Sea with the creation of artificial islands.[48] Such extensions of sovereign rights are frequently about access to resources rather than about extensions of sovereign territory, but the boldness of the moves made by China in the South China Sea, in Hong Kong, and at its borders with India stokes suspicions that it may one day seek to assert dominance over long-lost territories such as a large part of the Russian Far East.[49] Ultimately, international relations expert Marcin Kaczmarski argues, China and Russia understand regionalism differently and have divergent views about international cooperation at the regional level: "China defines regionalism in functional rather than territorial terms and sees its project as an inclusive one. . . . Russia, by contrast, interprets regionalism in spatial and historical terms, seeing it primarily as a way to maintain its influence in the post-Soviet space and as a barrier to the exercise of influence by other actors."[50]

In the last decade, China has embarked on a gigantic and unprecedented infrastructural project seeking to place itself at the center of a global trade network. The Belt and Road Initiative (BRI) was announced to the world in September 2013 in a speech by Xi Jinping.[51] A project stretching across more than sixty countries and incorporating almost two-thirds of the world's population, the BRI has taken the historical Silk Road "as a metaphor for regional trade networks, cultures of diplomacy, and the harmonious relations that come from the free movement of ideas, people, technologies, and goods."[52] Focusing on connectivity and movement, the BRI is notably amorphous.[53] Its spatial and temporal boundaries are unclear and its objectives vague—a flexibility that has allowed China to situate virtually any project within its remit. At the heart of the BRI is the concept of rejuvenation and renewal—overcoming a "century of humiliation" and placing China once again at the center of the universe.[54] If, as sociologist Tim Winter notes, signed contracts do not necessarily lead to finalized projects given that the BRI covers harsh landscapes where political and economic conditions can change rapidly, the force of the narrative lies in proposing a new geocultural imaginary beyond the concept of the nation-state.[55] The amorphousness and elasticity are precisely the point: China envisages the BRI as open and inclusive, a malleable network with unspecified borders.[56]

Russia, by contrast, aims to create an exclusionary space with clear boundaries, framed by a Soviet geopolitical imaginary with Russia at the center. Russia's Eurasian Economic Union (EAEU), the landmark project of the Putin administration, was launched in 2010 as a customs union between Russia, Kazakhstan, and Belarus, with Armenia and Kyrgyzstan acceding in January and August 2015.[57] While not as ambitious as China's BRI, the EAEU is still a trade bloc with significant clout: it has an integrated single market of 180 million people and a GDP of over $5 trillion. The goal is to develop the EAEU into a powerful supranational union of sovereign states, uniting economies, legal systems, customs services, and military capabilities in order to form an entity to balance the European Union and the United States.[58] Putin has further stated that his aim is to enlarge the customs union to all post-Soviet states, excluding the three Baltic EU member states, prompting former US secretary of state Hillary Clinton to describe the EAEU as a move to re-Sovietize the region.

These ambitions do indeed appear to be motivated by a desire to reestablish Russia's standing as a world leader following the collapse of the Soviet Union, which Putin famously described as the "greatest geopolitical catastrophe of the century."[59] Attempts to resurrect a defunct geopolitical entity on an old-school political imaginary of containment and border nationalism have not helped Russia in Asia, however. As professor of law and politics Sergei

Radchenko writes, in order to truly become a Eurasian power, Russia should focus instead on opening borders, on removing barriers to the flow of goods, capital, and people, and on encouraging cross-border communities that would "tie Russia to this region linguistically and culturally in ways that would support the notion of an Asian identity." For all intents and purposes, he concludes, Russia has been left on the sidelines of the "Pacific century."[60] Because of its insistence on border control, even to the detriment of a more flourishing economic climate (discussed in Chapter 3), Russia has also failed to fully benefit from China's BRI project.[61] Russia's eagerness to trade with China, tempered as it is by anxieties regarding an influx of Chinese migrants, has led to the feeling in Russia that it has been left in the cold, and to the sentiment in China that Russia is a difficult country to do business with.[62]

Paradoxically, the very ambitions of the BRI to establish connections have also created pockets of remoteness. Roads and corridors do not always annihilate distance—they create nodes of legibility and state presence, but in the process they also increase the remoteness and illegibility of border areas outside their immediate scope. As new hubs are created, facilitating the collection of customs taxes and centralizing logistics, they bypass local economies and border trading posts.[63] In the rugged Pamir Mountains of Tajikistan, anthropologists Martin Saxer and Ruben Andersson write, "newly disconnected communities tend to the scraps left behind by the Soviet regime, while China's new Silk Road is roaring past only miles away."[64] Even large cities such as Tashkent are fearful of becoming just a conduit for Chinese products transported to European markets, with little local capture.[65]

China's growing influence is felt and discussed well beyond the borders of the People's Republic of China. In places that have a long and complex history of imperial relations with China, such as the Hunza Valley, in the autonomous Gilgit-Baltistan region of Pakistan, the PRC's renewed engagement in development and infrastructural investments evokes not just promises and expectations but also doubts and fears.[66] These anxieties are shared with most of China's neighbors: recipients of BRI projects, both near to and far from China, have concerns about mounting debts to Beijing and erosion of sovereignty.[67] The example of Sri Lanka, which, owing more than $8 billion to state-controlled Chinese firms and unable to repay the loans, was recently constrained to hand over its port of Hambantota to China on a ninety-nine-year lease, has sounded alarm bells for other recipients of Chinese investments. China's global investment and lending program can amount to a debt trap for vulnerable countries around the world, simultaneously fostering a climate of corruption and autocratic behavior in struggling democracies.[68] For Kazakhstan and Mongolia, neighboring China but traditionally in the Soviet/Russian orbit, suspicions regarding China's geopolitical objectives have a long genealogy. In a context where for decades the Soviet Union used the specter of China to ensure loyalty, fostering deeply entrenched Sinophobic sentiments, China's shrewd tactics to gain territorial footholds are only confirming assumptions about China's ambitions.[69]

These fears are not unfounded. China, like Russia, has witnessed the rise of authoritarianism in a context of rising nationalism on a global scale.[70] Following its policy of "peaceful rise" (中国和平崛起), which characterized Hu Jintao's leadership and which sought to assure the international community that China's growing political, economic, and military power would not pose a threat to international peace and security, China has demonstrated more assertiveness both at home and abroad. Since 2016, the Chinese government has been pursuing a ruthless policy of assimilation of the Uyghurs and other Muslim minorities in Xinjiang through political indoctrination, reeducation internment camps, biometric mass surveillance, and forced sterilizations of women.[71] China's heavy-handedness in its attempts to suppress Tibet, assimilate Hong Kong, and quell even mild signs of national sentiment in Inner Mongolia also speaks to Xi Jinping's authoritarian leadership and to China's newfound confidence in achieving its political aims.[72]

To an extent, these tactics find a counterpart in Russia's expansionist and territorial ambitions, notably its takeover of Crimea in 2014, carried out through information warfare, coercion, and the systematic distribution of Russian citizenship, or "passportization."[73] However, the many parallels conceal markedly different forms of authoritarianism. As political scientist Maria Repnikova writes, "Russia projects its strength mostly through aggression and political interference, while China is pursuing an intentional authoritarian governance model."[74] Russia's political regime has evolved into a system "described by scholars and observers as a 'no-participation pact,' with citizens exchanging silence for stability."[75] The vertical character of the personalized Russian system means that the country is under the Kremlin's "manual control" in that "very little gets done on any issue unless the president intervenes directly and forcefully"—something that is increasingly openly resented in Siberia and the Far East.[76] Anti-Kremlin restiveness in these regions has many causes, notably growing poverty (even destitution in some places), ethnic tensions, and lack of opportunity for the educated even in cities, as we discuss in Chapters 3, 4, and 7.

The Chinese system, by contrast, remains far more collective, institutionalized, and above all coordinated by means of the continued authority and pervasive reach of the Chinese Communist Party (CCP). Its governance structures are more complex and multifaceted than Westerners imagine, in that the CCP, while predominant, does not hold a total monopoly in domestic and economic power.[77] The Chinese political system has been more adaptive to public opinion, and the party in fact obsessively studies and responds to it, as we mention in the Coda. Regional leaders have been allowed greater freedom of maneuver than their Russian equivalents. Chinese journalists frequently cover critical social and political issues by deftly navigating the minefield of Chinese politics. On several occasions in past years they have been able to build relationships of fluid collaboration with party officials while engaging in guarded improvisation.[78]

China and Russia have also adopted different forms of personality cults. Putin has been keen to portray himself as a macho hero fearlessly standing up to Western aggression, handling wild animals and riding bare-chested—leading to a whole slew of memes depicting him riding tigers, bears, and eagles.[79] His image has been carefully curated to transform him from a gray KGB man into a sex symbol, with the aid of pop songs such as "A Man like Putin" as well as media stories about "women who have had erotic dreams about him."[80] Xi, by contrast, has adopted the image of a father figure and is often referred to as "Big Daddy Xi" in the public arena.[81]

These divergent political formations have important reverberations for the people living at the border. Many of the social, cultural, and political identities that had already taken shape and ossified during the last two decades of the Soviet period have hardened further.[82] Public and even some practical interactions at the border are informed by national, rather than international, logics and become fragile, difficult, transient, or even oppositional (see Chapters 3 and 4). The long border between these two gigantic, nationalistically oriented countries is not merely a line between two countries—it separates two entirely different worlds.[83]

ON THE RUSSIA-CHINA BORDER

In one way, however, Russia and China seem alike: both share the high-flown discursive style adopted by their leaders, which, floating unmoored to reality, evokes unpredictable reactions from ordinary listeners. There are subtle differences here too, which can be sensed from the words with which the phenomenon is described. In China, official public speech is often described as *guanmian tanghuang* (冠冕堂皇), meaning grandiloquent, ostentatious, dignified in form but insincere in substance. Such speech may be criticized when not face to face as *daguanqiang* (打官腔), speaking empty officialese. But a more prevalent reaction is likely to be *shuner bucong* (顺而不从), smiling apparent acquiescence that conceals inner nonagreement. All of this is part of the ancient tradition of *li* (礼), propriety, the creation of elegant, ritualized, and harmonious relations. In Russian, although the days of creaky Soviet officialese are over, leaders' *napyshchennnyi* (bombastic) and *vysokoparnyi* (high-flown) speech retains a certain habitus from the past. Splendid and magnificent, but with hints respectively of fluffiness and steaminess, this language inhabits its own political-discursive sphere, unchecked by raw actuality. *Pokazukha* ("put on for show"), a term that has deep foundations in Russian history, is designed to impress persons higher in the hierarchy, as we describe in Chapter 4, or indeed to bedazzle a foreign dignitary. In conferences between the two countries, the politicians' diverse habits of impression management have become part of the scene (Chapter 3), obscuring mutual understanding. Just as important, they separate leaders from the ordinary inhabitants of rough reality. The half-believed-in declarations and promises seem to have the effect of blinding officials' eyes to what they are not interested in seeing—everything that contradicts or cannot be made to seem a positive contribution to the plans announced. We discuss this phenomenon at several points in the book, especially in Chapter 3, regarding "unseen" labor migrations, smuggling, and poaching.

As our book demonstrates, significant, largely undocumented processes in the borderlands are happening outside of the purview of metropolitan powers in Beijing and Moscow. Their reverberations look set to go the other way—from the periphery to the center. One of these is arising through a combination of global climate change and population dynamics. As ever-increasing swaths of Siberia and the Far East undergo warming, with permafrost shrinking year by year, animal habitats, forestation, and water resources are shifting, often with unpredictable local effects, as we discuss in Chapter 6. We document how local populations are dealing with this situation: by economic invention, through new religious activities, or simply by uprooting themselves and looking for work elsewhere. And we bear in mind the observation that in the long run, perhaps only after decades but more or less inevitably, mass migrations are due to follow when certain previously inhospitable lands are rendered habitable and fertile. Historically, migrations and refugee catastrophes have been common in this region, including as recently as the early twentieth century. Will Russia "win the climate crisis," as environmental reporter Abrahm Lustgarten claims?[84] We cannot claim to answer this question; we can only point out that it will be resolved by whatever happens in future decades in the great expanses of the Russian northeast border region. Here the land suitable for agriculture and other kinds of production expands year by year, just as the population gradually contracts. Meanwhile, unsanctioned, inventive, fly-by-night ways of making a living are everywhere.

Some emergent interactions across the border bely a simple picture of two estranged worlds. As we mentioned earlier, one of these is occurring among the indigenous peoples that inhabit the borderlands. Chapter 4 describes vibrant movements among some of these peoples to reach for ancient common ethnic identities that predated the imperial-colonial impositions of Russia and China. Cross-border allegiances are emerging, along with historicizing and religious ways of thinking that are foreign to both the Chinese and Russian mainstreams. Both governments, especially China's, may succeed in placing a lid on these movements. But with the new webs of connectivity afforded by the internet and social media, this may prove difficult.

Ultimately, we find that the very existence of the border and the proximity of the two groups in this vast contact zone inevitably lead to cultural enmeshments. The stark urban contrasts we discuss in the book (especially in Chapter 7) conceal a complex cross-cultural process of borrowing, inspiration, and mimesis. Russian and Chinese border cities, while in many respects emblematic of their own nations, are becoming similar in different ways, making their differences commensurable. After decades when the international border remained closed, the mirroring effect provided by the juxtaposition of two dramatically different urban environments is leading to significant blurrings that challenge one-dimensional representations of the Russia-China interface. While they frequently fail to dispel mutual misunderstandings, cultural frictions at the border remain nonetheless productive insofar as they generate spaces of dialogue and collaboration.[85]

By penetrating what is actually happening behind the glowing stories put out by each government, *On the Edge* offers a unique analysis of the evolving Sino-Russian relationship. Each chapter focuses on one particular aspect of the interface between the two countries, incorporating the personal stories of borderlanders, both Russians and Chinese. This approach brings a human dimension to the analysis of a poorly known region and aims to reveal the complexity of local experiences and the ways in which people imagine a future for themselves.

BORDER SPACES

1

The two sides of the northeastern China-Russia border are roughly comparable in their far-flung distance from their respective centers. It is impossible not to sense this remoteness as one surveys the lonely, watery expanses of most of the border (see Figure 1.1).

But the sensation that one is standing at the edge of a country is still remarkably different in Russia from in China. This is because the two states have created utterly incongruent administrative and infrastructural systems. These have been built up over the centuries and are salted into people's accustomed practices and their assumptions about the way things should be. It is true that scholars have drawn attention to what these two great countries currently have in common—political centralization, authoritarian government, rapacious capitalism, multiethnicity, and the problem of control of the peripheries.[1] But it is also true that this generalization obscures the fact that each of these features can be variously understood and acted upon. The divergence between Chinese and Russian aims and methods has become particularly apparent in the twenty-first century, and the border makes them starkly visible. The routes and communication networks by which the periphery is linked to the respective metropolitan centers form increasingly dissimilar and differently weighted patterns. This

Figure 1.1. The Argun River from Lijiang in China.
(Photo by Sören Urbansky)

chapter explores these disparate spatial arrangements and explains briefly how they came to be.

Why after all does it feel so different to stand at the edge of China from Russia? We start with one of the most striking practical contrasts between the two countries: road transport. For China, the Belt and Road Initiative is a political matter, key to the continent-wide projection of the country as a global power. The main thrust of the BRI extends westward via Central Asia and does not penetrate into Russia's Far East. High-speed Chinese motorways come to an abrupt stop when they reach the Siberian border. But beyond spectacular multilane highways and toll roads, China has also built a vast but much less remarked-upon internal network of ordinary roads. All of this, arguably including the BRI, is integral to a long-standing Chinese policy that aims at development via investment in transport infrastructure. A famous saying is often quoted in this context: "If you want to create wealth, first build roads" (*yao zhi fu, xian xiu lu*). Along with efficient economic integration, the increasingly authoritarian government under Xi has intensified control over far-flung localities, including through road building for upgraded border patrols. As a consequence, even though China now has relatively few security concerns over its border with Russia, there are serviceable "national defense roads" running along much of the Chinese side of the border rivers, the Argun, Amur, and Ussuri. There are still some areas of roadless forest, but wherever there is settlement, all towns, villages, or local industries on the Chinese side are connected to one another by well-surfaced roads and linked to highways leading to the interior.

On the opposite bank in Russia, by contrast, no road runs consistently beside the border, and the few tiny villages mostly have to make do with dirt roads. In fact, Russia's main routes—the new Amur Highway, Route 297, opened by President Putin in 2010, and the nearby Trans-Siberian railway—were both planned to run at a distance of some 25 to 40 miles from the border. This means that settlements on the Russian side of the Amur are marooned at the end of their own transport spurs. To go from one to another it is necessary first to go inland to the main road, travel along it, and then set out again. In other words, it is impossible to journey along the thousands of miles of this border on the Russian side the way one can in China. One reason for this situation is very simple: the difficulty and expense of constructing a road through dense forests, cliffs, and swamps in a landscape that is hardly populated. A more weighty reason is the Russian preoccupation with sovereignty and security, heightened in Soviet times, which saw the great border rivers as convenient barriers, preventing people from either entering or leaving. Thus, border security is maintained not by building roads, as in China, but by their absence. There are in fact very few places where this long border can be crossed. Only the three land border crossing points have substantial traffic, by rail for freight and by bus for passengers, while the two river crossings, at Blagoveshchensk and Khabarovsk, have to make do with more inconvenient ferries.[2] Cross-border bridges over the rivers have been notably absent. This lack is symbolic; somehow the rivers themselves remain both physical and conceptual dividers, liminal spaces of separation. As we explain in what follows, a less immediately evident factor in this situation, but structurally important, is the geopolitical rationale upheld by Russian governments over a long history that established a particular "remoteness-creating" relationship to jurisdictional borders.

In China, by contrast, a far denser network of both railways and roads covers all inhabited land (Map 1). The result is a grid-like infrastructure, which in the 2000s was tirelessly updated and extended, with new roads driven even into unfriendly terrain, often in advance of projected settlements. This network serves a far denser population: the population of China's northeast is now about thirteen times that of the Russian Far East.[3] But it also reflects a different state attitude toward outlying lands, which seems to be shared by many ordinary Chinese—namely, that it is a good thing to expand into unused spaces, support new enterprises there, and discover and exploit any possible sources of income. These days the towns on the Chinese side of the border feel not like a lonely periphery but more akin to the avant-garde of a comprehensive civilization. Yet a paradox of the situation, which is similar in other Chinese frontier lands, is that while actual geographical remoteness and cultural difference is being erased in China as fast as possible, the center is simultaneously exaggerating the idea of there being exotic "natural wilderness" at its edges, both as its own desirable complement and also as carefully tended economic resources from which income may be drawn.[4]

In comparing the two systems, we want to connect the organization of material space (administration, communication, and infrastructure) with discursive space (how these entities are imagined and talked about). We first describe the existing Russian setup, turn to the contrasting case in China, and then take a look at rivers as borders and explain why bridges over them, linking the two countries, have been so notably absent. Finally, we discuss the changes taking place right now and the tensions between the results of the new thinking—new projects with vaulting, global-scale ambitions—and long-standing social values and obdurate realities. In this way, we set the scene for the themes explored in the rest of the book, which concern how life is actually lived on both sides of this border.

THE CREATION OF BORDER SPACE IN RUSSIA

The unorthodox but insightful Russian geographer Boris Rodoman argued that Russia is an "administrative-territorial monster" that creates a specific kind of vacant space at borders.[5] What he had in mind was the historical hypercentralized hierarchy of government and its associated radial infrastructure. This was first established during the reign of Catherine the Great in the eighteenth century, then became standard throughout the empire, and went on being reproduced up to the present day, even though it became out of sync with population movements and new centers of industry. There must be a vital motif that renews itself, Rodoman writes, that is written into the land like a matrix. But what is this? His answer is that the pyramid of subordinated places encapsulated within one another springs from the "anisotropic" character of Russian society. In physics an anisotropic object is one that has different properties in different directions, such as wood, which is stronger along the grain than across it. Such an object can be tough in one aspect but also apt to break up or dissolve when approached from a different angle. The anisotropic aspect of Russian society is that its vertical links are strong and its horizontal ones weak. It is this that is manifest in the administrative structure and in fact in the entire sociocultural landscape. The vertical power relationships are reflected in the radial roads that link the metropolis to the regional capitals, thence to provincial centers, to district centers, and finally to villages on the periphery. The drive comes from the center, to capture more resources on a linear trajectory in which what is in front is seen as open wilderness, conceptually "lower," and ready for the taking. Looking back from the periphery, the center is what matters. The only roads kept in good shape are those leading "upward" to the bosses. Meanwhile, the roads running "horizontally" between small towns or villages are neglected (often becoming impassable in bad weather) or simply do not exist. Similarly, bus service, mobile phone signals, and so on fan out from Moscow and from each provincial center, but they become more exiguous and may give out at the edge of each jurisdiction. The "monstrous" aspect of this is that it *creates* "remoteness" in the gaps between the skeletal radial lines, which can exist sometimes even quite close to a major city.[6] It is in the peripheries of each jurisdiction that the spaces involved are most stretched and the minor roads most likely to peter out.

> Anyone who has travelled even a little in our country knows that to penetrate across the boundary between *oblasts* [provinces] in the countryside, not on the main road that leads to Moscow but somewhere away from it, is like crossing a mountain ridge. You get the very feeling of being on a mountain pass, the place it's most difficult to get to, where there are no roads at all. . . . Everyone talks about the difference between Moscow and the rest of the country. Which of course is substantial; but more important is the socio-economic difference between the center and the edge of each district, however small. This is specific to Russia. . . . In each of our regions, whether an *oblast* or a *krai,* there exists a depressed zone at their borders and a vacuum that forms between them.[7]

This entire system goes with a sharply felt hierarchy of esteem. Anna Kruglova, a native of Perm in the Urals, writes that in Russia's highly spatialized politics, the significance of a city recedes according to its distance from Moscow. So Perm is mocked for its European pretensions: "It is indeed the last European city as one moves east and accordingly down in social position on one's way both from Moscow and Europe to Asian Siberia."[8] With some exceptions that we discuss later, state funding, which issues almost entirely from Moscow, follows this hierarchy.

In a process that accelerated after 2004 when Rodoman was writing, the state got rid of much of its rural support apparatus. Subsidized collective and state farms, mines, and rural industries were left to sink or swim on their own resources and collapsed one after another. During Soviet times, distances had been to a remarkable extent "conquered" by subsidized low-cost air travel, but now only one-sixth of Siberian airports and landing strips that had operated in the Soviet era still are used. Local air service is rare, expensive, and unreliable; buses and taxis refuse routes into the back of beyond. Along the Siberian borders with Mongolia and China this has left many people stranded in former production brigades, reachable only after hours (or days) on dirt roads and crossing rivers on pontoon rafts. Furthermore, when the Soviet enterprises gave up the ghost, with them went the entire social system they had supported and much of the associated employment: machinery workshops, co-ops buying the farms' produce, medical and veterinary services, bakeries, accountancy offices, public bathhouses, local shops, clubs, libraries, kindergartens, public transport services, and local road maintenance departments. People flooded out of the villages to nearby towns. If a village population shrank too far, the school closed, and with that the settlement was likely to decline into complete decrepitude.

Rodoman's "depressed zones" at borders expanded, while the ribbons of relative prosperity narrowed. Next to the Russian border with Mongolia, there are vast empty lands. The remaining Buryat and Russian villages of former collective farms are often hidden down twisting sandy tracks; any surfaced roads in the vicinity are kept maintained not for them but because the roads run between more important centers. When I (Caroline)

was traveling in the area, my eyes dwelt on the boundless luxu-
riant grasslands, sparkling rivers, and forested hills from which
a few enchanting pine trees spread into the plains. I wondered
aloud, "Why does no one live in this beautiful place?" But immediately I saw that this was a stupid question: who would want
to live alone and vulnerable in the midst of nowhere, with no
electricity and no road? The vacant land is owned by the Forestry
Department, I was told, and it would be a bureaucratic night-
mare to even attempt to buy a plot from them. As for the pines,
a Buryat villager cried, "How can you say they are beautiful? I
hate them. Each one sprung up out there reminds me that this is
where we used to have our fields—our good productive fields."
Many of the houses are boarded up. The people who remain
depend on their links "upward" to the district and provincial
capitals for pensions, medical services, banks, child benefits, re-
mittances from their adult children, and purchases of all kinds.
A similar situation exists in other vast rural sections along the
border as it winds its way along the Argun, Amur, and Ussuri
Rivers.[9]

In Siberia, the railways have been more important than the
roads as routes along which settlements have been established.
The roads of Trans-Baikal were separated from those of the Far
East by "the Gap," a 1,300 mile section of notoriously boggy and
treacherous unpaved throughway between Chita and Khabarovsk.
In 2010 the gap was eliminated by the construction of an asphalted
highway, Route 297, the opening of which was celebrated by Putin
driving along it in a Russian-made Lada Kalina car. As Dominic
Ziegler writes in *Black Dragon River,* "The road was above all a
political project, made in Moscow. The Russian Far East had for
too long hung off the edge of the realm. The new road in symbolic more than practical terms, was intended to winch it back
in."[10] But, already buckling in places after only ten years, Route
297 epitomizes the uncertainty of road infrastructure in a climate
beset by bitter subzero storms, glaring heat, melting permafrost,
drought, and flooding, in which the best-constructed roads can

become impassable rubble virtually before one's eyes. The new highway passes for the most part through wild, uninhabited lands, and hundreds of miles separate the filling stations and cafes along it. By contrast, a glance at the map shows hundreds of small stations strung along the Trans-Siberian and the Baikal–Amur Mainline (BAM) railways. These are vital points in the wilderness. Along the busy Trans-Siberian each station has accreted a settlement of houses, shops, garages, bars, and perhaps a school or a club. Villagers anticipate the trains and gather to sell produce to travelers, and they can take the slow local trains to visit neighbors or sell their produce in the nearest city. The railways are slow and overburdened, have been little modernized, and these days are held to constitute a hindrance to Russia's economic expansion in the east, but socially, to travelers, they are linear and easily understandable, unlike the wandering and often impassable roads that wind their way through forests to distant mining, hunting, and logging settlements.[11]

Several films about disorienting journeys have been produced in Russia, somewhat akin to the American road movie.[12] The Soviet-era theme of triumphant conquest of nature has long been abandoned. Now the idea is to embrace the journey as revelation, self-discovery, and cultural critique. It usually begins in a violent/ degenerate Moscow, but it leads to nothing idyllic: the car or truck takes the protagonists to grim places with no signposts, where there is no sense of location or destination. They wind up in places that represent the past, where people are stuck in the stupor of provincial life or pointless religious rituals. The car stalls, or the road leads into an impasse—to entrapment and death. In Zviagintsev's *The Return* (2003), Fedorchenko's *Silent Souls* (2010), and Igumentseva's *Bite the Dust* (2013), the road is no longer a vital link between center and periphery but a human-made path that leads to a place where the car can go no farther—to water (a lake, a river, a drowned island), which stands for death. As it happens, none of these films refer to the great Siberian border rivers, the Argun, the Shilka, the Amur, and the

Ussuri. But these rivers do in fact, not only in imagination, function in one particular sense as a journey's end: in a state security sense.

CLOSED PLACES: *POGRANZONA* AND *ZATO*

Even in tsarist times the government regarded borderlands as politically suspect and from time to time carried out policies to move or forcibly assimilate frontier populations deemed potentially disloyal.[13] The subsequent Soviet government's attitude was if anything more security-conscious, and it likewise removed suspect peoples (Chinese, Koreans, Buryats, Nanais) from immediate proximity to the border in Siberia and the Far East. Fear of emigration, regional separatism, and Stalin's determination to take control over peripheries turned the Far East into a militarized garrison province.[14] Between 1934 and 1936 the entire international border strip of the USSR was designated a closed security zone (*pogranzona*). Officially known as the Restricted Access Border Zone (RABZ), it continues to this day. In 2004 this strip was placed under the control of the Federal Security Service (FSB), which operates directly from Moscow with little coordination with the regional and local authorities. Fences mark its boundary, and barriers with guard posts are stationed on all access roads. Neither Russian citizens nor foreigners may enter unless they are registered residents or have FSB permission. In places the *pogranzona* is only around 3 miles wide. But elsewhere the FSB, which not only regulates but also benefits from all enterprises within the zone, has taken the opportunity to broaden it up to 62 miles (or to change the zone's boundaries from time to time as it sees fit). Currently, all the land along the Amur between the river and Route 297 is in the closed area.[15]

On land, the physical border is a complex structure. Military bases, some of which have short-range nuclear weapons whose only purpose must be to "contain China," are situated in the rear.[16] The border itself starts with a light fence marking the outer edge of the closed zone. A considerable distance beyond is the actual border: a low fence with warning notices, followed a variable length away by a plowed-up strip to show footprints, then a strong high fence, and in places lights, security cameras, and radar. Beyond this there is usually a further no-man's-land before the border fence of the foreign country. In the case of the rivers the border runs along the thalweg (deepest channel). The existence of the *pogranzona*/RABZ makes the situation at river and sea borders complicated and erratic. Whereas some formerly entirely closed port cities, such as Vladivostok, were "opened" after the collapse of the USSR (though certain restricted military pockets were retained within), other inhabited areas, including all riverside villages and parts of major cities such as Blagoveshchensk, remained closed—in the latter case subsequently opened, then partially closed again. In principle, this means that a casual traveler, particularly a foreigner, cannot enter these areas or travel down the rivers by boat without obtaining special permission beforehand. And yet, and yet . . . given the fitful changes to the boundary, the fact that thousands of people actually live and work inside the closed zones, and the high chance that road checkpoints are unstaffed, the actual enforcement of the restrictions is unpredictable. It is sometimes strict, sometimes not. The RABZ is essentially a buffer zone, and only the real border at the edge is truly hard. At its final perimeter, Russia does not shade off into an indeterminate and permeable remoteness but ends at a hard, multiply reinforced boundary.[17] The center may neglect vast tracts of in-between lands inside Russia, but the rim of the country is an object of focused attention and concentrations of diverse security-related installations.

If the *pogranzona* is a continuous strip of land, the "closed administrative-territorial formation" or ZATO (*zakrytoe administrativno-territorial'noe obrazovanie*) is different, a delimited site for secret operations. In Soviet times, whole cities had this status, and today it continues for military bases, prison camps, uranium mines, military exercise grounds (*polygony*), secret research facilities, and factories for the production of weapons, especially nuclear ones. Such sensitive operations and penal zones are often located in less-populated remote areas, and this means, as Rodoman would have predicted, they are often close to borders.[18] Not by accident, different kinds of screened-off operations are often located in a single place. An example is the closed town of Krasnokamensk near the Chinese border, which is the site of both a uranium mine and a labor camp, the one where the magnate Mikhail Khodorkovsky was imprisoned in the 2000s.

However, the multifunctionality of Krasnokamensk's ZATO is nothing compared to the diversity of operations found in the border region as a whole. It contains places that are totally off-limits and others that are in principle maximally open. The dense untouched forests enclose boggy wastes, sad wreckages, crude logging camps, and desultory agriculture redolent of the past. But at the same time, this is a field of miracles. For one can turn a corner and see the shiny steel grids and fluorescent high-vis uniforms of new construction. They are the advance markers of Russia's pivot to the East, of its urge to make itself a major player, economically, diplomatically, and politically, in the Asia-Pacific. Most of the Soviet military bases and factories that used to dot the frontier zone with China have long since been decommissioned. Their ruins may be a physical reminder of earlier hostilities, but discursively they have been cast into oblivion by the vibrant future now aspired to.[19] Media and websites display glowing images of technically advanced edifices under construction. One of these is the huge Amur Gas Processing Plant being built at Svobodny, near Blagoveshchensk, to service the Power of Siberia pipeline that in 2019 began to convey gas from northern Siberia to China.[20] The 1,850 mile pipeline and the plant are both heroic enterprises, built amid awesome difficulties of climate, geology, and distance. The plant will supply Siberian towns as well as process helium, ethane, propane, and butane for export. It will be one of the largest such plants in the world and is being constructed to international standards, with German, Chinese, and other international participation. So far $22.1 billion has been invested in the project, and at present 15,000 people, including a contingent of Chinese, are employed in the construction. The permanent workforce is planned to eventually drop to 3,000, with use of automated equipment control and local renewables-based power systems. In short, Russia's attempt to switch to a high-tech, value-added economic future is a reality, not a mere aspiration. Yet it is not easily disentangled from the Soviet and post-Soviet geographies in which it is taking shape.

This can be seen from the circumstances surrounding another spectacular project located near the Amur Gas Plant. This is the Eastern Cosmodrome (*Vostochnyi Kosmodrom*), the spaceport that is being constructed to replace Russia's aging facilities at Baikonur on land rented from Kazakhstan. The Cosmodrome, with its aspiration to vertical mastery of space and possibilities for panoptic surveillance, is a "hyperspace of sovereignty," a star in Putin's "global player" thinking.[21] But the spaceport's siting is also related to the old Soviet order. The spaceport was originally planned for the Far East coast, but that site was rejected on the grounds that falling debris would disturb ports and shipping; it was then decided to locate the spaceport near military facilities that were already producing and launching rockets and missiles. The Eastern Cosmodrome is being built near a Soviet rocket launch site at Svobodny (closed in 2007) and next to the small ZATO of Tsiolkovsky. This town, renamed in 2014 after Konstantin Tsiolkovsky, the great pioneer of astronautics, was formerly called Uglegorsk, and it manufactured the ICBM missiles launched from Svobodny.[22] Many of the Cosmodrome construction workers are housed in former military barracks at Tsiolkovsky.

The Cosmodrome can be accessed by the Trans-Siberian railway and Route 297, but even so, it has proved difficult to overcome the problems of remoteness for the construction of a complex, ultra-modern facility (Map 2). Air freight is expensive,

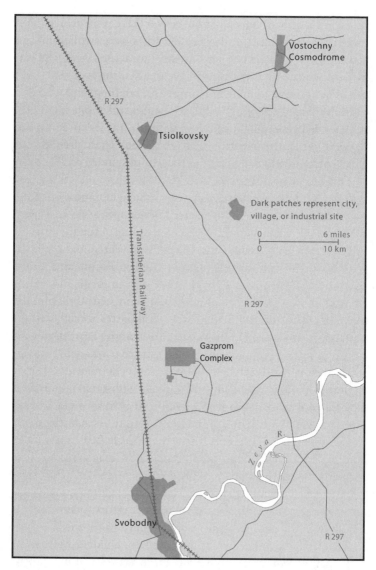

Map 2. Svobodny and the Vostochny Cosmodrome

and supplies proved difficult to assemble. There were delays. Contractors went into debt. The spiraling costs were swollen by corruption involving both officials and contractors. Many of the workers originally hired for the project fled the loneliness and mosquitoes; students had to be drafted in, but they went on strike when they were not paid for their work. Several unpiloted rocket flights have nevertheless been successful, but as of 2019 the Cosmodrome project was far from finished. There are Russian critics who say that the original idea was misguided and that the project now has "no meaning."[23]

A practical problem such critics may have in mind is that the project of turning the Eastern Cosmodrome into a vital regional center is at odds with Russia's continuing "administrative-territorial monster." The space industry's research and development facilities are centrally concentrated in European Russia, thousands of miles away.[24] The idea had been for the new Cosmodrome to boost the economy of the depressed Amur region, to create an innovation cluster that would attract bright young specialists. Instead, the accompanying "innovation hub" was built near Moscow, and only a skeleton crew was sent to Svobodny, the nearest sizable town to the spaceport. Located as it is in archetypal isolation, the spaceport, notwithstanding its ultra-modernity, cannot avoid being entangled in the former uses of these remote lands. And Svobodny, despite its name, which means "free," was also a ZATO, the site of the Baikal-Amur Lager (Bamlag), one of the largest camps of the Gulag system in the Stalin era.

The name Svobodny in fact refers to an agglomeration of facilities with an extraordinary multilayered history. It started as a small fishing-hunting settlement on the Zeya River, then became a gold rush town, then a Soviet labor camp for building the Baikal–Amur railway, and then, after the camp was closed in 1953, a town with a single factory manufacturing automotive parts and military equipment. The rocket launch site was built some 9 miles to the north of the town. As a ZATO, it was in some ways blessed.

During the Soviet period one of Svobodny's charms was its narrow-gauge "children's railway," built to link the town to idyllic Young Pioneer summer camps; almost all the railway's jobs (cashiers, conductors, station attendants) were performed by schoolchildren.[25] But after the factory closed in the 1990s, the town's population fell from 80,000 in 1989 to 54,000 in 2016. Svobodny became the town it is today: a quiet, dilapidated, melancholic place. Yet because of its transportation advantages—it has an airport, two stations on the Trans-Siberian railway, a road link to the Baikal–Amur railway, and a port on the river Zeya—the plan is for it to be transformed into a fast-growing industrial hub and dormitory town for the Gas Processing Plant and the Cosmodrome (see further discussion in Chapter 3).

However, it is the local authorities that actually have to bear the costs of the projected regional refurbishment. For example, Tsiolkovsky (population around 5,000), given priority because it is a ZATO, was supplied with an extra-large central heating plant in the expectation that the town would grow. But so far there has been no great inflow of residents and no corresponding income, and the cost is a drain on the local state budget. The result is that other projects are stalled. A nearby town, Romny, languishes in the forest at the end of 12 miles of earth road, and the entire Romny district, with 8,000 residents, is no better off. "There is no money for your road," said the embattled Amur governor, Vasilii Orlov, to a meeting of angry residents in August 2018. "It would cost around 700 million rubles and the entire income of Romny is barely a quarter of that. We have to pay for central heating plants for many settlements around here—and what happens, the population just goes on leaving. Leaving. Leaving. But we can't shut off the heating while people are still living there. And we cannot close down the villages and deport the residents either. That would be political illiteracy. Everything must be on a voluntary basis." To this despairing speech from the governor (who apologized for its frankness), a bitter voice from the hall responded: "So there are plans. And plans for what to do about the population. But potential investors are saying almost openly, 'First quit drinking and observe the law.' What with the traditions of Svobodny—the center of the Bamlag, the Amurlag, and later also the Svobodlag—not everyone has the strength for that."[26] We see from this that attempting to conform to Moscow's projections for the future in an obscure, depopulated location brings a host of contemporary problems and cannot silence memories of what happened in these same places before.

Strangely, from an outsider's point of view, the people living in ZATOs seem relatively content with their lot. Why do they not object to living in what might seem a prison-like enclosure? The stark fact is that the Russian Far East, which includes the vast area from Lake Baikal to the Pacific, is losing population.[27] People are moving away, generally to western parts of Russia. This is despite the fact that the main towns, Chita, Blagoveshchensk, and Khabarovsk, have many pleasant aspects of the typical Russian provincial city: they are unhurried, spacious, friendly, and unpretentious, with tree-lined streets, fine nineteenth-century mansions and cathedrals, and plenty of stores. But the 1998, 2008, and 2014 economic crises hit hard; there is a lack of opportunities and a feeling of insecurity and decline (see Chapter 3). By contrast, people living in "closed zones" have always had protected jobs, special supplies, and good-quality housing. Regionally speaking, they are privileged. As soon as their town loses its ZATO status, the benefits and security vanish. This has happened to a number of towns along the border after changes in military priorities and decommissioning of stocks of nuclear arms.

CHINESE GEOPOLITICAL SPACES AT THE BORDER

Black Dragon River (Heilongjiang) is the Chinese name for the Amur. Along with different names for rivers, towns, and mountains, a distinctively Chinese history of the region is taught in Chinese schools and displayed in Chinese museums (see Chapter 5). The Chinese and Russian accounts are very different, and extend even down to what ordinary people on either side of the border accept as truth about the source of the Amur River. In one Russian version, the source is the Ingoda, the northernmost of the inflowing rivers from the west, and definitely located inside Siberia; in certain Chinese publications, by contrast, the origin is the Songhua (also known as the Sungari), a river that has its source deep in the Changbai mountains, on the border with North Korea.[28]

With this Chinese attribution, a different geography swings into view: that of a vast river basin opening to the sea and encompassing both sides of the border. The physical reality is subject to a powerful representational structure very different from that found north of the border. If the Russian idea of the Far East is based on its history of west-to-east advances out of Moscow, subduing territories and indigenous peoples in linear moves until the Pacific coast is reached, the Chinese one is not linear but a series of concentric circles expanding outward from an inland central zone. Takeshi Hamashita has provided one of the best analyses of this Chinese vision.[29] Challenging Eurocentric history, he argues that this was a space combining a landed and maritime world. "The seas and the land should be understood . . . as part of a larger whole in which the land is part of the seas (and vice versa). The sea forms, in short, a road, a basis for communication and network flows, not a barrier."[30] The major principle that brought this far-flung and disparate world into a kind of unity was the system of tribute and trade relations that functioned from the Tang dynasty (seventh century) to the end of the Qing dynasty (1911). This was a conception of hierarchical order sustained by the Confucian "rule of virtue" in the person of the emperor / ruler. Backed by military force, it nevertheless allowed subordinate realms such as Korea, Japan, Laos, and Vietnam to assert themselves as "centers" vis-à-vis the smaller states and areas under their sway. Tributary states sent periodic tribute missions to the Chinese capital. These were not only political-diplomatic operations, involving exchanges of valuable gifts, but involved trade as well, since licensed merchants accompanying the envoy were entitled to engage in commerce at allocated places in the capital. China's land-sea orbit included settlements in lands that are now part of Russia, and the current major towns all had earlier Chinese names: Vladivostok, for example, was called Haishenwai (海参崴, "sea-cucumber cliffs") and was reached by boat.[31] Today, China's ancient sea-embracing vision is being brought to the fore again with its installations in the South China Sea.

China's vision of itself changed over the centuries, but at no point did it involve a single definite border; rather, it consisted of a cultural core in central China ringed by an expanding series of nested realms, gradually incorporating land on the margins via the Sinification of surrounding barbarian groups. The line between self and other lacked clarity and was subject to contestation and revision.[32] On land, imperial China had "inner" and "outer" realms, divided first by the Great Wall in its various manifestations. The Great Wall separated the *zhongyuan* (central plain) from the *saiwai* (beyond the pale), which was conceptualized as a zone of bleak deserts and bitter cold. Past that, beyond the mountains and stretching up to Siberia, was *beidahuang*, the dreaded Great Northern Wilderness. Exiles were regularly dispatched to languish in this outback, and in this respect the frontier region was used in a way similar to the Russian use of Siberia. However, the Manchu conquest of China in the 1640s brought a vision different from that of the Han Chinese, since the Manchu's own lands were in these outer realms and were designated sacrosanct ancestral territory. Manchuria, known in China as Dongbei (the Northeast), was separated from central lands by the Willow Palisade, beyond which Han were not permitted to settle.[33] The Great Wall had no particular significance for the Manchus—the allied princedoms of Inner Mongolia lay in an arc around it, and Outer Mongolia was an important component of the empire lying beyond even that. Yet fundamentally, once the Manchus had ensconced themselves in Beijing, they conformed to the Han Chinese vision. The legitimacy of the great Qing empire they founded, whose dimensions were inherited first by the Republic of China (1912–1949) and later by the People's Republic of China, rested on the Manchus' claim to status as members of the traditional Chinese order, which "enabled them to win the confidence of other Inner Asian peoples and bring them into the fold."[34]

Russia, from its first missions to China in the seventeenth century to establish trade relations, had difficulty—like Britain in the eighteenth century—in extracting itself from the Chinese conviction that the country was another gift-bearing tributary. At issue was the clash of two utterly different conceptual principles: the old East Asian hierarchical tributary order extending outward from the Middle Kingdom (Zhonghua) versus the treaty relations between sovereign states that underpinned international relations in Europe.[35] In the end, after elaborate one-upmanship ploys by both sides, the pacts that established the northeastern border, the Treaty of Nerchinsk in 1689 and the Treaty of Kyakhta in 1729, were defined as agreements between equally ranked sovereigns, an outcome attributable to the relative flexibility of the Manchu rulers, with their Jesuit advisors, compared to Han Chinese officials. But this did not prevent the Manchu Qing rulers from subsequently high-handedly cutting off trade with Russia, sometimes for years, as was customary with tributary states that displeased China. The Qing government needed to keep its northern frontier quiet while it dealt with new acquisitions and disturbances in the far west and south of its empire (a situation that has parallels today). Eventually, the Manchus came to the conviction, acquired from Han political thought, that their rule constituted the center of a world order, a historically evolved hierarchy of civilization surrounded by variously ranked barbarian peoples.

As their dynasty weakened in the late nineteenth century, the Qing were unable to prevent a trickle and then a flood of millions of Chinese immigrants into Manchuria, which became "perhaps . . . the greatest peaceful migration in history."[36] Still, it was images of Manchuria as a pristine land of "primitive" peoples unrelated to the Chinese that encouraged early twentieth-century imperialist incursions into the region by Japan and Russia.[37] Both countries, first Russia and then Japan, built railways across Manchuria with primarily military-strategic aims. For a period, this gave Manchuria, unlike the rest of China, an infrastructure similar to Russia's: scattered towns linked by railways that snaked through great areas of neglected underdevelopment. But after World War II, the old Chinese vision of expansion outward through concentric circles reappeared: peasant farmers were encouraged to settle in all empty lowlands. Further out in the Great Northern Wilderness Mao Zedong sent "class enemies" to state farms and prison labor camps near the border with Russia, making a far more determined effort to re-educate and transform minds by socialist labor than was attempted in the Soviet Gulag.[38]

Meanwhile, in the south of Manchuria and closer to China proper, the Communist Party took advantage of Japanese construction and established state-owned heavy industry, manufacturing, and mines. This zone became socialist China's "cradle of industrialization" and its wealthiest area from the 1950s to the 1970s. However, in the post-Mao era many of these factory towns declined into the country's largest rust belt, unable to adapt to rapidly changing markets and technology. Privatization led to millions of layoffs in the 1990s, and the subsequent economic growth was less vibrant in this area than elsewhere. The northeast as a whole is still known as the nation's "last fortress of a planned economy" and a relatively deprived region.[39] It was hard hit in a downturn between 2013 to 2017, prompting an exodus of young people to other parts of China.[40] China's high-tech industry and space facilities are located elsewhere.

Bitter memories of these violent swings lie behind the policies that inspire current Chinese structures of center-periphery relations. The problems look analogous to those in Russia's Far East, but the solutions are very different. With a more multicentered view than that in Russia, grand plans were issued to turn Manchuria into China's "Fourth Economic Engine," to rival the three capitalist-style powerhouses in the south. But President Xi in a state visit to the northeast in 2018—a deliberate mirroring of the inspection tours of Chairman Mao—declared that not private enterprise but the region's great state-owned enterprises (SOEs) would be supported and encouraged to become global players. The idea is to shore up the country's self-reliance in the face of US intransigence instead of relying on an open and liberal trade regime for continuing growth. Many regional leaders are glad. They have had to live with the effects of the previous policy of privatization, foreign investment, and corporatization of public assets and are nostalgic for a past when SOEs dominated the economy. In short, the new regional policies aim to shore up state employment and to even out economic and ethnic inequalities. Even more broadly, this is an aspiration to homogenize and "fill in" the entirety of China with harmonious "civilization." At least seven types of administrative entity are involved in this plan, and their nesting and ranking vis-à-vis one another create dense, impenetrable, and overlapping relations extending right up to the border.

In the 2000s, reforms aimed broadly at three areas: decentralization of power and delegation of rights, simplification and rationalization of administration, and gradual building of a government ruled by law. Fiscal decentralization in particular brought about de facto "taxation federalism," in which local governments acquired significant powers not only to retain a large portion of the taxes they collected but also to sell and rent out land, charge fees, create local legislation, and engage independently in investment, even outside China. This system of dispersion has been relatively fluid, in constant negotiation with central government.[41] Nevertheless, the general trend was in many ways the opposite of that ongoing in Russia, which has continued to be focused on centralization in the hands of the presidential apparatus, with reduction of the number of levels between the top and the bottom of the system, almost all taxes paid to Moscow, and a weakening of local self-rule. Decentralization was a key impetus for the astonishing innovation and growth that has taken place in China over the last two decades.[42]

However, Xi Jinping has recently recentralized many aspects of power, focusing especially on fiscal reform, security, military investment, control of the internet, and campaigns against corruption. In economic policy, there has been a move away from labor-intensive activities and toward value-added high-tech production, development of services and internal consumption, and attention to the environment, as we discuss further in Chapter 2. New high-speed roads and railways cut out spectacular routes, sweeping to the border with Russia, where they abruptly stop. This ultra-modern infrastructure ties in certain points on the periphery to central China, but as I (Caroline) observed, in Inner Mongolia it also has an undesired effect. People with low incomes avoid the new toll roads and expensive railways, the humble local roads become clogged with trucks, and inequality is in fact reinforced. In the cheery sociality of cheap roadside cafes there is a distinct feeling of separation from the well-off people who thunder past on the elevated motorways. Meanwhile, towns chosen for "redevelopment" become unrecognizable forests of high-rise apartments, inducing a sense of disorientation among older residents.[43]

Along with the massive infrastructural development, Xi has returned to older Chinese traditions of statecraft, calling for a merging of Confucian with Communist morality and the responsibility of officials toward "the people." Now, he reiterates, the market is to be firmly managed by the state. Overly hasty or unscrupulous entrepreneurs, including those investing abroad, are to be reined in. For disadvantaged regions, such as the northeast, investment has been poured in, not only for roads, railways, and new housing, but also for water supplies, sewage works, hospitals, cultural facilities, and telecommunications—but inequality,

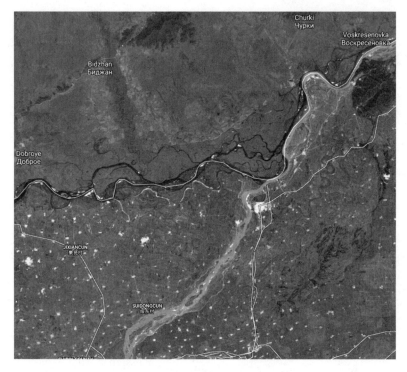

Figure 1.2. The two sides of the border at Tongjiang.
(Google Earth)

low wages, and lack of employment persist. Now the demands
for socioeconomic justice that come with rising incomes are more
urgent than before.[44]

A glance at Google Earth reveals sharply different patterns on
either side of the border. Figure 1.2 shows the border between
the largely empty Jewish Autonomous Region in Russia and the
uniformly settled Jiamusu county of China. Central to the picture
is Tongjiang town, located near the confluence of the Songhua
River with the Amur.

How are these densely populated Chinese borderlands organized internally? Two sets of statist players came to dominate

after the reforms of the 1970s–1980s: state institutions inherited from socialist vertical organization (central government, party and military bodies, and the enterprises owned by them) and municipal governments. China's internal politics unfolded as "an intra-state struggle over land between these two sets of statist players."[45] Their relative fiscal freedom encouraged the municipalities to become far more enterprising than the socialist land masters. From the early 2000s, their jurisdictions were extended out from town boundaries to include swaths of the countryside beyond.[46] The idea was to reduce differences between urban and rural citizens, as well as between various ethnic groups, and to spread economic enterprise. As geographer Youtien Hsing argues, such an expanded municipal region is not just a spatial unit defined by economic integration but should be understood as a "territorial dynamism, in which the administrative order sets the parameters for the restructuring of state power."[47] The dynamism was apparent through the municipality's engagement with a third element: private, non-state commerce. In other words, the municipality, rather than being a passive object of state policy, has become an active constructor and integral engine of the local state.

Manzhouli, the Chinese town on the Russian border, which we discuss further in Chapter 6, shows these processes in action. Its municipal boundary extends out to embrace a number of "zones": an industrial processing zone, a Russian industrial economic zone, a Russian-themed tourist park, a free trade zone 3 miles away, and the open-cast coal mines at Zhalainuoer (Jalan Nuur) 15 miles away, all of which are integrated by rail and road. In the free trade zone, small businesses include Russians selling such things as honey, cakes, and wooden carvings to Chinese tourists. Zhalainuoer, by contrast, is an archetypal state-owned location for heavy industry, with the accompanying environmental pollution. It was built, in fact, by the Soviets during the "friendship" period of the 1950s.[48] When we visited in 2014, steam engines of antique appearance still puffed slowly past faded concrete buildings. The place indeed had a rust belt appearance.

But coal is still needed, and long chains of dusty wagons clank their way to factories in the region. Zhalainuoer's enterprising citizens have taken the paradoxes of their situation in hand. With an eye to tourist income, they have opened a large modern Museum of Mining (with popular exhibits of steam engines), have built a colorful replica of St Basil's Cathedral in Moscow, and have also reached back in time to concoct an almost surreal "archaeological park" for tourists, with statues of dinosaurs and mammoths. We see from this that in China the complex arena called "the state" includes more inventive, self-reflective, and subtly multivocal local initiatives than the monocentric and rigid equivalent in Russia.

In its way, the landscape along the Chinese side of the border is almost as heterogenous as the Russian one. In Manzhouli, downtrodden rubbish-strewn shacks from the Maoist era still exist not far from gleaming shopping malls. In Hunchun, smart new apartment complexes stand alongside the already peeling entrance arch to the deathly quiet Russian enterprise zone. But any shabby remnants of the past are insignificant beside the towering ramparts of the new housing and industrial estates that have been funded by large-scale debt and land revenue machinations on the part of municipalities. The incentives for officials to demonstrate "development" (and then move on to a higher post) has resulted in the construction of "ghost towns"—whole schemes that are largely deserted (see Chapter 7). Projects to create impressive public buildings and elite housing in order to increase land prices and hence enhance municipal revenues occur all over China.[49] On the border they are particularly striking, in contrast to the more modest and often faltering schemes in Russian areas where such large credits are not available.[50] Caroline visited one elite gated development outside Yanji, near the border with North Korea and Russia. Hoping to attract ambitious business buyers, it was named Davos City and constructed in "Spanish style," with red tiled roofs, classical gazebos, and flowery gardens. The developers were falling over themselves to sell, for purchasers at this inconvenient out-of-town spot had been very few. The chances of coming across such globally attuned exotica across the border in Russia are close to zero.

However, the description given so far of two different life-worlds ranged across from each other is only part of the story. For one thing, China and Russia have in common both a practical problem and a potential opportunity: the rivers themselves. Even if "natural borders" are never entirely natural—they must be negotiated, and the seemingly obvious dividing line does not signify the same thing to the different parties involved—we should not forget that great rivers have their own physical properties and can never *just* be borders.[51]

THE RIVERS: WATERY EXPANSES OF CONTACT AND DISRUPTION

According to international agreements, the line of the riverine border runs along the thalweg, which forms the main navigation route. Because of border regulations and the exclusion zone on the Russian side, the rivers cannot serve as an ordinary public transport route for either country.[52] Yet the Shilka, Argun, and Amur are navigable, though they are shallow in parts, and confusing with their twists and turns. Historically, these rivers were some of the main routes by which the Cossacks first explored the Far East in the seventeenth century. It was possible simply to float people, animals, and goods down them on rafts. Waterways became the lines of flight for peasants escaping serfdom and religious persecution in central Russia. Later, political leaders reimagined the rivers as supreme passageways for Russia's achievement of its Eurasian destiny. By the mid-nineteenth century, when Moscow turned away from Europe, Russian leaders were projecting a route to the Pacific, and the glow of the Amur, one of the very few rivers in Asiatic Russia flowing eastward, came to transcend the grim connotations of the name Siberia. Here lay a land from which wealth would be garnered from gold, coal, and productive agriculture.[53] Even though the actual prospects for shipping at the Amur's mouth were only sketchily mapped, a bonanza in exports and imports was anticipated. Regaining control of the Amur from the Chinese became an obsession. This was achieved first by military expeditions and then by the "unequal treaties" negotiated with the weakened Qing by General Nikolai Muraviev-Amurskii in 1858 and 1860. Russian peasants were encouraged to settle the land as fast as possible, and the rivers became busier than any toilsome road on land.

Until the Trans-Siberian railway was built, passengers took to river steamers for the 1,428 miles between Sretensk on the Shilka and Khabarovsk on the Amur. Mail also traveled this way, tossed into the hold in vast leather sacks. Convicts bound for Sakhalin were towed behind in prison barges.[54] By 1900 the summer months saw regular boat service taking motley passengers to and from the river ports: Russian fur merchants, Chinese traders, peasant settlers, gold miners, Cossacks, engineers, river officials, European and American prospectors, adventurers, priests, brigands, and generals. Zigzagging between villages on either side, small mail boats would drop anchor to take on local passengers. Evidently cultural influences went back and forth across the river at this time: a British traveler describes "slither-limbed, pale-faced" Chinese with no money wanting a cheap passage, some "dressed in native attire, blue-bloused, baggy-breeched, with greasy little skull caps, others in ill-fitting Russian caps and leather boots, and one wearing Chinese lower garments but with a red and yellow striped blazer and an old English straw hat with a yellow and blue band."[55]

Over its history, the Russia-China border has opened and closed—or more accurately, its operation has enabled some people to pass and barred others in variable ways at different times.[56] The period at the beginning of the twentieth century, when China was weak and subject to imperial advances on all sides, was a time of maximal opening. The Amur hardly func-

tioned as a border. Instead, it is better understood as a system of
arteries draining great rivers from inside China as well as Russia,
and thus connecting a rich array of cultures and lifestyles and facilitating the flow of goods. Nevertheless, the passage was always somewhat treacherous: in many places the rivers divided
into tortuous side channels or snaked around looping bends. In
winter, they would be heaped with lumpy ice; in summer, there
were fast-running currents in some places, whereas in others the
flow was interrupted by countless islands, shoals, and sandbanks.
Both torrential rains and droughts could unpredictably change
the river's course, so it became unclear where the border actually
was. Every couple of years, heavy thunderstorms, premature
freezing, epidemic diseases, or floods would wreak disaster. The
hazards of such changeable natural conditions interfered with imperial colonization policies. The settlements along the Amur ordered by Muraviev-Amurskii "started out as tiny, bleak villages
and they have remained like this to the present," while flourishing
cities elsewhere on this vast drainage system, such as Harbin, on
the Songhua, owed little of their prosperity to their proximity to
the river.[57] In this riverine landscape, islands were places of uncertain sovereignty, and the chaotic movement of people and illegal trade were constants (see Chapter 2).[58]

The river's haphazard activity not only disturbed international
relations but also could turn ordinary lives upside down. The following Russian account from a village near Khabarovsk gives
some insight into local attitudes, both to the river and to ways of
gaining a living in these parts:

> My friend, now a land surveyor, was de-mobbed from the army with
> his party ticket in his pocket and he needed work. As bad luck had
> it, the village shop had no keeper and our brave sergeant was sent to
> take over. He hadn't a clue about trade. . . . No surprise, my friend
> was ruined. Fearing an inspection, he pored over the accounts time
> and again, and was reduced to drying out crusts of bread. Who knows
> if they'd have been useful, because suddenly there was a massive flood
> and the shop got washed away with all its provisions. "I stood on a

hillock," he said, "and saw the boxes and bottles swept away down the current, and I grimaced, but my soul was singing. Hey, that time was ended! I bowed deeply to Old Father Amur and vowed never to have anything to do with trade again. . . .

The Amur has various names, and one of them, "Black Dragon," is as good as any. It expresses the snake-like form of the river, its brownish water, and its uncontrollable, unpredictable character. And the gloomy black of the basalt rocks on its shores.[59]

CROSSING THE AMUR: PHANTOM BRIDGES AND AMBIVALENT INFRASTRUCTURE

If transport today along the rivers is sparse, what about the connections across the border? In 2020, by far the majority of cross-border traffic is by rail. Railways have long been established in Russian political culture as a means of "opening up" (*osvoeniye*) lands to be taken over and developed. There is something grand, solid, and admirable about railways as they plow through the tunnels, mountains, and seemingly endless forests of Siberia. Built at such harsh cost, at first by convicts and later by volunteer labor, they were national (all-Soviet) endeavors that at least by the 1960s–1970s invoked comradely "socialist internationalism." The station architecture of the Baikal–Amur Mainline represents this concept.[60] The imaginative and exuberant styles of each station represent the sponsoring cities throughout the Soviet Union that sent crews and designers to the heroic enterprise. But the Russian railways have not been modernized, and now the idea of railways trailblazing on behalf of the whole country has been taken up by China. A rail freight line was the vanguard of China's New Silk Road link to Europe in 2017. However, there is a hindrance at the Russian and Mongolian borders: the technical problem of different gauges (Russia's wide, China's narrower). This is one reason the main crossing point between the two countries, the land border between sleepy Zabaikal'sk and bustling, brightly lit Manzhouli, tends to be a bottleneck. Long freight trains trundle slowly through, carrying timber, minerals, and metals southward, but there are vast marshaling yards where hundreds of train cars wait for customs clearance or to have their bogies (chassis) changed.

Building bridges over the border rivers has been a much more fraught matter. At the time of writing (winter 2020–2021) there is no functioning bridge for road passenger traffic over the Amur. It is not just that such bridges require technical feats of engineering, or that they are costly because their foundations alter currents and make further water management schemes necessary.[61] Bridges are politically symbolic in a way that does not seem to apply to land crossings.

Water systems shared between countries, such as the Tigris and the Euphrates, the Mekong, and the Rio Grande, create possibilities for cooperation or obstruction, but almost always one nation holds the advantage. Today in our case, that is China. The Chinese, unlike the Russians, do not see the Amur in terms of defensive security. Rather, aware of increasing water scarcity in China, Beijing is interested in harnessing the river for intensive manufacturing use (paper and pulp production, chemical processing) and for irrigation of intensive agriculture. Beyond that, building cross-border bridges has a quite different resonance in the twists and turns of each country's history of political thought. The contemporary official Chinese discourse screens off the historical conflicts associated with boundaries such as the Great Wall or the Amur River. The Great Wall, for example, has now been reimagined as a "cradle of communication and fusion" and a "bond" linking different civilizations.[62] Once such a vision is conceived, China has the political and financial means to try to make it something like a reality. Reimagining borders as "bonds" can be seen as a natural outcome of the attachment of outer realms to China as the center. Hints in Chinese media—never fully official but often recurring—allude to the possible "return" of lost lands to China.[63] For Russia, on the other hand, the state border has historically been a sacrosanct closure, and it is an advantage if it happens to run along such a powerfully un-cozy river as the Amur; any bridge would pose the risk of uncontrolled incursions. The saga of the Blagoveshchensk–Heihe bridge, long since announced but still not yet functioning, is testament to these antinomies.

We should clarify first that Russia under Putin has been an energetic builder of many ambitious, beautiful, and excellently engineered bridges inside its own territory. So is not the difficulty of construction but the destination of this bridge that seems to have been the problem. The Blago–Heihe bridge has been held up for more than thirty years, as a condensed record sent to us in 2015 by a former resident of Blagoveshchensk describes:

> A railway bridge across the Amur (Heilongjiang) was proposed in 1988, when two border cities Blagoveshchensk (Russia) and Heihe (China) saw the start of the great cross-border shuttle trade. In 1991 the Chinese National Planning committee approved the bridge. In November 1992, a company called Most ["Bridge"] Ltd. was created in Blagoveshchensk. The idea was that this company would accumulate money from ordinary people in return for vouchers and invest them in the building of the cross-border bridge. In 1994 Presidents Yeltsin and Jiang discussed and supported the construction of the bridge. In 1995 Russia and China signed an agreement—but that was the high point of the bridge-dream. In 1996, in the government's program for social and economic development of the Russian Far East there was only one short sentence: "The geography of Eurasian transit *might be affected* by the construction of a bridge across the Amur."[64] This unclear statement was repeated in various strategies and programs, while the bridge still existed only on paper. In 2003 China proposed building the bridge, both railway and vehicle, at their own expense. In 2004 all relevant Russian committees approved the construction of the bridge, including even the FSB. A start date was set— December 2004—and in 2005 Heihe officials said they hoped to finish the bridge that year. But straightaway Russia became "anxious" about the monopolistic position of China if China were to be the sole investor. In 2008 Amur Oblast saw the appointment of a new governor,

and he started his term with an announcement of the necessity of the bridge. He was replaced by the next governor, who made the same announcement. In 2012 a real bridge appeared—but it was only a seasonal affair of floating pontoons. And that bridge did not work for months, because its use (not construction) was not approved by Moscow. In 2013 the mayor of Heihe announced that everything was ready for the construction of a proper bridge and the Amur governor was also eager to start the project. Nothing happened. Russian expert advisors were warning that "a bridge is not only a connection between states, but also a tool of intrusion," and regional officers of the FSB made the same objection. However, in summer 2014 the Amur governor reverted again to the possibility of bridge construction.

The Black Dragon too played a role—a great flood in 2013 swept away early stages of construction. But by 2018, the Chinese side had built their approach road and some spans of the bridge. The Russians also had started construction, but then their builders stopped, because they had not received instructions from Moscow on how to set up the border crossing controls. The next Amur governor, Kozlov, worried that this border sovereignty issue would take far longer to agree than building the bridge. Meanwhile, talks had to be held with anxious private investors.[65] And Kozlov had yet to reach agreement with Lu Hao, the governor of Heilongjiang, about whether people driving personal cars would be allowed to use the bridge, something for which there was considerable demand from middle-class Chinese tourists visiting Russia.[66]

This saga reveals first that the building of this bridge involved a multifarious assemblage of actors, from presidents through regional governor to local mayors, as well as the FSB, private funders, construction companies, and "Russian expert advisors." The various Chinese agencies were consistently in favor of construction, but the Russian side was divided and hesitant. A major pattern that emerges is a disjunction between the provinces and Moscow: while the Amur Oblast governors were in favor of the bridge, or at least publicly declared themselves so, the powers in the capital, including the FSB, had a more erratic and/or negative attitude toward it. One Russian high advisor told us in 2015 that this particular route was problematic: military strategists were warning that this was the route by which Chinese tanks might enter Siberia.

After years of waiting for the proclaimed bridge to appear, the inhabitants of Blagoveshchensk were cynical. In 2015, the same author saw the bridge as just one fantasy created in the hot air of international relations:

> The story of the phantom bridge across the Amur is not the only one in the chronicles of cross-border cooperation. Amur Oblast has an imaginary free economic zone, while Primorsky Kray [the region on the Pacific coast] has a dreamlike trade and economic zone, as well as the illusory "Tumen River Triangle" development [a long-running, unrealized plan to link the economies of China, North and South Korea, Russia, and Japan].[67]

By spring 2021, the bridge was finally built on the initiative of the regional governors of Heilongjiang and Amur. Each side was constructed separately, but the Russian part was financed from China, the debt to be repaid by fees charged for crossing. Currently it is planned to be a freight bridge only, and, due to the COVID-19 pandemic border restrictions (see Coda), it is not yet operative. Our local informant said she thought Russia's concern with border security would continue to hold up its opening to passenger traffic. She added that the citizens of Blagoveshchensk were glad that the bridge would not link the two cities directly (it crosses the river some 20 miles away from Blagoveshchensk), as people do not want the pollution, heavy-goods storage depots, and marshaling yards associated with freight transport in their city. The citizens would make do with the present arrangement (ferries in summer, buses across the ice in winter) to reach the Chinese side, with cable cars as an enjoyable pipe dream for the future.

One Chinese perspective on the long delay reaches back into history. An article in the government-linked *Global Times* suggested that the holdup was not due to lack of economic demand on each side but more a question of "collective consciousness shaped over the long course of history." It reminded readers that Chinese tour guides tell their groups not to photograph the Triumphal Arch in Blagoveshchensk because it celebrates the visit of Crown Prince Nikolai in 1891, which was associated with Russia's victory in acquiring Chinese-occupied territories along the Heilongjiang River. The massacre of these Chinese in 1900 "left a scar" (see Chapter 5), even if the two sides "now enjoy a clear border." Noting that the population of Heilongjiang is 38.12 million, while that of Amur Oblast is barely 800,000, the article quotes a Chinese expert who observed, "While the Chinese think about how to develop faster, the Russians prioritize security." In this view from China, the bridge would "heal old wounds."[68]

So what made the Russians overcome security fears and actually build their side of the bridge? And not just this bridge—the final spans on the Russian side of another railway bridge across the Amur were erected in March 2019, connecting Tongjiang with the tiny Russian settlement of Nizhneleninskoe in the Jewish Autonomous Region (see Figure 1.2). This bridge too had been delayed for years, to the great annoyance of the Chinese companies who built their side of it.[69] Why the unlocking? The answer to this question lies with Russia's bold new development policy.

"OVERTAKING"

In 2014, President Putin signed federal law No. 473-FZ, authorizing "Territories of Advanced Socio-Economic Development" (TORs; sometimes translated as "Advanced Development Zones," ADZs).[70] The idea was to jump-start development in the disadvantaged Russian Far East, and soon other impoverished regions, by selecting certain small enclaves for unbridled capitalist investment.[71] Putin's previous policies had had a different, inclusive approach, aimed at giving state support both to vast underdeveloped regions of Siberia and the Far East and to their opposites, the richest and most technically innovative spots in the country, such as the

Skolkovo business area in Moscow. But the results of such programs in the impoverished regions were minimal. How on earth
to turn around Russia's perennial problem? The program of TORs
was a radical and bold idea: abandon most of those vast tracts in
the Far East to their fate and focus instead only on certain chosen
spots to attract large investments—including, or even mainly,
investments by foreigners.

Immediately, some commentators called the law an "act of national betrayal."[72] What shocked attentive Russians is that these
new entities would be "spaces of exception," administratively and
legally detached from the rest of the country. When early versions
of the plan were unveiled, people complained that TOR territories would not coincide with existing boundaries; that they would
be exempted from regular civil law and would not be subject to
the local authorities; and that they would have different regulations regarding taxation, privatization, town planning, forestry,
customs, licensing, employment of foreigners, labor laws, ecology,
and licensing. Nevertheless, the new formations went ahead under
the direct oversight of the president. In the Russian Far East,
TORs are managed by a vast Moscow-based state company, the
Far Eastern Development Corporation (FEDC), which is in charge
of all investment flowing into the designated spots.[73] Combining
the idea of the internationally competitive special economic zone
with state-approved development projects, the aim is to create
maximally attractive conditions for global investment, including
attracting back to Russia money oligarchs had taken abroad.[74]
The incentives include zero tax on land and property, virtually
no tax on business profits for the first five years, and provision
of infrastructure by the Russian state. It so happens that the great
majority of the current eighteen TORs are located on Russia's
land and sea borders, including the border with China. In fact,
we have already touched on three of them: two were set up specifically for the construction of the bridges over the Amur and
the associated infrastructure, and the third was created for the
gas facility and other associated plants at Svobodny.[75]

Typing "Lenin's road" in Russian search engines unleashes an ironic cornucopia of photographs of upended cars, muddy tracts, and potholes. But what do local actors say about TORs? A TOR is not merely a set of contracts; it is also just as ideological a fantasy as Lenin's road. A key word here is *operezhayushchii*, which is usually translated as "advanced" but means "overtaking," a term associated with imagery that leaves the old Soviet posters looking tame by comparison (Figure 1.3).

Wild words have been flying back and forth regarding the TOR system, both for and against. The optimists invoke the idea of Hong Kong ("one country, two systems"), and some suggest that ambitious TOR projects are the Russian Far East's only chance for development.[76] But critics talk of "black holes." According to the economist Yury Boldyrov,

> it [law 473-FZ] is a complete crime. The statement that our power has no strategy is absurd, there is an unambiguous strategy in absolute continuity with the "wild 1990s." The goal is to hand over everything under long-term contracts, in such a way that international and not Russian law will protect the oligarchy. And further, this law 473-FZ is full of falsity. For example, "socioeconomic development." What has this law got to do with that? In today's world, socioeconomic development is [things like] the scientific and medical advances at Akademgorodok in Novosibirsk or Arzamas [site of a large machine-building plant]. But what this law in fact introduces, in one or another form, is dictatorship.[77] TORs are brought into being in order to draw resources from the earth or set up manufacturing processes that are too expensive and ecologically problematic to be done under ordinary conditions. Morally, this is a crime against the people, and the realization of the program will be parasitical on all sorts of other funds.[78]

It was further objected that the incoming "residents" of TORs would be able to eject existing inhabitants at will, since normal legal safeguards on property would be lifted, and rather than hiring locals, they could bring in foreign workers in the numbers and under the conditions they chose. Meanwhile, the state would

pour in money to fund the necessary infrastructure. The benefits would go to the investors, and would they—especially foreign investors—care about the interests of the local population? Each TOR is to last for seventy years. But the arrangement is renewable, and this has raised alarmist fears on sovereignty grounds. Some journalists, TV talk show hosts, and others have speculated that "the Chinese" will regard the territories as their own and start "behaving as masters" inside Russia. A different prediction was that people prepared to invest in the "remote corners" (*glukhie ugolki*) of Russia would be thin on the ground, for the TORs would still be poorly insulated from the prevailing, off-putting local conditions: foot-dragging bureaucracy, corruption,

Figure 1.3. TOR poster (*facing page*): "We are setting off to overtake."
Soviet poster (*this page*): "Our road was shown by Lenin, All others are
crooked and dirty, We will be green only in years, but in deeds and
life we will be red." (politrussia.com; yaplakal.com)

and lack of trust in the provincial leadership.[79] The TORs might
be set up on paper, but nothing much would happen.

In the event, there was a fierce scramble as Far Eastern districts
competed for the right for their places to be included in the list
of TORs. But few foreign "residents" came forward. Over the
past decade Chinese businesspeople have been happy to trade
with Russia, but not to invest in companies located there under
Russian jurisdiction.[80] An article by one of China's foremost experts on cross-border cooperation, based on firsthand research,
was blunt about the reasons: unclear legal security, crumbling

infrastructure, poor transport, weak management, corruption, and a lack of mutual understanding and language skills.[81] Even when investment is directed toward the theoretically welcoming TORs, enterprises face problems: as well as the general economic downturn in Russia, there is a lack of trained local workforces and the likelihood of extraction of "administrative rents" (bribes, kickbacks) by the FEDC. Thus while the eighteen TORs in the Far East licensed in 2019 contained around 330 declared enterprises, only 79 of these could claim to be operational—and in practice, even fewer were working.[82] However, the TORs for Svobodny and the two bridges over the Amur did attract Chinese companies and have actual achievements to their credit. How should this be understood in relation to the central theme of this chapter, the contrasting administrative-territorial orders of Russia and China?

On the one hand, the TORs can be seen as breakthroughs in several ways. Since they directly link Moscow with the enclaves, they cut through the layers of the Russian administrative hierarchy. Instead of the "nineteenth-century thinking" that Victor Larin suggests lingers within the government, TORs insert, or hope to insert, a frankly global capitalist rationale.[83] As territorial-legal exceptions, they breach the age-old spatial order that condemns the lacunae between the regular administrative jurisdictions to neglect and inconsequentiality. Most significant of all, these internal "offshore" projects, each personally vetted by Putin's executive manager, Yury Trutnev, were intended to bring China over the border. It is the president's sovereign might that enabled him to do this. His close connection with the FSB is crucial here, for many of the TORs are inside the *pogranzona* controlled by the security service, and some of them have been set up in the very places that are most redolent of the old defensive thinking—the closed ZATOs. Amid the many and varied kinds of "out-of-bounds" places along the border, some ZATOs have metamorphosed into TORs. The formerly closed city of Vladivostok is now a free port.[84] The nearby ZATO of Bolshoi Kamen', where previously nuclear submarines were manufactured, has been transformed into a TOR, into which international funds are poured for the decommissioning of nuclear arms, as we discuss further in Chapter 3. Thus, the most prohibited and secretive of places have become in a sense the most open—that is, open to global "residents" wielding substantial capital. In several sites, closedness and openness are intertwined in ways that are difficult to disentangle. For example, the military rocket/missile sites at Svobodny remain closed ZATOs, yet people in Blagoveshchensk hopefully anticipate that free-spending Chinese tourists might be attracted over the border to excursions around the Eastern Cosmodrome nearby.[85]

On the other hand, Russia's historical standoff between economic development and the politicized security of the periphery remains. Natalia Ryzhova, one of the foremost experts on the region, argues that it is the metropolitan perception of "national space" that gave rise to the experiment with TORs in the first place. To counter the substantial regional autonomy grabbed during the 1990s under Yeltsin, Putin declared in 2000 that the Far East region was "an inseparable part of Russia," and in 2002 he emphasized its "enormous strategic significance for the whole country." The region's serious demographic, migratory, infrastructural, and environmental problems, the president said, hindered Russia's ability to achieve its duly prominent role in the Asia-Pacific area.[86] Thus, Ryzhova argues, it was continental regional security understood in realistic terms, not economic feasibility, that in fact inspired the TOR scheme. The hypercentralized political will, hierarchical personal patronage, and disregard for local social circumstances characteristic of the Russian system remained central to their implementation. In this light, we can see the TORs not so much as an anomaly with regard to the old spatial order but rather as an example of a new version of it, or a resetting that still has to struggle to free itself from active aspects of the old one (see also Chapter 3). The two bridges over the Amur are cases in point. For while the TOR investment will enable the building of storage facilities, logistics centers, and so on, thus creating jobs near the bridges, it remains to be seen if, when, and in what way the FSB will authorize crossings at will by ordinary citizens of Russia and China. The legislation created to manage the TOR is an example of "a state's struggle with itself," as Ryzhova aptly remarks.[87]

TORs are a sign of a far wider process. By sovereign right Moscow has created a "state of exception," and by the same stroke of the pen Putin legitimated a notable erosion of Russia's border exclusivity.[88] By contrast, the international "development zones" in China, while seemingly similar to those in Russia, did not spring from an abrupt edict but were an established model going back to the 1970s, and they were set up not by Beijing but by provincial and local governments in fierce competition with one another for mobile capital.[89] The theme of local initiative provides a link to Chapters 2 and 3, which will look at political and economic relations in the borderlands "from below." In many diverse kinds of spaces and activities, these borderlands are witness to mixings and contacts—this time initiated by the local people themselves.

STANDOFF IN THE BORDER RIVER

2

PRESSURES ON THE BORDER

Geographers have argued against the popular assumption that borders arise inevitably as boundaries between populations that are "naturally" different from one another.[1] The China-Russia border in general, and in particular the island in the Amur that is the subject of this chapter, confirm how mistaken that assumption can be. There was nothing inevitable about the borders established in the seventeenth and eighteenth centuries, for there were no consolidated culturally different populations to be separated. The sparse indigenous inhabitants were herders, farmers, fishers, and hunters who lived scattered throughout the river basins and forests, and for them the border was nothing but an alien imposition. It was not until the twentieth century that the borderlands were populated en masse by Russians and Chinese. We discuss the dislocation of the indigenous peoples in Chapter 4. Here we attend to the complex matter of the ways in which the two dominating political cultures, each having its distinctive imagination of history, intersect at the border with ongoing local processes of security, economic development, and ecological concerns. Our case study—a small island that was divided in 2008 into a Russian half and a Chinese half—shows how these multiple countervailing pressures came to be crystallized in particularly concentrated and symbolic forms in one locale.

State governments are often called on to justify the location of their borders, and in this regard the political geographer Anne-Laure Amilhat Szary makes a seemingly arcane but actually very pertinent distinction between the "law of nature" and "natural law."[2] The former refers to whatever exists on the ground and is justified empirically, but "natural law" is in effect a moral claim: not what is, but what ought to be. Though the expression "natural law" is not used by either Chinese or Russian statesmen, something like "natural law" is what both countries had in mind throughout the nineteenth and twentieth centuries when each of them claimed the entirety of the Amur up to the opposite bank (if not farther) as rightfully theirs.[3] All islands in the rivers were thus subject to irresolvable dual claims. In the end, when seeking to put an end to numerous disputes about islands in the Argun, Amur, and Ussuri, the politicians had to reach for an alternative to the deeply felt views of their compatriots, an alternative that they found in the "law of nature": the border would follow the thalweg wherever it happened to be. Yet, as this chapter will show, natural law–type moral sentiments have not disappeared.

The island discussed in this chapter exists under the awkward dual name Heixiazi (Chinese side) and Bolshoi Ussuriiskii (Russian side). Its two sides are administered by the authorities on each bank. It has ceased to be subject to any common policy, and the separate parts are inevitably drawn into the disparate local processes and policy swings in each nation. If we zoom out to consider the whole region, we can see that the tensions inherent in the situation arise in great part because both postimperial formations struggle to control their underdeveloped peripheries. There are panicky Russian fears about a flow of migration spilling over from China that might combine in some disastrous fashion with independence movements in the Russian Far East. Meanwhile, China's rapid but uneven economic growth is putting pressure on employment, land, and the environment in the northeast, resulting in the emergence of dissatisfied marginalized citizens who have little alternative other than to exploit local resources even more intensively in order to try to achieve the prosperity found in other parts of the country. The Chinese government has become aware of this problem and is seeking to curb the negative effects through policies under the banner of Xi Jinping's "China's Dream." These envision eradicating deep poverty and at the same time building an "ecological civilization." This is no empty slogan: virtually all of the lands bordering Russia have been designated as specially protected "ecological function areas" supported by a budget increase from 6 billion yuan in 2008 to 62.7 billion yuan in 2017. The new policy is to prioritize biodiversity, soil conservation, and flood mitigation in these areas while restricting farming, mining, and logging, and forbidding them altogether in nature reserves.[4] However, taking land out of circulation or limiting its use only creates increasingly intense competition for the remainder, and this has obvious implications for the seemingly empty areas over the border in Russia. We discuss the wider economic and environmental issues further in Chapters 4 and 6; here we describe the effects of such pressures as they are concentrated in one small place.

The very oddity of the position of this small, bounded, and yet "unnaturally" divided island has made it a focus of both states' attention and a target for their changing policies. There is therefore something systemic (or "state embedded") about the way each side of the island has evolved, but the actual implementation has occurred through the activities of a variety of individual actors. These people, as we will show, can be found from the very top to the very bottom of the sociopolitical hierarchies in each country, and they have had differing motivations. The result has been that even over a short period, the very status of the two parts of the island—what they are said to be *for*—has undergone a chameleon-like metamorphosis. If anything, the differences between the sides have only intensified. A main reason for this is that the Chinese side of the island has become a showcase for environmental policies, whereas the Russian side has not. In Russia, ecology is barely mentioned in regard to the status of the island, while dreamlike international economic investment looms large. In the most general sense, the conjunction at this border of two radically dissimilar ways of relating population, economic development, and environmental damage is part of the global ecological crisis of humanity in the twenty-first century. But the pressures are made actual through the effects of individual decisions.

DIPLOMATIC MANEUVERINGS

It is useful first to understand *ethnographically* how these two states operate strategically in relation to each other. In recent years, after countless preparatory meetings, agreements between Russia and China and joint planning decisions have been shown off in the glare of publicity at international meetings, such as the Eastern Economic Forum (EEF), hosted by Russia annually in Vladivostok since 2013. The stated aim of the EEF is to encourage investment in Russia's resource-rich yet underpopulated Far East, but this goal is secondary to Russia's global political aims. Consequently, bilateral talks between Russia and China now take place against the backdrop of potential multilateral alternatives.[5] Russia has recently been playing the Indian card, attempting, for example, to attract investment from Delhi in the Vladivostok area. A flavor of the ambience can be seen in the language of an Indian observer's assessment. "Russia's evolving Asia-Pacific strategy," he writes,

> is premised on the following postulations: the West is on a path of irreversible decline, and Asia will remain the engine of growth in the near future; a strong partnership with China is key to its growth and to offset the US influence in Eurasia and Pacific; it must reinforce ties with key regional players such as Japan, South Korea, Vietnam and India to attract capital and to prevent China from becoming a regional hegemon; and finally, a close integration of Siberia and the Far Eastern region to the economies of the Asia-Pacific is essential for its regional stability. . . . Bringing India on board can be seen as a part of Russia's broader strategy to balance China's expanding influence in the region.[6]

This statement exposes a hovering contradiction: Russia needs China economically, even as it strategizes to forestall China's "regional hegemony." In these ambiguous circumstances, we can begin to see why a seemingly important element of the 2018 EEF, the drawing up of a new program of Chinese-Russian cross-border economic collaboration for the period 2018–2024, ended up being sidelined. President Xi Jinping had arrived in Vladivostok with an imposingly, almost threateningly large suite of regional officials, with their many proposals and big budgets. Meanwhile, Russia was holding massive military exercises with Chinese participation at its Tsugol proving ground near the border. But despite the "trusting relationship" with China proclaimed by Putin at the 2018 EEF in the spheres of politics, security, and defense, the new economic program was modest. In the words of a Russian observer:

> In the end, the EEF fell into a well-trodden rut . . . : the same record number of attendees, the same dozens of agreements worth astronomical sums that are far from certain to be implemented, the same hype around the top restaurants, and the endless closing of major roads to the public to allow official corteges to pass unhindered by traffic. In terms of these parameters, the forum is a complete success.[7]

The bureaucrats delayed publication of the proposed cross-border projects. There was also silence on the disappointing results of the previous 2009–2018 program. And the new program avoided mention of key issues: the ambitious Russian TORs (see Chapter 1) were left out, as was the construction of cross-border expressways requested by the governments of Heilongjiang and Jilin. And barely mentioned was the long-planned collaboration on the island in the Amur that is the subject of this chapter. According to knowledgeable insiders, the decision to omit these points was made on the advice of the Russian Ministry of Foreign Affairs, the reasons being that the Russian side doubted the economic gains to Russia of the proposed ventures, and in any case was unsure about the possibility of getting agreement for them from the security powers.[8] After delays during which several previously agreed plans were quietly dropped from the final document, only a tiny number of joint projects already under way, notably the two bridges mentioned in Chapter 1, were given definite dates for completion, while other promising undertakings were vaguely worded. Even the official joint report, *Russian-Chinese Dialogue 2018,* concludes that, compared to political and strategic cooperation, economic interaction has always been the weakest link in Russian-Chinese relations.[9]

Presiding over all this for Russia was the supremo Yuri Trutnev, whose recently centralized role combines mastery over both the development of the Far East and regional cross-border collaboration. During the years of negotiations he faced an array of powerful—yet changing—Chinese regional leaders. Furthermore, as political journalist Ivan Zuenko remarks, despite Russia's readiness to hypercentralize power in a single pair of hands, the "traditional bureaucracy" (the Ministries of Finance and Foreign Affairs and the Federal Security Service) "are fully capable of blocking any initiative Trutnev and his team might come up with."[10] In short, the high-level deliberations at the EEF, so resonant regarding global governance, left the cross-border economic investments hanging in the air. Almost all of the joint projects in the new plan are just potentialities that might or might not produce results. The border economy was left in a state of irresolution; in this situation, each region has had to make do as best it can. This chapter describes one such case.

ONE ISLAND IN TWO COUNTRIES

Let us now focus attention on the island, a desolate, sandy place of marshes, shrubs, and glinting waters near the middle of the long border. Covering approximately 130 square miles, it is the largest of many islets at the confluence of the Ussuri and the Amur. By an agreement in 2004 that was put into practice in 2008, the western half of it, along with the nearby smaller Tarabarov, Vinogradnyi, and Koreiskii islands, belongs to China, while the

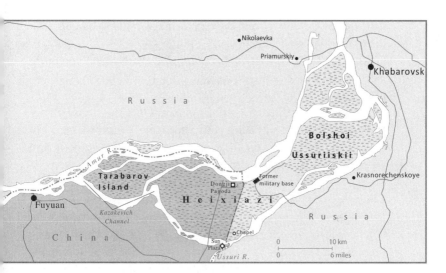

Map 3. Heixiazi and Bolshoi Ussuriiskii

eastern half belongs to Russia. Nevertheless, each country still uses its own names for the whole: the Russians call the main island Bolshoi Ussuriiskii and the main adjoining island Tarabarov (see Map 3), while for the Chinese the entire archipelago, which including tens of islets, is known as Heixiazi Island (黑瞎子岛, Black Blind Island[11]). This naming habit, which also applies to the maps produced in each country, reflects inherited "law of nature" imaginaries and the fact that both Russia and China had historically claimed the whole area. The 2004 agreement, however, resorted to the international convention of the thalweg. This happens to lie closest to Russia, and the whole island should therefore have become Chinese territory.[12] But a concession was made to Russian security concerns, and the island was divided roughly in half, north to south, in order to provide a protective buffer to Khabarovsk, the capital of the Russian Far Eastern Region, which lies across the water from the eastern end of the island.[13] The only

Chinese town in the vicinity, the smaller Fuyuan, lies a short distance from its western point.

Manchu Qing Dynasty maps marked a swath of land on both sides of the Amur as theirs, including the island, where a border post was set up in 1854. In 1901 fifteen families of the Hezhe indigenous group moved onto the island. Others soon migrated from both Russia and China, and a total of 47 families lived on the island in 1928.[14] At some point a Russian village quietly appeared on the east bank of the island, opposite Khabarovsk. This place, and indeed the whole island, was called by Russian locals Chumka, meaning "plague-struck." This was probably because it was used as a quarantine base for ships and livestock from China. Locals also say that the name arose because in tsarist days there was a strict rule that dogs dying from rabies could only be buried away from the city on the island.[15] In either case, for local Russians, the island was "ours," but a place apart.

In 1929, however, the island was invaded by the Soviet Union. The weak National Government of China ceded it and the adjoining islands as part of the Khabarovsk Protocol, by which the Soviets reasserted the earlier tsarist control over parts of Manchuria. After 1949, the Communist government of China rejected the protocol and claimed the islands as part of Fuyuan county, the easternmost province of the country. However, the Soviets ignored this claim and built an army base on Bolshoi Ussuriiskii, aiming to control the Amur and Ussuri waterways and protect Khabarovsk against potential Chinese invasion. The indigenous families were removed (see Chapter 4), and the Soviets refused to grant China navigation rights in the adjoining waters. Hostility between Maoist China and the USSR subsided after the demise of the Soviet Union. Nevertheless, there was popular anger in both countries at the 2004 agreement. This was especially the case in Russia, for after the breakup of the USSR, the country's redefined contours evoked in the public mood nothing but a sense of loss, and "giving away" even half of a small island was sharply felt as a loss of sacred Russian land.[16] In 2005 Siberian Cossacks demonstrated in Khabarovsk. Alarmist maps appeared on the Russian internet illustrating various alleged nefarious Chinese activities, such as setting fire to Russian dachas (summer cottages) on the island and provocatively waving flags in their newly reacquired territory. Characteristically, such maps show Khabarovsk but not Fuyuan.

Leading up to the 2004 agreement, a so-called irrigation war had been brewing. Both countries had been carrying out hydrotechnical construction to strengthen the riverbanks but also, and more importantly, engineering works to induce the main currents to flow along particular lines desirable to themselves, providing legitimation for the eventual border.[17] But the Black Dragon was also following its own bent, whatever human efforts were made. A Russian blogger wrote anxiously:

> The channel dividing the island from Kazakevich village on our bank got shallower and shallower, no matter how many attempts were made to deepen it, and this reduced any small chance of Russia establishing its international legal rights to the island. And on the other side the Chinese filled the channel with bargeloads of sand, so as to attach their bank more quickly to the developed parts of the islands. Our neighbors did as they wanted, silently, without emotional declarations, unlike us.[18]

The island, the subject of so much emotion, is controlled at a distance by two cities that embody the Russian-Chinese political-cultural difference. Khabarovsk, with a population of about 570,000, is an archetypally governmental place. The site was seized by the Cossacks from the native population in the seventeenth century (and today the town is named after one of them, Yerofei Khabarov); it was soon recaptured by the Manchus, however, who called it Boli, and it remained part of the Qing Empire until the Aigun Treaty in 1858, whereupon it was ceded to Russia. The city then became a military base and industrial center, with state offices, cathedrals, a university, museums, theaters, high-tech medical centers, and a TV station added over the years. The palatial residence of the tsarist governor-general of Siberia was located there. When President Putin decreed in 2000 that Russia would be divided into seven new federal districts (*okrugs*), Khabarovsk was made not only the seat of the governorship of the Khabarovsk region (*krai*) but also the seat of the plenipotentiary presidential representative for the entire vast Far Eastern *okrug*, which now stretches from Lake Baikal to the Pacific, from the Arctic Circle to the North Korean border. Khabarovsk spreads spaciously along the riverbank, disperses into villages, and then peters out as deserted marshes and dark forest take over.

Fuyuan, by contrast, was a tiny outpost in the Great Northern Wilderness (*beidahuang*), a speck in an expanse of untouched forest and wetlands. But after 1949 four waves of "land reclamation" saw northeast Manchuria intensively populated, first by 100,000 demobilized soldiers sent to "support the border regions" (*zhibian*), then by 450,000 "educated youths" sent for reeducation during the Cultural Revolution, then in the 1970s and again in the 1980s when thousands more reclaimed expanses for agriculture (wheat, rice, soybeans) by advanced mechanized methods.[19] For many years the life of frontier people was hardship and toil: living in primitive housing heated by wood-fired stoves, farming and fishing surrounded by a primal forest realm of black bears, deer, tigers, snow hares, leopards, and wild boar. But by the 1980s most of the forest had been cut down and the wetlands drained. More migrants arrived. The population of Fuyan town rose from 27,000 in 1985 to 50,000 in 2000 and is well over 100,000 today, with an additional 70,000 still working in the state farms established by the soldiers in the 1950s.[20] In short, the area became an important part of China's "rice basket," the region that feeds the whole country. The town proper became the center of a densely populated county that borders Russia along both the Amur and the Ussuri.[21] Heixiazi Island lies to the northeast of this well-farmed plain. In short, the island straddles a riverine zone between two towns that embody quite different histories and interests: centuries-old government in Russia and recent agricultural expansion in China.

For decades, the island had dozed as a Soviet militarized border zone, without a bridge to the mainland (though the ice was crossable in winter). Part of it was made a Soviet collective farm with a village. In 2008 the army moved out of its base, though the empty ruined barracks and some former support staff still remain. Russian residents on the Chinese side had to move, and most left the island altogether. The former collective farm village, which once had around 500 inhabitants, steadily lost population. Many of the houses were converted into dachas for the townsfolk of Khabarovsk. So after it was divided and the border established, the island began to lose most of its inhabitants. Yet it remains a potent symbol. For the Chinese, it is the easternmost point of their country. For the Russians, it is land valiantly won and rightfully theirs. It is in this symbolic-cultural vein that diverse structures have been erected on the island (a tall pagoda on the Chinese side and a Christian chapel on the Russian) and that local bloggers from the two countries expostulate about it.

BUILDING SYMBOLIC MARKERS

A Chinese blog, prefaced by a phantasmagorical map of the vast territory that ought to belong to China, including much of Central Asia, southern Siberia, the Russian Far East, and Sakhalin, complains that the whole of Heixiazi should be Chinese land.[22] The accompanying photographs—of Russians raising cows, erecting warning signs, planting potatoes, visiting a grandmother—are implicitly an affront to Chineseness. Next, photographs of the island's "enchanting scenery" and a hillock said to be a sacrificial site of the Daur people are interspersed with pictures of a Russian gunboat and soldiers measuring off the border line. Photos of "fertile pasture" and "fresh flowers wilderness" follow. Russia's state boundary marker is then shown, with the small brick Orthodox Christian chapel in the background. In the foreground is the river with a fishing boat and the caption "The Chinese fishermen are near at hand . . . [but] cannot [land] on the island." The chapel was deliberately constructed in 1999, says the blog, and it became the real Sino-Russian boundary marker. No one goes to this church. The building is just "an excuse," the blog claims, because in truth the whole island should return to China.[23]

Mirroring this picture of an idyllic, sun-drenched, fertile island, unfairly divided and marred by signs of alien culture, Russian blogs focus on the foreignness and astonishing smartness of Chinese installations on the tragically lost land.[24] The chapel has been given an inscription: "And one in the field is a warrior" (*i odin v pole voin*). This alludes to its lonely role as an outpost. The phrase works by reversing a well-known Russian saying (also the title of a film about World War II): "One [man] in the field is not a warrior" (*odin v pole ne voin*). The inscription is saying that one lone fighter *can* be a warrior. As for the golden cross on top of the chapel, a Russian blogger observes that it is "easily visible from the Chinese bank—either as a symbol of God's protection of us from foreigners, or alternatively, as a sign of Christian humility."[25]

In fact, every so often a regiment of soldiers and their families are transported to the lonely chapel for a *krestnyi khod,* a Christian procession. And this is but one of several activities that mark this rim of Russia as the boundary of a religious realm. Two communities are particularly zealous in upholding this idea: Trans-Baikal Cossacks, who after decades of repression for their desperate anti-Bolshevik stand in the civil war have reappeared as a patriotic volunteer militia, and the Old Believers, historically exiles in Siberia, who have always upheld the ideal of a sacred space separated off from the realm of the Antichrist. Activists from these two groups have gotten together in recent years to educate young acolytes by reenacting the heroic journeys of their seventeenth-century founder heroes. On one occasion, using two handmade rafts named after two of these heroes, Pyotr Beketov, the Cossack explorer and fortress builder, and Archpriest Avvakum,

Figure 2.1. The team of the Old Believer raft starting their journey on the river Shilka.
(Photo by Dominic Martin)

the exiled Old Believer martyr who was burned at the stake for his opposition to secular and foreign influences, the groups sought to reconstitute the ancient idea of sacred Russian territory. Sailing down the Shilka and on along the Amur, they sang hymns, visited churches on the Russian shore, and studiously ignored the Chinese bank (Figure 2.1).

On the island, apart from building the chapel, the Russians left things almost as they were. The Chinese, however, carried out plans to turn their side into an ecological tourist park. This was an ideological as well as commercial venture, and the pagoda was an important symbolic feature. Built of shining white stone with nine stories and a pinnacle, the Dongji (East Pole) pagoda rears up 81 m high, reached by a flight of stairs leading from a wide circular platform. Guarded by statues of giant chimerical beasts, the whole edifice is edged with tall pillars intricately carved with dragons. As architectural structures, pagodas originated historically as the Sinified form given to Buddhist stupas containing sacred relics. However, the new pagoda on the island has no religious meaning. It stands, rather, as a reification of Chineseness, of cultural magnificence, of the notion of a vista from on high. The same ideas are reiterated at a second towering monument known as Dongji Plaza (Sun Plaza), constructed at Wusu, a hamlet on the mainland just across from the chapel on the island. The plaza was designated a prime national ceremonial destination, and a new "expressway" was built to access it from cities to the south. It is called Sun Plaza because, being the easternmost tip of China, it is the first place in the country to receive the sun's rays in the morning. Advertised across the country, it has received thousands of visitors; no doubt older generations remember the revolutionary song "The sun is red, the sun is rising, from China appears Mao Zedong." Visitors are also encouraged to take tours, crossing to the island on a newly constructed bridge. They stroll along raised walkways winding through the ecological vistas and tended wetlands, admiring the tall, elegant pagoda rising among the marshes.

How would an external eye see the island's curious bifurcated situation? In 2016 Bruno Maçães, a Portuguese diplomat, visited the Russian side. Entering was "as difficult as you might imagine. You must be accompanied by Russian border guards and before anything else a long interview with a secret service agent awaits. I was asked about every imaginable detail about my previous life and all the papers I had with me were examined and photographed." Portugal, he was informed, is an enemy country. Why so? Because Portugal is a member of NATO. Following an elaborate political discussion with the FSB officer, Maçães talked briefly with the less sophisticated border guards. They seemed to agree with the idea that the main reason for the division of the

Figure 2.2. The monumental Chinese character for "east" at Sun Plaza. (CGTN)

island was the implicit promise that China would help Russia develop the whole area with strong investment and millions of tourists.[26] However, Maçães's *razvedchik* (the FSB security officer) said all this was nonsense, and that sometimes he could not understand what the people in Moscow were aiming to do.[27] Certainly no Chinese cash had reached Bolshoi Ussuriiskii, which was almost completely deserted and mostly still in ruins. What struck Maçães most forcibly was the symbolism: the tiny Christian chapel, which is surrounded by wilderness, is dedicated to St. Victor the Martyr, to commemorate the soldiers who died fighting to defend the borders in the Far East. The giant Sun Plaza on the promontory opposite features an enormous sculptural representation of the Chinese character for "east" (*dong*) topped by a golden ball (Figure 2.2). "Is this a proclamation that the east is Chinese?" Maçães wonders. He concludes his article with a final thought on this symbol. The plaza, he writes, with the monumental Chinese character pointed at Khabarovsk, looks from above unmistakably like a warship, a destroyer named *East*. This interpretation is supported by at least one Chinese website, which describes the plaza promontory, with the motherland at its back, as looking like "a sharp-edged warship bow cleaving through the waves towards the east."[28]

But symbols such as the chapel, the pagoda, and the *dong* character obscure the fact that neither country is a monolith, and there have been practical disagreements and swerves over policy in both of them. In far northeast China, these have focused on the conflict between agricultural productivity and ecological preservation of the wetlands. In Russia, the clash is over economic development of any kind versus the demands of security. Here we try to piece together via the specific case of the island how the process of decision-making in different administrative structures produces such divergent effects.

CHINESE DEVELOPMENTS

The Chinese central government began to consider taking action over its environmental problems in the late 1990s. There was a new understanding of the importance of wetlands in flood control and of the pollution caused by agricultural chemicals. The country was opening to the world, becoming aware of international NGOs and donor agencies, and seeking to repair its image in the post–Tiananmen Square era. Importantly, regional officials were willing to take leadership and learn from mistakes in handling the environment.[29] Severe problems had become apparent in the vicinity of Fuyuan: the reclaimed land was losing fertility, sometimes drying out, and streams were polluted. Excessive tree-cutting, overfishing, and overhunting had slashed wildlife populations—the population of magnificent Amur tigers was down to single figures (see Chapter 6). The Fuyuan county government took action. In 1993 it proposed creating a nature reserve—though perhaps less for altruistic reasons than as a way of attracting funding and as a career opportunity for the officials.[30] The project was approved at the provincial level, and in 1994 the director of the county's forestry bureau, Zhang Xixian, was appointed to establish and manage the reserve, which was called Sanjiang (Three Rivers) Reserve. Its headquarters in Fuyuan now manages three reserve areas along the Amur and Ussuri, though initially this did not include Heixiazi Island. Zhang was a true enthusiast for environmental values, and the reserve was set up as a local initiative. But soon it met an answering warmth from the capital. Zhang was encouraged and instructed by Ma Zhong, a professor of environmental studies in Beijing, who had been one of those youths "sent down" to Fuyuan for reeducation after the Cultural Revolution.[31] Ma became the linchpin connecting the reserve to the central government. After one of his reports, the Finance Ministry and the National Environmental Protection Agency sent a team to Sanjiang, and following their report the reserve was elevated to a national-level nature reserve.[32]

This sudden rise in status brought conflict with several agencies (the state farms, the Land Reclamation Bureau, and the State Forestry Administration). It also caused a turnaround in the attitude of Fuyuan's municipal officials, for Sanjiang Reserve was no longer under their authority; in fact, its management had priority over them. Moreover, the municipality stood to lose tax income from the farmers in the belts around the protected zones, who now paid rent to the reserve. Logging and fishing were prohibited in these zones. Increases in population were no longer to be welcomed. Farmland was not to be expanded—in fact, it was to be reduced and converted back to wetland. In other words, all the previous indicators of "success" as far as the town officials were concerned were beginning to look negative, and this was bad for their careers.[33] Local migrant workers, desperate to make a living by farming, hunting, and fishing, were also opposed to the reserve. Economic prosperity and environmental protection were at loggerheads, and there were regular infringements on the reserve. But in practice, many small crises were resolved by "talking things over," helped by the fact that leaders of the different organizations in Fuyuan were sometimes close relatives.[34]

Interestingly, the proximity of the border was a key factor in the complex set of relations involved in this standoff. The People's Liberation Army (PLA), whose units were stationed in the area to reinforce the border with Russia, took on extra duties. The army not only enforced the government's nature protection policies but also became a surprising champion of the new environmental values. Soldiers took up planting trees, rescuing animals, making nesting sites for birds, and participating in environmental education projects. For them, protecting nature was linked to patriotism—they were encouraged to see love for the land itself as part of their Chinese identity. The army's hierarchical military structure became an efficient conveyor in disseminating the new values cultivated in Beijing to the local populace. But they also injected a patriotic-military interest: the soldiers instructed villagers that proper use of land is connected with border defense. This produced a striking counter to the Russians' "irrigation war" fear that the Chinese were dumping sand in the river to attach the island to their side. Perhaps the trucks espied from afar had in fact been doing the opposite, for it seems that Chinese civilians had been *digging out* riverbank sand for domestic building purposes. Now, however, because of the Sanjiang Reserve, this practice was forbidden. The soldiers reinforced the ban with patriotic argument, teaching that when the bank became eroded the river's central line moved toward China and hence reduced the national land area. They proclaimed, "Digging sand means selling our homeland for private gain."[35] Meanwhile, military resources (boats, telescopes, personnel, offices and observation stations) were made available to the management of the reserve.

Both the reserve and the Fuyuan municipality were underfunded by the government and had to seek external income wherever they could. The reserve managed to obtain international grant aid, but the town encountered difficulties on all sides.[36] The vigilance of the PLA limited the municipality's usual income from illicit "fees" for turning a blind eye to illegal logging, fishing, and land grabs; the state farms were under a separate jurisdiction and contributed nothing to the budget, meanwhile tarnishing local reputation by infringing on the reserve lands. With every legitimate square meter of farmland crammed full, yet tax income from agriculture down, one official raged, "Fuyuan wants economic development. . . . What bonuses come out of your reserve?"[37] It is not surprising that municipal officials put two and two together and realized that the riverine ecology *could* be put to use for development—via promoting commercial ecotourism. Heixiazi Island was the ideal spot. It was too marshy for agriculture, and near enough to benefit from the glamour of the reserve without actually being in it. The whole district was included in an "ecological function area," which gave a cover narrative to the ecotourism project. Less strictly regulated than the reserve, Heixiazi had prospects for what some would see as an oxymoron: intensive "ecological development."

Then in 2013 the Black Dragon thrashed its tail. The Amur burst its banks in a vast flood. Virtually the whole island disappeared under water. The Chinese "ecological walkways" and bird-watching platforms were swept away; many of the Russian cottages were upended. Most of the Russian population was rehoused in Khabarovsk, leaving only a defiant fifty or sixty permanent residents on the island. But the Chinese quickly repaired their structures and finished construction of two bridges to the island. Tourism revived, and it was said that 600,000 visitors were arriving every year.[38] The Russians also built a fine bridge, but seemingly as part of some project that evaporated, for the asphalted bridge turns into a dirt road leading to the former army base and does not reach the populated area of the island. As for the border fence dividing the island in two, it is a dead zone. Chinese and Russian roads do not go near it, nor do they meet at any point. It is not possible to cross the border from one side of the island to another.

Soon the power of Beijing descended over Fuyuan again. In 2016 President Xi Jinping decided on an inspection visit to the far northeast, including to the island. Alarmed at the economic decline in the region, he declared that there were too many inefficient small household farms around Fuyuan; they should be amalgamated into cooperatives and "revitalized" by advanced technology in order to provide food security for China. During a tour of nearby indigenous Hezhe villages (see Chapter 4), Xi dropped a bombshell about commercial logging: it was to be drastically curtailed. "Lumbering in the past was necessary," he said. "Protections are now also necessary."[39] Though Xi mentioned that alternative employment would be sought for the thousands of forestry workers who would be out of a job, clearly the full stop to logging would increase the population pressure on the border area mentioned earlier. Proceeding to Heixiazi, Xi made another devastating announcement: the island was not to be used for development of any kind, including for leisure. He instructed: "All existing infrastructural objects must be rebuilt in such a way as to service only the preservation of ecology. The environment must be preserved in pristine form."[40] One can only imagine how these pronouncements were received by the municipal authorities. But they had to obey, as the island was now included in the reserve territory. Visits were restricted to Chinese citizens only, and even they needed to obtain special permission to visit.

As it happened, Xi's strictures coincided with central party and state campaigns, also masterminded by him, that pushed patriotism as a means of bolstering authoritarian government and could not be ignored by any citizen and especially not by officials. What next happened in Fuyuan revealed that however pressing the need was to keep the economic machine turning, that took second place to the power play involved in demonstrating regional loyalty to Beijing. So for several months before the triumphant celebration of the seventieth anniversary of liberation in October 2019, Fuyuan laid on, or was instructed to lay on, an outburst of popular national fervor. An ecstatic flag-raising ritual was held at Sun Plaza and daily in the Fuyuan town center.

The enthusiastic media endowed Fuyuan with new epithets (China's "East Pole" and "Oriental First Whistle") and redescribed it as a "patriotism education base" as well as being a "national ecological demonstration" area. Large numbers of tourists, local cadres, students, soldiers, and "the masses" were gathered to watch the first ceremony. The attendees, wearing smart uniforms or colorful ethnic dress, pinned flag badges on one another's chests, waved small national flags, and sang anthems to express their devotion to China. It is not known how long the daily flag-raising rituals, which also seems to have been seen as a greeting to the rising sun, continued after the anniversary on October 1, 2019, but it is significant that similar ceremonies were held in Mohe, now designated "Arctic Village," the small town on the Amur that is China's northernmost tourist attraction, just as Fuyuan is the most easterly. In both cases, their peaceful freshness, beautiful scenery, and ecological purity were hailed as points of national pride that every year would attract "hundreds of thousands of people from all over the world"—and presumably also provide a flow of income.[41]

No public event on China's borders happens by accident. In Hunchun, for example, the bank that faces across the river to the grim poverty of North Korea hosts a children's fun area, a dance floor where couples sway slowly under lanterns in the trees in the evenings, and many cheerfully noisy roast-meat-and-liquor joints—all surely intended to demonstrate China's prosperity, so lacking in the dark huddle of the village across the water. Similarly, the performances of optimistic flag-waving patriotism in Mohe and the Sun Plaza face across the river to Russia.

President Xi's strictures may have consigned Heixiazi to a strictly ecological purpose, but this did not put a halt to projects in the area. Wusu, the site of Sun Plaza, was scheduled for development into a large town. On the island, a stylish saucer-shaped conservatory was designed for a botanical garden. Also recently added to the existing border barracks and watch tower are a carefully tended lotus lake and an "ethnographic village" of the

Hezhe people.[42] As a further tourist attraction and to match the island's name, one hundred black bears were introduced in 2020. If they are housed in the new "zoo" mentioned scornfully by Russian observers, the bears may suffer a similar fate to wildlife held in enclosures elsewhere in the borderlands, such as the miserable squawking birds in cages in a nature reserve at Zhalong or the dejected tigers languishing in a field near Harbin witnessed by Ben Whately in 2005.[43] It is more likely, however, that the island will indeed become an ecologically appropriate sanctuary for endangered black bears, even though elsewhere in China these bears are farmed in grim conditions to produce medicinal substances, and across the border in Russia they are hunted extensively and the parts smuggled across to eager Chinese customers (see Chapter 6). In other words, by presidential edict, the "bear park" looks set to become an artificially "pristine enclave," a lesson, and a showcase to neighbors. In anticipation of increased outreach, in 2017 an expressway was built to the island, accompanied by hopeful statements that it "will eventually connect a new transnational road crossing over the Amur to the Jewish Autonomous Oblast and to Khabarovsk."[44]

In contrast to what was happening on the Chinese side of the island, the Russian side was sunk in a far more profound uncertainty. For the question of its fate brought the metropolis and the periphery into contact in a configuration different from that seen in China—one that is more contradictory and more confusing.

ON THE RUSSIAN SIDE OF THE ISLAND

In Khabarovsk, the governor since 1992, Viktor Ishaev, had opposed handing over any territory to China, and in protest of the 2004 agreement he had limited freedom of navigation on the Amur and Ussuri. He had proclaimed the need for economic development of the island, which technically was part of the city. The federal decision to cede half of it hit the public "like thunder in a clear sky."[45] The city erupted in protest, meetings were organized, dissenting letters with tens of thousands of signatures were sent to Moscow, and student movements were in ferment. But suddenly and strangely, Ishaev disappeared from public view, said to be "on leave" (though it is recorded that all governors of Russian regions had signed the handover documents for the island, according to protocol). It thus appears that he had deserted his constituents in their protests. As pointed out in a local online article, his silence was related to the fact that 2004 was also the year in which governors ceased being elected and would henceforth be appointed from Moscow. Why get into a conflict with "the power vertical"? Before long, possibly as a reward for his loyalty to the center, Ishaev was promoted—he was appointed as the presidential representative (*polpred*) for the entire Far Eastern Region. Now he came out in favor of *not* developing the island. "The builder of the Russian bridge to Bolshoi Ussuriiskii should be given the award Hero of China, not Hero of the Far East," he snarled. "It's a joke that constructing a bridge will lead to economic development of our region. They [the Chinese] are building their bridge to use the island for transit and trying to push us to do the same. What will we carry over this bridge? We have nothing to take. Should we become just a transit territory?" Evidently, he was attending to voices from the security services in Moscow.

The next governor of Khabarovsk was Vyacheslav Shport, and, being keen on promiscuous economic advances, he took a different view. In 2011, he supported an imaginative cornucopia of projects for development of the island, including a business center, a port for large and small shipping, a hippodrome, a Cossack village, a Russian-themed amusement park, an aquapark, an ethnographic center focusing on the indigenous peoples of the Amur, and a water leisure complex. He was hopeful that all of this would be done jointly with the Chinese, perhaps even funded by them. Russia promised to invest 19.3 billion rubles, but it never found the investors. The 2013 flooding put paid to this plan. In any case, there were high-ranking security officials in Moscow whose clout projected downward through the presidential representative,

Ishaev. It seems that Shport, who was one rung down the hierarchy, was kept in the dark about their discussions. An article that alludes to these details concludes that the governor was stymied: "If Shport takes any step—the *polpred* [Ishaev] will block it. For Viktor Ishaev that's a matter of principle, of philosophy."[46]

So what to do with the island? In 2014, there was talk of housing refugees from eastern Ukraine on Bolshoi Ussuriiskii. A year later, the federal authorities came up with another plan that would have built docking piers for domestic and foreign tourist cruise ships envisaged as sailing north up the Amur all the way to the Sea of Okhotsk. Once again, investors could not be found for this project. As for following China's ecological vision for the island, this had low priority. There was no need; Russia already had a countrywide system of reserves, protected areas, and national parks (see Chapter 7), including the vast Bolshekhekhtsirskii Reserve near Khabarovsk, located in a forested mountain range with a rich concentration of flora and fauna, including tigers.

Still, ambitious plans for development continued to be generated. In 2014, Aleksandr Galushka, minister for development of the Far East, declared that Bolshoi Ussuriiskii would become a TOR (see Chapter 1); it was to be designated for tourist recreation and celebration of the national traditions of the people of Russia.[47] However, in a contrary move in the same year, that path was firmly closed and Moscow's security-conscious policy was confirmed when the Russian bridge to the island was closed—even though it had been ceremonially opened only a year before. Travelers encountered concrete blocks, guards, and a barrier, and only residents holding permits were allowed through (Figure 2.3). In other words, Bolshoi Ussuriiskii returned to its old state of exception, the status of a particularly neglected restricted-access border zone.[48]

By 2017, although the Russian bridge to the island had been reopened, it became clear that no development on Bolshoi Ussuriiskii would be possible without the installation of a checkpoint

Figure 2.3. Entry to the Russian bridge to Bolshoi Ussuriiskii Island in 2014. The noticeboard states: "Attention! Border zone." (Photo by Natalia Ryzhova)

at the Chinese-Russian border on the island. So far, this has not been built. Even so, at the Third Far Eastern Business Forum held in Khabarovsk in 2018, fresh dream-like plans were proclaimed by enthusiastic entrepreneurs. Again, the island was to become a TOR—now imagined as a site for high-tech industries, robotics, and biotech, and even including a stock and commodity exchange for the whole Russian Far East. The inhabitants would get roads that would clear themselves of snow and be furnished with stations to recharge electric cars. Vertical farms would adorn the land. Drones would buzz through the air. The revivified island would attract Russians from across the country.[49]

However, later the same year the long-ruling Governor Shport, identified with Putin's United Russia party, which had recently lost popularity due to pension reforms, was swept from power in elections. Meanwhile, his predecessor, Ishaev, was arrested for corruption. There was still no news about the checkpoint. Now there was a sudden change of plan. Immediately after his inauguration the newly elected governor of Khabarovsk, a local populist named Sergei Furgal, cancelled all extravagant projects. Instead, declaring the need for grassroots economic development, he ordered the restoration of the Zarya (Dawn) collective farm on the island, saying that livestock should be a priority.[50]

Around one hundred Russians are now said to keep houses on the island, determined to remain where most of them have spent all their lives. But most housing units are deserted; there is no running water, central heating, or indoor plumbing; electricity is uncertain; and schools, medical centers, and shops are all on the mainland. Access to the city is not straightforward: there is a summer ferry (which does not operate every day), an unofficial pontoon bridge, and a track laid over the ice in winter. The island's dirt road to the new bridge is not always passable, and in any case, the mainland end of the bridge is located some 12 miles from the center of Khabarovsk. Marauders and thieves wander with impunity, as there is no police presence on the island. Aged residents were prostrated with despair when their cottages were burned down by arsonists scrounging for scrap metal.

People look out of upper-floor windows and envy the "garden town" on the Chinese side. Their first wish is a modest one: that the pontoon bridge across the strait, which serves as a de facto road to the Russian mainland, would be officially licensed as a road and thus available for use by a school bus. But try as they might, they were unable to get access to any officials in the Khabarovsk administration, let alone to the governor.[51] "Since the flood I've become disillusioned with the powers [*vo vlasti*]," said one man. "I was faced with the indifference of the administration, and since then I rely only on myself." Some are struggling in the courts for recompense for their losses in the 2013 floods, but "not everyone has the strength to fight. Some agreed to be resettled, but many won't leave their homes."[52] The islanders are quintessential examples of the ordinary people who feel that the earlier social contract with the government, based on substantial pensions, tax concessions, and subsidies, was broken when Moscow oversaw the transfer of huge sums to tax havens and elite projects in the Far East, with no benefit to them. It was such alienation from the higher "powers" that lay behind the rout of Shport and the election of Furgal in 2018.

A recent report highlights two residents whose stories are telling.[53] Lyubov Suslova worked as a teacher on the island for forty years. She lives on a retirement pension now and has no intention of leaving. Her house was ruined, not by the flood but by a crooked demolition crew that removed most of the roof. Part of the house soon became black with mold and uninhabitable. When the authorities sent a bulldozer to pull down the house, Lyubov stood bodily in its path. She moves onto the balcony during the summer and lives in her old bathhouse during the winter. In this tiny dwelling, "behind the padlocked door, a changing-room serves simultaneously as Suslova's entrance way and kitchen. She doesn't have much. There's a teapot, a single burner hot plate, a dim lamp, and bedding spread out over the sauna bench where she sleeps."[54] The islanders struggle together to live with the mud, the lack of supplies, the lapping water, the absence of drainage, and the aggravation of being cut off and ignored. We are reminded that these very malfunctions are what bring a sense of belonging and relating in many remote Russian communities—feelings not only of anger but also of unity and camaraderie.[55]

Valentina Adelbaeva migrated to the island seven years ago with her family. They sold their previous apartment in Yakutsk and brought the building materials for their house to the island. Not defeated by the flood, they rebuilt their house and it is now a rare comfortable, well-furnished two-story place with a farm and a sturdy fence. The floods, Valentina recalls, brought President Putin to visit the island, together with his envoy Trutnev and Governor Shport. Where else would the three dignitaries come to tea but at her house? At one point, Putin turned to the Adel-baevs and said, "Will a million [rubles] be enough for the repairs?" Amazed, they replied, "Yes!" Putin then looked at his envoy and said, "If it's not enough, add some more." But as Valentina summed up, "I don't know how many years have passed and we never saw any million. They [the Khabarovsk authorities] say, 'Putin made the promise. Go and ask him.'"[56]

In autumn 2019, the governor of Khabarovsk announced a state of emergency: the Amur had flooded again and thousands had to be evacuated along its banks. Russian houses on Bolshoi Ussuriiskii were inundated. It is not known how Lyubov Suslova or Valentina Adelbaeva fared in this latest disaster. A year later the Chinese pagoda was standing strong. Meanwhile, the Russian authorities were still "limply" (vyalo) talking of introducing cattle farming to the island, or alternatively, in complete contrast, a fi-nancial center for cryptocurrency.[57]

STATE HIERARCHIES AND CREATED WILDERNESSES

Through the example of Heixiazi/Bolshoi Ussuriiskii, we have tried to show that a view from the border illuminates how China and Russia actually work across the distances between the me-tropolis and the distant rim. Of course, this is a specific site that is not representative of the whole border. Yet it does illustrate some important points. On the very broadest of criteria, it is prob-ably true that China is beginning to look more like Russia: in both countries there is increased centralization, nationalism, pa-triotism, and state authoritarianism. But, by definition, Chinese and Russian nationalisms have their own trajectories; they are pulled apart by the dissimilarity of the established ways in which each hierarchical system works.

The case of the island demonstrates that the "social stuff" between the border and the capital is different in the two coun-tries. In China, this space is filled with a dense complex of mul-tiple and overlapping agencies. Between the president himself and the penniless laborer there intervene tiers of party and state officials, ministers, academic advisors, specialized bureaus and administrations, banks, municipal go-getters, state farm bosses, company directors, tourist guides, soldiers, border guards, managers of the nature reserve—and countless office workers, farmers, fishing folk, and lumberjacks struggling to make a living. Jostling and striving, the people running the midlevel organizations are also in intense communication and are prepared to make adjustments to one another—while at the same time being lassoed in by the high command. This elastic interaction enables them to work out how each can obtain some benefit from a common enterprise. The repeated speedy transformation of Hexiazi and the turning of Fuyuan into a site for demonstration of frontier patriotism is an example of this.

The material from Russia suggests, by contrast, a starker, linear structure, with many fewer players having effective agency. It is by virtue of their posts, more than their energy or character, that individual politicians can take action. These positions are ultimately uncertain, dependent on political protection from above in the narrow line of the power vertical. This means that priorities emanating from the secretive space above have to be sensed in advance—each official's antennae face upward. But this does not help when there is a sudden shift in the hierarchy. As we have shown, when a crack opens between the Kremlin and the distant province, Moscow normally turns the screw. Three months after Furgal's electoral victory over the president-supported candidate in Khabarovsk, which was a shocking affront to Moscow, Putin abruptly decided to switch the seat of the Far East *okrug* from Khabarovsk to Vladivostok, thus significantly curtailing Furgal's power and financial resources. In the Russian system, as Alexey Chadaev, a former Kremlin aide, wrote, money from Moscow whistles over the heads of regional bosses like ordnance aimed at some other target.[58] And for officials down the line, support from the tiers below cannot be counted on—not from provincial organizations, political parties, or even in any straightforward or conclusive way electorates. This means that links lower in the chain become attenuated or wildly variable, or even break off almost entirely. For example, when Furgal was arrested and replaced by a Kremlin nominee in summer 2020, the city of Khabarovsk erupted into mass protests against Moscow's "theft" of "our man." In sharp contrast to the patriotic fervor paraded at Fuyuan across the river, it was anti-Kremlin defiance that flared in Khabarovsk.

The reedy, windswept expanse of Heixiazi/Bolshoi Ussuriiskii demonstrates how the differences between China and Russia are manifested materially, architecturally, socially, and emotionally in the island's changing state. The island's old Russian name, Chumka (plague-stricken), has not been forgotten. It seems to express something of the no-man's-land quality of the place. Most recently, airy plans having evaporated, the island has again become a liminal place for both countries—more precisely, set up as two different kinds of wilderness—leaving it with a primarily symbolic role. The Chinese half somehow contrives to combine its sequestered ecological status with showy tourist attractions such as the pagoda, but the Russian side is complex in a different way. The chapel with its defiantly Christian and military associations stands alone, but this side of the island is also inhabited. The people living there cannot be characterized as abandoned or apathetic. On the contrary, because they have individually chosen to remain in the midst of "nothing," they have an independent spirit. They push back on the central system from its edge, a position where, as Chapter 3 will show, obedience is not a virtue.

MAKING A LIVING IN THE
CROSS-BORDER ECONOMY

3

Chapter 2 ended on a note of stalemate and separation at the Amur River island under divided sovereignty. But such disconnections are only part of the story. Russia and China also interact economically in numerous ways, and the overall trajectory shows an increase in such engagements. This bland statement tells us little, however, about which parts of the two economies extend across the border, and consequently little about the nature and scale of interactions. In both countries there have been a number of surges of enthusiasm, followed by periods of disengagement, but the Russians and Chinese have not experienced these surges at the same time. As a result, there have been times of misunderstanding and tension in economic interactions. Lying behind this is the shifting balance between official, large-scale, and in principle legal operations, on the one hand, and the numerous undocumented, small-scale, and legally dubious activities, on the other. In China, the relation between these two has been fairly constant, with a tendency to submerge or close down the latter. But in Russia, the picture is more turbulent and confusing, and this affects cross-border as well as regional economies. Our focus in this chapter will be on these informal dealings as ways of making a living, with farming, the jade trade, and sea fishing as examples. But none of these can be understood only as ethnographic examples divorced from the larger patterns lying beyond economics.

The "cultures of capitalism" differ in Russia and China, if only because culture in general, from conceptual-linguistic categories to work ethics, from gender relations to religion, is so different in the two realms.[1] The cultures of capitalism differ also because current capitalist activities take place amid the remnants of previous non-capitalist structures and involve people whose habits were formed in those earlier eras. If everyday commerce (or "petty capitalism," in the expression of anthropologist Hill Gates) has arguably been a thread throughout Chinese history with only a brief gap during the Cultural Revolution, after which it was supplemented by mass state-managed capitalism, Russia established a far longer regime (seven decades) that was not just non-capitalist but anti-capitalist.[2] The USSR created an entire socialism-inspired environment (and culture) of resource extraction, wealth distribution, built structures, communal services, and labor trained to work in certain ways, much of which abruptly became redundant in the 1990s. In contrast to the virtual tabula rasa on which China built new border trading cities (see Chapter 7), Russian capitalism, which took up a no-holds-barred version of neoliberal capitalism, operates amid inescapable socialist vestiges: visible physical ruins and human habits that still cling. This is the complex terrain that interests us in this chapter: not only the contrast between Chinese and Russian ways of doing business, but also their inevitable entanglement with processes that lie beyond a narrow understanding of capitalism.

In the broader historical picture, the importance of its enormous Far Eastern territory for Russia was political, not economic. As an economy, the region never paid its way and had to be subsidized even in the relatively prosperous 1970s and 1980s. On top of support for the civil economy, the Soviet state devoted huge sums to the military complexes located there and to the upkeep of the troops that formed a large part of the region's population. In a long historical view, we can see a pattern of subsidy followed by neglect. Injections of workers and finance for production and infrastructure went in waves. The 1930s–1950s introduction of

Gulags and forced settler labor was followed by a lull, then succeeded in the 1960s–1970s by "organized labor" (*orgnabor*), construction troops, and Communist Youth League (Komsomol) volunteers for projects such as road building and the BAM railway. When authoritarian socialist forms of peopling the economy ceased in the 1990s, and particularly when most of the military were withdrawn, a period of neglect followed; resource flows and employment withered, and people started to move back to central regions. A skeleton state sector was left when Moscow's solicitude evaporated. Meanwhile, what were the options for the remaining ordinary (non-state-employed) inhabitants? They had little choice but to turn to informal and illegal means of survival. These activities were "invisible," as the political scientists Leonid Blyakher and Vasil'eva argued, in the sense that the state turned a blind eye and the people engaged in them were no longer mentioned in official reports.[3] When the central government's attention was directed elsewhere, "the region's population declined perceptibly (sometimes by almost a third), but the 'invisibles' came into their own. More precisely, the entire intraregional space became 'invisible' to the state. The only essential task that remained was that of defending the border."[4]

In China, by contrast, interest in the northeast has always been as much economic as political. It has also been more sustained than in Russia, with the central government support for heavy industry that was initiated by Mao being reiterated by Xi in recent years and the increase in the farming population more or less constant. But now farmlands are full up and also subject to competing pressures (Chapter 2). Today, the *hukou* household registration system continues to tie rural people to their place of birth even if they go elsewhere to find work. The rules are assiduously followed up with the help of digital technologies that regulate migrants' limited access in a host of life decisions, such as obtaining health care, good-quality education, property rights, and insurance. People with an urban *hukou* are comprehensively privileged over villagers. As writer Xiaowei Wang observes, "The *hukou* system reveals the unabashed directedness of socialist central planning."[5] The millions of rural migrants who wash up in great cities are not "invisible" to the state in the same way as in Russia, and although they are infrequently mentioned in glowing reports of achievements, officials and factory managers are well aware that China's economic miracle depends on their work and on maintaining control of their conditions of existence. However, the priority given to economic growth, while intended to achieve loyalty through increased prosperity, also creates a potential threat to the country's stability. Digital technology and complex logistical systems of supply and transportation are advancing not only in manufacturing but also in farming, drastically reducing the need for human labor. For this reason millions of "peasants" (see discussion later in this chapter) look set to become unemployed, and most of them do not have the education or technical training to access opportunities in the formal workplace.[6]

On both sides of the border, therefore, there have been good reasons for "hustling" of various kinds to have flourished: illicit casual labor, selling scrap, hunting, fishing, forestry, gold mining, shuttle trade, and so forth. But each of these is an engagement with the global circulation of commodities. And that is not mediated through Moscow or Beijing, as the ideal of a coherent national economy would stipulate; rather, it often works sideways, directly across the borders, particularly between Russia and China, but also via networks extending to Japan, Mongolia, and Korea. How would the central powers deal with all this intraregional activity? And is there any point of articulation between it and major state projects?

If we stand back, it is evident that the main flows of cross-border trade are dissimilar: the majority of Russia exports to China are hydrocarbons and other raw materials, whereas China supplies Russia with financial resources, migrant labor, business start-ups, electronic equipment, advanced machinery, and a multitude of consumer goods.[7] Furthermore, although these two-way flows have approximately the same dollar value, they have very different importance for each country: China is Russia's main trading partner, whereas Russia is only the twelfth in China's list of partners and receives less than 2 percent of its exports, well behind countries such as India, Singapore, or the Netherlands (2018 figures). Chinese businesses are far more active inside Russia, in farming, construction, the timber industry, real estate, import-export trade, and the provision of food, than the other way around. For this reason, the chapter focuses primarily on economic activity inside Russia.

Russia's oil and gas pipelines and rail freight transport are run by huge metropolitan companies that involve little cross-border face-to-face contact, particularly with local inhabitants. The Transneft company's East Siberia–Pacific Ocean (ESPO) pipeline carrying oil from Western Siberia to the Pacific has two spurs to China branching off at Skovorodino, but it produces scant employment at this somnolent leafy town in Amur Oblast. Similarly, Gazprom's Power of Siberia gas pipeline snaking from northern Siberia via Blagoveshchensk into China is a big player in the Russian export economy, as we mentioned in Chapter 1, but it employs mainly non-local experts and specialist workers; plans to extend its range for the "gasification" of the scattered settlements of the Russian Far East have hardly started.[8] Other major exports to China, such as petroleum products, machinery, valuable ores, and coal, are produced elsewhere in Russia, and the goods are then merely transported through the borderlands on long trains.[9] Military production also fails to support the regional economy as it used to: the Soviet army bases and factories that used to employ hundreds of thousands of people almost all closed down in the 1990s. Some military enterprises focused on export continue in Vladivostok, but most production was moved to central Russia and modernized.[10] Thus, the border regions do not necessarily benefit from the fact that Russia's overall economy is dependent on exports and that China figures so large as a major purchaser.

Russia's fears of becoming a "resource appendage" of China sit uneasily alongside anxieties over the looming uncertainty of future demand for natural gas from its giant southern neighbor, which is developing its own sources of gas. The Russian government is now directing attention to other export sectors.[11] In particular, responding to China's trade war with the United States, Russia is expecting to increase its agricultural and food exports to China exponentially.[12] This is important for the borderlands, since much of the new production is being done not by Russians but by Chinese farmers working inside Russia, as we discuss later in this chapter.

"HUNTING GROUNDS" AND LAW-FREE HINTERLANDS

The larger picture, however, is that economies in the Russian borderlands are dominated by the appropriation of natural resources by Russian citizens themselves. State agencies, megacompanies, small businesses, and individual foragers all take part in activities that exist in parallel to their lawful operations. Beyond the hydrocarbons, more readily accessible resources also come from the land: timber, gold, gems, ores, herbs, "medicines" from wild plants and animals, hunting products such as fur and meat, ginseng, wild cannabis, fish and crustaceans, and even fresh water to be bottled for export. To this we can add detritus of the socialist era left for the picking, such as scrap metal, copper wire, or disused railroad ties. The situation could be understood theoretically as a resource frontier of capitalism or as "salvage accumulation,"[13] but we introduce instead the more closely focused and political analysis of a regional specialist. Leonid Blyakher, a political theorist resident in Vladivostok, envisages the country as made up of "hunting grounds" in which the lowly "hunters" are preyed on by "stationary bandits"—that is, state or state-linked actors.[14] Everything in such a territory is divided among three actors: the higher predators (the "stationary bandits"), the hunters (the producers), and the enemies (anyone able to prevent appropriation of the "food," such as honest policemen). The rest is just a neutral environment. The base extraction consists of the everyday, routine practices of the population—in other words, the thoroughly informalized economy. In the 1990s mafia-like local crime bosses set up "food chains" of extraction on their territories that amounted to social hierarchies, and soon some of these were robust enough to acquire regional dominance, all the while preserving their partial invisibility to the state.[15] But beginning in the 2000s, with the general improvement of the economy following the rise in the price of oil, many midlevel informal enterprises—fishing boats, forestry plots, sawmills, small manufacturers who had established themselves in sections of bankrupt factories, cinemas, bakeries, private clinics, transportation and storage services, or motor repairs—were able to find a more solid footing. Now they needed to make links outside their territories and to acquire a degree of stabilization and legalization, sometimes with a view to cross-border trade. This need the crime bosses could not satisfy: they were themselves outside the law, and conflict between them kept their sway limited to their own territories. But "stationary bandits" on the rungs above, especially the regional barons (governors, mayors), were able to provide what was needed. They "sold" a certain security of economic transactions in return for the political loyalty of the producers and a due cut of the profits (bribes and kickbacks).[16] Insofar as the regional barons themselves were legitimate figures, all those gathered within their cartels now were to some degree legalized. However, as Blyakher continues, the barons' desire to monopolize their own "feeding troughs" required setting in place strong controls and the expansion of the apparatus of repression—and this put increased pressure on the small businesses.[17] The barons took enthusiastic—if self-interested—part in the government's "war on corruption," and the result was that although tiny operations resolutely distanced from the state largely remained in place in rural areas, they declined in the cities. Meanwhile, the midlevel businesses that had entered into relationships with the barons were caught up in a murky multilevel system of control. Yet this too was informal and resulted in a paradox: only those who carried out the conditions of informal agreements (beyond the law), demonstrating their loyalty by illegal payments upward and support for the right electoral candidates, were able to carry out legal business.[18]

By the 2010s, the system had changed yet again—thanks to Putin's reforms, the regional barons were losing power to appointees of the centralizing state. Harsh controls were put in place to prevent "theft"—that is, the appropriation of serious spoils by "enemies," or anyone other than the nominated predators. The latter were now backed by a solidifying high-level network made up of the mega-companies tied to the central powers, with support from the state agencies that extracted "administrative rent."[19]

The increased pressure on resources from these larger and stronger predators left the struggling subordinate firms down the chain unable to maintain their legalized operations. The result was that many of them revived the old shadowy practices of the 1990s. After 2014, with the sanctions and the fall in the ruble, the mega-companies were propped up by state subsidies and contracts, and for this reason they were deeply concerned to keep up their legal status. But for small businesses, retreat into the shade into concealed forms of predation was increasingly attractive. Sometimes this was the only way to survive—anything to avoid the eye of the state and the heavy "costs of legality." We later describe two examples of this process, in the jade trade and in fishing.

According to extensive interviews carried out by Blyakher, economic rationalities have changed even in the quasi-legal operations. Small firms have abandoned long-term planning. Immediate returns and "living cash" (rather than bank transfers) are what count. Rather than use their own workshops and personnel to produce goods, they have started to farm out the work. For example, a business producing snacks and hot meals does not have its own chefs or kitchen but gets the food made "to order" by unregistered folk cooking at home. The firm thus saves on wages, rent, and equipment, and the cooks—who might be underpaid teachers, librarians, or students—get a sporadic source of additional income. Even more precarious than gig economy contracts in the West, this "to order" system has spread to many spheres where the talents of underemployed people can be drawn on. And it links in with the lowliest economic sphere of all: the dacha where chickens, sheep, or pigs are reared ostensibly for one's own use, the garage used to make furniture, the repair business in a back room, or the one-person transport firm. The profits from each individual enterprise are tiny; to control all of this is practically impossible, even though the hungry security and policing services roam the land. Much of the population is simply providing for its own subsistence.

These activities in such alegal hinterlands proliferate in ways that are invisible to officialdom. Mobile phones with exchangeable SIM cards are used to make arrangements; barter can sometimes be used instead of money, which helps to keep deals out of view. For example, Ayuna, a retired Buryat former teacher, used her village dacha near the border as a base for her potato business. She would employ a local man with his battered truck for a month in autumn to collect sacks of potatoes from even more elderly housebound Russians in nearby villages. Selling the potatoes for money in Ulan-Ude, she bought supplies of oil, sugar, detergent, salt, cigarettes, and other basic supplies, and during the year she packed them into her decrepit car and took them around to her clients as payment in advance for next year's potatoes. Wiry and active, Ayuna lived on her own, and she enjoyed the bargaining. She kept the entire business in her head—names, dates, prices, verbal agreements. Her barter business thrived and expanded to include a Kyrgyz partner and exchange of potatoes for meat over the border in Mongolia. Incessant calls on a number of mobile phones kept all this going, with a careful eye to changing prices across the region. In remote spots phone signals from Russian suppliers may be absent, so borderland folk regularly also keep Chinese phones and SIM cards.

Chinese phones are particularly useful in the shuttle trade operating across the border, another way that local people can obtain money income. There are two main methods. One is for individuals to sign up as "shopping tourists" with a local transport company, aiming either to make purchases on their own account or on order for someone else. They book seats online on a packed bus going to a Chinese border town such as Manzhouli, scour the town for bargains, lug the goods back through Russian customs (with which the tour company has normally made some arrangement), and then sell the items at a higher price back home. An alternative is to hire oneself out as a shopper-carrier for a Russia-based (but these days usually Chinese-owned) retail company. In this case, the boss takes the orders, hires a van and around six or seven carriers, and the same weary team may shuttle across the border several times a day, purchasing mostly bulk items ordered for resale by owners of stores in Siberian towns and villages. In both cases, the device to avoid customs charges renders the whole operation illegal: the pretense is that the goods are for personal use by each carrier. Bribes are routinely paid to border and customs officials. Phones are essential to these operations: checking on prices, making orders, contacting helpers in China, arranging storage, alerting friends to customs officers' schedules, and so forth. They are also integral to a third way in which the shuttle trade has evolved to integrate with internet shopping. Russian customers increasingly buy goods online through Chinese platforms such as Taobao. The problems here are how to pay when Chinese firms do not recognize Russian credit cards and how to ensure delivery of the goods when the Russian postal service takes lengthy routes and involves considerable expense at customs. The shuttle service can bypass these problems, especially collection and delivery of the items, which is carried out by the same informal methods (after a quick call, "Sasha" will meet you at a specified place to hand over the items you ordered) as the non-internet orders.[20]

Some of the trade formerly carried out by shuttle folk has been taken over by larger import-export companies—for example, the informal trading that used to extend to South Korea or central

China.[21] But Russia's shifting of customs inspections for wholesale businesses away from the Siberian border to a central site near Moscow, ostensibly to curb local corruption, has resulted in delayed orders and higher prices in Siberia, since many legally imported goods from China have to travel on extraordinarily long and illogical journeys to reach a destination just across the border.[22] A consequence is that the informal cross-border shuttle trading is still needed. True, it has lessened in recent years with the decline in the ruble's purchasing power. It remains backbreaking and risky, for there is always a chance of devastating fines or even arrest.[23] But it still is a way to obtain goods cheaply, and for uncounted people in almost any ill-paid profession it is a means to make extra income. Meanwhile, the same hard-pressed population faces a countersurge of shoppers coming from China. The ruble slump after 2014 made Russian goods attractively cheap for the citizens of Heihe, Manzhouli, and other north Chinese towns. For the first time, large numbers of ordinary Chinese tourist-shoppers were visibly present in Russian streets—and they were disconcertingly confident, well-dressed, and affluent.[24] Simultaneously, incoming Chinese farm workers were becoming a known-about but far less visible presence in outskirts and villages. With this observation, let us turn to the tenor of social life in the rural borderlands, the inescapable weight of history on it, and the ways it is, and is not, being affected by its proximity to China.

SUSPENDED ECONOMIES, BITTER MEMORIES, AND INCOMERS

In a village called Voskresenovka, perched above the Amur, the main street is quiet—no Chinese, indeed almost no one at all. Vegetable plots and a winding path slope down to the shore. But the riverbank is empty. Two iron pipes, with planks fixed on top, project into the water. The steamer from Blagoveshchensk used to dock at this contraption. But for a long time now the steamer has not come. The villagers say that a cutter arrives in autumn to take their potatoes to sell in the city. But right now, in summer, no boat stops here. The river slides slowly past. It is not beautiful or grand, write two melancholy Russian journalists: "The Amur does not have to be attractive; it is enough that it divides us [from China], just as the line of the sunset divides day and night."[25]

The Voskresenovka school once had 600 students from the surrounding villages, all them founded by Cossack settlers more than a hundred years ago. But there are barely 200 pupils now and only seven in the class for the youngest students. Irina Nikolaevna teaches there. She longs to leave, and she stays only to look after her sick mother. She carries a pail of slops to feed the pigs and gives breakfast to the two journalists, potatoes fried with tomatoes and tea with honey, and then she puts on a smart suit and blouse before setting out down the muddy street for the school. "That is how a rural teacher should go to work," comments the village head, Olga Gavaga, "like a princess surrounded by pages." Standards are kept up in this village. But it is telling that one of the pupils has painted a mystically sad painting that hangs on the school's canteen wall. It depicts the sacking of Moscow by Napoleon. Nothing remains of the old capital except two church domes rising out of smoking ruins. All the inhabitants have been killed or fled, as have the French soldiers, too. But Napoleon himself has survived. The young artist pictured him in his legendary bicorn hat sitting in a little boat in the Moskva River, angling for fish.

The lifeblood of Voskresenovka has almost stopped flowing, write the journalists. Once there was a large state farm (*sovkhoz*) here. Old Ivan Dolgerev, who was born in a Gulag lumber camp and battled his way through a career in hard-bitten collective farms to end up as a party man and director of the state farm, remembers his achievements: how he managed to build up a herd of 500 breeding cattle, and how, by hook or crook (employing Armenian builders), he established a tractor station, cowsheds, pigsties, schools in each village, kindergartens, clinics, housing for the villagers. There was even a telephone exchange with 600 subscribers. "We lived! We lived!" he exclaimed. But soon after Dolgerev retired in 1998 the *sovkhoz* was dead. "In two years—an empty space. I went round to the villagers begging everyone: 'Take what you worked for, privatize it, become independent.' But no one responded. The new boss handed over our forest to the Chinese. The cattle were slaughtered—all just for money. I could not sleep, I thought I would die, it was so sad. The village had had ten years of good life. Is that a lot? Or a little? But I did come to understand one thing," said Dolgerev with a contorted smile. "It's true that I put in so much effort, and another threw it to the wind. But my heart is not rotting in vain. Because the truth [*pravda*] is with me, and no one can take that away from me."[26]

There are other places in the Russian borderlands where there is not just quiet poverty but true despair. Zabaikal'skii Krai is one of the most deprived of the border regions, and here people write blogs with titles such as "From the Bright Past—to the Dark Future," giving descriptions of closed schools and shops, broken bridges, roads washed away, ruined farm equipment, boarded-up houses, and everywhere the scourges of alcoholism and illness.[27] In such places, there is chronic indebtedness and people easily fall prey to the mirage of pyramid schemes and multilevel marketing scams.[28] Villagers perforce depend on their "private subsidiary plots," a term lingering from Soviet days when these patches were allotted as concessions from the primary collective farms. Potatoes, vegetables, perhaps a few chickens, a pig or a cow, together with hunted meat, mushrooms, and berries from the forest—the mostly elderly villagers can conjure a decent subsistence from very little. But even so, this is a terribly harsh way of life.[29] Water has to be pulled up by hand and carried from wells, a mountain of firewood sawn for winter, snow shoveled by hand even to reach a neighbor's house. Floods, long bone-hard winters, animal epidemics, and mosquito-ridden summers have to be endured. Roads may be impassable for lengthy periods. Even electricity may be uncertain. Physically this life is not so different from how things were fifty years ago—except that now there are no jobs and villagers still have to find some way to pay for the outside help they need for plowing their plots, buying gasoline and fertilizer, transporting firewood, et cetera. Many rely on occasional sales of hunted meat, fish, and berries from the forests. As for regular income, pensions and state allowances are the main source—if we do not count illegal activities, on which more later.

In many villages, there are also one or two larger commercial farmers (*fermery*) who may employ a few local people as laborers. These commercial holdings are often based on privatized sections of a former state or collective farm and owe their existence to political connections giving access to initial credit. But in regions like Zabaikal'skii Krai even this more prosperous class is on the edge of going under. People say that since "the crisis"—which in Russia could refer to several dates since 2000—fodder and fuel prices have risen two- to threefold, and shop prices too, but not the prices the farmers get for their products. Dealers with access to transport take advantage of the remoteness of farms from markets.[30] If these larger farms fail, all the tiny household farms dependent on them for machinery, fuel, and fodder may collapse too.

Finally, in some places incoming wealthy investor companies and agribusinesses intervene from on high. Throughout Russia, these external investors, dubbed "Muscovites" no matter where they actually come from, form a separate class that hardly interacts with local society.[31] They lease relatively large holdings to managers, with the products often aimed for export. Many of these companies and managers are Chinese, as we describe later. Very often they employ Chinese migrant labor.

MIGRATIONS

The rural depression affects cities such as Chita, the capital of Zabaikal'skii Krai. Even the most enterprising people are affected by a general sense of futility, and many of them decide simply to abandon the cities of these border regions. But as they move out, a greater number of villagers and inhabitants of smaller towns move in.[32] This migration is in many ways similar to that in rural China, but with one important difference: the Russian villagers are better educated than their Chinese equivalents.[33] With the stable and varied career structures of the collective and state farms gone, farming looks more than ever a dead end and young people are better equipped to grasp urban opportunities.

Russian scholars call seasonal labor migration *otkhodnich-estvo*, from the word *otkhod*, "to depart" or "to break with," originally a nineteenth-century term that has its roots in serfdom, when people were legally tied to a domain. When peasants ran away, this "departure" was understood as a problem for government. An echo of that old system is the fact that, as in China, Russian citizens today are registered with a permit to live in a given place and *otkhodnichestvo* is still seen as problematic— people strike out from their villages and towns, fail to reregister anywhere else, and are effectively lost to state governance and statistics (there is far less surveillance of migrants than in China). Today, rural "departure" is a mass phenomenon. Sociologists have calculated that there are some 15–20 million such migrants seeking their fortune throughout Russia.[34] From villages, they flood into cities such as Chita, Khabarovsk, and Ulan-Ude. And if they find no way of gaining a living there, they set off seeking work, anything from housebuilding in western Russia to cleaning fish in Kamchatka. It is not only dire necessity that impels people to move. Other reasons are a desire for education and a life away from farming, youngsters' dreams of "conquering the city," or simply the wish to escape personal problems and find happiness in a new place.[35] Mobile, enterprising, prepared to live far from families, adept at escaping state controls, independent-minded, these "departed" (*otkhodniki*) are largely ignored in public policy—even as sociologists warn of the sociopolitical tensions they create by accepting low pay.[36]

Let us briefly make a comparison with China, where there has also been a mass rural-to-urban migration, but with far higher numbers of people involved. In 2002, Zhang's classic study *Strangers in the City* estimated China's "floating population" at 100 million rural migrants. By 2017, the number had grown to 230 million, about 17 percent of the population.[37] Many of these are farmers displaced by land grabs of municipalities, mines, or expanding businesses (or an unholy combination of all three). Whereas Russia's cities have been able to absorb the migrants fairly easily, accommodating them in dormitories, cheap communal apartments, and limited social housing, China's huge flood is more indigestible and presents a threat the government is determined to avoid: a potential "Latin American scenario" of unruly shantytowns. This is why, as we mentioned earlier, the government has consistently tried to contain the flow, by refusing to allocate the migrants residence rights (*hukou*) in the city.[38] Discriminated against as "peasants" (*nongmin*), they experience unfairly low pay (even non-payment), harsh and dirty conditions of work, and little access to medicine and education for their children. Even after several reforms and the abolition of the formal difference in rights given by urban and rural *hukou*, the expression "eating bitterness" (*chi ku*) remains apt; it refers to enduring hardships yet somehow managing to forge ahead.[39] In China, the multifarious precarious ways of earning a living, such as being a street vegetable seller, itinerant bicycle repairer, garbage recycler, storekeeper's drudge, occasional prostitute, and so on, have until recently been more visible than their equivalents in Russia, where public order is more officious and the police more intolerant.

Under Xi Jinping matters have been changing. The "New Urbanization" policy now embraces a fresh wave of rural migration, rethinking it not as an untidy flow but as a planned process masterminded by the state. The goal is to equalize and harmonize the population of the whole country (see Chapter 1). Unlike in Russia, where starkly different standards of living hardly figure in Moscow's priorities, in China they are a source of concern and action. For example, "radical poverty"—mostly diagnosed among indigenous peoples in remote areas (see Chapter 4)—is to be eliminated by forcefully relocating "backward" farmers to nearby cities and training them for "civilized work." To prevent the emergence of an underclass in great cities, access there is regulated, while a new middle class is to be created in smaller towns. The idea is that these people will buy homes, buy durable goods to fill those homes, and keep the economy turning by stimulating domestic demand.[40] A second goal of the "New Urbanization" is the transformation of rural life: to do away with scattered plots and old-fashioned methods and bring in agribusinesses and scale up high-tech production. But the transformation is far from complete. Meanwhile, countless people are caught grasping at thin air—dispossessed from their homesteads or pastures, or stuck in villages and unemployed for most of the farming year, and having no contacts to smooth entrance to a city. These people are available for alternative work, including contracts across the border.

So let us return to Russia. It was in the context of emptying villages that in 2015 the Zabaikal'skii authorities announced the plan to rent out 115,000 hectares (285,000 acres) of underused agricultural land to Chinese investors at a symbolic rate of US $5 per hectare. There was an immediate storm of protest, since people were convinced that the work on these farms would be given to Chinese and not to Russians.[41] Fears were inflamed by the media, in particular a terrifying film released the same year, *China—a Deadly Friend*, which became an instant online hit. It features the dire prediction of a long-bearded priest, Archimandrite Seraphim Vyritskii, that Russia will be split asunder: Japan will take over the Pacific Rim, while Chinese men will swarm into south Siberia, marry Russian women, and by tricks and deception come to dominate up to the Urals. Taking advantage of Russian kindness and hospitality, the incomers will force local people out of their homes and take over their farms. The country will be driven to destitution, but the Chinese will make big profits.[42] Despite such scares, the Zabaikal'skii plan was seen on high as a potential savior for the region and was approved whether residents liked it or not. After all, no one else wanted to take up farming or to invest there.

Perhaps we can see these abandoned lands as the antithesis of the "hunting ground." The predator has eyes on other places than weed-choked former fields and semi-abandoned villages of elderly folk. Putin's 2016 scheme to give one hectare (2.5 acres) of free (but remote) land to attract new active settlers to the Russian Far East has not been a success.[43] So, in the absence of other interest, the Chinese were invited in. A look at how Chinese live and work in Russia explains much—not only their motivations, way of life and effectiveness, but also why the villagers in places such as Voskresenovka see so little of them.

CHINESE FARMERS

A detailed research study by a team from BBC News Russian covering all five regions of the Russian Far East calculated that in 2019 Chinese farmers were working a total of 872,000 acres.[44] This is approximately 16 percent of the land presently suitable for agriculture.[45] Most of that land is leased; only 15 percent held in ownership.[46] The largest single concentration of Chinese farmers is in the Jewish Autonomous Region. Throughout the Russian Far East, there simply are not enough Russians able or willing to cultivate the swaths of empty land under present conditions. But while the governor of Amur Oblast refused to accept Chinese, the governor of the Jewish Autonomous Region welcomed them. A local official commented with a bitter laugh, "I'm not sure how many Chinese are farming here. But it's certainly more than the number of Jews!" She counted two Jewish families in her district.

The invasion of Chinese people presaged in *Deadly Friend* has not materialized. The huge and growing demographic imbalance on either side of the border does not necessarily translate into large-scale migration. The sources vary wildly on the numbers of Chinese migrants involved—from the official 29,000 said to live in the Russian Far East (census of 2010) to the 300,000 to 500,000 mentioned in other estimates as present in Russia as a whole.[47] It is clear that the vast majority of Chinese citizens arriving in Russia by legal routes come as tourists, as students, or in transit and leave quickly. Relatively few have visas lasting over nine months, and only a tiny number apply for citizenship.[48] Since 2006, Russia has imposed quotas on work visas. In any case, whether their presence is legal or not, a large proportion of the Chinese farmers are seasonal workers, staying for the growing months only. Others may live in Russia for a number of years but maintain their *hukou* and smallholding at home, aiming to return to China. Meanwhile, there are also Russian citizens "with Chinese roots," as the media puts it—that is, people who settled after earlier waves of migration. But even they have been emigrating back to China.[49] So overall, clearly a mass influx does not threaten Russia. Yet Chinese farming has a big economic impact and even more a social and political one.

Putin-era Russian policy has consistently prioritized capitalist large-scale farming over private smallholdings. Most Chinese farmers arrive in Russia as contract workers for big Chinese-owned companies. This means that the migrant workers face a situation different from what they were used to in China, where peasant family farms still predominate, especially in the center and south of the country. Many had become used to the broadly egalitarian village communities of the household responsibility system introduced in the 1980s, when communes were replaced by family-based farming with long-term land-use rights. Even though the household plots became unequal over time and some "peasants" (*nongmin*) moved from subsistence farming to higher-value, market-oriented agriculture, the rural Russian setup establishes a more definite social inequality, as we mentioned earlier. But taking on a low social status in Russia means little to the Chinese workers when the money to be earned is weighed against the precariousness of and discrimination against internal migration at home. One reason for taking on migrant work is that average farm sizes in China over the past decades have been shrinking: from 1.7 acres in 1985 to less than 1.2 acres in the 2010s.[50] And in almost all parts of the country there are pressures on the availability of *any* land for farming, notably from urban and industrial expansion and soil degradation. Another push factor is that agribusinesses, which are spreading in northeast China, dispossess people of family farms but do not provide alternative work. Instead, the *nongmin* are moved to newly built town apartments with compensation payments—and there they are left marooned, often to vegetate.[51] The remaining villagers find their tiny plots an ever more exiguous safety net for their families.[52] All the more reason, then, for a family member to take time away to earn money in Russia.

The major pattern is for the Chinese enterprise to lease farmland as a joint venture with a Russian company. On this land it establishes a fenced compound, locked at night, in which the Chinese workers sleep, eat, and socialize. The main crop is soybeans, though there are also wheat, rice, maize, vegetables, and pigs.[53] People work hard ten- or twelve-hour days; there is little drinking or partying. The workers, the vast majority male, do not try to make friends with Russian women. They go back to China for festivals, holidays, and slack periods. They keep in touch by phone with relatives in their home villages. Far from expropriating Russian houses, as predicted by the grim priest of *Deadly Friend,* the workers hardly visit Russian villages, except to buy cigarettes or a bottle of beer if there is a local store. Most do not speak Russian, not even the night guards of the compounds, whose task it is to deal with Russian intruders. And those who do know a few words clam up when Russians try to start a conversation. Furthermore, these farms are not usually connected with one another. Gathering workers for the Russian farms is usually done on a village basis all over China by local recruiters who take charge of all expenses (travel, food, visa, accommodation). It has been estimated, for example, that around 10 percent of the population of one small area of Dongning county in Heilongjiang province works in Russia.[54] This kind of recruitment encourages the formation of almost closed Chinese communities inside Russia, which some locals describe as *kreposti* (fortresses).[55] Increasingly, the Chinese in Russia do not use rubles but the Alipay and WeChat online payment systems to access their bank accounts at home; these systems have been adopted by some Russia-based, though often Chinese-owned, companies, restaurants and stores, but are unavailable to ordinary Russian citizens.[56] Such economic and social separation is why it could be said in Voskresenovka, "There are Chinese in the Amur lands, but in a way, there are not."[57]

There is an important downside to the closed-off contract labor system: the more "invisible" workers are, the more they are liable to exploitation by their Chinese supervisors. This happens as follows. Russia imposes annually changing quotas on workers from China, with specific numbers being allocated to each district for particular types of work: commercial agriculture, construction, restaurant jobs, and so forth. Since these numbers do not accord with the actual work that needs to be carried out, mediators arrange illicit swaps between the districts; for example, fifty "farm laborers" accredited to an area where there is no demand for agricultural work may well end up doing construction work in a different district. This renders their presence and activity illegal. The bosses take the workers' passports and conceal the activity from the Russian authorities. In such a situation, reports Sayana Namsaraeva, who worked as an interpreter for one such Chinese team, the remarkable efficiency hides the fact that the workers are vulnerable to many abuses, such as bullying, overwork, squalid living conditions, or arrears of pay, and there have been several cases of Chinese workers running away in desperation, suddenly appearing "visible" as bedraggled protesters on roadsides, appealing to Chinese consular officials in Russia for help.

With the fall in the value of the ruble, it has become more difficult to attract Chinese workers to the large soybean farms. But there is plenty of room for individual commerce, particularly in vegetable growing and greenhouse horticulture, in which Chinese skills far outpace those of Russians. Land rent is much lower than in China and the demand for fresh fruit and vegetables is high. By hard work and ingenuity, a lone entrepreneurial Chinese migrant can "save" his whole village back home.

An example is an "insignificant peasant" from poverty-ridden Yongli village, near Harbin, a place where farm sizes were down to three-quarters of an acre per capita and there was no additional land to distribute to growing families with children. In 1994, this man joined a group organized by the township sent to grow vegetables in Russia, and later he struck out on his own, negotiated a lucrative greenhouse vegetable contract, and began to finance and recruit seasonal laborers from his village. By 2005 he had brought over eleven production teams. He had become a "big boss in Russia" (*Eluosi da laoban*); almost all of the earliest villagers who left for Russia under his direction became bosses of their own too.[58] Famed in Russia for their determination, hard work, and frugality, Chinese farmers succeed in creating businesses because commercial know-how is passed on within families and personal networks can be used to raise credit.[59] Furthermore, they also bring with them intensive agricultural techniques unknown in rural Russia. They import fertilizers, pesticides, advanced machinery, hothouse technology, and animal feeds. According to Russian locals, Chinese vegetables grow inconceivably fast and pigs swell to unheard-of sizes. Complaints are loud that the land is being polluted by plastic sheeting and chemicals and degraded by overuse, since the incomers are said to have no stake in the long-term health of the land (see also Chapter 6).

Russian policy has made it hard for individual Chinese incomers to establish themselves as a legal business entity. Obtaining a visa to work as a market trader has been impossible since 2006. Yet whether as a farmer, an artisan, or a trader, ways can be found through mediators and undercover payments for incomers to insert themselves into the chain of an existing market.

This can be done by taking out a sublease, by setting up with a Russian partner who fronts a new enterprise, or by using local villagers to sell the produce. Or, even better, by marrying a Russian citizen under whose name the business can be run. If we return to the banks of the Amur, an example is the conjugal pair Sasha and Angela, who have become successful marketeers in Magdagachi, a small town along the river from Voskresenovka. Sasha started life as Qin Chuanzhao, deliverer of newspapers. When he was eighteen he went to Russia in search of work, and in ten years much of the business of the town was in his hands. Angela, half Cherkess and half Russian, arrived in these parts as a child when her father was thrown off the Trans-Siberian for some misdemeanor. Together the pair came to own several markets and shops, and they are building a restaurant and hotel in nearby Shimanovsk. In the opinion of locals, marriage to Angela changed Sasha—he became "a different kind of Chinese." Now open and sociable, he abandoned the characteristic caution and evasiveness, they say. As for Angela, she was looking forward to the time when they could emigrate to China—"to Dalian, to the Yellow Sea! I went there once and have never forgotten it."[60]

THE JADE BONANZA

A Sino-Russian marriage also lay at the heart of one of the saddest and most remarkable economic ventures in cross-border trade. Jade (Ch. *yu*) has a supreme and sacred value in China, but in Russia the same mineral, called nephrite, is merely a cloudy stone, long ignored and at best used in cheap jewelry. The yawning gap in prices gives rise to an extraordinarily valuable trade (or "salvage accumulation"). In the early 1990s, Evenki hunters and reindeer herders (see Chapter 4) realized that the forests of Baunt in northern Buryatia contained a treasure trove. They were the only people native to these wild lands; they knew where it was possible to cross the rivers, where a path could be found through the forest, and where there was enough shelter to survive during the winter. An Evenki family was panning for gold when they realized they could also sell nephrite stones. It so happened that the wife was of Chinese origin (from a family settled for decades in Siberia), and she knew that the white nephrite found in Baunt had prime value in China—fetching prices many times higher than the more common green jade. Her own Chinese family in Russia could not access the deposits themselves; physically they were not able to venture into the forests. However, they were able to act as mediators to establish connections with buyers from China. Soon a network was set up to sell the stones and convey them across the border. The Evenkis set up a company called Dylacha (Sunshine), which operated at first as a "family-clan commune," a legal category set up in Russia and freed from taxes in order to support "small peoples of the North" in traditional employments (see Chapter 4).[61] Later, when Sunshine made big profits from mining, it changed its status to that of a regular business, applied for and obtained a license to mine for the nephrite at Kavokta in Baunt, and became one of the leading taxpayers of the region.

The raw stones were transported by truck over the Russia-China border with all necessary paperwork, in which the nephrite was documented as a stone for building and decorative purposes. The people who did understand the value of nephrite, the Chinese buyers, were kept at a distance and never allowed to visit the mining areas. Meanwhile, the Evenki miner-employees were forbidden to set up separate relations with the traders or to visit Chinese jade mines, jade workshops, or jade trading centers. Ignorant about the prices paid there, they were willing to accept very low wages. So it was the establishment of mutual social and geographical distance, ensuring ignorance at several points along the trade network, that lay behind the first ten years of commercial success of the Sunshine company.[62] The border officials did not identify the stones as jade, and the purchasers in China, located in Manzhouli, where the raw stones were cut and polished, also "had no idea" where the stones came from. This was convenient for them, since lack of knowledge meant they could claim the stones originated from a more prestigious site in China and therefore they could receive a higher price for the finished products.

By 2008, when the rest of the world was struggling with the global economic crisis, the sun was shining brightly on the Sunshine company. The Beijing Olympic Games created a jade fever in the market. It was decided to use jade in the winners' medals, with the precious white jade prominently inserted in the gold medals. Jade merchandise was mass-produced to sell to the hordes of visiting tourists. The Sunshine company made wonderful profits. It built an office in the nearest big settlement to the mines, set up other local businesses for Evenki, and gave up its gold prospecting altogether, deciding to focus on jade exports. Now, however, it was becoming evident that jade deposits had turned into a paradigm example of the "hunting grounds" mentioned at the beginning of this chapter.

What happened then was very dramatic. Beginning around 2008, the criminal world in Buryatia became aware of the immense profits to be made from the sale of nephrite. Illegal mining spread to several other mountainous areas of Buryatia. Criminal bosses hired teams of desperate and hard men and sent them out to the "hunting grounds" deposits. There was fierce competition between the gangs, and prime mining areas were divided up among different groups. These new teams were armed and guarded. Miners who strayed into the territory of another group were killed, and by 2010 there were assassinations among the criminal leaders. This became known as the "nephrite war." [63] Bosses from the city of Irkutsk took over the deposits in Oka district, and from Ulan-Ude they advanced on Baunt. On top of their own profits, they forced any local "illegals" to pay them a tribute. Soon the profits were so immense that the sale of nephrite became by far the largest income for the entire Republic of Buryatia. Now the "roving bandits" began to be joined by the stationary kind—corrupt officials were determined to receive their share. The Chinese intermediaries were forced to pay, and not just once but twice: they bought stones from the "bases" set up by the criminal gangs, and then were also made to pay a "tax" (state levy) for each truckload they transported. In such ways, the "nephrite mafia" achieved a strength and organization that was unheard of previously in the Buryat Republic. At this point the criminal world in Russia as a whole, which was highly interconnected, got interested, including the most powerful mafia boss in Moscow, Aslan Usoyan, known by his nickname "Grandfather Khasan" (*Ded Khasan*). Soon, though, the Grandfather was dead, assassinated in an interclan war in 2013.

The Russian legal and security organs determined to put a stop to the violence and criminality—and also to benefit from the nephrite trade themselves.[64] The Moscow-based state organization Rostekhnologiya set up some daughter companies in the region, under the patronage of the security services. Their first target was the most successful local operator, the Sunshine company. A legal case was filed against Sunshine on the grounds that it was mining outside its legally licensed territory. The Sunshine leaders argued that this was not true. They started a campaign that attempted to involve international agencies and even the Cree indigenous rights lawyer Wilton Littlechild. The Udege activist Pavel Sulyandziga, appearing with a defiantly non-Russian mustache and embroidered clothes, spoke publicly in support of the Evenki enterprise (see Chapter 4).[65] But by 2014, unable to contend with the Russian power hierarchy, they lost the case, despite many appeals.[66] Sunshine's huge store of nephrite was confiscated, the firm was closed down by force, and soon the directors fled to China.

However, with the takeover by a state-run company, the sky-high profits slackened. The old cultural distinction between "nephrite" and "jade" lost its commercial edge. Under state-regulated trade conditions, the old secrecy, the mislabeling of the stones at the border, and the pretense by Chinese traders that Russian stones come from somewhere in China have all ended. Now there is just one playing field in which everyone recognizes that the Buryat product is jade aimed for the Chinese market. The costs of taxes, customs, equipment, transport, and miners' wages rose to the point that Rostekhnologiya gave up and sold the Baunt deposit to another company, Zabaikal Mining Enterprise (ZME). Now there is a single, more or less transparent, but far less profitable cross-border sphere of extraction, processing, and trade. This can be seen from two facts: first, that there is Chinese investment in the ZME, and second, that Chinese specialists in selecting, carving, and polishing the stones are employed at the ZME's base in Ulan-Ude and are training Russian apprentices to learn this very culturally specialized set of skills.

POLITICAL AND SOCIAL REPERCUSSIONS OF THE CHANGING ECONOMIC SCENE

At the beginning of the chapter, we mentioned the history of Russia's alternating policies of subsidy and abandonment of the Russian Far East. The current era is one of subsidy—but, as we described in Chapter 1, only a few spots are subsidized, with the result that the cycle of subsidy and abandonment now forms a *territorial* pattern of glaring differences in wealth and opportunities. In this situation, we are reminded that economic activities are performed not in a vacuum but in a sociopolitical matrix in which whatever is actually carried out serves to benefit some actors and to exclude or damage others (and among these others we include animals and other living entities; see Chapter 6). In these final sections we examine briefly some of the political, social, and moral consequences of the recent trajectory of borderland economies.

Let us return first of all to the Territories of Advanced Socio-Economic Development (TORs) and examine the case of Bolshoi Kamen' (Big Stone), a formerly closed (ZATO) port town near Vladivostok. Even though it has no port of its own on the Sea of Japan, China has so far been hesitant to commit to large investments in this (or any other) Russian port.[67] Foreign companies complain that municipal authorities often prevent them from working and that customs offices do not properly observe the zones' tax concessions.[68] It is becoming clear that the Russian government is heavily subsidizing the Far Eastern TORs, if only because the state is legally responsible for providing TOR infrastructure and these enclaves are currently functioning mainly as platforms for Russia's state-linked giant companies.[69] Nevertheless, in some ways, the Bolshoi Kamen' project is a success. Big Stone is being utterly transformed by Moscow's designation of the town as a TOR. Six new micro-region housing developments are being built, with more than 5,000 new apartments and a population rise of 20,000 people expected in the next five years. The state has earmarked 25 billion rubles for infrastructure development, with a new central heating plant, electricity station, hospital, and schools. The Kremlin is providing 99 percent of this funding, with the aim of making the city attractive to future workers of the TOR's main accredited company (*rezident*), the Zvezda (Star) shipyard. This yard, which as of 2020 is being reconstructed, is to be the biggest in Russia, building nuclear-armed ships for the navy and tankers to exploit the Arctic routes.[70] Numerous smaller companies have been applying to join the TOR. Vladivostok, just across the bay, is also thriving by regional standards: by 2018, 141 new enterprises had been set up in the sprawling territories of the city's free port, of which 95 were in a TOR.[71]

In this new entrepreneurial situation, a value reorientation is taking place, especially in education. Unlike in the past in the Russian Far East (and elsewhere in Russia today), the new school funding is not provided by the municipality but by the private corporations of the TOR. There is now a Zvezda-supported shipbuilding college, and there are "school-institute-enterprise" courses where pupils join "the big team of Rosneft" (the oil giant) even as schoolchildren. The local university has a close connection with Gazprom (the state-owned natural gas company), with the explicit aim of producing "market-competitive graduates for our base partner." Gazprom provides thousands of internships and training programs throughout Russia. This is a move toward the "human capital" approach, in which the student is encouraged down a single track into employment in the energy industries. In these privileged pockets the younger generation seems to be making a cultural shift, which is a historic one for Russia—leaving behind the old Soviet reverence for the intellectual and creative professions (see also Chapter 7), which are now seen as superfluous, and eagerly targeting the so-called world skills in mathematics, computing, business, and engineering that are in demand. Furthermore, they are beginning to conceive of themselves as subjects in the global market for specialist skills. This market is now dominated by China, especially in the Asia-Pacific region. Classes in Chinese language are in high demand. Students are imagining a future for themselves that embraces not just collaborating with China but migrating there for well-paid work.

Yet, looking at the wider sociopolitical matrix, we see that all of this is bringing tensions. First, despite the legislative "state of exception" that characterizes TORs (see Chapter 1), the resident companies have not in practice been able to extricate themselves from administrative entanglements, from both above and below.[72] And second, the actual operation of the TOR is proving socially divisive in a way that reflects and exacerbates rather than heals differentiations already present in the border economy. It is not just that not all of the trained and hopeful students can find jobs in Zvezda and other mega-companies but also that the "global players" tend to avoid hiring locals for a whole swath of ordinary jobs. A study of the personnel sections of newly established firms in the Bolshoi Kamen' TOR found that department heads see the local labor force as "marginalized people," untrained and unwilling to work. "The dearth of labor forces us to search for qualified people in central Russia, in other regions where we have branches. Actually, we just take our own people and relocate them. That is because there are no good workers here in the Far East," said one TOR manager in 2017.[73] These recruits, including migrant shift-working *otkhodniki,* have to be paid a special regional hardship allowance, 1.5 times the salary paid for the same job carried out for the firm in central Russia. The companies expect locals to accept lower pay packages. Even so, they are not hired, and this is not just because of company policy, as one company director planning to join the TOR explained in 2017:

> Locals do not want to work for us. At all. How come? In some locations, we did not find even one man who wants to work for us. Just one woman, she comes, cooks and goes away. All our other employees are shift workers. Maybe there is an alternative employer, other positions? No, it's just us for a hundred kilometers. In fact, the only alternative is illegal fishing or poaching. Everyone here earns money in this way. They tell us they can work for us only in winter—from May to October they are all busy. This means they must earn more [than we would pay them] during the fishing season. I'm not sure it's that much more, but yes, they get money from these activities. Moreover, that is their habitual way of living. . . . They have always lived here. But they started poaching predominantly only after the collapse of the Soviet Union. And I think that ethnicity does not really matter. Some of them may be Evenki, others Russian, it makes no difference.[74]

We learn from this that having had to adjust to a new reality after the end of the Soviet Union, twenty years later many disadvantaged people were thoroughly accustomed to their new way of life and not eager to abandon it. They took to informal niches, from teaching, taxi driving, and trading to poaching the diverse natural resources around them (gold, nephrite, coal, fish, forest berries, wild-growing cannabis, astragalus roots). They processed, transported, and smuggled, sending most salable items to China. In Vladivostok, they also imported used or stolen cars, trucks, and heavy equipment from Japan, creating a whole sub-economy of gas stations, repair shops, pools of mechanics and drivers, and sales agencies employing tens of thousands of people.[75] One way or another, interwoven with trade and transport, most of the economy of the region came to depend on the informal automobile business. Networks were flexible yet robust, tightly tied to local social relations at one end, roping in border guards and inspectors, and ending with agents in other Asian countries at the other.[76] For informally employed people the creation of the TORs, with their unfamiliar structures, was not a solution. On the contrary, as happened in villages near Svobodny, it could leave the excluded and disadvantaged feeling "like lepers."[77] And sometimes it was a catastrophe. For the great new companies might well be intent on capturing the very same resources the ordinary folk were taking informally—as we showed in the case of the jade trade.

THE PACIFIC COAST: ANOTHER "HUNTING GROUND"

The emerging social divisions are more complex, of course, than a face-off between mega-companies and locals, for there are also enterprises that are squeezed in between. They are caught in a shifting limbo between metropolitan lawmaking, regional bureaucratic machinations, and local brigandage. To illustrate this point, we take the case of a fish processing company in Bolshoi Kamen'. A subsidiary of the partly state-owned Dobroflot, this firm found itself subject to President Putin's "investment for quotas" law launched in 2017.[78] The idea was in principle a good one: to allocate fishing quotas to companies only if they invested in constructing factory ships and canning factories in Russia rather than selling their unprocessed fish to China, as they had been doing (with the result that Russian consumers were buying the less-than-fresh, and needlessly expensive, cleaned fish imported back from China).[79] But a problem soon hit the Dobroflot subsidiary: it built the factory but did not get the quota. This was a "bureaucratic" matter, allegedly a question of a minor technicality—an altered specification in the filleting machinery. This hitch meant that Dobroflot's booming fishing and canning operation went ahead on an illegal basis, without a quota, and only after an expensive court case in Moscow did the company receive a quota for 2020.[80] Further squeezing came when all the companies in the Bolshoi Kamen' TOR received a dressing down from the new governor of the *krai,* Oleg Kozhemyako (appointed in 2018 by Putin to replace the bribery-tainted previous governor). He accused them of moral faults: lack of transparency in pricing and ignoring their "social obligations" in the city. To these ironies—for Kozhemyako was no stranger to the usual machinations of regional officials—we can add the most crucial Achilles' heel of the "investment for quotas" scheme, which is that the quotas are impossible to police in practice. The seas off the Russian coast are beset with poachers and even armed pirates. Some of these are desperate North Korean fishers, some Chinese, some from Japan, but a large number—in tiny boats, adept at hiding amid the fogs and island creeks, and well capable of fending off foes—are Russian citizens.[81] Dobroflot's fishing quota, obtained at such cost, was undermined from below by the other participants in the maelstrom of the Far East coast, a restless population of ordinary folk who have turned alegal, with some even becoming outlaws.

The criminal barons contesting one another in the wild 1990s may have been killed—such as Grandfather Khasan, mentioned earlier in connection with the jade boom—but their successors have started to reappear.[82] The defiant culture of the underground world has not disappeared. Notably the veneration of the criminal "king" (known as the "thief-within-the law," *vor-v-zakone*), the observance of strict rules of behavior including a vow to avoid any contact with agents of the state, and the "crowning" of successor "thieves" so the tradition can be carried on. The clothes, the slang, the aggressive style, and the inter-gang fighting spread from the "zone" (the prison camp system) into villages in the borderlands.[83] Beaten back by the *siloviki* (police and security forces) in the 2000s, these attitudes still permeate certain circles, such as those engaged in cannabis gathering and the drug trade or in illicit mining, where participants often circle in and out of prison camps.[84] One of these areas is illegal fishing off the coast of Vladivostok. We have chosen this as an example because it illustrates how "criminal acts" emerge in what is more generally a way of earning a living.

The individually owned small boats operating visibly (quasi-legally) in Russian waters face bankruptcy. In 2016, fishers in Vladivostok received 75 rubles per kilo (34 rubles per pound) for their catches of pollack, while the retail price was 200 rubles. Most of the difference in price went into the "gray schemes" of fly-by-night firms mediating between the non-VAT-paying fishers and the VAT-paying Russian buying companies (although frozen fish is 60 percent of Russia's food exports to China, the export trade is highly monopolized and not open to individual fishers unless by smuggling).[85] Meanwhile, from their meager 75 rubles the fishers had to pay for their ships, fuel, nets, cold storage, and packing materials, and in many cases for various forms of help given to their home villages.[86] The temptation to turn illegal, to do everything as invisibly as possible, is almost impossible to resist. As is also the case with the widespread illegal fishing in the Amur, there is no shortage of Chinese firms willing to take part in cross-border schemes.[87] Furthermore, they pay in cash, unlike most Russian fishmongers.

On August 9, 2017, as the Vladivostok media reported, Roman Klimenko, Valerii Dvortsov, and Dvortsov's son-in-law set off in their cutter, deliberately failing to inform the border control and coast guard, taking forbidden nets on board for trawling salmon.[88] They were not supposed to be fishing for salmon at this time of year, which was set aside for the fish to spawn. They relied on a "cuckoo," an informer paid to follow the movements of border patrols and send a signal to the poachers to move to a safe cove; with the cutter's 300-horsepower engine, they reckoned they could make a fast escape. But this time heavy fog blinded the "cuckoo," two inspectors' boats appeared out of nowhere, and an officer boarded the cutter. Normally, the fishers could have expected a fine. But the problem was that Dvortsov had just been let out of prison on probation, and therefore he now risked a new, more severe sentence. He seized the inspector, intending to throw him overboard. Miraculously, the official managed to jump from the cutter back to his own boat. Klimenko then gave the cutter full throttle, rammed the inspectors' vessel, and disappeared rapidly into the ocean, hiding in the fog. The inspectors returned to shore and witnesses were sought. A fisher said he had observed the incident from afar, just as described. But then, threatened by Dvortsov's allies, he changed his testimony, saying that he what he had actually seen was the officers firing at the men in the cutter. Further, it seems that Dvortsov had phoned a friend on land, reporting that it was his cutter that had been rammed by the inspectors' ship and that he had been wounded. This friend failed to inform the police about the phone call. On August 11, the bodies of Klimenko and Dvortsov washed up on a beach. Dvortsov's son-in-law disappeared without trace.

The consequences of this murky incident are interesting with regard to the theme of this chapter, making a living. The fishing folk of the coast raised a storm of protest on social media sites, threatening and insulting the border guards. They even planned to picket the office of the local branch of the border section of the FSB, though they had second thoughts and gave up the idea. They were supported by considerable local opinion, with many citing the lack of work, high prices, and general poverty. It was then pointed out that though not everyone has an expensive cutter and specialized fishing nets, everyone has to make a living. "Just try offering such a man stable work for 50–60 thousand rubles a month" was one comment made in an online forum. "He'll refuse! Because in one good season fishing salmon or crab he can earn enough to spend the whole winter lying on his sofa and spitting at the ceiling. That's why anyone who prevents him fishing, like the border inspectors, is an enemy with whom it's necessary to fight."

It is significant that in respect for these realities, the local courts do not punish poachers and smugglers with the full force of the law. They do not confiscate the fishers' boats, for instance, which would deprive them of a living. Fines are used where the law stipulates prison. As of 2018, the poachers were subject only to "administrative" law, not criminal sanctions, according to the local media.[89] A way of life is thus allowed to continue. In fact, it seems to suit a great many people very well.

So perhaps we can conclude this chapter with the thought that Russian citizens have managed to create their own more or less satisfactory economies "from below." Whatever the statistics might say, "the poor" are not actually so poor. The eminent sociologist Simon Kordonskii even suggested that there is something mythicized about the "algorithm of poverty" automatically employed by ordinary people when addressing officials. Among themselves, however, people will not say they are poor, just that "we live like everyone else." This means cobbling together something extra—whether by hook or crook, like Ayuna the potato trader, or by money sent by a "departed" son or daughter, or through a hunter's sheer toughness and determination in the snowbound forests.[90] The idea that village physical conditions have not improved since the 1970s can be indignantly denied. "We have made improvements," people say. These are small but important things, such as a new (Chinese) type of insulation for the walls, or an ingenious method of heating the outside toilet. The extra income does not always come via chains of transactions leading to China, though a great deal of it does.

In coming years, the intercountry situation is likely to change. As global warming makes swaths of Siberian wilderness suitable for large-scale agriculture and at the same intensifies migratory pressure from dry regions of Asia, notably including part of China, a warmer Russian Far East with a longer growing season may well become an irresistible target for Chinese investment.[91] However, in the present, big Chinese investors are not pushing as hard at the Russian door (nor is it being held open as wide) as the two Great Leaders like to proclaim. In this situation, the regional economies in the Russian Far East have to sustain their own momentum. As the jade and fishing cases show (and these are only two of many other possible examples), the Russian everyday borderland economy keeps itself alive through its own specific form of capitalism, by means of densely interknit webs of informal economic setups that link municipal officials, businesspeople, lawyers, the *siloviki,* and the people. Sayana Namsaraeva, a member of our research group, told us that her experience of living in Russia through the 1990s made her aware that in the absence of the state, what really mattered were human relationships. That, we confirm, is still true today even though the state has made a comeback, and it is to these relationships, in particular among indigenous peoples, that we turn in Chapter 4.

INDIGENOUS PEOPLES
OF THE BORDERLANDS

4

In 2014, I (Caroline) was researching cross-border contacts in towns and villages along the Russian border with Mongolia and China. One brief encounter was memorable for its unexpectedness. In the solemn emptiness of the newly built Orthodox Christian cathedral in the border town of Kyakhta I noticed a smiling, Asian-looking man acting as a servitor to the priest. Intrigued, I started chatting with him, thinking he might be Mongolian; but no. "I am Nanai," he said, naming an ethnic group that lives far away to the east, along the lower reaches of the Amur River. I asked if his relatives back at home had contacts with the Nanais on the other side of the river. He replied simply, "There are no Nanais in China." The response surprised me because the people called Nanai have always inhabited both banks of the border river. Admittedly, the population living in China is known in Chinese as Hezhe (Hezhen), but still, the man's comment seemed remarkable. Was it that there had been such an absence of contact over the border that he simply did not know of their existence? Or was it that he *did* know about the Hezhe but saw them as so unlike his own people that they no longer counted as "us"? The puzzling question of the different ways in which indigenous peoples position themselves in relation to the wider world is the main theme of this chapter.

Many ethnic groups, of greatly varied size and political weight, are native inhabitants of the borderlands. What happened to these various peoples is enormously revealing about the values and structures of the Russian and Chinese modes of government. While they now live lives very different from their ancestors', the indigenous peoples have maintained their own distinctive ways of "going about things"—at a tangent to the majoritarian Russians and Chinese, and with kinds of sensibilities, memories, attitudes to the world, the landscape, and social relations that we have not met so far in this book. What is interesting is that this is now enabling a rethinking of identities and the potential for an overall shift in the interethnic pattern established during the twentieth century.

The indigenous peoples belong to two major linguistic and cultural groupings. Using the names commonly accepted today, they include the Mongolic-speaking, previously mainly nomadic pastoralist and Buddhist peoples, the Buryat, Barga, Horchin, Khamnigan, and Daur; and the Tungusic-speaking, shamanist, and formerly hunting, reindeer-herding, fishing, and farming groups, the Manchu, Evenki, Nanai, Hezhe, Oroch, Oroqen, Negidal, Ulch, and Udege.[1] In using the term "indigenous," we do not wish necessarily to imply autochthony or origin in this territory—for these peoples were all mobile and in the depths of history may have come from other areas—but simply refer to the ethnic groups whose forebears were present in the area of the present border before the advent of Russian and Manchu-Chinese rule in the seventeenth century.[2] From that time, they began to be incorporated into social statuses, places, and institutions not of their own making. This has been a continuous process extending to the present, eroding languages and cultures, and the indigenous peoples can be seen in this sense as postcolonial subjects. But it is important to point out that they took initiatives to strengthen or change their situation—adopting new identities, migrating, attempting to secede, adapting their economies, switching language or religion, setting up trade links, and intermarrying with other groups. The result today is a complex mo-saic of indigenous peoples, often living not only adjacent to but also mixed among older and newer settler populations. We have chosen to discuss some peoples of the borderland rather than survey them all, and our main focus, amid all the possible topics of interest and importance, is on their engagement in what the anthropologist Madeleine Reeves calls "border work"—that is, on the ways in which they maintain the border as a line of sepa-ration or, on the contrary, make strenuous efforts to bypass or overcome it.[3]

Sheer numerical size of population matters in the strategies open to different groups, as we discuss later.[4] But it is also important that the numerically larger peoples (Buryats, Bargas, Khorchins, and Manchus) have long traditions of literacy in their own languages and scripts, and their own scholars who composed historical, religious, ethical, geographical, ethnographic, and medical works, as well as translating sacred texts from other lan-guages. If the smaller, non-literate, now separated groups such as the Nanai-Hezhe or the Oroch-Oroqen had local transborder cultures, these more numerous peoples had been part of far wider transcontinental networks for centuries.[5] That long, complex his-tory is not adequately represented by the tropes of "minorities" and "tribes" used in the standard Marxist accounts found in the USSR and China. In this context, our use of the word "indige-nous" for these larger peoples has to be carefully nuanced. Many Buryats, for example, have long viewed themselves as cosmopoli-tans, citing the long history of their Buddhist links with Mongolia and Tibet, and they would reject the connotations of "indige-nous" as implying traditional, backward, or in need of being saved.[6] Nor would they all agree with being characterized as "au-tochthonous": for although some Buryat groups' earliest history is located in the area around Baikal, many others know the pre-cise dates in the seventeenth or eighteenth centuries when their ancestors arrived from distant parts of the Mongol world. Never-theless, all Buryats are devoted to the places, mountains, rivers, and steppes they now regard as *their* homeland, not that of in-comers of other ethnicities, and in this sense would agree they are *korennyye* (Russ: "rooted," "indigenous"). When their kind of indigenous history-making, which combines attachment to precise spots with a tradition of transnational journeying, is reinvigorated, as is happening now, it produces a completely different perspective from that of the imperial/colonial rulers.

The remark from the Christian Nanai in the cathedral opens up several themes important for this chapter. Our aim is not only to give some information about the indigenous peoples living along this border but also to convey a sense of their various perspectives, feelings, and hopes for the future. Understanding their various pasts is crucial. Until the 1930s–1940s, the two sides of the Argun and Amur were culturally and economically a common frontier space.[7] The border was too porous, too long, too thickly wooded, or too marshy to be effectively patrolled. For fishing people such as the Nanai-Hezhe, with their boats and relocatable dwellings, the rivers and their islands were the vital center of their lives, not a dividing line. And in this they were not alone, for as we mentioned in Chapter 1, in the early twentieth century traders, bandits, gold prospectors, Cossack detachments, opium growers, smugglers, and others, of a variety of ethnicities, also crossed back and forth over the state boundary more or less at will.

In the countless arrivals and departures of this border very few groups have been able to remain in one place over generations. There is, though, an almost invisible layer of old settlers who are just as "rooted" as any indigenous group. Arriving as banished or resettled peasant farmers, they had to build houses and clear the land with their own hands; they hunted, fished, and gathered, turning the land into their own. Villages of exiled Old Believers have clung to the same places in Zabaikalia since the early eighteenth century, and the same is true of the tiny remote settlements of peasants sent in the nineteenth century to colonize the area that is now the Jewish Autonomous Region. Hardy and self-reliant, their descendants stay out of public life and count themselves as *korennyye* in relation to all the later waves of incomers: farmers, miners, teachers, administrators, merchants, and builders of cities. Along the Amur many of these "rooted settlers" rebelled against the Soviet in the 1920s, were defeated, and emigrated, leaving almost empty land behind. This explains the strange formation of the Jewish Autonomous Region: the Soviet solution was to send tens of thousands of "working Jews," people whose accustomed artisan and trade occupations were now forbidden, to farm and populate the vacant lands. A year or two of grim deprivation and lack of promised supplies was enough, and most of these Jews fled. In the 1950s–1960s further (non-Jewish) cohorts were sent in, now mainly for mining and manufacturing.[8] Analogous turnovers happened elsewhere in the borderlands, above all as a consequence of punitive exile and deportation in the 1930s–1950s, but throughout it all, in hamlets here and there, there are Slavic small farmers living much as their ancestors had done, at arm's length from the authorities, and they are just as "rooted" as the peoples whom we are terming "indigenous" in this chapter.[9]

The repeated settlements of Slavic and Han farmers pushed the small reindeer-herding, fishing, and hunting peoples into remoter areas but did not cement state control. Between 1911 and 1925 a series of bitter uprisings of (and between) indigenous peoples undermined state sovereignty in the whole region. Several insurgencies erupted in Barga, in Inner Mongolia, after the mass arrival of Chinese settlers from the east had pushed Horchin Mongols westward, dislodging other Mongols in turn and arousing much mutual resentment.[10] In Barga (see Map 1), Mongol and Daur leaders periodically attempted to wrest autonomy from China up to the late 1920s. But by far the larger migrations were from north to south, as indigenous people fled Russia in waves. Some of these crossed into Mongolia, and more migrated into China. The northeastern Manchuria steppes and forests came to be dotted with the incomers' hunting camps and herding settlements. Soon they were to be joined in this capacious land by hundreds of thousands of central Russian refugees fleeing the Soviet regime, in this case mostly settling in cities, such as Harbin, Hailar, and Dalian (Russ: Dalny).

Three long-term consequences of this period of uprooting reach into the present day. First is the continued determination of the states, especially Russia, to clamp down on the border, both physically and ideologically, and never allow such a loss of population again (see Chapter 1). Second, there is the metropole's never quite extinguished fear that remote regions contain "wild" indigenous people who might appear from out of the Siberian forests and create havoc in Russia. One such person is the shaman Aleksandr Gabyshev. In 2019 Gabyshev undertook a Pied Piper–like journey on foot from Yakutia-Sakha, via Buryatia, heading for Moscow with the intention of exorcising the "demon" Putin from the land. As he trudged slowly on, Gabyshev conducted rituals, gained publicity, and collected a band of followers. But he only got as far as Lake Baikal. Moscow's extraordinary overreaction was evident: he was arrested, diagnosed with insanity, and forced to return to confinement in Yakutia, and armed, masked OMON forces were sent to beat and arrest his supporters.[11] The incident sparked outrage in the Buryat capital, Ulan-Ude, where shamans are respected as spiritual healers of illness and misfortune. Gabyshev's arrest, combined with unrest about electoral corruption, gave rise to angry demonstrations by thousands of people, all of which revealed the gulf of suspicion that separates Moscow from the remote provinces (see also Chapter 3).[12] The third consequence to reach out from the past is the renewed sense of their own vulnerability that took lasting hold among the native border dwellers. They saw how easily they could be suspected of the disloyal desire to separate themselves yet again, and to this day extreme caution is their watchword.[13] In the next section, we delve further into this situation, showing that it was never constituted simply by a center-periphery relation, but also featured unstable articulations that either involved a third player (the foreign "other side") or shifted the parameters altogether by turning the ethnic periphery into its own kind of center. We suggest that it is this equivocal field that is now the arena for the emergence of new social groupings.

A REBELLIOUS PERIPHERY?

It is legitimate to ask if the indigenous peoples, poised in such a historically volatile borderland, pose a threat to the stability of the Russian or Chinese states. In both countries, metropolitan fears of uprisings in the peripheries were compounded by attributing an alien, "irrational" and "easily influenceable" nature to the indigenous peoples.[14] Kristina Jonutytė's examination of the media furor in Russia around the case of the shaman Gabyshev shows that this attitude is still current today, and we suggest that it cannot be divorced from the twentieth-century history of the elusive practices of the border people.[15] Even before the advent of the socialist regimes, the two central governments were anxious about "their" people succumbing to the attractions of the other side. Late Qing and Early Republican Chinese officials noted with alarm that Tungusic Solon hunters living near the Argun and Amur spoke Russian, gave their children Russian names, had been widely converted to Christianity by missionaries, and were engaged in trade across the border; some had even taken Russian citizenship.[16] Fearing that Russia could make use of these people in its steady expansion in Manchuria, a series of measures were undertaken to counteract Russian influence and win back the Solons. They were to be converted from "primitive" hunting to farming, educated in "civilized habits," and given land, livestock, equipment, and schools. But it turned out that the Solons were not just potentially disloyal; they were also unruly. A good number refused to become farmers and escaped to the forests. In 1922–1923 there was an armed uprising of Solon against oppressive Han Chinese governors and merchants, which killed several officials and disturbed much of the border region.[17] Shortly after, there were similar uprisings in Russia, such as the "Tungus Republic" set up in northeast Siberia by Tungus and Sakha-Yakut groups in 1924–1925 in revolt against the local Bolsheviks' racist terror tactics and expropriations. Its declared, though doomed, aim was to secede from the USSR.[18]

The secessionist Pan-Mongolian Government initiated by Buryats, Bargas, and other Inner Mongols in 1918 in Dauria, a station on the Trans-Siberian railway, threatened to throw aside the entire binary imperial rule of the borderlands. Supported by the rabidly anti-Soviet Cossack general Grigorii Semenov, its goal was to set up a great theocratic Buddhist state invoking the spirit of Chinggis Khan, encompassing the whole of Mongolia as well as large sections of Russian and Chinese territory. No government in the region or the world at large supported the Pan-Mongol enterprise, and it rapidly collapsed. But amid the violent, chaotic fighting of the civil war, Buryat Buddhists set up another secessionist theocratic state under the leadership of a charismatic lama ascetic, Samdan Tsydenov, who assumed the title Nomun Khan. This was put down by the Bolsheviks, but its pacifist and Tantric religious ideals, under the name "Balagat movement," remained vital for thousands of Buryats throughout the 1920s (and despite decades of repression the ideals were revived in the 1980s).[19] These very diverse movements—the militaristic Semenovites, the peace-loving Balagats, and the Pan-Mongolists—became potent bogeymen for Moscow, all of them signaling native insurrection. Stoking the fears in the metropoles was the continued flight of Buryats, Khamnigan, and Evenki across the border.

However, beginning in 1931 the Japanese invasion of Manchuria enforced militarization of the Chinese side. Indigenous hunting peoples such as the Oroqen were treated with contempt. The Japanese colonizers forced them to provide hunted meat for their troops, enslaved men and women, and used them in human experiments. The Japanese oppression, together with epidemic diseases, reduced the Oroqen population by at least half. Meanwhile, the Soviet imposition of the border security zone, internal passports, and other security measures in effect sealed off the border from the north. As historian Sören Urbansky writes,

"During the 1930s, the Soviet-Japanese arms race . . . transformed the borderland into a no-man's-land strung with barbed-
wire fences."[20] Both countries worked hard to infiltrate spies se-
cretly into the other side. They favored indigenous hunters and
herders as agents because of their knowledge of the land and their
tracking skills. Those who had fled the USSR for China became
particularly suspect, each country fearing that their respective
spies planted among them were double agents.[21] Later, with the
Stalinist purges of 1937–1938 and hysterical accusations of Pan-
Mongolism and "spying for the Japanese," the leaders of large
indigenous peoples such as the Buryats were decimated. It was at
this time also that most of the Chinese remaining in the Soviet
Union were deported and virtually all of the 171,000 Koreans in
the Russian Far East were moved to Central Asia. The indigenous
herders and hunters living in the immediate vicinity of the border,
such as Buryats, Nanai, and Oroch were forced into resettlement
in the interior. Hundreds of Buryat Buddhist lamas in monasteries
close to the border were executed or sent into exile in distant
Gulag camps.[22] In the Russian Far East, place names derived from
local languages or Chinese were systematically changed to Russian names (see Chapter 5). In Maoist China, "class enemies,"
including more prosperous members of minority groups, were
"sent down to the countryside" for reeducation by labor in the
harsh semi-famine conditions of the communes in northern
areas.[23] The border became a sterile militarized environment and
more or less impenetrable. By the time of the Sino-Soviet split in
the 1960s, for indigenous people the merest hint of "nationalism"
or contacts with kin living over the border became a punishable
crime (see also Chapter 5). Thus, local people's experiences of dislocation, fear, harassment, ideological dragooning, and sometimes terror went hand in hand with the strengthening of state
sovereignty and a divide-and-rule approach to administration. In
the long run, the border sterilization policy proved highly effective: the two governments ensured that this region could not be
as culturally independent or rebellious as Tibet or Xinjiang.

There have been no large-scale migrations of indigenous people across the border in this region for almost a hundred years. At present, while some leave their native lands for another location elsewhere in the same country, very few migrate to the spaces right across the border. Instead, upward mobility enables energetic and better-educated individuals to merge into the urban society of nearby towns and metropolitan cities. But this vertical integration, which usually goes with loss of native languages, coexists with something very different: the emergence of new "horizontal" subjectivities and previously unknown kinds of wider social association. This implies not physical migration but a shift in perspective. There are mental alignments and disjunctions that did not exist earlier. One of these is the disconnect between ethnic attachment to a locality and the fact that economic opportunities are far away (see Chapter 3). But others concern the more psychosocial questions that are the themes here: self-understandings that are distinct from state-imposed identities; the emotional presence of hitherto buried memories that differ from public memorialization; the spiritual devotion to homeland places but at the same time the emergence of new cross-border quests; and a desire for globalized liberal modernity that grates against renewed conservatism in certain cultural patterns. These complex processes have brought into the open vibrant, unofficial associations that do not match the state administrative entities, even when the latter, such as "autonomous" provinces and districts, were designed to represent ethnic populations.

Absent, dormant, or barely thinkable in earlier periods, the new attachments have been made actualities in people's lives by the pervasive spread of digital technologies. These days, people can manage without running water in their homes, they can cope with snowed-in roads, but cellphones, TVs, and laptops are essentials.[24] Cellphones enable close kinship relations to be maintained at a distance, and they help labor migrants cope with loneliness and hostility.[25] But most significant in relation to the theme of this chapter is the almost universal use of smartphones to create social groups with their own conversations. Most of these are personal circles: associations of school classmates, co-villagers, members of a profession, or graduates of a college. Often they are closed to outsiders, operate in either Russian or Chinese, and are specific to one country or the other. But some are platforms for new cross-border social groupings, which, as we describe later, switch back and forth between virtual and very real physical existence.

While digital technology helps people reorder and extend their views of the world, it is also policed by the metropolitan powers that be. Once an online group has been set up with its own name and rationale for existence, its registration immediately places it in the digital public sphere. This is heavily monitored in both countries, but particularly in China, which not only has a firewall to prevent access to Western search engines but also allows government access to personal data on messaging systems. Controlling media of all kinds is central to all state-led projects, but particularly relevant to this chapter is the state's patrolling of historical memory in the service of current visions of national integration. Personal identities and online communications therefore intersect with the political sensitivities of states and may (or may not) adapt to their unpredictable swerves. For people trying to navigate their daily lives, the situation recalls Ismail Kadare's evocation of the dilemma of an Albanian translator in the 1970s.[26] A former bourgeois, he had adapted to Soviet domination and perfected his Russian—till his country fell out with the "revisionist" USSR and sided with China in the 1960s. He then laboriously learned Chinese and made a fine living, only suddenly to become aware that the rigid Albanian Communist Party had quarreled with Mao too, over his rapprochement with Nixon. Chinese translations were no longer required. He despaired to himself: "Henceforward he would be doubly undesirable, as a survivor of two detested eras—that of the bourgeoisie and that of the Chinese. People would point to him as the worst of time-servers."[27] In pointing to this example, we concur with the approach taken by Martin Fromm, the historian of East Asia—to move away from the conventional dichotomy of "state propaganda" versus "empirical truth" and seek instead to describe the interpenetration of local experience with the official enterprise of producing history.[28]

One main reason both governments see the now globalized "politics of indigeneity" as problematic and even dangerous is because in both China and Russia the *sine qua non* of state sovereignty is complete control of territory.[29] But indigeneity rests on narratives of autochthonous or prior settlement, on "belonging" to a particular land, as distinct from abstract citizenship, and it undermines state claims based on conquest, imperial purview, international treaties, superior civilization, and so on. Seeking to deal with such ineffable claims in their own ways, both states resent the interest of international organizations and NGOs and decry their depiction of the "plight" of indigenous peoples. Both countries claim that their constitutions already provide carefully planned support for their minorities. But what do they provide and for whom exactly? Are the constitutional rights different in China and Russia, and are they legally enforceable? These questions are so fundamental that we need to address them first, before turning to the main theme of the chapter, which is to show how border peoples understand their present situation by means of the production of "situated historical truths" along with flickering new imaginaries.

STATE CLASSIFICATIONS, RIGHTS, AND DEVELOPMENT POLICIES

The contemporary list of different "peoples" is essentially the outcome of successive governments' attempts to create order among mobile and amorphous groupings that historically split up or consolidated, and sometimes changed their ways of life and ethnic allegiances. During this long process the various populations were given a confusing variety of names, mostly quite different from those used today in either China or Russia.[30] It would be fundamentally incorrect to see any of these peoples as "pristine."[31] Even today's smallest and most peripheral-seeming groups, such as the Oroqen and Khamnigan, were closely tied to, or took active part in, imperial hierarchies, trade, fur tax or tribute (see Chapter 6), and military formations. Effacing such traces and memories was integral to the twentieth-century Communist campaigns to transform these societies, and then subsequently to recast their earlier history as romantically pure but also as savage, illiterate, dirty, disease-ridden, and generally in desperate need of progress.

The two socialist governments began with similar tasks. Jettisoning earlier imperial ways of categorizing their populations, new projects of ethnic classification were carried out in the 1920s and 1930s in the USSR and in the 1950s in China, in both cases according to principles laid out by Stalin: he had decreed that a stable "nationality" is determined by a common language, territory, economic life, and culture.[32] The problem was that in these border areas Stalin's four elements did not necessarily coincide. Nevertheless, the two socialist governments ordered that classification be carried out and appropriate names given; these classifications remain the basis of the state-recognized nationalities today.[33] Over time, however, the policies in each country toward these groups diverged, and today they differ greatly.

For the people themselves, while the given ethnic categories are recognized in official contexts, other identities that are just as deeply felt surface on other occasions.[34] This availability of alternatives is why many indigenous people easily switch who they say they are, depending on whom they are talking to. To foreigners they are likely simply to use the broadest category, *rossiyanin* ("citizen of Russia," as distinct from *russkii,* "ethnic Russian") or *zhongguoren* ("Chinese citizen," as distinct from *hanren,* "ethnic Chinese"). In local contexts there are a variety of nuanced alternatives to suit the occasion. Khamnigans, for example, may call themselves Buryat in the Buryat capital city but would never do so back in their home village. Even for officially recognized ethnicities in both Russia and China there has been a certain possibility of choice. Many indigenous people in the past, inventing a suitable ancestry, sought registration either as ethnic Han or as Russian to avoid repression or enhance social status. Conversely, majority nationals have sought registration as minorities to obtain access to economic and social benefits, in particular exemption from the one-child policy in place in China from 1979 to 2015. In Russia from 1997 on, ethnicity was no longer entered on passports. Welcomed by most as a sign of equality of citizenship, the measure was opposed by many from among indigenous groups who feared that with no documentary proof of their status they would lose benefits.[35] At present, Russia, but not China, allows its citizens to acquire dual nationality.[36]

In Russia the result of the ethnic categorizations was a hierarchy of political-administrative representation, roughly according to population size. Larger groups such as the Buryat were recognized as nationalities and allotted Autonomous Soviet Socialist Republic (ASSR) status, which meant they had a governmental apparatus with a president, ministries, a judiciary, and their own constitution. In the 1920s, the Buryat-Mongol ASSR was the only ASSR in the borderland. It was therefore designated as a beacon of socialist progress, ideally placed to shine its progressive light on neighboring China and Mongolia, which of course made the implementation of policies for reeducation, collectivization, hygiene, and urbanization all the more urgent there.[37] The less numerous Evenki were assigned an autonomous district (*okrug*) in central Siberia, while the other Tungus peoples, including Evenki living widely scattered outside their *okrug*, were accorded the status of "indigenous small peoples of the North" (*korennyye malochislennyie narody severa*, KMNS).[38] This last status continues to this day and is a cornerstone of Russian policy. Experienced anthropologists have shown convincingly that the numerical benchmark of KMNS status, conditional on having a population under 50,000, has "forced a dichotomization into small-numbered and non-small-numbered people and created a peculiar type of identity politics based on group size."[39] We suggest in this chapter that these divergent strategies are central not only to identity politics within Russia but also to intraethnic relations across the border.

The rights and privileges of KMNS apply only to people living in territories recognized as "indigenous homelands." Therefore, obtaining registration of such lands is central to small-group strategies. The privileges are substantial. Provided they are engaged in "traditional pursuits," KMNS are exempt from land tax, military service, and income tax; they have a lower pensionable age and special priority rights to hunt, fish, and gather resources in their lands. All of this is so attractive that since the end of the USSR the number of groups applying for and succeeding in attaining KMNS status in the Russian Federation almost doubled, from twenty-six to forty-five. Central to the policy is the right to form "family-clan communes" (*rodovaya obshchina*) to use ancestral lands for traditional economic pursuits, as we mentioned in the case of the Evenki company Sunshine in Chapter 3.[40] Such recognized community organizations have the right to take part in public affairs, but in practice they exercise very little political power. And while they can take legal action, regional power structures make it difficult for them to obtain justice.[41] Furthermore, some KMNS groups lack designated territories altogether, or have them allocated in desolate areas, or have their precious wildlife resources trampled by commercial companies with impunity. The consequence is that people belonging to the most precarious, smallest, or most scattered indigenous groups often have to seek illegal or dangerous sidelines for extra income. Their villages suffer from far greater unemployment, sparse medical services, poorer education, and more alcoholism than the Russian population as a whole.[42] All of this influences the ethnic politics of the "small-numbered." They center their efforts on getting good-quality land registered as indigenous territory, keeping away outsiders and predators, and jealously guarding the land's resources as well as the equipment (vehicles, fuel, guns, fishing tackle) needed to use it as they would like. As we will discuss later, this exclusivist focus is very different from the expansive, inclusive attitude of the large peoples of Siberia, such as Buryats, Altaians, and Yakut-Sakha.

In China all of the indigenous peoples, whatever the size of their population, were classed as "small ethnic minorities" (少数民族, *shaoshu minzu*), and some of the less numerous groups were artificially amalgamated with dissimilar others.[43] Most, but not all, achieved recognition in the form of "autonomous" districts (mostly called Banners in northeast China) within a unified, hierarchical system. However, unlike in Russia, this ethnic representation is structured in such a way that it does not provide enforceable land rights.[44] The irony here is that China has not hesitated to sign international agreements to protect indigenous rights. Such protocols present no problem, since China simply declares that it has no indigenous peoples (*tu zhuren,* "people of the land," is a term applied only to foreign cases, such as Australian Aboriginal peoples)—all its own citizens are majority or minority Chinese and equally native to the country.[45] This stance has been adopted to forestall any accusation that China itself is a colonial power in regions such as Tibet and Xinjiang. Representation in local government and encouragement of minority culture is expected to provide sufficient protection. The statewide policy of equal and harmonious development described in Chapter 1 dictates overriding any indigenous opposition in the interests of the economic modernization of China as a whole.

Since the early 2000s, the "ecological migration" (*shengtai yimin*) policy has demonstrated that minorities have no priority in rights over land. All over China, any peasant farmers, herders, or hunters seen to use land extensively in non-modernized, economically low-profit ways have been liable to compulsory relocation. The claim is that their traditional methods keep them in poverty and cause ecological damage—the opposite of the KMNS policy in Russia. Although one declared aim is to rehabilitate environmentally affected areas, in practice the effect of "ecological migration" is often to create openings for industrial development, mining, tourism, and so forth.[46] The indigenous minorities have been greatly affected by these various policies. For example, three culturally and economically diverse groups, now all called Evenki, were subject first to titular amalgamation into an ill-assorted and scattered ethnic category; then, during the commune period, they were both swamped by Han incomers and relocated; finally, "ecological migration" dislocated some of them into further newly built sites beginning in 2003.[47] Some indigenous peoples are glad to leave isolated villages under ecological migration programs, but others miss beloved places and dread the move to towns or concentrated settlements. They are afraid they will be faced with inadequate compensation payments and either unemployment or low-level uncongenial work such as street cleaning. A consequence of these programs in steppe regions near the border is that grasslands may be cleared of people and herds for "rehabilitation," which in practice often means that the land becomes host to forests of wind turbines. In Inner Mongolia in 2011, there were protests when local governments failed to curb ecologically destructive mining companies in former pastures.[48]

A distinctive feature of Chinese policy, far more pervasive than in Russia, is the encouragement and commodification of "cultural heritage." Items such as clothing, artwork, utensils, architecture, musical instruments, epics, songs, and dances, so long as they are "traditional," are recognized as having a museum-cum-commercial value. Immense work is put into collecting, preserving, and reproducing such items. Some of them are designated for museums and archives, but most minority artifacts are now also up for general sale. Only recently have indigenous people been able to sue for intangible cultural heritage rights.[49] Local festivals and ceremonies have become key events to promote the wearing of ethnic dress, performance of traditional dances, and so forth. At the larger festivities, Chinese officials posted to indigenous areas often appear in benign patron/funder mode.[50] The festivities then take the form of the staged joyful presentation of community "culture" in its most brilliantly colored form to the officials, and ideally also to the external world, with TV filming and interviewing of elders an essential part of the proceedings. The "cultural heritage" extracted and performed in this way *is* the culture as far as state institutions are concerned, and it is increasingly valued by them primarily as a way of attracting Chinese and international tourism. "Ecological" and "ethnographic" tourism has become a central state policy for economic development. Well aware of this, ethnic minority leaders in some places, such as Oroqen townships, are able to use the cultural heritage policy creatively, diverting funding to their own more practical projects for local communities.[51]

There are many complexities and ambiguities to this situation. On the one hand, with minorities caught up as they are in the immense, rapidly enriching, and fast urbanizing networks of China, it is politically a lost cause for them to hope to have full control over particular territories and work them in traditional ways. Furthermore, they may not even want to do that. Barga Mongols, for example, often hire Chinese to do the tough herding work for them and scheme hard to educate their children in the hope that they will leave the countryside forever.[52] No one lives in a felt yurt any longer. Yet at social gatherings they sing heartfelt songs about nomadism and the beautiful and beloved pastureland. And the very same largely invented festivities to which the officials are invited usually have a religious core, or perhaps a separate private ritual sequence, that stems from the old culture passed down by elders.

This is the case especially at the *oboo* rites that are devotedly performed by all of the Mongolic peoples in the Chinese, Russian, and Mongolian borderlands. *Oboos* are cairn shrines where prayers and offerings are made to ancestors and spirit-masters of the land, as we discuss in detail later. *Oboo* cairns can be moved if absolutely necessary, and new ones can be set up. But still, in all cases the rites show the persistence of a deeply felt relationship between a given community and a homeland. What is interesting is that while some ceremonies are socially circumscribed to a particular clan or village, the same kind of *oboo* ritual can be a vehicle for the gathering of people from thousands of miles away across the border.

We hope by this point to have given a preliminary sketch of some factors that lie behind the different situations and diverse attitudes of indigenous peoples in Russia and China. But a fuller understanding can only be conveyed by more detailed case studies.

A PEOPLE SPLIT APART: NANAI AND HEZHE

In both Russia and China a few settlements have been given special status as "ethnic villages" and set up to support indigenous culture and attract visitors. But the two countries do this very differently. First, we should note that history has scattered the Nanai and Hezhe and that they do not all inhabit ethnic villages, nor is the population of these places entirely made up only of the designated ethnicity. This is particularly the case in China, where villages were integrated into huge multiethnic communes in the Mao era and are now incorporated in wide "townships" in which Han people and the Chinese language dominate almost everywhere.[53] Throughout the frontier zone it is rare to find a monoethnic settlement. Indigenous people tend to be multilingual. In Shenehen near Manzhouli we met, for example, a Daur driver who took for granted his own fluency in Chinese but also spoke Buryat, Evenk, Manchu, and Mongolian along with his native Daur. Furthermore, even in the ethnic villages, the old life of hunting and fishing in the wild is long gone. Now both activities are strictly limited and only legal at certain times for people with licenses. The restrictions are similar in both countries, but otherwise there are many divergences.

In the Hezhe ethnic village Zhuajizhen (抓吉镇) on the Ussuri River 7 miles south of Fuyuan, residents' prospects have transformed since it was included in the tourism complex of Heixiazi Island (see Chapter 2). The villagers had lived from modest fishing, farming soybeans, rice, corn, potatoes, and raising a few sheep and goats. Now the mudbrick-thatched roof or concrete cottages have been replaced by showpiece varnished wooden houses, white stucco villas, and four-story apartment blocks. The Square of the One Hundred Cooking Pots, a paved area in the shape of a giant fish, was constructed for the tourists. The fish's eye is represented by a giant decorated cauldron swinging from tall poles, and the outer contour of the fish consists of a curved awning that shades the 100 brick cooking stoves—designed, it seems, for mass feasting on fish. The center of the plaza is adorned with bronze-painted sculptures depicting Hezhe people engaging in their traditions: fishing, wrestling, sitting round a campfire, and so forth. This fanciful construction was much damaged in the 2013 floods, and a Russian tourist visiting it a year later found it deserted.[54]

The plaza has since been repaired, and when the governor of Fuyuan arrived on a visit, he gave an unclear speech that nevertheless revealed the true purpose of the village's transformation: "To preserve the ethnic customs of the village for future projects for greening and improvement of the territory and infrastructure. Officials should support village rebuilding and the developments on Heixiazi Island; they should integrate tourism with rural and urban policies and play their part in the district [Fuyuan] and province [Heilongjiang] in order to achieve urbanization."[55] A Russian blog describing the transformation pictured a tipsily grinning Hezhe villager, happy with his lot; a sour Russian comment was that the splendid new housing in Zhuajizhen village was just *pokazukha* (put on for show) to impress the Nanais on the other side of the border.[56]

Indeed, this relentless improvement contrasts with the Nanai settlement of Sikachi-Alyan, likewise designated a "national village" and tourist site, located on the Amur not far from Khabarovsk. Urbanization is not the goal here. Instead, Sikachi-Alyan is advertised as a place to see ancient relics: engravings of whorls, fish, animals, and human-like faces on the black basalt boulders on the river shore. Unlike the tourist attractions in the

Chinese village, these are genuine, and Russia is applying to UNESCO to accord them international recognition. The petroglyphs are many thousands of years old, made by unknown predecessors, and the Nanai revere them as the placings for spirits. The village, which contains people of several ethnicities as well as Nanai, is half deserted. Its ethnographic focus is a small, informative museum located in the basement of the only new construction, the Culture Center—a multifunctional building also containing the administration, the club, and the kindergarten. In the museum the brilliant intricate embroideries of the old Manchu-esque ceremonial attire jostle strangely with rough-hewn utensils and wooden images of spirits.[57] Nearby, empty reconstructed traditional houses and fish-drying sheds form an "ethno-tourist complex." Otherwise, the village has been left in all its post-Soviet authenticity—battered wooden houses, rutted roads, rusting car wrecks, and TV antennas (Figure 4.1).

A Russian adventure tourist, videoed picking his way among the boulders excitedly discovering engravings here and there, commented that no doubt in China such a place would be full of counterfeits, but, he said with a laugh, "in Russia we haven't got anyone to make fakes." In this place, he said, looking around, people live extremely poorly.[58] The villagers too complain that there is no work, and fishing is strictly limited. Much of their income comes from selling souvenirs—embroidered slippers, dolls, mats, and, at the pricey end, shaman's costumes and fish-skin coats—in the Culture Center; occasionally children put on a dance or elders perform ceremonies for tourists for a fee.

The petroglyphs are left unguarded. When the villagers were informed that the engravings were valuable "cultural heritage," they set someone to guard the site and charged 100 rubles per visitor; instantly, though, they were forbidden to do this by the district administration on the grounds that permission had not been given and the fee not agreed with the Ministry of Economic Development.[59] Each season, the boulders disappear from sight when the murky Amur is at high water. When they reappear, the

Figure 4.1. A house in Sikachi-Alyan, 2013.
(Photo by Natalia Ryzhova)

most visible engravings are the bright new ones chipped by tourists ("Oleg and Tanya were here").

The "ethnic villages" in each country are indicative of the general situation of the two groups: the Hezhe in China are engulfed in development, while the Nanai in Russia are languishing for the lack of it. The Nanai villages of the lower Amur are depopulated, the fishing stocks are depleted, the waters are polluted, and the people are racked by the social ills of unemployment, alcoholism, drug addiction, and premature mortality.[60] In sharp contrast, the Hezhe have become a tourist attraction, but they are also part of a diversified regional economy, including agriculture and small business along with fishing. It is relevant to such comparisons that there are only 4,600 Hezhe (as of 2018) and they are scattered in small groups across Manchuria, whereas there are

12,000 Nanai (as of 2010), most of whom live in villages strung along the lower Amur. But still, why do the two populations hardly recognize each other?

Borderland people are not necessarily enthusiastic about establishing relations across the frontier just because they have been told that people of their own ethnic group are living on the other side. And if they do travel across for business, belonging to the same ethnic group does not in itself ensure mutual trust.[61] For such relations to thrive there have to be other powerful factors at play. We have already mentioned the role of population size and Russia's KMNS policy in identity politics. The "small-numbered" groups define themselves exclusively, assert their uniqueness, and almost perforce emphasize the "traditional" aspects of their culture, whereas for the larger peoples it is advantageous in the politics of their titular republics to be more numerous and powerful. They cannot forget Moscow's history of splitting them apart, and therefore they include in their self-definition all related groups, even those living in other regions.[62] However, sheer size and the corresponding stance in the regional political situation is not a sufficient explanation. The Khamnigan, one of the smaller, more obscure and downtrodden of borderland groups, provide a counterexample. Despite lack of numbers and with no recognized administrative unit to call their own in China, Russia, or Mongolia, Khamnigan enthusiasts are currently embarking on the expansive version of identity politics. To explain this, we suggest that a second crucial factor is the nature of the historical dispositions present in some groups but not others.

Among today's (Tungusic) Nanai-Hezhe, there is little knowledge of the Manchu-dominated past. Their common ethnic history is not taught in schools. In the 1980s and 1990s one elderly Nanai shaman was the subject of several earnest Russian ethnographic expeditions as a rare repository of memories of customs and rituals.[63] However, in the last few years the handful of aged shamans have died and attempts to replace them failed (the initiates all met untimely ends). Shamanic practice in its ancestral variant has been forgotten, and the younger generations have no interest in it.[64] It has been replaced with New Age spirituality, evangelical or Orthodox Christianity, or new Russian-language versions of shamanism using a vocabulary of "energy points," "extrasensory perception," and "cosmic powers."[65] It is these recent enthusiasms and not ancestral traditions that now define Nanai concern for their lived environment of rivers and forests. These "situated truths" link Nanai to contemporary modes of spirituality that have burgeoned across many postsocialist regions. But New Age faiths are far less evident in China. The spiritual worlds of the two peoples are increasingly distinct. Most Hezhe seem content to acquiesce in the state-defined definition of "culture," with shamanism defunct and "native lore" consigned to festivals and museums or tourist attractions. Unlike in Russia, mystical shamanic oneness with nature was never a strong element of their official image. This image recalls, rather, a soldierly past when, like the Chinese Evenki, they were sent to guard the border with Russia.[66] For all their occasional sardonic comments, Hezhe people recognize that the state has indeed been good to them. In Jiejinkou village, party leaders from Harbin turned up one day with Chinese workers who started painting lurid aquatic murals on the walls of the houses. "This is your history!" they said. "These are Hezhe legends!" A Hezhe resident said to anthropologist Ed Pulford, "We didn't have a clue what they were talking about," but he was not annoyed and just laughed cheerfully.[67]

A brief flare of popular interest in visiting the people of the other side when the border was reopened is now virtually extinguished. These days contacts between Nanai and Hezhe are largely reduced to official cultural delegations, invariably headed either by a Russian or a Han Chinese, and usually consisting of the same "important people." In fact, such meetings serve as separators, since the people attending them "act as citizens of the PRC or Russia, not in the mode of Nanai-Hezhe shared identity."[68] Crucial in the evaporation of common identity is the lack of interest in cross-border kinship links. These used to be sustained by the overarching system of clans (*hala*), which had been used by the Qing as structures for local rule and tax-gathering.[69] But the *hala* lost those functions with the demise of the empire and socialist reorganization. Today ordinary people's knowledge of their *hala* is sketchy, and Nanai talk instead of their *rod*, a Russian term denoting a few generations of immediate kin living close by.[70] When in 2014 the ethnologist Shiro Sasaki asked members of the Udinka clan (*hala*) on the Chinese side whether they knew that there were clan kin on the Russian side, no one knew and no one was interested.[71] In 2012–2013, he found a similar response from Udinka people living in Russia near Khabarovsk: they had no idea about clan relatives in China.

Like other Tungusic peoples such as the Evenki, Udege, and Orochon, the Nanai use informal exchange networks to solve immediate practical problems.[72] These are necessary, especially for clandestine hunting and fishing (getting equipment, selling the meat or furs or fish) and for smuggling, but they are not a vehicle for regular group relations to bridge the bureaucratic-political barrier of the border. Sporadic and tolerant of mishaps, such links between individuals are easily broken off, as anthropologists have shown from fieldwork among Evenki living on the fringes of Buryat settlements in Russia. They describe stubborn personal independence and attachment to idiosyncratic refractory ways, such as the Evenki preference for walking on foot through the forests rather than using vehicles on roads.[73] Sometimes Evenki isolate themselves. One group of reindeer herders living near the BAM railway refused, to everyone's amazement, to have a bridge built to their village. They talked about the "peace" of the taiga, their objection to aggressive outsiders, and their desire to maintain their own culture.[74]

With such habits of stubborn disengagement, the tiny number of activists among the Tungusic peoples have little open support. One is the Nanai campaigner Leonid Sungorkin, based in Khabarovsk, who is leader of the Union for the Protection of the

Culture, Rights and Freedom of the Indigenous Peoples of Priamur Region, founded by himself. In 2014 Sungorkin told anthropologist Ed Pulford of his dream to reunify the Nanai and the Hezhe by creating a joint ethno-park on Bolshoi Ussuriiskii Island.[75] The unreality of this, given the political high stakes of the stalemate on the island (see Chapter 2), went along with Sungorkin's atypical evocation of ancient history, which depicted the Nanai as oppressed by the Chinese, like all Manchu-Tungus peoples.[76] Sungorkin's dream evinced little interest among his fellow Nanai. His hassling the authorities about the dire situation of Nanai in the here and now is another matter. Oddball nonconformist though he is, Sungorkin follows the KMNS pattern of territory-focused identity politics. The first problem was that the main area of Nanai settlement, historically called Boli, was now occupied by a major Russian city, Khabarovsk. The task was to get that area of land registered as a pre-Cossack indigenous homeland, for without this, no KMNS organization could be set up. Surprisingly, this was successfully negotiated, but Sungorkin's other petitions for guaranteed fishing quotas, forest land for settlement, special pensions, and care for invalids have fallen on deaf ears.[77] Successive ministers of culture either refused to meet Sungorkin or brushed him aside when he pleaded for state support for Nanai-language schooling, dedicated publications, and a theater troupe. He wanted to stand for election but, amid xenophobic abuse, was turned down by one party after another, even the opposition parties. The ostensible grounds for the rejections were that he was the subject of a pending lawsuit for alleged offenses committed in his youth.[78]

In relation to minority politics in Siberia, Sungorkin's unsuccessful battles fall in the same category as that of the Evenki head of the Sunshine Company (see Chapter 3) and the Udege indigenous rights activist Pavel Sulyandziga. In the 1990s, Sulyandziga successfully organized protests against Hyundai's attempt to exploit virgin forest for logging[79] and he helped establish prosperous reindeer-herding, hunting, and fishing enterprises in the Far East.

He became a leader of the RAIPON indigenous rights association and spoke at international conventions. But his support for Sunshine and outspoken allegations of "present-day serfdom" of indigenous peoples drew the wrath of the authorities ("go and sit in the tundra," they said, and tore the page with a US visa out of his passport). Soon he was suspected of spying for the West and accused of separatism for advocating an indigenous zone free of military presence. Like the head of Sunshine, Sulyandziga was indicted for corruption and forced to flee Russia.[80] All three indigenous leaders failed in their attempts, but in their awareness of international indigenous rights struggles and their support for one another they are perhaps a harbinger of the emergence of a new platform.

Precarious though the situation of indigenous activists is in Russia, they have been able to publicize legitimate concerns in the context of volatile electoral politics. In China, by contrast, numerous low-level protests are hidden as much as possible by the state-run media.[81] True, the Chinese government's recent "rule of law" policy (*fazhi*) and law popularization campaigns (*pufa*) enable local lawyers to use the courts—sometimes successfully—to argue on moral grounds for justice on behalf of peasants and other disadvantaged people such as minorities.[82] But even if some Hezhe have taken the step of going to court to defend their cultural intellectual property, we have no evidence that they take any interest in the struggles of their former brethren over the border.

Let us now turn to people seeking, on the contrary, to overcome the separation forced on them by the border. Many Buryats now actively cultivate contact between the dispersed populations of Buryats living in Russia, Mongolia, and China, and some of them also welcome identification with the Barga, who are officially considered a separate nationality settled in China and Mongolia. These are large populations: there are some 500,000 Buryats and 88,600 Bargas.[83] Yet this is not an overtly political movement. Rather, it is seen by participants as a way to assert a new broader identity, revitalize culture, and create occasions of common sociality. After 1991, the Buryats' regional status as a beacon of socialist modernity fell away. Now it is the presocialist past they turn to, and the talk is of recovering lost unity with other Mongol populations. What lies behind this enthusiasm, and how does it manifest itself?

BURYATS AND BARGAS: COMING TOGETHER?

In 2013 I (Caroline) used to drop in to Solbon's Buryat restaurant in the Chinese border town of Manzhouli, themed to attract customers from across the Russian and Mongolian borders. Solbon is a Shenehen (Shinehen) Buryat, the grandson of refugees who fled from Russia to Manchuria to escape revolution and war. On the wall, beside a bar stacked with bottles, hung an immense genealogical chart (*ugiin bichig*) (Figure 4.2). It detailed the patrilineal descendants of Khoredoi, the mythical ancestor of the eleven clans of the Khori Buryats. It was unusual among such charts, however, since it showed how the same clans are shared by the Barga people. Dating the first historical ancestors of the combined people to the eighth century CE, it named the key descendants, numbering the degrees of distance of each from the origin and culminating in sixty-one generations from the first ancestor. Proudly announced at the top was that this is the genealogy of the *nagatsnad* (mother's brothers) of the Golden Clan of Chinggis Khan.[84] I stopped by the restaurant frequently and I saw how people would go up to the diagram to peer at it and point to their putative place in the scheme.[85] I noticed other details as well: that the genealogy had been put together by experts from two Buryat associations, that it referenced nine academic histories and genealogical compilations (though it disclaimed completeness), that Barga Mongols were its key financial backers, and that its designer was one Baldandorzhiin Ad'yaa of the Bayaud clan (*obog*). In other words, it was the creation of multiple cross-border collaborations.

The chart shows that these collaborators are able to use patrilineal kinship as a way of conceptualizing the relations between

Figure 4.2. The genealogy in Solbon's restaurant, Manzhouli, 2013.
(Photo by Caroline Humphrey)

many thousands of people living in three different countries and classified today as different ethnicities, an immense feat of historical imagination. The Barga Mongols are people of the same ethnic stock as the Khori Buryats. In the sixteenth century a large body separated off and migrated from the Baikal area into east Mongolia. Later, in the eighteenth century, the Qing settled some of these people in two waves in the region of Manchuria now known as Barga (see Map 1).[86] China counts them as Mongols, not as Buryats. Thus, by folding them in with the Buryats, this chart is creating new "knowledge" for ordinary people (non-scholars). We use the word "knowledge" rather than "myth" because Buryats, at least on ritual and rhetorical occasions, hold that genealogies ideally can and should be true, which is a relevant fact from a social point of view. Having a skeleton map of the eleven clans in their heads and knowing themselves to be a member of one of them, Khori Buryats can use such genealogies to place themselves in a transborder "world" that is an alternative to territorial, state-administrative, or class divisions. Furthermore, such kinship schemes have their own internal hierarchy and political-relational logic—this means, for example, that the Barga Buryats are able to think of themselves as the "mother's brothers" (a senior and honored status) in respect to the acclaimed Khalkha Mongols' Golden Clan that ruled in Mongolia. Now, this is a claim, and not many Khalkhas would agree with it, for the ethnic belonging of the early ancestors is disputed. It rests on shaky historical evidence and is a matter rather of the idealizing and localizing of ancient personages and of a habit of thought that classifies whole groups of people as being related in the same ways as individuals. The important point here, though, is that such mega-genealogies ignore the national categories assigned by twentieth-century Russia and China, instead shifting the reference points for identity centuries back.

What, though, was the impulse that lay behind the making of this genealogical chart? It has no relevance in contemporary official politics.[87] Nor was it of any practical use as Solbon sat behind the bar organizing his business dealings on his mobile phone. Aged around thirty, cheerful, adept, and multilingual, he was the center of an ethnically diverse web of clients, organizing transport and contacts for transactions across the Mongolia-Russia-China borders. He also owns a hotel where his traveling contacts can stay. His muttered tones and indirect allusions suggested the confidential, possibly illicit nature of many of these deals. The menu in Solbon's restaurant was adapted to a cosmopolitan clientele: Russian dishes, Chinese concoctions, Buryat dumplings, Korean kimchi, and all kinds of drinks were plunked down on the wooden tables by his cooks, who seemed to know most of the diners and stopped to chat with them.

In contrast to this multiethnic business life, the notion of the clan is brought to bear in a monoethnic register, that of the countless social and religious events that Buryats cram into the short summer months. They include calendrical festivals, weddings, *oboo* rituals, memorial gatherings for the deceased, birth celebrations, song festivals, sports competitions, and ethnic get-togethers that revive the *yokhor* circular folk dance.[88] Clan kinship is increasingly meaningful for many Buryats, a basis for a feeling of identity with people beyond the immediate family; it exists alongside other collective identities such as living in the same village or having been in the same class in school or college. Let us give an example, which shows the essential and structuring role of the mobile phone in bringing the abstract idea of "the clan," one of the same ones mentioned in the chart, into real-life existence.

Tsyben, a middle-aged man from the Aga district in Chita Oblast, Russia, is a member of the Bodongud clan of the Khori Buryats. He decided to organize a group to participate in a Sagaalgan (Lunar New Year) festival at which the clans would vie in sportive competitions, such as mass tugs-of-war and "breaking the bone."[89] However, apart from relatively close kin, Tsyben did not know who the descendants of the ancestor Bodon were. He sent out a message on the Viber app to around five fellow clan members, asking them to pass it on. In the first hour twenty others had signed up; this became more than eighty in the first day, and three days later he had almost a thousand. In this way Tsyben discovered that a large number of Bodonguds, previously unknown to him and mostly living in Mongolia, were keen to join the festival in Aga in Russia. However, Viber is not used in Shenehen, the main area of Buryat settlement in China, and no Bodonguds answered his call from there. The same would have been true if Tsyben had used Facebook, which is popular in Mongolia but blocked in China. If he had used the Chinese WeChat application (Ch: Weixin), popular with the younger generation, he would have had many responses from the Shenehen Buryats, but fewer from Mongolia.

The summer festivities (*naadam*) of the Buryats and Mongols have always featured masculine competitive games (horse racing, wrestling, archery), and the tradition was gratefully taken over by the Communist Party in the Soviet era as a popular platform for speeches, exhortations, and "socialist emulation," which pitted collective farms or factories against one another. At these events the formulaic recital of production results was sweetened by song contests, dances, and oratory, along with the traditional sports events. Today, it is usually villages (*selo*) and districts (*raion*) that replace the Soviet enterprises as the competing groups. But clans also appear and are even becoming the initiators. They are socially innovative precisely because they bypass administrative structures, are non-territorial, and branch out beyond the borders of Russia.

The return to public life of clans, subclans, and local lineages—all disapproved of and half-forgotten during Soviet times—has been encouraged by shamans. Their occult abilities enable them to perceive and disclose that offended ancestors are behind their clients' problems. The shamans therefore require people to search in family and state archives to find out about these long-dead people and make ritual recompense. Meanwhile, the overarching large clans of the Khoris and other groups have become the subject of intense genealogical interest. Each of the eleven Khori clans, for instance, has been equipped with a unique colored banner, an emblem, a totem animal or bird, a war cry, and a verse summarizing the clan's unique moral character. The clan's name is written in vertical Mongolian script, thereby asserting Buryat belonging within the greater Mongol sphere. Each clan has its own forum on social media, as do most subclans. Scholars produce detailed histories of clan migrations, settlements, battles, and heroic figures. All of this is producing new knowledge for young people, many of whom barely knew about clans previously or thought of them as just obscure preoccupations of aged relatives.

Clan leaders dressed in ceremonial silk gowns parade the flags, making a splendid phalanx at public events (Figure 4.3). The most notable of these is the all-Buryat Altargana *naadam,* a great cross-border celebration that takes place every two years, rotating among the regions where Buryats live.[90] The festival was initiated in 2004 by Buryats living in Mongolia. By 2012 the Altargana held in Aga, Chita Oblast, had around 10,000 participants, and more recent celebrations have also drawn in Buryats from all over the world, including the United States, Australia, Hungary, and Britain.[91] Each delegation holds up a banner and parades its identity. Such showing oneself to the "outside world" in one's own cultural manner is a matter of pride for formerly marginalized indigenous peoples.[92]

This expansiveness combines with deep roots in communities. Even small villages prepare for the Altargana. Local dance troupes, singers, and sports teams compete in preliminary rounds, performing before traveling commissions that choose the winners to take part in the great event. Winners of the horse races, wrestling matches, beauty competitions, and contests in other skills get tremendous kudos and publicity. Organizers comment on the difficulty of reconciling the resulting fierce rivalry with the idea that the festival is about Buryat unity. Setting up the festival largely as a series of competitions inevitably emphasizes differences (of

Figure 4.3. A group of Buryats pose with clan flags, Altargana, Dadal
Somon, Mongolia, 2014.
(Photo by Jargaliin Chinggis)

dialect, precedence, genuine "Buryat-ness") among the various
components of "the Buryats." However, this is no problem to
many participants, since it enables them to celebrate the precolo-
nial, pre-border tribal entities that they counterpose to the "artificial" present-day situation.[93] Somehow there prevails a spirit
of openness, fun, generosity, eagerness to meet unknown distant
relatives, and willingness to overcome the difficulties of reaching
the event across borders and windswept steppes. There is strong
social pressure to attend, partly because taking part is believed to
have a collective spiritual benefit—it not only raises the *hii mori*
("wind-horse," or inner spirit, fortune, or luck) of every individual
who, for example, touches the winning wrestler or racehorse but
also uplifts the confidence, well-being, and strength of all groups
that take part.

The Altargana is framed as an ethnic event, and what is original about it is that, unlike the great Mongolian *naadam,* which is based on Mongolia as a territorial country, it is conceived as a transborder or even global experience of ethnicity. The model—creating community by seeking quasi-mythical shared ancestry—was copied by other historically minded Mongolic peoples: the Bargas set up their own annual cross-border *naadam,* called Bargazhan, and even the Khamnigan are attempting the same.[94] Altargana has its own "people's" geography, which periodically superimposes itself on state boundaries. Attendees use their own native cross-country routes to reach the festival rather than making a detour to the few official border crossing points. They arrange for the border guards to let people through illicitly. This practice points to the ambivalent relation the Altargana—and other facets of Buryat ethnic resurgence—has with the state.

One of the high patrons of the Altargana is Damba Ayusheev, the Khambo Lama, who officially presides over all Buddhists in Russia, including the Tyvans, Kalmyks, and others. However, he has a particular take on his role. Rather than seeing himself as manager of a federation of regional Buddhist organizations, he is an ardent advocate of the supremacy of "indigenous Buryat Buddhism." In his view, this version of the faith should not only saturate Buryatia and dominate the other Buddhist regions of Russia but also act as an attractor to Buddhist devotees across Mongolia and north China. His idea seems paradoxical: Buryat Buddhism should be rooted in archaic rural life, with small monasteries founded at the heart of each village, along with the reintroduction of indigenous livestock species, traditional herding practices, and patriarchal forms of kinship, but at the same time, it should form a center that fans outward and claims "religious sovereignty" by outperforming shamanism, other Buddhist schools, Christianity, and New Age movements.[95] The Khambo and his followers aim to achieve this goal by recreating a strong monasticism and by revealing their own more powerful, intrinsically Buryat miracle-working deities. Two of Ayusheev's sacred revelations have indeed proved extraordinarily popular: the deity Yanzhima, discovered in Barguzin, who grants fertility to couples unable to conceive, and the preserved remains of a previous Khambo Lama, Itegelov (1852–1927), who, sensationally still "alive," grants believers' wishes and sacred protection against misfortune. Increasingly, believers do indeed flock from Mongolia and China to these miracle-working sites. The forthright Ayusheev does not aspire to prominence through religious learning; rather, his project is ambitious in a different way. It positions itself as a moral system, relying on its conservative interpretation of indigenous (i.e., Buryat) traditions. Thus, it stands implicitly against all "foreign" (Tibetan and Western) Buddhist influences and adherents. This stance places Ayusheev as a would-be competitor to the Dalai Lama for religious influence in north Asia.[96] It is not surprising that, in practice, Ayusheev's "traditional *sangha*" is contested by many in Buryatia and throughout Russia. But he has a trump card: possession of the supreme treasure, the sacred body of Itegelov.[97] With this beacon and other recently discovered holy sites to attract adherents, he has been able to cast the Tibet-supporting Kalmyks into the shade and at the same time configure a new Buryat-centered temporal and spatial world for his followers.

We have described high aims that circulate across the border, but how do people put them into practice? An occasion that reveals the kind of pitfalls that can occur in cross-border ceremonial events occurred in 2015 in Kurumkan, a Buryat village some 250 miles north of Ulan-Ude. Kurumkan, tucked away between craggy snow-topped mountain ranges, is in the Barguzin Valley, which has long been identified with Bargujin Tukum, a place mentioned in the thirteenth-century *Secret History of the Mongols* as the homeland of the legendary ancestress Alun Goa; it is also the Bargazhan held by the Barga Mongols to have been their ancestral homeland. Beginning in the early 2000s, the Bargas had started holding their own Bargazhan *naadam* festivals, rotating between Mongolia and Chinese Inner Mongolia. But then, by reaching deeper into history and hence beyond the state-defined ethnic categories, Barga intellectuals started to publish histories and genealogies that unified the Barga with the Buryats, like the one we found in Solbon's restaurant. In 2014, a relaxation of the border regime enabled visa-free group travel to Russia, opening the opportunity to hold the next Barga *naadam* in the distant homeland itself. The event was organized by Gombo, a Barga elder from Mongolia. The goal was for the Bargas to make contact with and pay respects to their ancestral protector deity, the spirit-master of Baragkhan Uula, the holy mountain that looms over Kurumkan. The local Buryats welcomed the idea, seeing a chance to elevate their status with other Buryats; some even started reinventing themselves as "Barga Buryat."[98]

However, Gombo's phones and social media had been working too well. Hundreds of people arrived in Kurumkan from far and wide, completely overwhelming the supplies of food, accommodation, and gasoline available in the village. The ATM machine ran out of cash, credit cards were unusable, and the guests were unable to change their Chinese and Mongolian money into rubles. Furthermore, one of the visitors' buses broke down on the rough road to Kurumkan, meaning that a large group arrived too late for the mountain ritual at the Gulmakta *oboo*. And the difficult situation continued: since all the gasoline had been used up, no one could leave, and the overly numerous guests were forced to stay longer than anyone had planned. The hosts were humiliated by this disaster. Soon afterward, complaints began to surface. Why had the Chinese Bargas brought their own shaman to conduct the rites at the Gulmakta *oboo* instead of asking a local shaman or getting a blessing from the resident Buddhist lamas who worship there regularly? Why had they done their ritual on the wrong (inauspicious) day and erected a *serge* (ritual post) without permission? They had polluted the sacred site by digging latrines for the crowds too close to the *oboo*, and they had rudely driven their cars right up to the monument and churned up the land. After the guests had left it was further alleged on local social media that the many who spoke only Chinese among themselves must include spies who dressed up in Mongol clothes as Bargas but in fact were strangers inspecting Barguzin for the chance to exploit the natural resources there later. Soon that dry summer a dangerous forest fire flamed uncontrollably close to the village, covering everything in ash. It was concluded that the spirit-master of Baragkhan Mountain had been angered and was punishing the Kurumkan villagers. Opinions varied about the reason for his fury. Either it was because the villagers had failed to ensure that their guests behaved in the ritually correct way, or it was because the Bargas, whose ancestors were accepted to have been the more ancient inhabitants, *had* now established themselves as the legitimate custodians of the holy site, and the mountain spirit had therefore ceased to give protection to the locals.[99] Either way, we see on what delicate grounds the new ethnic links are being made. Not that the problems in Kurumkan caused the cross-border ties to be broken; the next Barga *naadam* was held in eastern Mongolia in 2018, and some "Barga-Buryats" of Barguzin made the long journey to take part.

What is remarkable is that practical reasons do not explain this kind of extension of relationships. The groups involved, who live up to 2,000 miles apart, have few meaningful economic interests in common. In terms of national politics, there is nothing to be gained from setting out on the uncomfortable and expensive journeys involved, or from hosting the crowds of visitors. Perhaps the explanation for these events is that by working through their own historical-mythical time, the Buryats and Bargas are taking "time out" from all the major state structures of Russia, Mongolia, and China. The ceremonies take place within a completely different rationality, and the identities they celebrate are sprawling indigenous, non-state-regulated ones. "We were split apart by borders," is the underlying thought, "and now we will meet together in our own way."

All of these cross-border festivals, pilgrimages, *oboo* rituals, and so forth are avowedly "non-political." Yet the respective governments recognize that there is something self-generated, anarchic, and potentially subversive about these gatherings. Once again, China and Russia have approached this issue differently. China does not allow Altargana inside its borders. The event cannot be controlled by the Chinese Communist Party; it involves a conception of Buryat that cannot be confined to the "Chinese minority" idea, and no doubt it is seen to smack of dangerous nationalism. Altargana is too multitudinous and freighted with foreign politicians to be classified along with the events that China does allow, such as ice festivals or beauty contests. The Russian government, in contrast, allows the gatherings, but whenever possible tries to defuse their specific ethnic content. It does this by top-down domination, attempting to reframe Altargana as a Soviet-style "international" event by sending state representatives to make speeches and award prizes, as well as by trying to insist, to Buryat annoyance, that all regional residents (Armenians, Ukrainians, Russian Old Believers, etc.) should be invited to take part.

These emergent transborder Buryat-Barga-Mongol worlds have an interesting relation to the official nation-building policies of Russia and China. In present conditions, they cannot be a reprise of the early twentieth-century Pan-Mongolian political alliance, which is the unmentioned elephant in the room. Nevertheless, it cannot be an accident that the enthusiasm for cross-border sociality has arisen among the Buryat and Barga, for sections of both peoples had risen in flashes of independence-seeking that played on cross-border alliances several times in their history.[100] These "cultural" movements run counter to the socialist-era dogmas, but, curiously, they seem to have an affinity with the era of Putin and Xi Jinping. The Soviet policy had been to position the Buryats as a "progressive" Siberian people and cut them off from their "backward" Mongolian ancestry. As mentioned earlier, many were moved from immediate border areas, their national name was changed from Buryat-Mongol to Buryat, a dialect markedly different from Mongolian was chosen as the official language, and the history taught in school stressed their voluntary adherence to the tsarist empire and their admiration for Russian civilization. Chinese policy, meanwhile, enclosed the Bargas and Shenehen Buryats in a China-centered world in which they had to demonstrate their loyalty to China. This was done, contrary to the Russian narratives, by producing a history of the Buryats that stressed their Mongol origins.[101] Following the government line, the Chinese Buryat historian Abida presented all Mongols as an integral part of the long and glorious heritage of the Chinese nation. He depicted the Russian Buryats as victims of colonialism, a sad fate analogous to Chinese humiliation at the hands of rapacious European imperialism. But both of these socialist-era official histories contradicted the memories of elderly Buryats.[102] It was in starting to speak again about their own understanding of historical loyalties that the way was opened for the appearance of the transborder assemblages we have described. Today, when state alternatives to the socialist-era accounts have yet to be devised, Buryats can present the festivals for public purposes as a reflection of the warm Sino-Russian relations under Xi and Putin. Meanwhile, Ayusheev's Buryat Buddhism project chimes well both with China's hostility to the Dalai Lama and with Russia's attempt to regain its soft-power clout in Inner Asian spheres. However, the underlying impetus of the festive events is actually completely different: to create a separate celebratory space in their own lands for people divided by the great imperial powers.

5

FRIENDS, FOES, AND KIN
ACROSS THE BORDER

NINO'S STORY

I (Franck) met Nino on my second visit to Blagoveshchensk's Confucius Institute. Nino was a minor celebrity at the institute, where she had been attending Chinese language classes for a few years. Her connection to China was unusual, and Nikolai, the institute's director, had arranged a meeting so that she could tell me her story. Nino was as warm as she was eccentric. Dressed in bright colors, an unusual choice for a Russian woman of sixty-four, she explained that she didn't quite fit in Russian society—a comment indirectly supported by the eye-rolling and sideways glances frequently exchanged by the members of the staff as I chatted with her.

Nino was born in Ukraine. When she was twelve and a Young Pioneer, she began exchanging letters with Deng Shuhua, a Chinese girl of seventeen from Bei'an, a small village in Heilongjiang province, halfway between the city of Harbin and the Russian border. The two girls became good pen friends, exchanging letters for about two years. Then, in 1966, letters stopped coming. With China in the grip of the Cultural Revolution, it had become dangerous for Shuhua to write to someone in the Soviet Union. She had to destroy all the correspondence, pictures, and presents Nino had sent her. But Nino hung on to everything and for years wondered what had happened to her friend. Over the

Figure 5.1. Deng Shuhua and Nino, reunited in 2013.
(Courtesy of Nino Dulskaya)

years Nino and her husband lived in many countries around the
world, and in 1986 they eventually settled in Blagoveshchensk,
across the river from China.

As relations began to thaw between the two countries, Nino
decided to study Chinese, and she enrolled at the local Confucius Institute. Asked to choose a Chinese name for herself, she
picked Shuhua. Moved by Nino's story and hoping to help her
find her friend, the institute's director at the time, Lu Chunyue,
mobilized her friends, acquaintances, the local police, and news
organizations in the neighboring province of Heilongjiang. After
several months, in 2013, Shuhua's picture was eventually spotted
by the son of an acquaintance, and the two friends were once
again in touch. The story was later picked up by a local Chinese
TV station, which did a short documentary on their reunion (see
Figure 5.1).

Nino was eager to stay in touch with Shuhua, and she cher-
ished their friendship. During our chat she repeated several times

that she felt more at ease in China than in Russia, where she felt judged and not socially integrated. Eager to show off her Chinese friend, she suddenly decided to call Shuhua in the middle of our conversation, and passed the phone to me. The person at the other end spoke no Russian and was clearly confused, so I gave her the phone back. Unfazed, Nino repeated the few Chinese words she knew and eventually hung up.

THAWING RELATIONS

Nino's story, well known in Blagoveshchensk, is in many ways emblematic of the relations between Russia and China in the second half of the twentieth century.[1] It echoes the familiar stories of broken friendships and estranged family members following the Sino-Soviet split that led to the closure of the border between the late 1960s and the collapse of the Soviet Union in 1989. As the relations between the two countries deteriorated, the existence of cross-border kinship and social ties suddenly became a liability. One of our interlocutors, Andrei, explained that his family had successfully concealed their Chinese heritage during the latter part of the Soviet period. For Andrei, who had red hair and typical European features, it had been reasonably easy to do so. But for Russians who had phenotypically Asian features, alternative family stories had to be painstakingly reconstructed. Many tried to pass as members of another Asian group—Koreans, for instance. Maria's family, ethnically very mixed, had to resort to such practices, especially because of her grandfather's high social position. The political atmosphere was such in those years that her grandfather even concealed his heritage from his own wife, who only found out after several years of marriage. On the Chinese side of the border, similar pressure existed. The few small Russian communities scattered in Heilongjiang province gradually became monolingual, with only a handful of Russian words such as *lieba* (from the Russian *khleb*, "bread") surviving in domestic contexts. As in Russia, individuals with mixed heritage also sought to conceal their background, some dyeing their hair black in order not to attract undue attention.[2] In recent years, these fully Sinicized Russians have garnered widespread attention. Dong Desheng (董德升), also known online as "Uncle Petrov" (彼得大叔), is one of China's 15,000 ethnic Russian citizens. His video feed has more than a million subscribers who enjoy his "unsophisticated humor and unconstrained optimism" delivered in perfect northeastern Chinese dialect (*dongbeihua*). His videos have also generated much interest because they challenge assumptions about Chinese culture and identity.[3]

The period of border closure was characterized by pervasive suspicion and constant propaganda on both sides. In border cities such as Blagoveshchensk, slogans such as "Border under lock" and "You are living on the border, stay vigilant!" were continually reiterated. During the Cultural Revolution (1966–1976), Chinese counterpropaganda was blasted across the Amur River. In recounting stories about this difficult period, interlocutors in Blagoveshchensk recalled that even innocuous behaviors such as looking at the other side of the river with binoculars could potentially lead to being questioned by the police. By the time the border reopened in the late 1980s and it was safe again to reestablish contact with the other side, in many cases all details about relatives had long since been lost.[4] For Andrei and Maria, China was as mysterious as it was for most of Blagoveshchensk's inhabitants. In the late socialist period, study of the Chinese language had been actively discouraged and many faculties of Sinology in both Russia and Mongolia were closed down. With the border hermetically sealed, borderlanders knew virtually nothing about their neighbors on the other side, in spite of living a few hundred yards from them.[5]

It was precisely this sense of the unknown that drove so many Russians to cross the border in the early 1990s to see for themselves what China was like. This ethnographic curiosity was compounded by the sudden opportunity for Russians to purchase items that were not, or no longer, locally available. For both sides, the sudden opening of the international border meant a propitious meeting of complementary needs. Over the last two decades this intense flurry of commercial activity has been a defining factor of dynamic development for the two towns. For Russian border towns such as Blagoveshchensk, Khabarovsk, and Ussuriisk, whose financial support from Moscow had suddenly evaporated, the Chinese goods and produce available across the border provided a veritable lifeline. From a Chinese perspective, the presence of a large community of consumers was a godsend. Tiny hamlets such as Heihe, opposite Blagoveshchensk, or Suifenhe, neighboring Ussuriisk and Vladivostok, turned into sizable towns (see Map 1). Manzhouli, a once sleepy Chinese town close to the Russian and Mongolian border, is now China's busiest land port of entry, through which 60 percent of all imports from and exports to eastern Europe transit.

Over the last three decades, Russian and Chinese border towns have existed in symbiosis, and local governments on both sides of the border have sought to foster closer ties and further cooperation. An annual swimming event across the Amur River is organized between Heihe and Blagoveshchensk every spring, and numerous events such as art exhibitions are organized jointly by the municipalities of sister towns. Throughout this border region haunted by history, a narrative of Sino-Russian friendship is consistently employed by local authorities, and all negative aspects of recent history are silenced for the sake of good neighborly relations—at least officially.[6] Thus, neither Blagoveshchensk's nor Heihe's museums mention the tragic events of June 1900, when thousands of Chinese men, women, and children lost their lives at the hands of the Russians (but see further discussion later in this chapter).[7] In fact, the only museum in Heihe is dedicated to Sino-Russian friendship, specifically to the numerous Chinese students and migrants who studied and worked in Russia and the Soviet Union.

This sense of goodwill and common desire to move past the trauma that characterized much of the second half of the twentieth century is clearly visible in border cities, particularly on the

Chinese side. The Chinese cities of Heihe and Manzhouli prominently feature Russian symbols such as bears and Russian nesting
dolls in what is also partly a cultural appropriation for their own
domestic tourists. Russian border towns such as Blagoveshchensk
have a very different emphasis, with an accent placed on Russian
historical presence in the region (see Chapters 1, 4, and 7), but
the discourse of friendship is also prominent there. Slogans pro-
fessing eternal Sino-Russian friendship, ubiquitous for a few years
following the establishment of China's Communist regime, are
enjoying a second wind, excising from history the decades of suspicion and enmity.

If these narratives of friendship are dominant in public spaces
and tourist brochures, Sino-Russian friendships remain un-
common at a personal level. Both communities have grown accustomed to each other, and Russians in particular were spending
a lot more time in China, at least until a few years ago, when
Western sanctions—and the consequent devaluation of the ruble—
made it less economically profitable. For residents of border towns
such as Blagoveshchensk, weekend trips to Heihe meant access
to goods not easily available in Russia, as well as access to entertainment such as restaurants, karaoke bars, and saunas. Over
the last decade, Russians in the Far East have gained familiarity
with Chinese culture. Russian infatuation with Chinese food in
particular has led to a proliferation of Chinese restaurants in Blagoveshchensk, which are now three times as numerous as establishments serving Russian food. This transformation of the local
dietary landscape has brought with it a slew of new practices and
tastes, such as competence in the use of chopsticks and a fond-
ness for Chinese alcohol (*baijiu*).

The preferential visa regime that allows Russians to spend up
to thirty days in Chinese border towns without a visa has also
meant that, to many Russian borderlanders, China no longer feels
exotic.[8] In conversation, many Blagoveshchensk residents emphasized the sense of familiarity and closeness they associate with
Heihe: "It's not really China. Heihe is an area of Blagoveshchensk
[*Heihe—eto rayon goroda*]. It's a place where you go spend a

weekend, have nice Chinese food, and have fun with your friends." The liminality of Heihe is tied largely to the fact that one can navigate it without knowing a single word of Chinese, since most Chinese in Heihe, like in Manzhouli or Suifenhe, know at least basic Russian. And although the city may differ in its cultural outlook, the frequency with which Russian visitors bump into friends and encounter familiar faces there lends the experience a certain sense of familiarity.

This very familiarity has been encouraging deeper forays into China by Russian borderlanders in the last decade. Whereas in the first few years Chinese border towns such as Heihe provided one-stop destinations for all commercial and leisure needs, Russians who are now more economically savvy and equipped with a better knowledge of China have been keen to travel further afield, to Harbin, Beijing, and even cities in the south. Increasingly, Heihe is seen as too provincial: poor, "backward," and with a limited range of goods. It is also no longer seen as exotic. The restaurants have adapted their menus to Russian tastes, but that's precisely what is making them increasingly unattractive. However, in the early days this hybridity eased Russian familiarization with a neighbor from whom they had been estranged for decades and whom they were curious to discover.

The first few years of the 1990s were characterized by a mad rush, Andrei explained, with more than 2,000 people a day pushing and shoving to get on boats to cross the river.[9] "It was really crazy. You didn't see many intellectuals [*intelligenty*] then." At the time, as described in Chapter 7, Heihe was little more than a village. The only restaurants available were street stalls, and most commercial activities also took place by the roadside. As Andrei recalled:

> You would see old ladies sewing Adidas trousers right there on the street. On one side they would have the material, on the other the trousers ready to wear. They sold these to Russian visitors who knew full well they were fake goods, but they were very cheap. They were very bad quality, though, and wouldn't last long. At times the seams would fall apart even before you had reached the Russian shore.

Andrei began his import-export career as a shuttle trader, or *kirpich* (literally "brick"), purchasing large amounts of goods in China and carrying them back across the border—the commercial activity that, as discussed in Chapter 3, characterized the early 1990s. Like other traders, Andrei realized in the late 1990s that delegating the actual cross-border transport and having a team of *kirpichi* bringing goods from China would lead to higher returns. These managers of brigades of *kirpichi* are commonly known as "lamps" (*fonari*).[10]

These different ways of operating also require closer personal ties between Russian and Chinese businesses. Andrei's Chinese partners became good friends, people he could trust fully. Given the way local Chinese businesses operate, trust is crucial—even if, as we will discuss later, trustworthiness does not necessarily equate with friendship. Deals are rarely made in writing, and payment tends to be in cash, which is carried in suitcases. Despite strong cultural reluctance, Russians trading with China have thus learned of the necessity to keep commercial and personal relations deeply intermeshed.[11]

Trust and connections are also crucial to deal with the frequently corrupt customs and border officials on the Russian side who have the power to hold up shipments indefinitely.[12] Maxim, a local businessman, explained that he owned no fewer than six companies, precisely as a way of coping with unpredictable issues. Russian customs officials sometimes freeze the accounts of a company while they investigate it, or confiscate merchandise. You can take them to court; Maxim, for instance, won several cases against them. But if the goods are intended for a specific event, such as New Year or International Women's Day, then having your merchandise returned to you at a later date is useless. "This is why I own several companies," explained Maxim. "This way I can ensure I remain operational."

Here the Russian concept of *blat* and the Chinese system of *guanxi* (connections) operate in commensurable ways. Through friendship, Russian businesspeople are able to access and benefit from existing Chinese networks. Similarly, Russian friends can facilitate for Chinese businesspeople the acquisition of property in Russia. These partnerships have largely emerged out of mutual need, through commercial collaboration. Most traders, like Russian shoppers in Chinese border towns, started their business with the help of *pomogaiki* (helpers), Chinese intermediaries with sufficient knowledge of Russian to facilitate commercial transactions. Over time, some of these connections have solidified into friendships.[13]

Personally, Maxim had few Chinese friends. His experience so far had been that friendships between Russians and Chinese go through various stages. There is a lot of enthusiasm (*vostorg*) at the beginning, but these friendships are rarely strong; they tend to remain unsteady. Because his friends were also business contacts, he felt that he never knew to what extent he could trust them. The only Chinese he considered a true friend was someone who studied Russian at university in Nanjing. But despite their friendship, this Chinese friend once confessed to Maxim that even a bad Chinese would still be closer to him than a good Russian. For Maxim this was a perfect example of Chinese nationalism: "They make a big distinction between Chinese and non-Chinese." When I asked him whether that was not the case for Russians too, he was emphatic that nationality didn't come first in the friendship equation with Russians. "If he's a friend, then he's a friend [*esli drug, znachit drug*]."[14]

The experience of Ivan, a PhD student in economics at Blagoveshchensk's state university, was more positive. He spent a lot of time in China and spoke fluent Chinese. He had a close Chinese friend who considered him his best friend and even asked him to be the best man at his wedding—not a common occurrence in China, as Ivan proudly pointed out. Ivan previously worked as a manager for a number of firms, and his insights into local business practices convinced him that informal networks were key to the trade between China and Russia. He gave me the example of car and truck imports from China, which witnessed a sharp rise in 2006. Such equipment is very expensive, and there's no money in the Russian Far East to buy and resell it. Pointing to the image of a huge truck adorning the cover of his recently completed doctoral thesis, he told me that such a truck costs no less than 1.5 million rubles, well beyond what local companies can afford. However, thanks to their informal networks, Russian businesses in the region were able to obtain this equipment without providing any money up front; they would pay the Chinese once the truck had been resold. The need for such equipment in the Amur *oblast* is limited, so businesses act as intermediaries between China and cities in western and central regions such as Moscow and Saint Petersburg, to which the connections of local Chinese businesses rarely extend. As Ivan was keen to emphasize, such trade would be simply impossible without trust and strong friendship networks.

Cultural and linguistic fluency is crucial to the success of Sino-Russian friendships and continued commercial connections, and the importance of the Chinese language is something the city of Blagoveshchensk has been recognizing more and more. Chinese has become one of the most popular foreign languages there, ranking a close second after English. Around 1,000 students study Chinese full-time, while another 1,500 study it as a minor subject in evening classes. Another 250 students are enrolled at the Confucius Institute, including a class of retirees who study free of charge twice a week. In addition, the institute is providing free classes for government customs and administration officials, with a view toward facilitating international contact and exchange.

In part, this growth reflects a stronger interest in Chinese language and culture, but for the majority it simply represents a key to future success. It is also the recognition that the future of the Russian Far East is firmly tied to China. For residents of the region, working with China is a given (*zdes' bez Kitaya nekuda*)—something that interlocutors were keen to stress. The growing interest in the Chinese language is therefore mostly strategic.

Chinese is seen primarily as a useful tool to guarantee access to the international labor market as well as a means of outmigration.

SHIFTING WORLDVIEWS

Irrespective of individual motivations, linguistic and cultural engagement with China has led to better knowledge of the country, and this has significantly impacted local Russian worldviews and geopolitical imaginations. A closer examination of attitudes of Blagoveshchensk's residents, particularly those of the younger generations, highlights the current coexistence of two competing geopolitical mental maps, one with Moscow as the primary reference point, the other resolutely turned toward China. Interviews carried out with three classes of students at Amur State University suggest that differences in worldviews are to an extent tied to social background. Students who have had little or no personal experience of China are predominantly from families of the former "socialist intelligentsia": their parents are educated professionals such as teachers and doctors, who had a high social status during the socialist period but have limited financial resources today. The fact that the vast majority of these students have been to Moscow and cities in western Russia suggests that their worldviews (or at least those of their parents) remain firmly anchored to Moscow and the West. By contrast, for children of traders who have had extensive contact with China, Moscow appears to have lost much of its relevance as a cultural benchmark. Most of these students have not visited Moscow, and their responses overall underscored the sense of unbridgeable distance they felt separated them from the capital. For this group, the future was unquestionably found in the East, specifically in the cities of eastern and southern China such as Shanghai or Shenzhen.

The growing importance of China as cultural benchmark has been paralleled by a decrease in Moscow's capacity to shape ideas of the future and modernity. Particularly among Blagoveshchensk's economically more successful social strata, the megalopolises of southern China have largely eclipsed the lure previously emanating from Moscow and Saint Petersburg. While some segments of Russian society remain attached, culturally and geopolitically, to the models inculcated during the socialist period, it is likely that the current trend favoring China will continue to expand given that the old socialist intelligentsia tends to be less financially successful. Chinese and Asian cultural models are also gaining ground among the younger generation through anime and martial arts. And it is from China that fashion trends predominantly originate—although, as we discuss later, these trends tend to be global rather than specifically Chinese.[15]

These differences emerged sharply in interviews conducted with high school and undergraduate students at several educational establishments in Blagoveshchensk. These differences were also conveyed graphically through drawings they were asked to make of the two border towns. In addition to the physical differences between Blagoveshchensk and Heihe, which are explored in more detail in Chapter 7, representations also shed an important light on mutually held cultural assumptions. The children of the old intelligentsia tended to emphasize differences, depicting the twinned cities of Heihe and Blagoveshchensk as separated by an abyss or even as distinct planets (Figures 5.2 and 5.3).

By contrast, the students who were more familiar with China focused on the links between the two sides, in terms of either economic exchange or cultural relations. Being more knowledgeable about China, and in some cases proficient in Chinese, they held views of China that were more nuanced than those of the other group. Their assessments tended to be positive, and many of them had also traveled to the southern cities of Shanghai or Shenzhen. Nastya, a twenty-year-old female student, was especially enthusiastic about China. "I love China, I love everything about it," she explained. "I can't wait to move there after I graduate."

The majority of the children of traders spoke some Chinese, and a couple of them were fluent. One, Alexei, worked as an interpreter for a number of local companies. In the middle of my

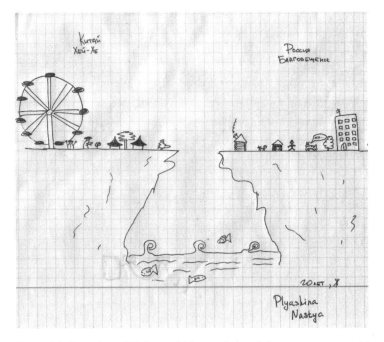

Figure 5.2. Drawing of Heihe and Blagoveshchensk by a twenty-year-old Russian student.

discussion with the class, his phone rang, and he left the room for a few minutes—another booking. For Alexei, as for most of his classmates with his social background, interaction with China had always been part of his life: "People who come to Blagoveshchensk find it strange that we live on the border with China. But China is not exotic to us." Another student added she had been going to China on a regular basis since the age of five. Like Alexei, she spoke Chinese and planned to relocate to southern China after graduation. There are just more opportunities there than in the Russian Far East. A couple of students explained that they felt that Russians were actually more compatible with Chinese than with western Europeans or Americans: "The Chinese have

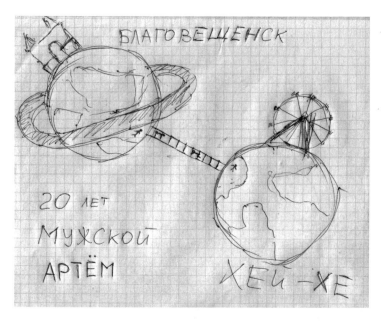

Figure 5.3. Drawing of Blagoveshchensk and Heihe by a twenty-year-old Russian student.

similar ideas about culture, family, friendship. They are not that different from us." The consensus is that the cultural differences, while substantial, are not unbridgeable.

Familiarity and similarities in worldviews do not extend to romantic entanglements, however.[16] When I (Franck) asked the children of the traders whether they could imagine marrying a Chinese, I was met with resounding nos, including from Nastya, the student infatuated with China. When I pressed her for the reasons, she explained that "the Chinese don't know how to love" (*Kitaitsy ne umeyut lyubit'*). Nastya, like the majority of her class, felt that the Chinese are not as open as Russians emotionally. Their notion of love is not the same, according to her; they are less romantic, more instrumentalist and transactional. Her views reiterated in this sense what other interlocutors in the Russian Far

East told us and the other researchers in our project. For most Russians, the assumption is that a marriage between a Russian and a Chinese will be pragmatic. For the Chinese partner, in most cases a male, marrying a Russian signifies higher social status in China as well as access to permanent residence and better economic opportunities in Russia.[17] For a Russian woman, marrying a Chinese is also perceived to be a marriage of convenience, as Chinese men tend to drink less and be more helpful around the house. In the eyes of many Russians, a Chinese husband is a safe strategy, but rarely a first choice. Igor, a Russian businessman in his late twenties, explained, "Russian women who marry Chinese men are usually older and less attractive."

These assessments reflect, in part, a reluctance to acknowledge the very real transformations that have taken place across the Sino-Russian interface, as well as the rise of China internationally. As anthropologist Ivan Peshkov writes, Russians have found it difficult to accept that Chinese forms of modernity have come to challenge the cultural hierarchy taken for granted over the course of the twentieth century.[18] In the early 1990s, Chinese media started reporting the growing number of international marriages—primarily between Chinese men and Vietnamese women. About a decade later, stories about the growing number of successful Sino-Russian families in northeast China began to be published. As anthropologists Elena Barabantseva and Caroline Grillot note, whereas Vietnamese brides are regularly depicted negatively as opportunists and sources of national insecurity, Russian brides have been welcome as a positive development, helping to raise the quality of the population.[19] One particularly popular story in December 2014 described the happy marriage of a self-made Chinese businessman in Ukraine who made many Chinese netizens jealous of his beautiful Ukrainian wife.[20]

While the economic standing of that particular Chinese businessman might suggest a transactional type of marriage based on financial resources, interviews with Russian and Ukrainian brides carried out by Elena Barabantseva reveal that their unions were prompted primarily by physical attraction and romantic love rather than economic factors or, as many Russians assume, the inability to find a husband at home.[21] However, Russian women living in China with their Chinese husbands commonly expressed that "they felt objectified by the Chinese marriage culture, were not fully accepted by their Chinese family and struggled to adapt to their foreign migrant wife status in China."[22]

The notion that the Chinese marry for pragmatic reasons, in order to stay in Russia or because of social status, is well entrenched. The stereotype that the Chinese—and Asians overall—are long-term planners is one that is not specific to Russia but is largely shared with the West. Chinese anthropologist Yunxiang Yan writes that when he was doing research for his book on love and intimacy in a Chinese village, he encountered difficulties in framing the results of his study.[23] As he recounts, in Western literature the Chinese way of life is conventionally depicted as a corporate model in which rationality prevails to the detriment of emotion.

These stereotypes were not supported by interviews carried out with Chinese students. On the contrary, the idea of romantic love recurred in several of their depictions of Blagoveshchensk, which included trees, flowers, and animals (Figures 5.4 and 5.5). These positive associations were confirmed by follow-up interviews with the students. Several of them emphasized the more prominent place of nature in the Russian city, with its wide leafy avenues and many trees. One Chinese student also explained she felt freer in Russia, and several of her classmates said they wanted to stay in Russia after graduation.

The positive associations with Russia made by the Chinese students in their drawings are due in part to their personal experience as young adults enjoying freedom away from home. Indeed, interviews with their counterparts—a class of young Russians studying Chinese in Heihe—also revealed positive views about China, and to some extent about Heihe as well. The romantic

Figure 5.4. Drawing of Blagoveshchensk by a twenty-year-old Chinese student.

Figure 5.5. Drawing of Blagoveshchensk by a twenty-year-old Chinese student.

aspect, however, was entirely missing in Russian drawings as well as in interviews.

Wei, a Chinese girl in her early twenties from Changchun, in Jilin province, who was completing her degree in economics, was very forthcoming about her love for Russia and Russians. She had convinced her parents to let her study in Russia. She didn't speak Russian before coming to Blagoveshchensk, but she had been interested in the country for a long time. She said she loved being in Russia and wanted to stay in the country—though perhaps not in Blagoveshchensk itself—after she finished her course. She cooked Chinese food in the dorm for herself and her roommates. Her best friend, a vivacious Russian girl, taught her how to cook Russian food. The last time she had gone back home she prepared Russian food for her family, but the experience was not exactly a success: her dad said it was OK (*hai keyi*), while her mom preferred not to comment. When I asked her whether she had a boyfriend, she said no, but she added that she much preferred Russians; Chinese boys are too sly (*khitry*), while Russians are kind (*dobry*).

Wei appears to be an outlier, however, and differences between Russian and Chinese students remain vast. When questioned about Sino-Russian romance, Russian students struggled to think of even one mixed couple among their acquaintances. The few examples given were invariably between Russian women and Chinese men, never the reverse. Interestingly, this particular gender configuration is also the dominant one in other parts of the former Soviet world, including Mongolia, and it does not appear to be a recent phenomenon.[24] Unlike the typical colonial situation where intermarriage normally meant Western men taking native wives, historian Mark Gamsa writes, the main arrangement at the Sino-Russian border, in both urban and rural settings, was Russian women marrying Chinese men. The reverse, while not unknown, was much rarer.[25] When asked to reflect more deeply about these sexual arrangements, students in the various classes initially suggested that the gender imbalance prevalent in the region, with more Chinese men than women (see Chapter 7), favors this particular configuration. But Sino-Russian romantic entanglements are also clearly inflected by gender ideologies. The consensus among the Russian students as well as throughout local Russian society was that while Chinese men tend to make good marriage partners, Chinese women do not. As mentioned previously, it is widely believed that Chinese men drink less on average than their Russian counterparts, and that they also help with domestic chores, such as cooking and cleaning. By contrast, unlike in the West, where Asian women tend to be imagined as docile and submissive, Russians view Chinese women as difficult and capricious.[26] A couple of students also believed that Chinese women, at least the ones living in the northern borderlands of Heilongjiang, did not sufficiently take care of their appearance. Blushing, a young female student explained, triggering embarrassed giggles in the class: "Many of them don't shave." On a purely aesthetic level, both sides agreed that Russian women are beautiful—at least when they are young.[27] As they get older, the students said, they tend to get fat.[28]

The low incidence of marriages is clearly not the whole story, and the numbers of official registrations conceal many pragmatic arrangements such as Chinese businessmen taking young Russian women as lovers. Prostitution is also common on both sides of the border.[29] In the late 1990s, several casinos opened in Blagoveshchensk, attracting many Chinese from across the border. As these businesses developed, the Russian city, then nicknamed "Blagovegas," also witnessed a rising number of local Russian women engaging in prostitution. As both the Chinese and Russian governments decided to crack down on casinos—the Chinese because of the illegality of gambling, the Russians because of the growing levels of attendant criminality—the bulk of the social interaction between the two populations shifted to Heihe.[30]

Prostitution still exists in Blagoveshchensk, but it is now less overt. Russian sex workers are able to attract higher prices in China, where their exoticness is highly prized, and Russian "girls" have become prominent in the big northern cities of Harbin, Dalian, and Beijing, as well as further afield, in Shanghai and Shenzhen. A number of Russian women in China also work in the entertainment industry as acrobats, dancers, models, and singers. Even though the majority of them may not engage in prostitution, the line is not always clear, and financial rewards are often part of an equation that includes protection and semi-legal immigration status.[31] In addition, the propensity for Russian women, both at home and abroad, to "dress sexy" and "weaponize" their femininity has led to an unfortunate mental association for many Chinese between Russian women and prostitution.[32]

Chinese sex workers are, I was repeatedly told, totally absent in Blagoveshchensk, as "no one would even look at them." While our research appears to largely support these statements, it does not mean that Chinese women do not engage in prostitution. Heihe, like all Chinese cities, has its fair share of saunas and massage parlors, which both Chinese and Russians patronize. Some Russian women also engage in sex work in Heihe, where they advertise as strippers. But Heihe is less attractive in terms of financial rewards, and it is also too close to home, so Russian sex workers prefer to travel further south, to the Russian quarter of Yabaolu in Beijing, as well as to Shanghai, Shenzhen, and Singapore.

EXOTICISM AT THE BORDER

Despite claims of expertise by both sets of borderlanders on the basis of their geographic location, there is actually a lack of knowledge about each other, and cultural stereotypes on both sides of the border are still strong. In a 2019 study, Ed Pulford writes that Russian and Chinese tourist consumption patterns privilege an engagement with simulacra and stereotypical representations of their neighbor over direct contact.[33] If the drawings made by the students suggest an incipient fracturing of worldviews and geopolitical orientations—notably among the children of traders who are linguistically competent and have grown accustomed to Chinese cultural norms—the assumptions made by several of the teachers show that in the general population the cultural gap remains wide. Before I interviewed the Chinese students studying Russian in Blagoveshchensk, I explained to their teachers that I would ask the students to draw the two cities. Independently of one another, all three teachers assured me that the drawings would not be interesting for me, and all gave me the same reasons: "The students will draw things as they are; the Chinese can't think symbolically."[34]

Older than their students, the teachers first experienced China as young adults, after many years of intense propaganda. It was therefore not surprising that their ideas of China tended to be both more negative and more entrenched. Interviews carried out with a group of retired women at the Association for Elderly People (Assotsiatsia pozhilykh lyudyei) was in that sense illuminating, as during their formative years they had been subject to more polyvocal views—both the intense hostile propaganda of the 1960s and the earlier positive narratives of Sino-Soviet friendship. The chairman of the association, Sergei, was a very friendly man in his seventies. He had been running the association as a volunteer for many years and was protective of his flock of retirees, mostly women, who attended the classes run by the association. With sparkling eyes and a wide smile exposing a mouthful of gold teeth, he explained that the classes were run on an ad hoc basis: "People come and ask whether a particular class is available. If there is enough of a demand, then we'll try and source a volunteer to teach the class." For the Chinese language classes, the two instructors were loaned by the city's Confucius Institute (Figure 5.6).

In addition to Chinese language, other classes running at the time of my (Franck's) visit were computing, psychology, flower arrangement, and Chinese paper-cutting. Sergei explained that the Chinese language classes were really conversation classes, intended to familiarize people with the language and to make it easier to travel to China and buy things. But occasionally someone

Figure 5.6. A Chinese language class at the Association for Elderly People, Blagoveshchensk, 2014.
(Photo by Franck Billé)

would register with a desire for deeper knowledge. One man, for instance, attended classes for a while and then decided to pursue his study more seriously at the Confucius Institute. He was determined to learn Chinese in order to go to Sochi as a volunteer to help with foreign visitors during the 2014 Winter Olympics. There was a lot of demand for such spots, but he knew English and Chinese, so he was successful in securing one. At sixty-four he was one of the oldest volunteers. He is a bit of a local hero.

Two of the chattiest students, Marina and Lyudmila, were eager to respond to my questions—and to ask questions of their own. Both had been studying Chinese for a couple of years and greatly enjoyed it. "We only study how to speak, not write, unfortunately," explained Lyudmila. But Marina was satisfied with the way the class was organized, as she felt they were too old to learn the script. They both expressed regret they had not had the possibility to study Chinese sooner, although it was something they hadn't really considered until recently. Lyudmila wished there were classes every day—twice a week was not enough, and her progress had been slow. With China so close, having a better command of Chinese would be very useful, she felt.

Both Marina and Lyudmila were very positive in their views of the Chinese. Their imaginary of the country is one of a hardworking and resilient people. Interviews with other people in their late fifties and sixties suggest that Marina and Lyudmila are not outliers. Irina, who worked at Blagoveshchensk's city library, recalled that in the 1950s and early 1960s there was a fir tree (*ëlka*) in the middle of the river. "Chinese and Russians would meet there for celebrations," she explained. "At the time they were friends. But then the events at Damansky Island happened [see Introduction] and the two sides became enemies." Her colleague, also called Irina, recalled that her grandmother used to cross the frozen river on foot in the winter when she was ten (so just before the Revolution). She would go there to buy candy and other things. Heihe was dreadfully poor then. At the time it was called Sakhalian (萨哈连), which is the Manchu equivalent of Heihe (meaning "black river").

This older generation grew up at a time when the two countries enjoyed friendly relations, and when Russia was routinely described as the "elder brother" benevolently guiding a less enlightened "younger sibling." Despite China's meteoric economic development, the notion that China is somehow less advanced is an enduring one that permeates analyses and punctuates discussions. And if some journalists have warned about a complete reversal of economic and cultural hierarchies, in which China is no longer Russia's "younger sibling" but has now become the "wise elder sister" (*mudraya starshaya sestra*), the dominant sentiment for this older generation is one of camaraderie, a feeling of a common socialist history, of common struggle, and of common battles against a common enemy, Japan, during World War II.[35]

A CULTURAL CHASM YET UNBRIDGED

Regardless of actual attitudes, whether China inspires fascination or anxiety, the border marks a sharp fracture between the two countries, a fault line between two cultural and racialized worlds. Despite its proximity to the border—it is in fact the Russian city closest to China—there is little indication that Blagoveshchensk is located in the Far East. Unlike Heihe's street signage, which is trilingual, in Chinese, English, and Russian, street signage in the Russian town is in Russian and English.[36] Chinese influence is also conspicuously absent from the city's soundscape. Radio and TV stations play Russian, American, and European music, never Chinese. No Chinese movies are shown in the cinemas, and no bookstore or kiosk carries Chinese books or newspapers. In any case, most Russians would be hard pressed to name a single Chinese writer.[37] In spite of the presence of the Confucius Institute, established in 2007 and located within the State Pedagogical University, China's soft power appears limited.[38]

Surprisingly, this is also true for the many Russian students studying Chinese. The interviews conducted with them suggest that while China is perceived primarily as a place where forms of modernity are visible and deployed, these forms are not seen as specifically Chinese. If the hypermodern megacities of the south such as Shanghai and Shenzhen are attractive, it is predominantly because of the cosmopolitan aspects that they appear to offer. These cities are consistently described as international, places where you might bump into Europeans, Americans, or Africans. In other words, it is not Chinese culture itself that is perceived as modern, but the space in which these forms of international and cosmopolitan modernity are found.[39] I was even surprised to hear Marina and Lyudmila admit they would happily swap their Chinese classes for English ones if a teacher for those classes suddenly became available. While they enjoyed studying Chinese as a window to opportunities beyond Russia, English remains the premier linguistic passport, capable of providing access to international travel and exotic experiences.

On the Chinese side of the border, where Russian is spoken by most borderlanders at least at a rudimentary level, the situation is not substantially different. There too, Russian is important for pragmatic reasons, but a real dialogue appears to be lacking. Heihe residents' knowledge of the Russian language is essentially commercial.[40] It allows traders to interact with customers but does not extend much beyond basic exchange. In interviews, local Russians were keen to emphasize the existence of a Sino-Russian pidgin that is used by traders to communicate.[41] What was especially striking in these discussions was perhaps not the existence of specific terms but the persistent affirmation that a form of pidgin was in use between the two cities. This insistence concerning the emergence of a Sino-Russian pidgin has been the subject of recent articles and book-length studies by several Russian scholars.[42] While the classification of these linguistic forms as true pidgins remains somewhat contentious, what these scholarly discussions do index is the embryonic emergence of local identities that diverge from national norms and bridge the cultural and linguistic divide.[43] The enthusiasm of academics for the topic clearly extended beyond actual practice, however, as only a few interlocutors were able to cite more than two or three words of this pidgin.[44]

Druga was a term routinely given as example of the emerging linguistic hybridity of the Sino-Russian borderlands. A Chinese-accented form of the Russian *drug* (friend), *druga* is a term heard ubiquitously in markets—the standard word used by Chinese traders to hail customers. While it is also used by some Russians to address Chinese, its usage by Russians and Chinese is situated, and resonates, very differently. For Chinese traders it is one of a handful of Russian words that they have acquired to conduct their commercial activities; for Russian customers it is a corrupt form of a common word, funny-sounding and signaling illiteracy.[45] But it indexes a genuine intermingling of influences, a mimetic back-and-forth that we can also see deployed in the context of urbanization, as described in Chapter 7. The Russia-China border, so distant from Russia's and China's capitals, is a place of immanent hybridity—despite the entrenched mutual distrust and cultural incomprehension.

SIMMERING RESENTMENTS

While taking a stroll in Heihe on the frozen surface of the Amur River, I (Franck) was hailed by a young Chinese woman carrying an infant. "It's OK, you can walk home, it's not far," she joked in Russian, assuming I was from the other side. As we exchanged greetings, she took her baby's hand and waved: "Say hello, say hello to our Soviet friend [*sulian pengyou*]." The usage of the term "Soviet," especially in the mouth of someone so young who had no personal memories of the Soviet Union, is testament to the enduring good-neighborly sentiments that prevailed in the 1950s between the Soviet Union and the newly formed People's Republic.[46] In fact, in contrast to other European powers, Russia continues to occupy a privileged position vis-à-vis China. Despite the territorial losses associated with the 1860 Treaty of Beijing, Russia is rarely placed in equivalence with Britain or France in Chinese narratives of national humiliation.[47] China and Russia, as mentioned previously, are acutely aware of their common socialist history and common political struggle, and the current joint narrative of "eternal friendship" does resonate with many people at a certain level.

Resentment and antipathy nonetheless exist, stoked by stereotypes, ignorance, and occasionally condescending attitudes, especially on the part of Russians. In spite of China's meteoric development, most Russians continue to view their Chinese neighbor as less developed and less cultured, and these attitudes frequently color social exchanges. Russians in Heihe and other Chinese border towns can be heard addressing Chinese traders and middlemen with the familiar pronoun *ty,* for example.[48] Unequal status was also embedded in the very discourse of fraternal relationship at the height of Sino-Russian friendship. China's position as the younger sibling was coded as one of political guidance and cultural nurturance, but it also had more derogatory undertones. The expression "our lesser brothers" (*brat'ya nashi men'shie*), occasionally used in contemporary Russia to refer to the Chinese, can also be used to refer to animals. This discourse goes both ways, however, with the Chinese referring to the Russians as *da maozi* [大毛子], the "big hairy ones."

Even when they hold no sentiments of cultural superiority, Russians' directness can easily be misinterpreted as haughtiness or as a lack of friendliness. Largely in reaction to this, traders in Heihe have in turn become more abrupt and less amenable to bargaining. Over the three decades since the border reopened, relations have never reached the levels of friendship and mutual understanding official narratives suggest. Below the surface, one finds palpable levels of apprehension, anxiety, and resentment in both border communities. Rather than a meeting point for a mutually beneficial relationship, the 2,500-mile border remains, despite the few rather exceptional cases discussed earlier, a line dividing two worlds, two civilizations.[49]

As previously mentioned, the only museum in Heihe is dedicated to Sino-Russian cooperation and specifically to the Chinese who studied and worked in the Soviet Union. But another museum, in the Chinese village of Aihui, 25 miles downstream of Heihe, has a very different focus.[50] The Aihui museum is dedicated to the infamous "Blagoveshchensk massacre" of June 1900, when, in retaliation against the Qing army for firing at Russian military boats sailing along the Amur River, a group of Russian volunteers and Cossacks armed with axes and bayonets drove the Chinese population out of the town and forced them across the river. Many Chinese were brutally killed before they were thrown into the water; others either drowned or were shot while swimming. On that fateful day, up to 5,000 Chinese died—with fewer than 200 managing to cross the river.[51]

The Aihui museum displays photographs of old Blagoveshchensk, a multimedia diorama, and a chronology recounting the fateful events. Unlike most museums in China, there is no entrance fee, but tickets are issued only upon presentation of a passport, since Russian nationals are not allowed to enter. As I (Franck) approached the modern structure housing the displays, walking on a sinuous path along which were erected memorial stones bearing the names of the "Sixty-Four Villages East of the River," I was met with hostile gazes from several Chinese visitors.[52] "Russians are not allowed here," hissed a man as I walked past him, prompting my taxi driver, an outspoken woman in her early forties who had decided to accompany me into the museum, to snap back, "He's not Russian, he's allowed to come in!"

To Russians, the museum remains shrouded in mystery, rumored to include terrible photographs as well as anti-Russian statements. The museum's exhibits, hidden from Russian view and excluded from the dominant political narratives of Sino-Russian eternal friendship, constitute an important point of articulation of Chinese historical memory and source of underlying resentment. Russians also have heard that yearly commemoration of the event takes place on June 2, when residents of the neighboring city of Heihe allegedly deposit into the river little paper boats containing a candle, one for each departed soul.[53]

On the Russian side of the border, if anti-Chinese sentiments are not especially strong, significant levels of anxiety are nonetheless present. To pursue a theme already mentioned in Chapter 3, in the early 1990s, a number of Russian political figures frequently warned that "Chinese migrants will flood, or have already flooded, into the country's vast and increasingly less-populated Far Eastern region."[54] These statements, particularly when they were made by politicians based in Moscow or Saint Petersburg, were often based on ignorance. As Russian scholar Viktor Dyatlov has pointed out, people in Moscow tend to imagine the Russian Far East as a wild place where bears and illegal Chinese immigrants are ubiquitous.[55] Xenophobic narratives were also promoted for political gain, with some politicians from the Russian Far East purposely exploiting anti-Chinese sentiments to obtain political and economic support from Moscow at a time when subsidies were dwindling. If these anxieties remain potent in Moscow and in regions of Russia far from the border, they have considerably abated in the Russian Far East itself—in part because the threat of impending waves of Chinese overrunning the Russian Far East has failed to materialize, and also because of the realization that China is inescapably part of the region's future.[56]

The potent brand of Sinophobia witnessed elsewhere—in Mongolia or Vietnam, for instance—is largely absent in the Russian Far East, but the years of propaganda and decades of insulation have left their marks.[57] Russian fears of becoming a "resource appendage" (see Chapter 6) are strong, as is the sense of demographic imbalance between the Chinese side and the Russian side. This imbalance has been one of the factors impeding the erection of a bridge across the Amur River (see Chapter 1), as Russians feel a permanent structure would allow free passage for untold numbers of Chinese. Anxieties about China's vast population and the comparative emptiness of the Russian Far East are also voiced through half-serious, half-facetious claims that the Chinese are penetrating into Russia "in small groups of a hundred thousand each" (*nebolshimi gruppami po sto tys'ach chelovek v kazhdoi*). Demographic imbalance accounts as well for Chinese culture's lack of visibility in Russian border towns and for the emphasis on historical markers. In the city of Blagoveshchensk, as noted earlier, very few public signs are found that include Chinese characters. The statues that dot the urban landscape overwhelmingly celebrate explorers and military leaders. Unsurprisingly, there are no model Chinese villages in

Russia, and no counterparts to Heihe's "Russian tourism streets" (see Chapter 7).

A similar reluctance to engage with the Chinese presence is perceptible in depictions of the region's past. The main museum of Blagoveshchensk is the Amur Regional History Museum (Amurskii oblastnoi kraevedcheskii muzei).[58] A large two-story building, the museum retraces the history of the city and the region from prehistoric times to the present. It describes at length the Manchu, Nanai, and other ethnic groups in its history of the region prior to the arrival of Russian settlers, but makes no mention of the Chinese. Yet most of the major Russian cities in the region, such as Vladivostok, Khabarovsk, and Ussuriisk, originally emerged around 600 CE as Chinese settlements. Traditionally, the Chinese name for Vladivostok was Haishenwai (海参崴); Khabarovsk was called Boli (伯力), and Blagoveshchensk was known as Hailanpao (海兰泡). In contemporary Chinese official documents, these cities are now referred to by their Russian names—that is, Fuladiwosituoke, Habaluofusike, and Bulageweishensike—but these transliterations have not wholly displaced their former names; in informal conversation, older Chinese names often resurface. These older names index the enduring national "body map" held by some Chinese, who are imagined by the Russians of the Russian Far East as remembering the exact location of the old ginseng patches abandoned by their ancestors and yearning to reclaim possession of them.[59]

As historian John Stephan noted, in the 1970s, as the relations with China deteriorated, Soviet archaeologists and historians began cleansing the territories included within Russia's borders of any Chinese historical presence by renaming more than a thousand locales.[60] If until then scholars had been vocal in arguing that Chinese sources were essential to reconstruct the prehistory of the region, notably of the Priamur, Primorye, and Sakhalin, references to Chinese presence contracted into cryptic footnotes, and by the 1980s students were being taught that until the nineteenth century no Chinese had ever stepped into the Russian Far East.[61] In our conversations with museum staff and academics, this reluctance to acknowledge the presence of Chinese in the region was routinely emphasized. "The region is claimed by the Chinese but not on the basis of a Han historical presence," explained a history professor at the State Pedagogical University. "Many indigenous groups lived here, such as the Evenki, Daurs, and Mohe. Because China is a multiethnic state which includes these nationalities, Chinese claim the land is Chinese." For Russians this is at best an indirect claim. And because the Russian Federation itself is a multiethnic nation, of which many of these groups form an intrinsic part (see Chapter 4), Chinese claims are seen as essentially baseless.

Russian reluctance to acknowledge cultural and geographic overlaps also extends to Russian communities within China. One of the fifty-six ethnic groups that make up China is the Eluosi zu, a Russian national minority based primarily in northern Xinjiang but also found in Manchuria, in Heilongjiang province. Many of the Russians who live there are descended from refugees who fled Communist violence in the 1930s and then married locals. Now mixed and mostly monolingual, like Dong Desheng, the farmer presented at the beginning of this chapter, they tend to be seen by the Russians as Chinese.

In China, however, they are classified as ethnically Russian, on a par with Tibetans, Mongols, and other minority groups (*shaoshu minzu*). During and after the Cultural Revolution, most ethnic Russians switched their ethnic affiliation to Han and sought to assimilate as completely as possible in order to avoid being seen as spies and traitors.[62] By the 1964 census, the Russian population in China had plummeted to a mere 1,326. Russians now number around 15,000, many having changed their ethnic category again, partly to benefit from programs of affirmative action, in particular in their university entrance examinations. No longer a threat to national unity, the Russian minority (*Eluosi zu*) is viewed favorably and with much curiosity, as testified to by the popularity of the fully Sinicized "Uncle Petrov," as discussed at the beginning of the chapter.

The two governments' official narratives are keen to portray the Sino-Russian interface as one of close friendship, but actual interactions suggest a lack of genuine engagement as well as "plenty of mutual distrust behind the curtains."[63] On the Russian side the dominant drive is to keep the two communities separate and distinct. This can be seen in the reluctance to build a bridge or issue visas, and in the heavy militarization of the border zone, reinforced by the creation of exclusion zones.[64] On the Chinese side, by contrast, we see a process of blurring of distance and co-optation of otherness whereby the exotic qualities of Russia are adopted and exploited for commercial and touristic purposes. On neither side do we sense an authentic affection for the other that is based in social interaction or personal experience. Overall it merely feels like the two sides are trying to make the most of their geographic position.

Nino's story offers in this sense a narrative of international friendship that is neither threatening nor destabilizing for either country's view of itself. It celebrates the reunion of long-lost friends but does not touch on the traumatic history that defined much of the recent history of the two countries. It does not hint at the hybridity and messiness that exists in the borderlands, the loss of family members, or the alienation experienced by borderlanders on both sides. The focus on the long-distance friendship between a Russian and a Chinese also obscures the complex ethnic entanglements that are inherent to the region. As discussed in Chapter 4, the ethnic landscape along the sinuous Sino-Russian border is a patchwork of ethnicities, languages, and cultures. Many of these straddle the international border. When the border closed, it not only sliced through whole communities but also transformed people into Chinese and Russian citizens, socializing them into differing languages, worldviews, and geopolitical orientations.

In an article about the Shenehen Buryats, a community of Mongolian-speaking exiles in China, Marina Baldano retraces the attempts at reunification that followed the reopening of the international border. She shows that the initial burst of excitement at the prospect of reconnecting with kin and acquaintances was quickly followed by the realization that the two communities had developed very differently.[65] Furthermore, the role of cultural and linguistic intermediaries that the Shenehen Buryats had assumed they would adopt as a matter of course was complicated by divergent cultural expectations and different ties to their respective governments, although as the example of the restaurant owner Solbon showed (Chapter 4), a few individuals have been able to become successful mediators in the Mongol-Barga-Buryat middle ground between China and Russia. A situation not dissimilar to that of the Shenehen Buryats in China was experienced by the "old Chinese," tiny communities left in Siberian Russia after most of their compatriots had been repatriated in the 1930s. They likewise managed to retain a distinctive culture and even occupation (they specialized in vegetable growing in Buryat collective farms). On occasion some of them became intermediaries between cultures, as we described in the case of the Sunshine jade business, which did not end well. The focus of intense Russian mistrust as well as a takeover, the Sunshine leaders had to flee Russia for China in the end. If ethnic division and cultural alienation are inherent to the operation of most political borders, the experience of the communities living in the Soviet Union and the rest of the socialist world was particularly intense. The creation of very different groups on both sides of the border is something that was experienced in other socialist regions—between Mongolia and China, for instance, or between Georgia and Turkey.[66] In the case of Russia and China—two countries with very little cultural overlap—differences appear especially difficult to bridge.

Though we have discussed the challenges experienced by the numerous ethnic groups indigenous to the region in renewing former ties, the vast majority of inhabitants on both sides of the border are members of their nation's respective majority groups. Large population transfers—from Ukraine and the western regions in the case of Russia, from southern Heilongjiang and other northern provinces in the case of China—have reinforced differences between the Chinese and Russian populations. The immediately visible somatic differences in the population of cities at the Russia-China border make the two environments oddly bipolar: apart from Russians and Chinese, one sees very little distinctive ethnic diversity. This contributes to the peculiar feeling of crossing from one world into another. In both Heihe and Blagoveshchensk, the idea that the river marks a civilizational fault line is very much present in the minds of local people. The assumption of both Russians and Chinese that they are fundamentally different from each other is in fact shaping interactions between the two groups. As a result, one frequently hears from Russians who live a stone's throw from the bustling markets of China that they inhabit a remote place, abandoned, far from everything.[67] If this feeling is due in part to the hub-and-spoke-like spatial formation of the Russian Federation (discussed in Chapter 1), these statements also index a sense of unbridgeable rupture—a rupture that ubiquitous political narratives of eternal friendship or heartwarming stories about two pen friends reunited after decades of absence ultimately fail to alleviate.

6

Manzhouli, China's largest land port, through which close to 60 percent of all Chinese exports transit to Europe, is known informally to Russians as the city of cupolas and matryoshka dolls. A full-size Chinese rendering of Russian culture (see Chapter 7), it is also a center for trade and processing of Russian raw materials and natural resources, particularly timber. A visitor to this Chinese border boom town is immediately struck by the ubiquitous smell of wood. For Russians, the mounds of sawdust also speak to a worrying trend: that of a fast-developing and energy-hungry neighbor eager to tap into Siberia's vast—but finite—resources. The massive quantities of timber omnipresent in Manzhouli that hail from Russia are processed in China, by Chinese workers, for Chinese and other non-Russian customers.[1] The Chinese are also involved in the timber industry in remote villages throughout the region, specifically with sawing, transport, and marketing.[2]

If China's recent breakneck economic development has transformed the Russian Far East into an important extractive zone in the last couple of decades, the region has long been a crucial source of raw materials for both China and Russia. Indeed, the pristine forests of northeast Asia have been at the core of empire-making for both countries. From ermine and sable pelts to tiger skins, from ginseng to fungi, pearls, gold, and more recently jade, medicinal herbs, and timber, the wealth of natural resources found in this part of the world has been a great source of state and personal enrichment as well as a way to bind indigenous populations to empire through well-developed systems of tributes and vassalage.

As was discussed in the preceding chapters and will be developed further in this one, much anxiety at the prospect of seeing the Russian Far East overrun by Chinese intent on acquiring natural resources continues to pervade Russian media and informal conversation. In fact, however, the harsh physical environment of *beidahuang* (Great Northern Wilderness) itself long proved a discouraging factor for Chinese migrants. As James Reardon-Anderson's historical study showed, Heilongjiang was populated gradually and reluctantly: "These pioneers were reluctant to move in the first place, those who moved were reluctant to stay, and those who stayed were reluctant to change the world around them or their own ways of adapting to it. They expanded the realm of China more by replication than by device."[3] Russians themselves are also greatly ambivalent about the region. The Russian Far East—and Siberia as well (their fates are closely intertwined)—is perceived on the one hand as a vast territory full of untold riches key to ensuring Russia's place in the world as a global power, and on the other as a terribly harsh environment. Securing and retaining control over such a vast geographical expanse has always presented important challenges for Russia, especially given its location on the edge of an overpopulated China. Convincing Russians to relocate east during the socialist period required financial incentives and other advantages. Since the collapse of the Soviet Union, the region has hemorrhaged demographically, losing around 20 percent of its population over the last two decades. The Russian Far East, just like the northeast (Dongbei) for the Chinese, thus sits at a juncture of contradictions. It is a place of fantastic wealth but also one of banishment. It is a natural reserve of pristine nature, but also one witnessing the steady depletion of unique fauna, flora, and reserves of minerals, as well as the pollution of Lake Baikal, the largest freshwater lake in the world. Previously on the remote edges of empire, the Russian Far East now finds itself at the center of new infrastructural geographies, crisscrossed by roads, railways, and pipelines.

A LAND OF VAST NATURAL RESOURCES

When I (Franck) met Igor, he was in his late twenties. A couple of years earlier, with few job prospects after finishing university in Blagoveshchensk, he decided to try his luck in Heihe. He moved to the Chinese border town, learned to speak fluent Chinese, and gradually built up a network of Chinese friends and business partners. When I spoke to him, he was making a living as an intermediary, buying Chinese goods for Russian customers and helping Chinese businesses trade with Russia. Gesturing at store signs displaying nonsensical strings of Cyrillic letters, he explained that he had helped various Chinese store owners correct and reprint their signs. "In the early 1990s, you would see store signs with random arrangements of Cyrillic and Latin letters that perplexed and amused Russian visitors, but most make sense now." However, a few still remain, and Igor pointed out to me a sign displaying an uninterrupted string of twenty Russian consonants.

As we sat down to have dinner at a local restaurant over a mountain of *jiaozi* dumplings, he launched into one of his favorite topics: hunting. As he explained, the coincidence of abundant wildlife on the Russian side and an increasing demand for animal organs on the Chinese side offers people like him valuable economic opportunities. "Bear paws are very expensive on the Chinese market; one single paw can be sold for as much as $500. Bear meat is another resource, as it sells at $100 a kilo. Russians rarely eat bear meat, but for the Chinese it's a valuable medicine.[4] The gallbladder [in Russian *zhelch'*, in Chinese *dan*] is especially valuable and therefore expensive."[5] One time he was approached by a Chinese who asked him if he could find one. "He was ready to buy it for ¥20,000. So I asked several people I know in Russia and one guy said he could sell me one for the equivalent of

¥10,000. I bargained, got it for ¥8,000 and so I made a ¥12,000 profit. It's easy to bring it; you just put it in your pocket. It's not metal, so they don't detect it."

The pride he expressed in having duped the customs agents was somewhat jarring in a context where he was frequently critical of Chinese smugglers who "stole" precious Russian resources. This particular irony speaks to the complex entanglement of legality, informal state practices, individual enrichment, corruption, and personal networks (*blat* in the context of Russia, *guanxi* in the context of China), that defines the Russia-China borderland.[6] As will be shown in this chapter, the line between legality and illegality is not always clear. Practices that are formally illegal are often ignored by authorities who recognize the realities of economic survival (see Chapter 3), but laws can suddenly become applicable when someone falls afoul of a powerful individual. This state of affairs is not exclusive to postsocialist Russia, having been a defining feature of both the socialist era and prerevolutionary Russia. While this situation is not unique to the Russian Far East, the rich natural environment of northeast Asia, with its wealth of animals, dense forests, and minerals, has placed natural resources at the center of social, economic, and cultural relations there.

Nature as Imperial Resource

The fur trade had long been crucial to Russian imperial aspirations. As early as the fifteenth century, Moscow secured its political ascendency over Novgorod through the fur trade. Russians exploited the existing antagonism between indigenous groups such as the Komi, gradually turning these communities into tribute-paying vassals.[7] The tribute system in turn led to the establishment of a network of fortified towns all across Siberia and the Far East. The Muscovites employed brute force to exact regular tribute (*yasak*) from the indigenous population, taking chiefs or members of their families as hostages to ensure that the required number of pelts would be delivered. This system of extortion was "accompanied by government regulations which were intended to prevent arbitrary violence" toward the natives, and to ensure they would not attempt to rebel.[8]

As the global demand for fur increased, notably in Renaissance Europe, sable and marten pelts gave Muscovite Rus its principal commodity of foreign exchange and provided the means for purchasing goods from abroad such as precious metals, textiles, or firearms.[9] Sable, with its dark color and luxurious texture, commanded the highest prices, and "the possession of a few pelts . . . could make a man in Russia prosperous for the rest of his life."[10] As a result, the opening up of Siberia led to a "fur fever" comparable to the nineteenth century's gold rush, and by the sixteenth century the value of Siberian pelts accounted for around 10 percent of the Russian state's total income.[11] As hunting grounds became depleted, the Russians moved farther and farther east. In fact, the rapidity of Russian advance eastward can be attributed precisely to this process of extermination of sable resources.

It was the pursuit of fur, not land, that drove much of Russia's rapid eastward advance and led to the encroachment upon Chinese imperial frontiers, eventually resulting in the establishment of state borders. A defining moment for the frontier history of northeast Asia was the establishment of the Albazin Fort near present-day Blagoveshchensk in 1650, but this event was preceded by many incursions by hunter-trappers and Cossacks who took advantage of the ill-defined limits of China.[12] As Russian incursions into Dongbei became more frequent, the relations Qing China entertained with its northern neighbors, and in particular with Mongolia and with Chosŏn, had to be reframed.[13] Until then, Dongbei—and to some extent Mongolia as well—had not been fully integrated in the Qing territory. The region was a special frontier protected by the Manchu court through a "policy of closing off" (*fengjin zhengce*), and Han Chinese were excluded.[14]

For the Qing, natural resources shared some of the meanings and values they had in the Russian Empire. They were a way to bind indigenous populations to empire as well as a means for state enrichment. Some goods, such as fur, had a true global reach and were "enmeshed in networks that extended from Beijing to Lake Khövsgöl, the Amur delta, Sakhalin Island, Siberia, Hokkaido, Alaska, and even Baja California."[15] But fur and other goods were also important symbolic objects. For the Jurchens, a Tungusic people who established the Jin dynasty (1115–1234) and who were ancestors of the Manchus and other local peoples, ginseng became a unique symbol of their identity.[16] For the Manchu rulers of the Qing Dynasty, pearls, sable, and ginseng initially were the primary items gifted to their neighbors and later became symbolic objects of Manchu ethnicity. There was intense demand for furs at the Manchu court itself. Local tribes were contracted to hunt for them and supply the capital, where they were carefully graded by a dedicated bureau and then used as payment to courtiers, officials, and Mongolian princes according to rank.[17] All of these resources were dependent on activities such as hunting and gathering, which were seen as integral to Manchu identity. These traditions required the preservation of a space separate from the rest of the Han population; the Qing divided Manchuria into several regions, confining the Han Chinese to Shengjing, the Manchus to the northeast, and the Mongols to the northwest.[18] This goal of this policy was to protect local tribes from the majority Han Chinese population and to preserve untainted Manchu ethnic traits and practices in Manchuria.[19] Historian David Bello and others have argued that this division also made ecological sense given the mutual incompatibilities between Han agriculture and alternative practices, such as Mongol pastoralism, more suited to borderland ecologies.[20] The ecological conditions of Manchuria and Mongolia, Bello writes, "dominated by comparatively dry and cold forest and steppe, precluded agriculture as the primary means of environmental interaction."[21] While these analyses are somewhat problematic given that Han settlers have managed to farm larger areas of Manchuria, including the region near Tongjiang right on the border with Russia, the different ecology and the harsh climate conditions certainly made this more challenging than for central regions of China.

Beginning in the eighteenth century and intensifying in the nineteenth, changes in the political environment of northeast Asia led to a dramatic shift in the conceptualization and management of borders. Initially, Mongolia and the borderlands between Qing and Chŏson had functioned as buffer zones, but gradually settlers began moving into them.[22] Throughout most of the Qing period, the Manchurian provinces of Jilin and Heilongjiang "were kept off-limits to Han civilians in order to preserve the region as the sacred birthplace of the imperial court and the last bastion of the Manchus."[23] Mongolia, though formally under Qing sovereignty, had been placed under similar restrictions and was off-limits to Han settlers. But in the last decades of dynastic rule, largely in response to Russian territorial ambitions, the Qing reversed the policy and encouraged the settlement of sparsely populated Mongolia by Han farmers and traders.[24] Russian encroachment also compelled the Qing to incorporate its northern territories in less ambiguous terms.[25] The vast expanses of Inner Mongolia, largely settled by Han Chinese at the beginning of the twentieth century, and later those of Manchuria, proved increasingly attractive to Han farmers looking for arable land. On the eastern borders, the Qing had agreed with Chŏson to keep their common borderlands off-limits to civilian settlers. However, as ginseng became more and more scarce and people started to settle there, the two neighbors had to reconsider their agreement, as well as their understanding of territory and boundary.[26]

Thus, just as the expansion of the Russian Empire was directly tied to fur hunting, the boundaries of the modern Chinese state emerged through the exploitation of—and competition over—natural resources. The full integration of what were until then remote borderlands was accompanied by important population transfers. As indigenous populations were displaced (see Chapter 4), both the Chinese and the Russian states encouraged and sponsored the resettlement of their respective majority groups in the region, largely as a way to strengthen their borders. Known as *chuang Guandong* (闯关东; literally "crashing into Guandong"), the late eighteenth-century rush into Manchuria witnessed the resettlement of many Han Chinese farmers to the area along the Liao River, as well as Han refugees from northern China who were suffering from famine, floods, and drought.[27] The subsequent migrations of Han Chinese into Manchuria between 1890 and 1942 was one of the largest population movements of the twentieth-century world.[28] On the Russian side, population transfers were motivated less by the search for virgin lands than by a desire to populate empty territories as a way to secure them (see Chapter 1). They also came later, during the socialist period, when a combination of social and financial incentives and deportations led to the creation of a string of medium-sized cities (Chapter 7).[29]

Transfers of population to the borderlands were made possible and sustained by the wealth of natural resources, but this human presence also led to dramatic ecological collapses. Based on a study of Chinese, Mongolian, and Manchurian archives, historian Jonathan Schlesinger describes the steady disappearance of countless species of animals from the forests of Qing Manchuria, with sables first vanishing in the 1820s and 1830s, then squirrels in the 1860s, and all other valuable fur-bearing animals soon afterward.[30] This extinction process extended well beyond the region. Fueled by Qing demand for natural resources, animal populations in Southeast Asia and the greater Pacific began to face similar challenges.[31] In Inner Asia itself, trade in furs was soon supplemented by commercial exchanges around other natural resources, such as pearls, fungi, sea cucumbers (known as *trepang* in Russia and as *haishen* in Chinese), and precious metals including gold.

The preceding discussion suggests the existence of an intense competition between Russians and Chinese, and this is indeed the view often portrayed by economists and scholars working in international relations. However, this has not always been the case on the ground. When gold was first discovered, in 1883, in a tributary of the Amur, Russians rushed to set up "wild" (unlicensed) mines, including the settlement of Zheltuga, located on Qing territory, in the far north of present-day Heilongjiang province (around the location of Mohe, China's northernmost village). Independently governed, it became known as the "Zheltuga Republic." Zheltuga is the first recorded case of shared life in Manchuria, more than a decade before an influx of Russian settlers turned Harbin into a cosmopolitan city. In spite of the intense competition that prevailed, and although the Chinese constituted no more than 10 percent of the overall population in Zheltuga, the Russians made no attempt to exclude them socially or politically. On the contrary, "the Chinese are said to have participated in the election of Zheltuga's first ruler, and to have been represented by two of the ten appointed foremen."[32]

Natural Resources in the Present Day

Many contemporary situations present similar partnerships between Russians and Chinese. While there is limited social interaction between the two groups, as earlier chapters have shown, and certainly less than the official narratives of eternal friendship suggest, there is also comparatively little hostility. In the Russian Far East, the bulk of ethnic antagonisms is directed at recent arrivals from Central Asia and the Caucasus rather than at the hardworking and politically invisible Chinese. As a result of Russia's stringent immigration quotas and the drop in the value of the ruble, migrants to the Russian Far East are now increasingly coming from Central Asia, where they have come to dominate street markets—a development that has not been welcomed by all.[33] As a high school teacher named Maria confided, Central Asian migrants are Muslim, they tend to be uneducated, and typically they don't integrate. "Actually, their presence has made it much easier for Chinese," she said. "People think that the

Chinese are by far preferable. They work, don't create any problems, and they integrate easily in Russian society."

As will be discussed in the next section, fears of Chinese encroachment are recurrent in the media and informal conversation, but in no way do they compare to the vitriolic narratives that pervade the Mongolian media.[34] On the Chinese side, the quotidian friction caused by cultural misunderstandings has not translated into Russophobia, and apart from the occasional fistfight—mostly fueled by overconsumption of alcohol—the attitudes of Chinese borderlanders toward their northern neighbor are generally neutral, if not positive (see Chapter 5). Even in the 1960s, at the height of hostilities, there is anecdotal evidence that some form of commercial exchange continued to take place and that trade persisted, informally, across the Amur River.[35] Exchanges have therefore been informed by strong pragmatism, and this complicates Russian official reports and media representations, which generally tend to place blame squarely on Chinese poachers.

Research by sociologist Natalia Ryzhova on practices of illegality and semilegality demonstrates that Russian businesses and intermediaries are fully involved in poaching taking place at the border (see Chapter 3).[36] In a study of fishing practices in the Amur River, Ryzhova shows that Chinese poaching is made possible through the bribing of a number of Russian actors. Paying off inspectors ensures that fish caught illegally are not confiscated and can be traded. The shipment is then prepared for export through the procurement of quality control and veterinary certificates, which are submitted to customs for approval. An exporting firm, registered in the name of a Russian citizen but often just a front for the actual Chinese owner, can then export the shipment "legally" to China.[37]

The involvement of a large network of people who play at least some role in the "Chinese poaching" of Russia's natural resources is testament to the entanglement of traders, hunters, and fishers on both sides of the border, as well as to the difficulty of identifying who is a poacher and who is not (see also the discussion of sea fishing in Chapter 3). As in the case of Igor at the beginning of this chapter, fears of Russia becoming a "resource appendage" for China can become muted when the opportunity arises to make extra income, or when it represents economic survival. The general pattern for all informal resource business, whether it involves jade, wild animal parts, medicinal herbs, fish, gold, ginseng, scrap metal, or timber, is for the tough primary extraction to be carried out by impoverished Russian citizens, while most of the management, finance, transport, and processing, and of course the end purchase, is done by Chinese.

The collapse of state support for the logging industry after the demise of the Soviet Union has similarly led to the emergence of timber operators who export around 60,900 cubic meters of hardwoods to China annually.[38] The timber industry presents many similarities with the fishing industry described by Ryzhova. Illegal logging takes place in many forms, and includes logging without a license, logging in protected areas, logging outside of concession boundaries, illegal domestic movement of timber, undergrading timber, transfer pricing, and incorrectly classifying species to avoid taxation.[39] A common loophole here has been for people to apply for a so-called sanitary logging license allowing them to remove dead or dying trees, and then use this license as legal cover for the felling of valuable hardwood. As in the fishing industry, "customs inspections can easily be sidestepped through the use of forged legal documents or fraudulent declarations."[40] A recent Russian documentary entitled *Dark Forest* claims the timber industry is now fully in the hands of criminal gangs, beyond federal control.[41] New legislation was enacted in 2007 to combat this widespread corruption in the hope of saving the forests.[42] Tariffs were imposed on unprocessed timber but waived for processed timber, with the aim of encouraging the development of a wood processing industry within Russia. However, Russians proved largely uninterested in developing such an industry. By 2010, only a couple of Russian processing factories were in operation. By contrast, close to 10,000 small-scale Chinese saw-mills had mushroomed at the border. Because of imprecisions in the law (it does not adequately define "processed"), Chinese workers have been able to bypass the new regulations simply by cutting the trunks into planks, which then can be exported legally and tariff-free.[43]

By exposing a couple of prominent corrupt officials, *Dark Forest* was successful in bringing the situation to the attention of the Russian public. However, because of the region's endemic levels of corruption, it has proven extremely difficult to pursue lawbreakers. Moreover, the "cost of operating 'legally' in Russia, with its heavy burden of taxes and unofficial 'fees,' makes legal forestry largely unprofitable."[44] The illegal logging that takes place in the region in fact goes a long way to sustain the local population. As one of the Russian residents interviewed explained: "We live on the timber while it's still around [*My za schët lesa zhivëm, poka est' les*]. If there's no forest, we'll die." So dire is the situation for some locals that they are remunerated for their work in food and alcohol.

The view from the Russian capital—and the western regions overall—is that the Chinese are guilty of predatory practices that are decimating these primeval forests.[45] Yet if Chinese demand for timber has certainly exacerbated the issue, the situation on the ground is far more nuanced. As a recent analysis shows, the radical transformation of Russia's timber industry in 1992, when the Russian government privatized all state forest industry enterprises, led to an explosion of small private firms and exporters. "State agencies, due in part to declining budgets, have been largely unsuccessful in controlling these enterprises."[46] In fact, Russian forest service units (*leskhozy*), the very government bodies responsible for monitoring logging operations and maintaining forest health, are directly involved in illegal activities. They themselves cut, or issue licenses for others to log commercially, valuable ash, Korean pine, and oak forests.[47] Losses are compounded by extremely wasteful and destructive practices, with 40 to

60 percent of all cut timber estimated to be lost in the produc-tion process.[48]

Assigning blame to Chinese "greediness" is an oversimplifica-tion obfuscating the responsibility that Russian companies, and the state overall, bear for the rapid destruction of Siberian for-ests.[49] The wildfires that consumed vast swaths of Siberia and the Russian north in the summer of 2019—consuming over 12 mil-lion acres—were caused in part by high temperatures, gusts of wind, and dry thunderstorms.[50] But they were also made worse by a slow response by Russian authorities, who felt the projected cost of extinguishing them exceeded the projected damage that they would cause, and were compounded by changes in forest conservation laws. Indeed, following the adoption of the new forest code in 2006, forestry staff plummeted from 70,000 to 12,000. The forest itself was turned into "movable property"—a legal category making it easier to transfer to private ownership or rent—which directly contributed to placing it outside state control. Unsurprisingly, in 2008, only one year after the new law was passed, the number of fires in Russia was already forty-one times higher than in the previous year.[51] Official explanations, however, placed the blame squarely on illegal loggers, who were accused of using arson to conceal their activities.[52]

We saw in Chapters 3 and 5 that despite generally positive relations—and ubiquitous narratives about an eternal friendship—between Russians and Chinese, social exchanges remain limited. But local Russians tend to feel respect for the hardworking Chi-nese, whose presence has given remote villages in the region a new lease of life.[53] Thus, despite the illegal nature of logging, as well as the risk of heavy fines and confiscation of equipment, this in-dustry has grown to supersede farming as the main source of in-come for the rural population in parts of the Russian Far East, such as in certain districts of Buryatia.[54]

This state of affairs is hardly surprising if one considers the extent to which Chinese economic involvement in the Russian Far East has provided a veritable lifeline for locals. Vladimir Putin's strengthening of the state's hierarchical power structure (the "power vertical," *vertikal' vlasti*) has seen the Russian state recapture some of its influence on its long-forgotten eastern borderland, but disparity between the two sides of the border continues to grow. Russian anxieties regarding China's increasing involvement in the extraction of natural resources are by no means baseless. China's hunger for Russian fauna, flora, and mineral wealth has shaped the Russian Far East's economic and political landscape, and nowhere has this been more dramatic than with the jade mining business. As discussed in Chapter 3, jade is considered to be the essence of Chinese culture. In Russia, by contrast, where jade is known as nephrite, no cultural or economic value is attached to it. If this incongruence in value undeniably presents economic opportunities, the value of jade in China is attached to its geographic and cultural provenance: "To be valuable, jade objects should either be from archaeological excavations or antiquity collections or should be made from the same material as famous historical objects."[55] Russians who trade in this mineral need therefore to maintain a gap of misunderstanding and discrepancy in values.[56] They navigate a liminal space of trust and mistrust, knowledge and ignorance, authenticity and forgeries.[57] Overall, as anthropologist Tobias Holzlehner notes, cultural differences in consumption and specific ecological conditions play a crucial role, most particularly across the Russian-Chinese border, "where certain species of flora and fauna flourish in Russia that are in high demand in China."[58]

These cultural misalignments also contribute to a large extent to Russian anxieties about their borders. The Chinese not only want things that Russians also want (which would make things comparable and commensurable) but also are interested in goods that have no value locally. This creates an environment where anything is liable to being desired, commodified, and spirited away—in a manner that remains often opaque to locals. An example is the plant *Saposhnikovia divaricata*, which grows as a weed in abundance in Buryatia and Zabaikal'skii Krai. It was recently discovered to be highly valued for its medicinal properties in China, where it is known as *fangfeng* (防风, lit. "protect against the wind"). Now whole villages scour the countryside, dig up the roots, and make a good income, though the precise means whereby the roots are whisked across the border is not known to the people who harvest them. Russian governmental anxieties about precious Siberian resources leaking out in this way are compounded by very different cultural and social conceptualizations of "bordering"—a considerably thorny issue for two countries sharing such a long land border, as discussed in Chapters 1 and 2.

Perhaps nowhere else are these issues so dramatically evident than in Asia's northeast—the vast region bisected by the Sino-Russian border. From a Russian perspective, as can be seen in the monument to the history of Russian presence in the region (Figure 6.1), the demarcation line is imagined to be running south of the river rather than through it. Until Sino-Russian territorial disputes were finally settled, Moscow insisted on a China-bank boundary. While this is no longer the case, in the Russian popular imaginary the Amur River is Russian rather than shared, and this plays a significant role in discussions involving river usage (as in fishing) as well as in cases of water pollution—a genuine issue given the significance of the border river for Chinese local agriculture.

Narratives of "leakiness" are partly sustained by the feeling of having been bypassed by China (see Chapter 7), but the analogy extends beyond a mere metaphor. In 2017, China was reportedly considering plans to build a 620-mile pipeline that would transport water from Lake Baikal to parched Gansu province.[59] While ambitious, such a huge hydrologic project would not be China's first. In 2014, China inaugurated its South-North Water Diversion, a gigantic web of canals and reservoirs shifting trillions of gallons of water from the south to its northern provinces. It is also an eerie echo of Soviet mega-projects that saw the alteration

Figure 6.1. Monument to the history of Russian presence in the Amur region. The title reads "The Amur land was, is, and will always be Russian" (*Zemlya amurskaya byla, est', i budet russkoi*). (Photo by Franck Billé)

of the physical environment on a grand scale. One of the most ambitious plans—eventually rejected by the Soviet leader Mikhail Gorbachev in the mid-1980s—was to divert part of the rivers Ob and Irtysh to Central Asia, notably to replenish the desiccated Aral Sea.[60] The fact that such huge projects are now being implemented by China certainly generates considerable anxiety for Russia. But such ambitions to control and shape nature on a massive scale underscore the many similarities the two countries share, in spite of their vast cultural differences. The contradictions are in fact frequently internal, on both sides.

POLLUTION

While they recognize the hard work carried out by Chinese migrants, local Russians are frequently ambivalent about Chinese agricultural practices (see Chapter 3). *Plënka*, the plastic sheeting commonly used by Chinese farmhands, was a recurrent topic in conversations and interviews. Plastic sheeting is used as protection against frost but should be removed after the harvest. However, strict annual work visas imposed by the local authorities make this difficult to implement. As local businessperson Dima explained, "If they [the Chinese] were allowed to come here for longer periods, if they used the land for, say, ten years, then they would be more careful. But they come here for one year, so they feel it's not their land. And if you don't remove the *plënka,* in winter it breaks up with the cold, then bits of it fly all over the place. But it doesn't degrade biologically, it stays here."

His perceptive analysis that environmental degradation is directly linked to quotas is not self-evident to the Russian majority. In fact, the claim that Chinese practices are inherently deleterious to the environment is routinely expressed by local Russians and dominates discussions of the shared border river. Of course, these narratives are not free-floating and are tied to common Chinese practices.[61] But they are also framed by a wider discourse associating China with unbridled and environmentally noxious forms of capitalism.[62] Just like Western publics, Russians have become familiar with images of Beijing shrouded in thick dust storms—said to be the outcome of desertification and poor management of fragile landscapes in southern Mongolia.[63] In interviews and informal conversation, Russians voice concerns about a neighbor they perceive to be uninterested in environmental issues and therefore unlikely to introduce meaningful changes. An explosion at a petrochemical plant in Jilin province in November 2005 that led to benzene contamination of two border rivers, the Sungari (Ch: Songhua) and Amur, and to the death of local aquatic life confirmed Russian fears about the deleterious effects of Chinese economic growth. Water monitoring by Khabarovsk regional authorities indeed found phenol levels in the Amur River to exceed permitted levels by nearly 100 percent.[64] Russian regional officials have repeatedly voiced concern over China's industrial plants, estimated to be around 100 in total on the banks of the Sungari. On account of demographic pressure (the Chinese population near the Sungari is in excess of 50 million, while there are around 5 million people living in the entire Russian Far East), the total area of farmland in northeast China has increased dramatically, making use of large quantities of chemical fertilizers and pesticides.[65]

However, such Russian complaints make short shrift of similarities as well as complexities.[66] As discussed earlier in this chapter, the Russian Far East also battles with environmental degradation, as does Russia in general. The rapid loss of forest cover throughout the northeast may be fueled by Chinese demand, but Russian poverty, corruption, venality, and administrative inefficiency make that possible. Russia is in fact home to some heavily polluted towns. Norilsk, an industrial city in Krasnoyarsk Krai, within the Arctic Circle, is one of the most polluted in the world—by some estimates its nickel mines are responsible for 1 percent of global sulfur dioxide emission.[67] In the Russian Far East, the small village of Oktyabrskiy, on the outskirts of Krasnokamensk and located just 60 miles from the Chinese border, is another environmental catastrophe zone. The site of a uranium mine that for a time was the biggest in the world, today Oktyabrskiy lies neglected and poisoned. Radon gas and radiation coming from the uranium works as well as from natural mineral deposits in the soil are responsible for a high incidence of children born with malformations—three times higher than normal.[68]

The notion that China is incapable or unwilling to find solutions to alleviate its pollution levels is also misrepresentative of the situation on the ground. Beijing has made a lot of efforts in that direction in recent years, shutting down industries on certain days, restricting the number of cars on the road, closing coal mines, and prohibiting new coal-fired power plants in the country's most polluted regions. In the first four years after China declared war against pollution in 2014, the results were impressive, with cities having cut concentrations of fine particulates in the air by 32 percent on average.[69] Concurrently, China has been investing massive sums in renewable energy, both at home and abroad. A recent report by the Institute for Energy Economics and

Financial Analysis cites a global investment of $44 billion in 2017 alone. Indirectly aided by the Trump administration—the United States' decision to withdraw from the Paris climate agreement was an important catalyst for China's growing renewable energy dominance—China will increasingly be providing technology leadership and financial capacity in the growing green sector.[70] These positive measures come, however, at high human costs associated with environmental migration, as discussed in Chapter 4.

Having a centralized government able to dictate and implement new policies has certainly been helpful in effecting these changes, but it would be amiss to view China as a single-minded entity. On the contrary, as legal scholar Rachel Stern explains, the Chinese state is "a heap of loosely connected parts" with divergent perspectives on the wisdom of suing polluters. Her recent study about environmental litigation in China shows that pollution cases, while politically sensitive (*you yidian min'gan*), enjoy a "sliver of political opening that renders them less risky to complainants than other rights-related cases."[71] Politically touchy but not taboo, environmental cases sit near the boundary of the politically permissible.

According to Stern, grassroots action does not necessarily indicate nascent environmental consciousness. Most environmental cases are in fact filed out of desperation and compelled by an immediate threat: "So-called 'typical cases' (*dianxing anli*), a prominent phrase in the Chinese legal lexicon, nearly always involve compensation for economic losses."[72] Her assessment is consonant here with political scientist Maria Repnikova's findings on the limits of "speakability" in China and Russia.[73] In her 2017 book on Chinese media, Repnikova highlights the "within-the-system nature" of China's societal activism. In other words, criticisms published in the Chinese media tend to have a collaborative rather than antagonistic form.[74] Repnikova shows that the system carries both consultative and fluid dimensions, as the state creates "some input channels in policy-making while keeping the rules of the game intentionally ambiguous."[75]

In Russia, by contrast, the limits of critical reporting are clear to journalists—as are the penalties for overly harsh criticisms. Unlike in China, the objectives of Russian journalists and those of officials are frequently at odds: the state's management of media does not include mechanisms for people to let off steam, which contributes to the evolution of specific relations between journalists and the state.[76] Whereas in Russia criticisms are voiced more openly but are subject to harsh repression, journalists in China attempt to work within the acceptable limits of "speakability" and play a delicate game of cat-and-mouse. This complex positioning of environmental litigation and investigative journalism in both Russian and Chinese contexts highlights the similarities that bind the two countries despite an apparent stark contrast—a situation attributable, in part, to a similar authoritarian political trajectory over several decades.

A further hurdle has been the difficulty for both sides to collaborate on what are essentially issues affecting entire ecosystems not confined to national jurisdictions, such as the Amur basin. While there are grassroots movements in both Russia and China, they often lack the linguistic skills to join forces. The ties of Russian and Chinese environmental groups to large Western foundations are also different in both depth and nature. Groups in the Russian Far East tend to be professional, well-established, and skillful in securing international grants. Organizations in China's northeast, by contrast, are mostly environmental groups run by local college students, with larger Chinese NGOs mainly concentrated in places such as Beijing, Shanghai, or Yunnan. Whereas the Russian Far East, with its vast pristine forests, is considered a "hot spot" deserving attention from Western foundations and environmental NGOs, Heilongjiang province is primarily agricultural and industrial "as a result of industrialization and the state-organized large-scale land reclamation campaigns from the late 1950s to the 1970s."[77] Even when engaged on the same environmental project in a given biosphere, NGOs in China and Russia each tend to be better connected to the Western head office than they are to each other.[78] In recent years, NGOs in both Russia and China have found themselves on shaky ground, potentially labeled as "foreign agents." As Emily Yeh notes, NGOs in minority areas especially are weak and in retreat. Young Tibetans prefer instead to open companies that incorporate some social goals, since companies are regarded as commercial and therefore not subject to the same scrutiny.[79]

There are nonetheless a number of success stories. For example, in spite of these structural and political issues, both the Amur leopard and the Siberian tiger have made an impressive recovery. In 2000, there were only thirty leopards in Russia and just two in China, but at this writing they number close to ninety across both countries. The Siberian tiger was on the verge of extinction in 1940, with only forty individuals left, but as of 2019 there were as many as 540. While both species remain under threat due to poaching, habitat loss and fragmentation, excessive land exploitation, and unsustainable consumption of large tracts of virgin forest for the sake of development, recent binational efforts are starting to pay off. Cooperation between the two nations began in 1998 when Russian and Chinese biologists and scientists walked the border together and entered into a partnership. In 2001, Jilin province established the Hunchun National Nature Reserve, close to the border with Russia and North Korea, and there are plans to combine it with the nearby Wangqing Nature Reserve in Jilin province and Laoyeling Nature Reserve in neighboring Heilongjiang province, making it a huge nature reserve, 60 percent larger than Yellowstone National Park in the United States. More recently, the Chinese have created a bear park on Heixiazi Island, the Chinese section of the river island, as discussed in Chapter 2. One hundred northeastern black bears have been introduced, and the bear park has been widely advertised as a "bear paradise."[80]

Support for tiger and leopard conservation has also grown in Russia, with the creation of a system of protected areas that together cover the majority of the leopard range, thanks in part to support from Sergey Ivanov, the former chief of staff of Vladimir Putin. In June 2019, presidents Xi Jinping and Vladimir Putin signed a joint declaration that included reference to creating a transboundary park to protect Amur leopards and Siberian tigers, joint monitoring, and establishing nature corridors on the border.[81] In both Russia and China, the Siberian tiger is the flagship animal of the boreal forest ecosystem and a metaphorical figure standing for the environmental protection and benevolent paternalism that both governments seek to project.[82] The political persona of Xi and Putin are also intimately enmeshed in these narratives of national pride and strength evoked by the Siberian tiger. Putin in particular has used the tiger for various photo opportunities, seeking to portray himself as a hypermasculine hero.[83] While such strategies have been made fun of on the internet, where there are countless memes of a shirtless Putin riding tigers, eagles, sharks, and polar bears, the personal involvement of political leadership at the highest level has been decisive in these environmental success stories. As Barney Long, director of species conservation for the World Wildlife Fund, said in 2015 with respect to the Siberian tiger, "We're talking such a vast area in the Russian forest, that to make impacts across that entire area you really need high-level political support."[84]

In May 2014, Kuzya, a twenty-three-month-old Siberian tiger, gained wide popularity in Russia. Nicknamed "Putin's tiger" after President Vladimir Putin, who had a personal hand in reintroducing it into the wild, in October Kuzya—disappointingly for the Russians—swam across the Amur River into China. According to ecologists, the endangered Amur tiger was probably looking for better nutrition, but popular Russian and Chinese reactions to this opportunistic border-crossing also echoed very common narratives. Some in China joked Kuzya might be a spy, while some Russians suggested that he was seeking to escape Putin's authoritarian grip. Many Chinese microblog users predicted an unhappy ending—"How long before this poor tiger becomes a rug in some rich official's house?"[85] These facetious comments tapped into very real differences between the two sides of the border, notably in land use. Ecologists worried that while the tiger knew how to avoid people in Russia, it would be more difficult in that agricultural area of China. Overall, Russians saw their side as "more natural," a better place for a tiger.[86]

Matters pertaining to the environment, as discussed in this chapter, extend well beyond cultural attitudes to "nature" and "development," and are indeed metaphors of how the two sides see and imagine each other, and of the dynamics of their relationship overall. Thus the notions that China threatens to seep beyond its borders through poorly managed unruly rivers, or that its polluted atmosphere cannot be contained within its national boundaries, speak to entrenched ideas of an imperialist China eager to extend its territorial footprint. Chapter 7, on border urbanism, will continue this exploration of differences and similarities, highlighting the ways in which urban forms are metaphors for broader notions of modernity and development.

7

URBAN CONTRASTS

The borderlands between Russia and China tend to be seen by both countries as remote and undeveloped. While it is true that both the Russian Far East and the furthermost reaches of the Chinese northeast (Dongbei) are peripheral to their respective states, the borderlands are nonetheless a strategic region that has witnessed tremendous changes over the last three decades. One of the most remarkable changes over that period has been the mushrooming of sizable cities on the Chinese side. In Russia, Vladivostok, Khabarovsk, and Blagoveshchensk are important population centers of 600,000, 580,000, and 250,000 inhabitants, respectively. On the Chinese side, cities such as Manzhouli, Heihe, and Suifenhe, morphing out of mere villages, have grown rapidly. While modest in comparison to Chinese megapolises, they are important trade nodes, and in many cases have grown larger than their Russian counterparts (Figure 7.1).[1] Manzhouli in particular, on the border of both Russia and Mongolia, is a commercial hub of a quarter million residents and China's busiest land port of entry, accounting for 60 percent of all imports from and exports to eastern Europe. By contrast, its Russian counterpart, Zabaikalsk, is a small, largely defunct military outpost.[2]

An analysis of urban developments, particularly in the context of new and older border towns, is essential to understand the

Figure 7.1. Blagoveshchensk (*foreground*) and Heihe (*background*) in the late 1980s (*top*) and today (*bottom*).
(Amurskaya Pravda)

shifting dynamics in the region. Indeed, urbanization is not merely an index of economic development. The size, shape, and axis of these towns tell us a lot about the way Russians and Chinese see themselves and how they seek to portray themselves to their neighbors. Cities are also symbols of more elusive notions such as progress and modernity, and as such can help us track geopolitical orientations and cultural benchmarks. As we will see in this chapter, Chinese border towns tend to be compact, vertical, and luminous, while their Russian counterparts often have a

horizontal layout, a more dispersed footprint, and use lighting
more sparingly—the product of distinct cultural values and contrasting imaginations of urban modernity. Yet, as this chapter
will suggest, the very proximity of Chinese and Russian border
towns inevitably leads to processes of cultural enmeshment, borrowing, and mimesis.

While the two cities of Blagoveshchensk and Heihe that feature in this chapter are comparable in size, thirty years ago Heihe
was little more than a collection of a few houses (see Figure 7.1).
Demographic comparisons between Heihe and Blagoveshchensk
tend to be a little misleading, however. The population of Heihe is
officially 1.7 million, whereas "Blago" has only 225,000 residents—
but this dramatic contrast is due largely to differences in administrative division as well as in the very concept of "city." As
mentioned in Chapter 1 with regard to Manzhouli, in China "city"
is an administrative term denoting an expanse of land under the
auspices of a particular level of urban government. In that sense
a city may be urban in name only, and can often include large
expanses of agricultural areas, mountains, forests, or deserts.[3]
The urban district of Heihe, for example, includes six different
settlements that can be as distant as 60 miles from the town of
Heihe proper (Map 4).[4]

Chinese and Russian cities in the region also differ drastically
from each other both structurally and in terms of aesthetics, and
this is largely due to the way in which they have developed. Russian cities in the region are older than their Chinese counterparts.[5]
They were established in the mid-1800s as the Russian Empire
was seeking to assert its presence in Asia. They then grew further
during the Soviet period, largely through population transfers from
western Russia, Ukraine, and Byelorussia. Throughout Russian history the image of a seemingly boundless territory (*neob'yatny
prostor*) has been a powerful symbol of identity.[6] Moreso perhaps
than in other cultural settings, the marking of this geographic
space has been perceived as inherently tied to the country's destiny

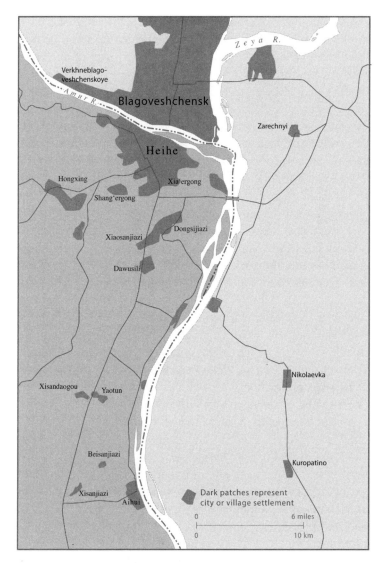

Map 4. Blagoveshchensk and Heihe

and to claims of modernity and "civilization." Because of a "persistent belief that all its territory must be populated to be possessed and governed," Russia saw the emergence of numerous midsize cities throughout the vast Siberian expanses.[7] As a result, Russia's demographic distribution contrasts starkly with other countries that have low population density, such as Canada or Australia, where distribution is less homogenous. Approximately 85 percent of Canada's population, for instance, is concentrated within 200 miles of the US border, where winters are less harsh; in the case of Russia, by contrast, such a clustering is largely absent. Russia's vast geography is dotted with medium-size cities, making it more reliant on transport.

The artificial nature of population distribution, long enforced through household registration (*propiska*), became painfully evident at the end of the socialist period, when the government was no longer able to subsidize distant settlements spread over its vast expanses. Even large cities in Siberia and the Russian Far East struggled and began hemorrhaging population; these departed residents gradually were replaced in part by an influx from surrounding villages, where living standards plummeted even more dramatically.[8] Given the highly centralized and centripetal model of Russian political space, as discussed in Chapter 1, moving closer to the center translates into better access to professional opportunities, health services, and education.

Soviet urban experiments and the peopling of the eastern regions, supported in part by financial incentives, coercion, and much propaganda, were not always resounding successes.[9] Historian Stephen Kotkin has written about the difficult beginnings of Magnitogorsk, a mining town in the Urals, where, instead of the new shining city they had been expecting, new arrivals were confronted with dreadful conditions of overcrowding and lack of sanitation.[10] A similar situation was found by Jewish settlers arriving in the Jewish Autonomous Region, created in the early 1930s in a remote part of the Russian Far East on the border with

China. Here again, the promised land turned out to be swamplands and forests completely lacking in infrastructure.[11]

Blagoveshchensk, the Russian city that features prominently in this chapter, was established in 1858 at the location of the Albazin Fort, the first Russian settlement on the Amur River. The foundation of Blagoveshchensk, whose name means "annunciation" in Russian, was symbolic. It not only marked Russian territorial advance eastward but represented a beacon of progress and Christian Orthodox civilization in a continent perceived as feudal, despotic, and stagnant. Blagoveshchensk, just like the similar outposts of Khabarovsk and Vladivostok, became in the space of a few decades a vibrant "center of economic life of the Russian Far East, matching the cities in European Russia in terms of size and architecture."[12] It grew especially rapidly in the 1940s through population transfers from western Russia and especially Ukraine. As a military town on the border with China, it had a surplus of men. In order to redress the gender imbalance, it was decided to create a local industry that would bring in women workers. As a result, the city became an important center for the textile industry. However, by the end of the Soviet Union and the planned economy, the textile industry had floundered.

Chinese settlement of the region, by contrast, has been more recent, only taking place at the turn of the twentieth century, when Han migration was encouraged in response to Russian encroachment.[13] As a result, a large influx of migrant settlers, mainly landless peasants from nearby Hebei and Shandong provinces, relocated to the region, and by the 1930s the population had grown to over 20 million.[14] Today the population of the northeast has grown to over 100 million. However, while Russians in the Russian Far East frequently assert that millions of Chinese are pressing at their border, the vast majority live in the southern part of the region, in the large cities of Harbin, Shenyang, and Changchun. As mentioned in Chapter 5, Chinese cities in the region's north developed much later, predominantly after 1990, in response to market demand. It is really after the reopening of the border in 1989, with new commercial opportunities, that China's very north began to truly transform.

While new Chinese cities do benefit from state incentives and tax breaks, their development post-1989 has been more organic insofar as their growth has not been reliant on large state-directed population transfers.[15] In spite of the region's bitterly cold winters, the prospects of economic opportunities and escape from the pollution of large cities have proven very attractive. As a result, unlike cities in the Russian Far East, which have developed very slowly in the last couple of decades, Chinese border towns have grown at breakneck speed.[16]

Outlooks also differ significantly. Residents of Russian border towns often complain of being in a remote place, far from everything, at the edge of the world. This is true even for a city such as Blagoveshchensk, even though it has been one of the principal conduits of trade for the Amur region. Chinese border cities, by contrast, have enthusiastically embraced their position on the border with Russia as a development tactic. As discussed later in this chapter as well as in Chapter 3, cities such as Heihe and Manzhouli have adopted a variety of strategies to attract both Russian and domestic customer bases. They have also been highly adaptable, knowing how to anticipate and respond to demand.

Two cities dominate this chapter: the "twin cities" of Heihe and Blagoveshchensk.[17] Standing across from each other on the Amur River, Heihe and Blagoveshchensk are the point along the 2,500-mile border where Russian and Chinese urbanisms come closest together. As cities of comparable size, they constitute a good case study for the urbanization trends and models currently seen at the Russia-China border. As an extreme case of cultural appropriation and mimesis, Manzhouli will also be discussed insofar as its characteristics have provided a blueprint for other border towns such as Heihe.

Economically codependent and culturally enmeshed, the twin cities of Blagoveshchensk and Heihe are nonetheless very different kinds of siblings. Structural differences between the two are immediately evident. Blagoveshchensk appears inward-looking, almost turned in on itself. The main avenue, Ulitsa Lenina, runs parallel to the Amur River, but at some distance from it. There are no large unobstructed vistas looking onto the other side. To a visitor, it feels as if the river were largely irrelevant. Similarly, the few hotels that are situated near the river do not capitalize on their location, with the best rooms facing away rather than toward the river. This could not contrast more with Heihe's layout. There, the entire city appears to be facing Russia, with the tallest and most modern buildings, including the best hotel in the city, standing right on the riverbank. This marked imbalance prompted a Chinese architect we interviewed to remark on the contrast, describing it as "yi zhang re lian tie zai leng pigu shang" (一张热脸贴在冷屁股上, lit. "a hot face pressed against a cold butt").

To a large extent, differences in layout are due to the two cities' respective histories.[18] Heihe is a new city that has grown and developed in response to cross-border trade with Russia. By contrast, Blagoveshchensk is much older and for the largest part of its history had no neighbor to look at. Originally founded as a military outpost in 1856, and heavily guarded and militarized in the second half of the twentieth century, architecturally the city retains a certain defensive quality, exemplified by the lookout posts found all along the riverbank, a legacy of the Sino-Soviet split (Ch: *zhong-su jiaowu,* 中苏交恶; Russ: *sovetsko-kitaiskii raskol*), and a reminder of the restricted access border zone.

In the first twenty years after the border reopened, Blagoveshchensk's riverbank remained undeveloped. Heihe's embankment, on the other hand, much like those of Hunchun and Fuyuan (Chapter 2), has been turned into a pedestrian promenade lined with trees, small parks, and, in the summer, cafés and small restaurants. The contrast becomes even more evident at night, for at nine o'clock every evening, Heihe's entire riverbank lights up. All the high-rise riverbank buildings suddenly sparkle in a wide array of bright colors, and a laser light dances across the sky. With pop music blasted through loudspeakers, the Chinese city takes on an air of festivity. Yet this is an ordinary day: two hours later the lights and the music will go off, only to return the next evening at the same time. To Russian onlookers, this is a light show clearly designed to impress them and lure them to visit the city. In a stark contrast, with no lights and no tall structures, Blagoveshchensk is barely visible from the Chinese bank.

These Chinese displays of urban modernity are not unique to the Sino-Russian interface and are indeed characteristic of Chinese frontier development overall, as several chapters in the collection by anthropologists Martin Saxer and Juan Zhang make explicit.[19] The kinds of cityscapes put forth by China at its borders are meant to be consumed differently: at a distance, and by various publics, including local and international audiences. This notion of distant enjoyment reminds us of the work of architects and urban theorists Robert Venturi, Denise Scott Brown, and Steven Izenour on Las Vegas. In their pathbreaking book *Learning from Las Vegas* (1972), they argued that the city was designed to be consumed at speed in an automobile. The common comparison of Heihe and Manzhouli with Las Vegas, while somewhat facetious, is thus certainly on point. Russian anthropologist Kapitolina Fedorova makes this very argument, noting that many parts of Manzhouli are not functional but rather are designed to be seen from the car or bus window on the way from or to the border.[20] Similarly, just as in Las Vegas, where the replica of an Egyptian pyramid or an Eiffel Tower—typically housing a casino and hotel complex—is employed for its exotic value, Russian churches or outsized matryoshka dolls index playfully the international and cosmopolitan nature of Manzhouli. Voided of its original meaning, the shell (the "duck" in the typology of Venturi, Scott Brown, and Izenour) is self-referential.[21]

More than simply denoting a lack of interest in its neighbor, the prevalent mood in Blagoveshchensk is one of protection and securitization. In contrast to the playful matryoshka and bear statues that dot Heihe's riverside walk, the Russian town's central symbols reflect an unambiguous intent to draw a clear separation between itself and its neighbor. Through its museums, monuments, and memorials, including a remaining Lenin statue pointing the way forward, the city is structurally insistent on defining itself as Russian rather than liminal. Thus, the architectural element that dominates Ploschad' Pobedy (Victory Square), Blagoveshchensk's central plaza, is a monumental arch bearing the inscription "The land of the Amur was, is, and will be Russian" (*zemlya amurskaya byla, est' i budet russkoi*). The same inscription is also found on a monument on the edge of the city, erected by Governor-General Korsakov in 1868—a large mural depicting the Amur River marking the border with China (see Figure 6.1). On the Russian embankment, a naval ship, a statue of a border guard facing China (Figure 7.2), and the presence of armed soldiers patrolling along the river further emphasize this insistence on protection and historical presence.

Russia's wariness of Chinese intentions is perceptible in the lack of a bridge directly linking the two cities. Despite repeated Chinese offers to bear the entire cost of the project, construction has been endlessly postponed for decades. While a bridge can be an undeniable economic boon to a border town such as Blagoveshchensk, Russian reluctance has been due in large part, as discussed in Chapter 1, to security concerns, since a bridge could facilitate the movement of Chinese troops across the border in the event of a conflict.[22] As a result, passenger crossings between Blagoveshchensk and Heihe have been handled by two services (one Russian and one Chinese) with complete monopoly over their respective citizens.[23] In the summer crossing is done by ferry, in winter by a special bus service over the frozen river. With the two cities only 500 yards apart, foot crossing in the winter could easily be done if it was allowed. But it is in the summer months,

Figure 7.2. Blagoveshchensk's embankment, with Heihe in the background, 2014. The statue is of a border guard with his vigilant dog. (Photo by Franck Billé)

when demand is highest, that the transport link is physically most cumbersome. As traders comment, "The goods have to be transported to the wharf, loaded onto boats, off-loaded on arrival and then loaded on trucks for their final journey—a triple process on both river banks."[24] As this book goes to press, a bridge has finally been built, though at some distance from the towns and not yet operative. As can be seen on Map 4, the bridge can only be reached via a 20 mile detour going east from Blagoveshchensk, across the Zeya River, and looping back south of Heihe.[25]

Blagoveshchensk, like Vladivostok and other sensitive sites along the border, was a closed city for much of the Soviet period. Not only was it closed to Chinese visitors, but Russians themselves, if they lived elsewhere, were able to enter the town only with a special permit. The city is no longer closed today, but this is an exception in the region. Indeed, neighboring villages and even suburbs of Blagoveshchensk have not seen a change in their closed status. While this situation often renders life along the border difficult for local Russians, it is generally accepted as a price worth paying to guarantee the security of the country. It also bestows a special status on those who reside in these zones, since the very lack of human access to the land abutting the border transforms the outer limits of the polity into a sacred space. An epigram attributed to communist revolutionary Sergey Lazo famously reminds Russian citizens that "not everyone is granted the right to tread the last meters of Fatherland." On the Chinese side, where no such protective zones are in place, neither Chinese nor foreigners are restricted from approaching the border. As one Russian interlocutor recounted, it was only when he stood on the Chinese side that he got to see two bears on the Russian bank. "The wildlife there is rich because people are not allowed to go. In fact, only our border guards get to see it."

AUTHENTICITY AND MODERNITY

As the city of Heihe lights up every evening, its sleepy Russian neighbor looks upon this spectacle with a certain level of ambivalence. "It looks really beautiful from here," "It's just a show to attract Russian tourists," and "They're powering these lights with Russian electricity they buy at discount prices; it makes me angry" were some of the comments our questions elicited. While the majority of respondents did not necessarily voice positive assessments, the importance of the light show for the city of Blagoveshchensk was undeniable. The topic regularly came up in conversation, and views of nighttime Heihe even featured among the very small selection of postcards, fridge magnets, and souvenirs available in Blagoveshchensk.

The symbolic significance of nighttime Heihe for Blagoveshchensk residents extends, of course, well beyond the image of economic success that the city of Heihe is celebrating and advertising.[26] For some, it is nothing but a glitzy façade of modernity, barely concealing poverty, dirt, and a rural, uneducated population. For others, it is the trademark of a new frontier town, built with the purchasing power of its Russian neighbor, and symptomatic of a renewed, economically confident China. For most, Heihe's bright riverbank is also a reflective surface, a mirror reminding uneasy onlookers of their own failings. Indeed, while Heihe is booming and expanding ever more rapidly, Blagoveshchensk remains beset by a host of administrative and political hurdles that together cohere into severe growth inhibitors (see Chapter 3).

However, unlike Blagoveshchensk, which is wholly visible to the external gaze, Heihe's exposed face tends to be perceived and described by Russian onlookers as a façade, a mirage.[27] This metaphor of surface as a cover extends seamlessly to ideas of deception and trickery, and to the binary opposition between superficiality and depth. By concealing the inner workings of the self/city, the visible surface remains a mere illusion. This dimension was made explicit by many residents of Blagoveshchensk in my (Franck) conversations with them. Heihe's riverfront development—the only surface of Heihe visible from the other side of the Amur—was consistently described to me as a Potemkin village, a visual trick performed by the Chinese. It was nothing but *pyl' v glaza* (sleight of hand), I was told—a show intended to attract Russian customers. Russian interlocutors pointed out the discrepancy they saw between the surface image of the city as a success story and emergent modernity, on the one hand, and the "real" Heihe, poor, dangerous, and with a low level of "culture," on the other. For them this discrepancy was reflected in the very structure of the city, with the tall modern buildings and the main pedestrian

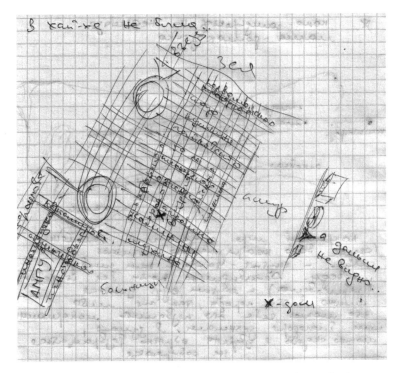

Figure 7.3. Drawing of Blagoveshchensk (*left*) and Heihe (*right*) by a twenty-year-old Russian student who had never traveled to China. Amur State University, Blagoveshchensk, 2011.

street along the Amur River contrasting with the roads further inland, where, allegedly, houses are falling apart and people are dressed shabbily.[28] The façade of Heihe was depicted as an elaborate sham, a commercial lure without any substance—and in fact, although Heihe may not have the suspected failings, much of the city's life is concealed from Russian view, as we describe later. The dual nature of the riverbank as advertising platform and concealment device was made especially clear in a drawing produced by one of the students (Figure 7.3). This student's depiction of Heihe, a city she had not visited, was limited to four buildings. As an explanation, she added, "I can't see any further" (*a dal'she ne vidno*).

The newness of Heihe and its rapid evolution from a settlement into a town also featured among the criticisms. Far from seeing this as a consequence of economic dynamism or a sign that China was able to catch up, the fact that "twenty years ago there was nothing there" appears to confirm for many Blagoveshchensk residents that this newfound modernity has no basis, no realness, that it is nothing but a billboard without any depth.[29] The presence of a supermodern city on the other side of the border is perceived not as a success story for China but as an abnormal humiliation of Russia.[30] As anthropologist Ivan Peshkov explains, this perception of Chinese border towns as inauthentic and nonmodern is due in part to their newness but also in part to their location.[31] Writing about Manzhouli, he notes that the town is seen as a phantom that only imitates modernity—appearing artificially in a region that is ultimately incapable of real progress. In such a perspective, he adds, "the border region is seen as inherently a 'zone of depression,' distant even from Siberian cultural centres. Anyone going to live in Manzhouli is ranked among the lowly, non-prestigious class of small traders."[32]

By contrast, for all its faults, Blagoveshchensk is described by its residents as real and authentic. In spatial terms, the horizontality of the city, with its wide tree-lined avenues and numerous parks, is regularly emphasized.

The opposition between horizontality and verticality, according to Chinese American geographer and theorist Yi-fu Tuan, is fundamental to the human understanding of place. These two different axes stand "symbolically as the antithesis between transcendence and immanence, between the ideal of disembodied consciousness (a skyward spirituality) and the ideal of earthbound identification. Vertical elements in the landscape evoke a sense of striving, a defiance of gravity, while the horizontal elements call to mind acceptance and rest."[33] Thus, as he explains in a more recent article, very tall buildings in a city's skyline mostly cater to the needs of business and financial aspirations, while "work[s] devoted to the body and to the running of government seem to require a feeling of stability and gravitas that is best projected by low-lying buildings."[34]

This equation of elevation with modernity does not seem to hold true in Blagoveshchensk. The surface of the city, and especially what is going on at ground level, appears to take precedence in assessments of development and modernity. In the early 1990s, as Sino-Russian trade was thriving, street markets started to appear in both Heihe and Blagoveshchensk. But if Russian buyers did not seem to mind the lack of quality and the ad hoc stalls and kiosks they saw in Heihe, the emergence of similar economic phenomena at home in Blagoveshchensk proved far more problematic. In Blagoveshchensk, just as in the rest of Russia, markets (pejoratively called "bazaars"—with clear orientalist connotations) were, and are, perceived as "dangerous places." Yet their footprint in the city kept expanding. As Caroline noted in an earlier text, "Bazaars, widely condemned as shady places of speculation, unmoral behaviour and lack of civilization, (re-)emerged as central nodes in trade networks and the universal centre for private consumption."[35] Market traders were seen by middle-class citizens as shady characters, particularly in the first decade after the collapse of the Soviet Union, when economic and commercial exchange remained heavily inflected by socialist moral precepts and a deeply internalized repugnance for "non-productive" profit obtained from buying and reselling. In a later article, Oleg Pachenkov suggests that these associations remain largely current. The open-air market is perceived as a shameful, almost criminal place, inhabited by the "downtrodden who feel that they do not measure up to social standards."[36]

This socialist morality was also linked with an ethnic dimension, since members of Soviet ethnic minorities often came to dominate economic exchange, with Russians relegated to the more passive role of buyers. Although Blagoveshchensk is not a rich city and therefore does not draw many incomers, it had attracted numerous Chinese market traders. However, they fell victim to regulations introduced in March 2007 prohibiting "foreigners" from selling at the market as well as near places where medicine and alcohol were sold.[37] Local Russians generally supported the new rule because they wanted Russians to trade; however, this decision merely led to the closure of the majority of open-air markets, their numbers plummeting from a total of around eighty to fewer than ten. During that time, consumer demand for goods never ceased. When the Chinese began to vanish, traders from former Soviet nations appeared. As a rule, each group has a specific niche: the few remaining Chinese sell goods produced in China, Tajiks sell goods from Europe, and Armenians and Azeris sell what Russians produce. Uzbeks focus on export, specifically to Yakutia, in the very far north of the country, since the city of Blagoveshchensk functions as an informal corridor for Yakuts. In Ulan-Ude, Chita, and other Siberian towns, the Kyrgyz have come to be major traders in cheap shopping malls where they sell goods mostly from China.

Another important aspect of these new economic spaces has been the overwhelming presence of women. As a group, women were hit particularly badly by the collapse of the Soviet Union and the resulting rise in unemployment and non-payment of wages.[38] Initially, many of them started selling items they owned at makeshift flea markets, and later they took a more active role in shuttle trade, importing goods from other towns as well as abroad. It is likely that the preponderant role played by women contributed in some way to the negative evaluation of open-air markets and bazaars in postsocialist Russian society. Women acting as independent, feisty, moneymaking traders jarred with the reappearance of conservative gender norms in the 1990s.[39] Indeed, the reversal of social roles attendant to political cataclysms appears to have been an important factor.

But if gender and social role upheavals are certainly central factors behind the Russian aversion to bazaars and open-air markets, what we wish to suggest here is that the very place where these exchanges occur has also contributed to the low status of these commercial forms. In both official and informal discussions, the driving argument that bazaars are primitive, uncivilized, and transitory and so need to be replaced with "modern" trading arrangements has frequently highlighted the lack of a physical structure for housing these economic exchanges.[40] Indeed, one of the reasons the March 2007 decision to close the Blagoveshchensk markets in the hands of the Chinese received widespread support was the related intention to introduce a more "civilized format" (*tsivilizovannyi format*), specifically a move from the street to an indoor space, and including a formal division between selling areas and storage areas/staff rest areas, as well as the presence of cash registers. The separation between "living area" and "shop" is often absent in Heihe, particularly in small commercial establishments, where the presence of a bed close to the cash register is a common occurrence. This lack of formal division is a particular point on which several informants commented during interviews. These were the kind of examples our Russian interlocutors would provide when discussing "primitive" and "uncivilized" commercial practices, the most primitive of all being the practice of selling goods directly on the street. In other words, the division between "uncivilized" and "civilized" was predicated on the space where the activity was carried out rather than on differences between economic systems (which tend to remain shrouded in mystery for most non-specialists, anyway). It is important to note here the dual meaning of the Russian expression *na ulitse,* meaning both "on the street" and "outside." The commercial activities are taking place not simply on the roadside but "outside," that is, outside of ordered human-made structures. This distinction is not merely linguistic; it is essential to the ways in which urban modernity is conceptualized in Russia.

When Chinese traders (often coming on tourist visas) started operating in Blagoveshchensk, they began by selling their goods and produce on the street, directly on the ground, on a tarp. Later, with some pressure from Russian municipal authorities, they started selling on stalls; in the last few years, most exchanges have been taking place inside dedicated trade centers. The shifts have been structural rather than economic, suggesting that ideas of "commercial modernity" are predicated primarily on the space in which exchanges take place.

To an extent, this is also true in the Chinese context, where a similar trajectory from open-air markets to shopping malls has occurred. However, the coexistence of both forms appears to be less problematic in China, where street markets remain common. Every morning between 6:00 and 9:00, for instance, Hailan Street in central Heihe is closed to cars and turns into a large street market. Farmers from all around the district come to sell fruit, vegetables, clothes, and other household goods, displaying their goods on tarps placed on the pavement. By 9:00 all the traders have gone and the "normal" urban activities of Heihe resume. The temporal bracketing of street market activities is ensured through a special time window enabling farmers to sell their produce without incurring fiscal liabilities. Without this tax break or indeed the possibility to sell directly on the street, it is unlikely farmers would be able to sell their goods in Heihe.

If these markets are not necessarily the image of successful urban modernity that Heihe municipal authorities are keen to project, open-air markets are not as problematic there as they seem to be in Russia. In Heihe such spaces tend to cater to the needs of a "modern," urban workforce—providing a breakfast of fried pancakes on the way to work, or access to fresh and inexpensive fruit and vegetables directly from farmers. In fact, even in large Chinese cities such as Höhhot (Huhehaote), the administrative capital of the Inner Mongolia Autonomous Region, the cohabitation of large avenues and street markets is common. In Russia, by contrast, these markets are largely perceived to be incompatible with ideals of urban modernity. To a degree, these ideals bear the imprint of Western economic models introduced in the early 1990s, but in some cases they seem to have developed earlier.[41] During the Soviet period, for example, there was a large *kolkhoz* (collective farm) bazaar in Blagoveshchensk at the intersection of two central avenues, on the location of the principal *yarmarka*, or trade center.[42] Deemed too close to the city center and to administrative and government buildings, it was moved three blocks away. This reluctance to tolerate open-air markets in central locations continues to be seen with the general displacement of shopping precincts away from city centers that is taking place in a number of Russian cities, such as Irkutsk and Saint Petersburg.[43] This consistent drive to displace and/or contain bazaars (in the literal sense of placing them into containing structures) appears to be predicated less on a reluctance to participate in the bazaars' loosely organized form of economic exchange than on their cultural associations with nonmodernity. This was indeed the official rationale behind the closure in 2003 of the dozens of flea markets that had emerged in Saint Petersburg about a decade earlier. In preparation for the celebration of the 300th anniversary of the city, open-air markets were eliminated in order "not to disgrace and shame the city in the eyes of the respectable foreign guests."[44] The sole surviving market, the Udelniy flea market, located in the city's outskirts, is not even mentioned in tourist guides.[45] Seen as incompatible with the modern face of the city, it simply does not figure in official discourse.

The numerous kiosks and other private commercial spaces that came to punctuate the urban landscape of postsocialist Russia in the 1990s, while not as problematic as bazaars, were also seen as not fully integrated within the city's fabric. Informally referred to as "lumps" (*komok*, from *kommercheskii kiosk*) or "commercial dots" (*kommercheskie tochki*), they tended to be perceived as "something that broke out of the existing environment (lumps) or as something that only punctuated it (dots)."[46] The disjunctive nature of these new commercial forms was also visible through the new naming practices that accompanied their emergence. Unlike the generic and descriptive names (such as Secondary School Number 17) that had previously mapped out the urban environment, private shops and kiosks were given exotic names in French or Italian, a tendency that anthropologist Sergei Oushakine sees as symptomatic of an attempt to "reconfigure public space by establishing new historical and geographic connections."[47]

As historian Dipesh Chakrabarty has argued, modernity is a notion that stubbornly eludes definition.[48] If in both Russian and Chinese contexts terms such as "progress" (Russ: *progress;* Ch: *jinbu*) and "backwardness" (Russ: *otstalost'*; Ch: *luohou*) continue to bookend the teleological march toward a modern society, what modernity itself might be remains very cloudy. What is perhaps clearer, for Russians and to a large extent for Chinese as well, is *where* that elusive modernity might be located. For Russians, modernity is undeniably "the West," or more precisely a fantasy of the West, imagined as sanitary and rational, that is, without street markets, and with all commercial activity contained within structures. The imaginary dimension is fundamental here: if in their urban development both Russia and China have global cities such as New York or Dubai in mind—an imaginary of these global cities, given that few in the region have visited them—they are not following a single, linear path.[49] In fact, structurally Heihe and Blagoveshchensk differ fundamentally from each other.

In their conversations with me (Franck), Blagoveshchensk residents routinely pointed out the town's rectilinear quality, and this aspect was frequently emphasized in drawings made by students (see Figures 7.3 and 7.4). According to Maria, a political scientist working at Amur State University, the Russian cultural preference for grid-like regularity as a marker of progress and modernity is particularly strong in a town such as Blagoveshchensk, which was a military outpost and retains this "Roman fort"

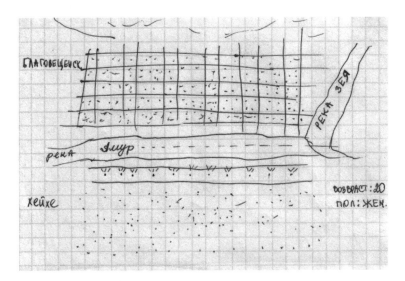

Figure 7.4. Drawing of Blagoveshchensk (*top*) and Heihe (*bottom*) by a twenty-year-old Russian student. Amur State University, Blagoveshchensk, 2011.

quality.[50] "We are still modernists here," she quipped. "Blagoveshchensk hasn't reached postmodernism yet!"[51]

While regularity in the urban road network is of course not exclusive to Russia—indeed, most American cities are built on a similar regular pattern—there is perhaps something specific in the cultural significance this appears to have in the Russian context.[52] As Yi-fu Tuan has noted, if for Americans the open plains figured in social imaginations as a symbol of opportunity and freedom, for Russian peasants, boundless space was seen primarily as a source of anxiety: "It connoted despair rather than opportunity; it inhibited rather than encouraged action. It spoke of man's paltriness as against the immensity and indifference of nature."[53] It needed to be conquered and enclosed in order to become safe.

Blagoveshchensk's grid layout was imposed from the outset, marking the town's place as beacon of modernity on the fringes

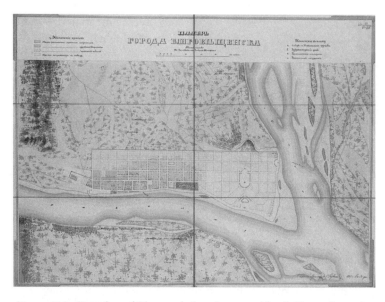

Figure 7.5. City plan of Blagoveshchensk, created by S. Krovrelin and dated December 30, 1869. The two small settlements marked on the Chinese side of the Amur River are now part of Heihe.
(Library of Congress, Meeting of Frontiers)

of empire.[54] This modern stamp is clearly visible in the city plan drawn in 1869 (see Figure 7.5), and is something that was in fact replicated in the creation of Russian cities across Chinese Manchuria. The cities of Harbin and Dalian, unlike the west European cosmopolitan and commercial treaty ports that emerged throughout China, were the first cities in China's modern history to be the subject of comprehensive urban plans.[55] Dalian was planned to have major roads radiating from the city center. A sense of formality and grandeur emanated "through the arrangement of broad boulevards connected at key nodes and junctions often landscaped as public parks, forming a more dense urban grain with minor streets serving residential or smaller commercial functions."[56]

Essential to this mesh-like horizontal layer is the materiality of the roads themselves. On this point, a fascinating tension between "structure" and "surface" emerged in interviews and informal conversations. While Blagoveshchensk's gridded road network was described as superior to Heihe's less rigid infrastructure, the actual surface of Russian roads was deplored. Tanya, a young woman in her thirties who lives in Heihe and works remotely, with her employer's main office in Blagoveshchensk, pointed out: "Roads in Russia are generally very bad. As the saying goes, Russia has two misfortunes: fools and roads [*v Rossii dve bedy: duraki i dorogi*]. Our roads in Blagoveshchensk are full of potholes and are often quite dangerous. When Putin came to visit, they resurfaced all the streets where his car was going to pass through. But only those!"

The higher quality of the road surface in China, by contrast, was a point consistently arising in all comparisons between cities. As with the riverfront discussed in the preceding section, the smooth roads of Heihe were read primarily through an imagery of deception and concealment. Metaphorically, this reading of the surface resonates with widespread Russian perceptions of Chinese culture as mysterious and impenetrable, and with pervasive Russian suspicions that Chinese operate in Blagoveshchensk behind "seemingly Russian" businesses.

Paradoxically, it is precisely beyond the surface—both behind the riverfront façade and underground—that clues to Heihe's continued urban growth and emerging modernity are to be found. If, undeniably, the city's riverbank is staged as a large billboard advertising the city's newfound wealth and economic prosperity, it may be rash to brush it aside as a mere illusion. Contrary to common Russian claims that all the tallest buildings in Heihe are pressed against the river and that they conceal an economic and cultural poverty, Heihe's hinterland is in fact where the newest and tallest developments are to be found. In recent years, a manic spurt of construction has taken place on the southeastern edge of the city, but because most Russian visitors rarely venture beyond the main shopping streets running immediately parallel to the riverbank, these developments have not been visible to them.[57] Yet it is in these inner layers, rather than the immediate façade, that the bulk of Heihe's urban modernity is found.

In fact, except for its central node overtly focused on Russia, Heihe is very much a typical Chinese city, displaying a strong preference for upward construction. Dutch architectural theorist Rem Koolhaas has pointed out this modern evolution in Chinese construction projects, concluding that "the skyline rises in the East."[58] Similarly, in an analysis of recent urban practices in China, Aihwa Ong has drawn attention to the emergence of hyperarchitecture and to what she terms the "spectacularization of urban success."[59] Of course, China does not have an exclusive claim to vertical modernity, but the preponderance of such forms in China stands out dramatically in comparisons of Blagoveshchensk and Heihe. In the former, high-rises are both less common and less central to the self-image the city seeks to project. In fact, the tallest, most modern structure, right in the center of Blagoveshchensk, is the Asia Hotel, a Chinese-made, Chinese-owned building. At 215 feet in height, the building dominates the city and offers panoramic views of Heihe from its top-floor rotating restaurant. It is also the best hotel in the city, and is advertised in Heihe as Blagoveshchensk's "Chinese people's hotel" (中国人的饭店).

In Heihe, the best hotel is the Heihe International Hotel (Ch: 黑河国际饭店; Russ: Gostinitsa "Mezhdunarodnaya"). Located on the riverbank, it is the tallest building in that part of town. It is also one of the buildings brightly illuminated at night. Despite its prime location and alleged Russian focus, it is mostly patronized by non-Russians. Overwhelmingly, it is Chinese businesspeople who stay there. In fact, in stark contrast to the many small businesses found at street level in its vicinity, the Heihe International Hotel is one of the few commercial places where Russian is not spoken. Unlike local shopkeepers who hail potential customers with emphatic calls of "Druga! Druga!," the hotel staff, from the reception desk to the bellboys, do not speak even rudimentary Russian.[60] A vivid symbol of the reduced role played by Russian purchasing power in the development of Heihe, and emblematic of the opposition between the economic realms of the horizontal and vertical planes, is that the Russian-language sign for the hotel lies on the roof, discarded and forgotten.

Interestingly, the "rooftop view" of Sino-Russian economic exchange finds an unlikely mirror image in the activities taking place below ground. Running directly under one of the main commercial streets where Russians come to shop is a long underground corridor focused largely on Chinese customers. The corridor is about 10 feet wide, with small commercial outlets on both sides, each side occupying roughly the same footprint as the main passageway. It extends for several blocks under Xing'an Street (兴安街), from Ying'en Road (迎恩路) to Dongxing Road (东兴路), with a food court at its western end. The corridor runs along a single east-west axis, except for a short section branching out from the middle of the corridor and extending south for one block. Unlike the space just above it at street level, where Russian shoppers are constantly hailed by shopkeepers and intermediaries (*pomogaiki*) and where shop windows display various signs in Russian, shoppers below ground are rarely greeted and nearly all signs are in Chinese. There are very few Russian shoppers. Below ground, as in Heihe's best hotel or around the urban development taking place on the southern edge of the city, Russians are conspicuous by their absence.

In fact, the majority of the goods on display, particularly in underground spaces but also more and more at street level, are now intended for the internal Chinese market. A clear indication of this trend is the increasing difficulties Russian women encounter when searching for clothes that fit them. Whereas in the early 1990s clothes were produced specifically for the Russian market, in recent years the focus has shifted in favor of local consumers. In part, this shift is attributable to changes in Russian customs regulations. In the early 1990s Russian shuttle traders could take home up to 100 kg (220 pounds) of goods per trip, but over the last decade the quota has been significantly reduced, down to a mere 10 kg a day. Recently the quota was again increased to 50 kg a day, provided the carrier has stayed for a minimum of three days in China. This means that the earlier *kirpichi* activity is no longer as profitable. At present, when individuals do work as *kirpichi,* it tends to be because they happen to be going to Heihe anyway, so they might as well bring the maximum quota of goods back with them and offset the cost of the trip.[61]

While the implementation of these new customs regulations has had wide repercussions for Blagoveshchensk residents, Heihe does not appear to have suffered. According to Ivan, an economics professor at Amur State University, currently only 5 percent of goods on sale in Heihe are targeted at Russian customers, with the remaining 95 intended for Chinese consumers. "Russia has merely been an accelerator for Heihe's development. The city has now gained its own momentum. Should the border close tomorrow, Heihe would continue to thrive. For Blagoveshchensk, however, things would become much more difficult."

If these economic trends are evident to economists such as Ivan, they tend to remain invisible to the general Russian population. Recurrent in interviews was the notion that Heihe was heavily reliant on Russians and that all construction was geared to them. And yet, as mentioned earlier, most of the construction currently carried out in Heihe takes place inland, well away from the riverbank. These misperceptions may be due to the lack of visibility of the new construction sites, found in parts of the city rarely visited by Russians, but they also index a reluctance by Russians to accept China's very real economic progress.[62]

Similarly, in interviews and discussions with Russians, verticality was rarely emphasized, even though the city of Blagoveshchensk also has a number of high-rise buildings, notably the hypermodern Asia Hotel. Instead, the elements consistently accentuated as markers of progress, modernity, and civilization were all located on the horizontal plane. They were the gridded structure of the transport system, the broadness of the roads, and the cleanliness of the pavements. This emphasis on a brand of modernity reliant on Soviet norms and the reluctance to engage with the forms of modernity deployed in Heihe have been partly sustained by the realization that Blagoveshchensk lacks the financial resources to compete with its Chinese neighbor.[63]

FRACTURED TIMELINES

"When visitors come to our city, they like to look at Heihe's lights from the Russian embankment," explained Dasha, a student at Blagoveshchensk Pedagogical Institute. "But because the two cities are so close, occasionally a visitor will not realize they're looking at China. They point at Heihe and ask how they can reach the city center."

Such misunderstandings feel particularly insulting to Blagoveshchensk residents. Originally an outpost of European presence in an uncharted East, the Russian city long perceived itself as a beacon of enlightenment in Asia, shining a light onto a dark and mostly empty space. Over the last two decades, as the small village of Heihe grew into a full-size city, Blagoveshchensk has seen its place as a model of modernity challenged and significantly weakened. This notion of being a beacon extends well beyond the metaphoric. The issue of physical illuminations is in fact crucial given the importance of electrification campaigns in the early socialist period and their significance with regard to modernity. Electric light, through its powerful association with notions of higher understanding and culture, was seen as the metonymic emblem of a single grand narrative, that of modernity itself.[64] The common power outages and thefts of copper and aluminum wire that since the early 1990s have occasionally plunged sections of Siberian cities into darkness are thus frequently seen as nothing less than the failure of this modernist grand narrative. As anthropologist Sergei Oushakine writes, people routinely complain of having been left in the dark (*ostavili v temnote*) and of being cut off from the rest of the world (*otrezali ot mira*).[65] In the context of Blagoveshchensk, the fact that it is the Chinese side that is now brightly illuminated is therefore symbolically potent as well as a destabilizing factor.

In spite of its relatively modest size, Heihe is one of the forty or so Chinese cities that announced, as early as the 1990s, their intention to become "global cities" (*quanqiu chengshi*).[66] In fact, Heihe's daily spectacle of lights is directed at the Russian city across the Amur just as much as it is at a domestic audience. With an equivalence between lighting and modernity that holds true in the Chinese context as well as in Russia, Heihe—and China overall—is challenging its subaltern position with respect to Russia. If until 1989 China was the Soviet Union's "younger brother"—a familial order that also described the relationships of the other Soviet republics to Russia—this hierarchy has now been upended.

For Russia, this reversal of hierarchies is much more significant than simply a loss of cultural relevance. It also implies the breaking down of a developmental model and a particular sense of unfolding history. With the collapse of the Soviet Union, Russia experienced an important loss, that of a promised bright future that has failed to come to fruition.[67] In a cultural and political context where Russia was imagined to be on the cusp of attaining socialism, future and present had come to be coextensive. This was aptly described by anthropologist Nikolai Ssorin-Chaikov with respect to his field site in subarctic Siberia, which was perceived as being in a constant process of construction "in which the end is constantly deferred, the initial point almost forgotten, and the most stable constructs are not what is being built but structures that are supposed to be mere tools of construction."[68] In an environment where the present was always about to materialize and where the temporary was permanent, the end of the socialist era led to a temporal fracture difficult to resolve, a break with its past as well as with its future. The current desire to reinvigorate Russia and to reinstate its global standing is thus the yearning for a glorious past, but it is also the mourning of an incomplete utopia, a nostalgic longing for a lost future yet to be realized.[69]

The Soviet Union's view of history was a long teleological march from feudalism to socialism by way of capitalism, along which the Soviet Union—and specifically Russia—would lead the world proletariat. For most Asian nations such as Mongolia (but also China, which many classified as "feudal"), the assumption was that the transition to socialism could bypass capitalism altogether. In such a context, the recent meteoric transformation of China into a global power while retaining Communist Party rule, rendering Russia's benevolent guidance obsolete, constitutes in effect a complete overturning of Russian assumptions regarding cultural hierarchies and linear development. These fractures in evolutionary timelines go a long way to account for Russia's general reluctance to accept China's claims of modernity at face value, and for its tendency to interpret China's urban development as an illusion without any depth.

In recent years, there has been much discussion in the global media about Chinese "ghost towns"—brand-new but barely inhabited cities. The origins of the term with respect to China—specifically the Kangbashi New District, a coal-mining boomtown in China's Inner Mongolia Autonomous Region—are traceable to two news reports, one by Al-Jazeera and the other by *Time* magazine.[70] These initial reports led to many media stories, accompanied by striking shots of endless urban vistas with not a single person in sight. These eerie photographs—some of them contrived, all eminently Instagrammable—have fed into a global imaginary unwilling to take China's rapid pace of development as genuine.[71] But as journalist Wade Shepard has noted, the planning of new cities is a long-term game whose natural timeline doesn't exactly match that of the global economy. The Chinese "ghost cities" that were so prevalently showcased in 2013 and

2014 are no longer global stories today: they have filled up to the point of being functioning, normal cities.[72] And rather than such new developments being a sign that infrastructure is outpacing demand, fueled by unsustainable debt and overinvestment, some analysts suggest that the Chinese Communist Party is instead attempting a "carefully controlled mode of urbanization and social transformation that is designed precisely to avoid the unpredictable effects of ad hoc and informal urbanization."[73]

Interestingly, this urbanization phenomenon, frequently criticized by Russians, was also the model on which Dalian was developed. As Edward Denison and Guangyu Ren write, at the turn of the twentieth century Dalian was a boomtown without any reason for a "boom," signaling ambitions that were novel and audacious, but also chimerical:

> Behind ambitious plans and exorbitant budgets there was an omnipresent sense of ephemeral opportunism lingering over Russian Dalian. The harbour had been built, but there were no ships. Not yet at least. Macadamised roads criss-crossed the empty plain on which the city had been laid out on paper but had yet to be built in brick or stone. One road had even been carved through mountains at considerable expense so as to reach the sandy coastal beaches where "future millionaires of Dalny will have their summer bungalows." But the millionaires were nowhere to be seen.[74]

MIMETIC RIVALRY

In spite of stark cultural and ethnic differences, the very proximity of Heihe and Blagoveshchensk, in combination with the distance that separates them from their respective political centers, brings the two cities closer together. Declared twin cities by their respective municipalities, they form an exceedingly odd pair. Structurally dissimilar but sharing a common geographical space, they are evolving along contrasting paths, and yet details in their development often betray the cultural influence each exerts on the other. The two cities are caught in a dynamic tension between integration and separation. In a financially symbiotic relation, the two administrations constantly seek to foster cooperation and goodwill. This mutual desire for integration is visible at many levels, particularly cultural. A strong partnership is seen by both parties as a guarantee for future success and development. To reinforce existing links, more and more international cultural events are being organized by the two localities, such as Sino-Russian art exhibitions or an annual swimming competition across the river, the Sino-Russian Heilongjiang Friendship (中俄友谊黑龙江).

Each city also stands to the other as representative of its nation. Their urbanization models and decisions extend therefore beyond the local: Heihe stands in for China, just as Blagoveshchensk is shorthand for Russia.[75] As mentioned earlier in this chapter, one of the core differences between these two cities is the extent to which Heihe (as well as other Chinese border towns) has sought to integrate Russian imagery into its development. From statues of bears to giant matryoshka dolls, Heihe markets itself as a liminal space, halfway between China and Russia. While to outsiders it looks like a typical Chinese city, to a Chinese audience the presence of Russian symbols (and visitors) feels exotic. For Russians living on the other side, this appropriation of their cultural symbols is not always seen positively, as when Heihe's municipal authorities introduced a new design for the city's trash cans in the shape of matryoshka dolls—eliciting much anger from Russians, who interpreted this choice as the making of a visual equivalence between Russian culture and garbage. In conversations with Blagoveshchensk residents, two assumptions dominate: that this urban furniture is there to attract tourists, and that these symbols are meant to make Russians feel at home and therefore spend more time and money on the Chinese side.

If this cultural liminality is clearly commercially motivated, the object of these seductive practices is, somewhat surprisingly, not China's Russian neighbors but a domestic audience. When Chinese border towns such as Heihe, Manzhouli, and Suifenhe mushroomed in the early 1990s, their prime resource was initially the Russian population just across the border. But with the ruble falling in value against the yuan (in 2008, 2014, and again in 2020), China is no longer the attractively cheap destination it once was.

The same foreign flavor dominates in all Chinese border towns, and perhaps nowhere more evidently than in Manzhouli. From a bustling hub for Sino-Russian trade, Manzhouli has now been transformed into a prime destination for domestic tourists.[76] Chinese traders who had spent time acquiring conversational Russian to conduct their business have switched their focus to the well-to-do from central and southern China who visit Manzhouli for its less polluted air and the chance to sample the foreign and mysterious culture of China's northern neighbor.[77] Some of the key items now sold in town to Chinese tourists are matryoshka dolls, exotic fur coats, and Russian chocolate.[78] As a result, Manzhouli now plays the role of "Russia" for the Chinese and "China" for the Russians.[79] With each side seemingly preferring a "simulacrum of the other over direct contact," it has become a phantasmatic city, a "place for constant intercultural dialogue as well as constant and inevitable miscommunication and misunderstanding."[80]

Albeit on a much smaller scale, Heihe has followed the same strategy to try to capitalize on its location and attain greater visibility. Heihe has a much smaller footprint than Manzhouli, and unlike Manzhouli, it is not positioned at a commercial crossroad between three countries. However, its location, right across from Blagoveshchensk, is unique. It offers Chinese tourists the opportunity to observe Russia up close without having to apply for a tourist visa. The boat experience offered to them takes them close to the Russian embankment before bringing them back safely to Heihe where, on an entire block of Hailan Street, they can purchase Russian souvenirs and delicatessen items. On the edge of the city, a model Russian village was also erected, presenting in idealized form a traditional Russian environment, complete with windmill, bakery, and even a small cathedral—a scaled-down model of Harbin's St. Sophia.[81]

These particular Chinese representations of Russia are largely positive, but they are not based in any real dialogue. The imaginary of Russia they project has been filtered through state narratives rather than representing the outcome of a lived experience. The model Russian village is in fact located next to another exhibit of "traditional Russia"—a full-scale replica of wooden barracks that served as the location for the filming of a famous story of wartime Sino-Russian friendship. The movie set has been turned into an exhibition space, and each building features props such as guns and uniforms as well as pictures of the main actors. Like other Chinese representations of Russia in the particular context of Chinese commercial consumption, this one portrays Russians as friends and allies.[82]

Geographer Joseph Rykwert refers to such miniaturizations as "mimetic condensation." He notes that even centuries ago, "pilgrimages to remote and sacred places were replicated for those who could not afford to leave home. The fourteen stations of the cross, which you may find in any Roman Catholic church, are a miniaturized and atrophied version of the pilgrimage around the holy places in Jerusalem."[83] This process was employed as a way to control, tame, and appropriate what was alien and remote.[84]

In China's contemporary context, this important insight is only a partial explanation for these replications. An excellent study of Chinese mimesis by journalist Bianca Bosker illustrates how Chinese mimetic practices—particularly in the context of architecture—are much more than simple reproductions.[85] Even in the case of faithful imitations, they frequently incorporate key living features that Chinese residents refuse to relinquish, such as auspicious orientation (*fengshui*). Overall, Chinese mimetic architecture appears to be less concerned with exact replication than with achieving a particularly Chinese vision.[86] This is visible to some extent in Heihe, but is especially evident in other border towns, such as Manzhouli.

Mimetic architecture is of course more than a border town phenomenon—the German Anting Town, British Thames Town, and Swedish Luodian Town in Shanghai's vicinity are good examples of this. But whereas these Shanghai suburbs were designed explicitly to convey a sense of living in Germany, Britain, or Sweden, border towns such as Heihe or Manzhouli have styled themselves as liminal places where local Chineseness is enmeshed with, and enriched by, the culture across the border.[87] These border liminalities extend well beyond the idea of overlapping frontiers between two cultural realms; they tend to draw on a wide range of Western architectural heritage, including Greco-Roman. Rather than try to achieve faithful copies, they have used Russia as one among several European inspirations to foster a convivial environment. Manzhouli has similarly capitalized on its position at the border between China, Russia, and Mongolia, and its buildings mimic European architecture. Interestingly, Mongolian culture, such as Buddhist monastic architecture, is not one that China is attempting to emulate, despite Manzhouli's proximity to the Mongolian border. Instead, Mongolia is represented by horse rides and yurt camps for the benefit of tourists. A number of theme parks have also sprung up close to the border gates (*guomen*)—for instance, Matryoshka Park features representations of famous Russian and Western personalities as disparate as Charlie Chaplin, Audrey Hepburn, and Jesus.

This surprising combination of heterogenous influences again indicates that Chinese mimesis is not a matter of slavish reproduction. The models these architectural copies have followed are all from the West, and largely from countries that at one point or another in history were China's colonizers. Chinese mimetic practices may thus be seen as a reappropriation and transcendence, on Chinese terms, of this colonial past. The confidence that underpins these practices is clear in view of the very scale of these reproductions. The largest matryoshka in the world is found in Manzhouli, not in Russia, and the fact that the Chinese lay claim to such an emblematic Russian symbol is certainly not lost on Russians.[88] Similar processes of "mimetic rivalry" are also at work in Heihe, where a massive Ferris wheel has been erected on the riverbank.[89] Not only is it much larger than the one in Blagoveshchensk, but it is also perfectly situated to be visible from the center of the Russian city. As a young student at Amur State University explained, "The new wheel they've built, twice as high as the one in Blagoveshchensk, is just across from 50th October Street, so that when people come to our city, the Chinese wheel is the first thing they see."

Chinese replication practices often seem very alien to Russians. There are, to our knowledge, no similar recreations of Chinese environments on the Russian side of the border. On the contrary, the subject of Chinatowns in the Russian Far East is presented as a nightmarish prospect and has been actively mobilized by Russian actors seeking to restrict Chinese presence in the region. Blagoveshchensk, like other cities in the Russian Far East, has thus not sought to style itself as a liminal space. The Russian city has also been very resistant to adopting practices seen in Heihe, such as the use of lights on prominent buildings.

Similarly, while Heihe's embankment had been turned into a pedestrian promenade, the Russian riverbank long remained undeveloped. It was only following Putin's visit to Blagoveshchensk in summer 2011 that funds were finally allocated to revamp the city. By October, excavation had begun and trucks were dumping sand all along the banks of the Amur to create prime riverfront real estate. A little over a year later, the first section of the new embankment opened to the public.[90] This came as a pleasant surprise for the majority of Blagoveshchensk residents, who had been steadfastly convinced the project would never go ahead. The popular consensus deemed the new riverbank development a resounding success, "much better than Heihe's."

Comparisons with Heihe are of course inevitable. As anthropologist Aihwa Ong has argued, urban transformations involve "unavoidable practices of inter-city comparison, referencing, or modeling."[91] In twin cities, and especially cities such as Heihe and Blagoveshchensk, which are located on a fault line between two different "civilizations," these processes are even more manifest.

The recent evolution of urban practices in Blagoveshchensk suggests that the Russian city has not been altogether immune to its neighbor's cultural influence. Local newspaper articles covering the design and inauguration of the new embankment thus made explicit reference to Heihe's, with no small dose of revanchist glee.

Sometimes urban influences are also traceable to the materiality of objects. Old Blagoveshchensk was built of solid dark red brick, but that is hardly used today. Because so much building material is imported directly from China rather than manufactured locally, new urban developments often have a very Chinese flavor. A case in point is the new trash cans that adorn the revamped embankment. Bought from China, they not only are identical to the trash cans found all over China but also bear Chinese-language instructions that distinguish recyclable items from non-recyclable ones, as well as Chinese-language stickers indicating the compartments where old batteries and cigarette butts should be deposited. Such aspects rarely register as "cultural influences," and in fact none of our interlocutors appeared to have noticed them. Yet it is precisely such material elements that together aggregate into a city's overall image and branding. What makes a city immediately recognizable as American, Russian, or Chinese is often seemingly insignificant elements such as road markings, mailboxes, and street signage.[92] Here Blagoveshchensk's very proximity to China, combined with an economic imbalance favoring imports from China, greatly facilitates the bleeding across the border of these Chinese urban forms.[93]

Other dramatic transformations in the course of the last few years have been the city's policies with regard to public illumination. Having long criticized Heihe's practice of nighttime "light shows" as garish, Blagoveshchensk now appears to be following suit. As the municipality's principal architect explained in a newspaper article, the city should elicit a festive mood (*prazdnichnoe nastroenie*) when you walk around it at night. If ideally the local authorities would like all buildings to be lit, precedence should first be given to historically significant buildings found on the principal thoroughfares. That these measures are Blagovesh-chensk's "tailored response to its Chinese counterpart" (*svoeo-brazny otvet kitaiskoi storone*) is clear from the priority given to the riverbank: even before the two central thoroughfares, Lenin Street and 50th October Street, the very first place to be illuminated was Krasnoflotskaya Street, a minor road running along the embankment, right across from central Heihe.

As mentioned earlier, a military feel and a strong emphasis on patriotism and national pride pervade Blagoveshchensk's new embankment. The fact that the construction of this kind of embankment has taken place at a time when Russia appears to be regaining confidence and is exhibiting the political will to stand up to the United States and Europe is not coincidental. In conjunction with this emphasis on nationalist and patriotic drive, Blagoveshchensk has also been witnessing a recent surge of interest in traditional architecture, as well as new constructions inspired by the first buildings erected in Blagoveshchensk in the mid-nineteenth century. According to Olga, an economics professor at Blagoveshchensk's Amur State University, these urban forms, just like the new embankment, are somewhat Disneyesque in their approach. "I don't like the new embankment," she confided. "It reminds me of Chinese copies, in the sense that they too try to mimic traditional architecture, but all they end up with are bad copies." In her opinion, the old buildings found in Blagovesh-chensk were already poor copies of the imperial architecture found in western Russia. "The prerevolutionary residents of the town were rich merchants but not necessarily well educated. They had often more money than taste. As a result, the buildings they erected in Blagoveshchensk had different aesthetics. The colors were too bright, even garish, not subdued like in Europe. The buildings were also inspired by different periods and styles—New Russian and Modern—but were in fact neither." For her, the new architectural forms currently seen in Blagoveshchensk seek to emulate the noble aristocratic style of Blagoveshchensk's pre-revolutionary period but are just poor thirdhand copies. In our conversation, Olga was especially critical of the embankment's gazebo (*besedka*), which she described as a parody—an attempt at projecting an image of aristocracy and taste, but ultimately tasteless and vulgar.

Her interpretation of this "neo-traditional" architecture is interesting, as it suggests that Blagoveshchensk's urban development, despite trying to convey an impression of historical weight, in fact closely resembles the mimetic practices typical of Chinese border towns such as Heihe or Manzhouli. As in Chinese border towns, the impetus is not to recreate faithfully a certain style but to draw inspiration from it. While in Heihe and Manzhouli the aim of including Russian architectural elements is to convey a sense of international flavor, in Blagoveshchensk the mimetic process serves to reinforce Russia's cultural and historic hold on the region. The presence of traditional architecture speaks both to a 150-year-old presence on the banks of the Amur and to a cultural predominance over China. These new, faux-traditional buildings in Blagoveshchensk constitute an attempt to reiterate the old architectural tropes of cultural dominance.

In spite of these ambitions, Blagoveshchensk's recent architectural projects clearly betray China's increasing power to influence and mold urban evolution in the region. In the last couple of years, the municipal authorities have reclaimed 110 acres of the riverbank's alluvial grounds with the view to building a complex of iconic buildings and hypermodern infrastructure, such as tall skyscrapers and a cable car linking the Chinese and Russian banks. Rather grandiose, especially given the modest size and regional importance of Blagoveshchensk, this ambitious project— just like the new policy concerning city illuminations—is clearly a signal being sent to Heihe.[94]

Other projects currently under consideration and/or under construction in Blagoveshchensk, such as Little Venice and Little Holland, are testaments to the significant influence exerted by China with respect to urban developments. After all, it is Chinese real estate companies who have access to the necessary funds, and the influence of their aesthetic can be seen in other border cities such as Vladivostok.[95] Little Venice is to be developed on a 22-acre vacant lot opposite Druzhba Park. The plans envisage the construction of a large complex encompassing trade, exhibition, and sport centers, hotels, cafés, and restaurants. The site, to be built in a Venetian style, will come complete with a canal and gondolas. The project is the brainchild of He Wen'an, the Chinese owner of the Asia Hotel in Blagoveshchensk. A further project called Little Holland, also owned by He Wen'an, is currently under consideration. If it goes ahead, it will create a residential complex of Dutch-style buildings over a network of canals in one of the city's riverside areas.

At first glance, Heihe and Blagoveshchensk are two very different cities, each one in many respects emblematic of its own nation. Yet a closer look at the recent evolution of their urban practices reveals considerable overlap through a dialogical process of borrowing, inspiration, and mimesis. This mutual cross-pollination does not mean that the two cities are becoming fundamentally more similar. But they are clearly employing an increasingly similar architectural vocabulary and becoming ever more commensurable. Blagoveshchensk's decisions to redesign its riverbank and to illuminate the buildings that line the Amur River are a sign of engagement and competition as well as self-redefinition. One-upmanship is not simply a passive copying of the other, but a more complex and inherently dialogical process whereby the "groups concerned are making claims to equality as well as to superiority."[96]

After decades of hermetic closure of the international border, the mirroring effect provided by the twinning of two dramatically different urban environments is leading to significant cross-fertilizations. The evolving relations of this odd urban pairing are perhaps best understood through anthropologist Anna Tsing's fertile metaphor of friction.[97] "Friction" in this context denotes primarily an affective force, not reducible to negative or positive outcomes, but potentially spanning both. Friction stands here as the generative energy produced through the physical and involuntary coming together of two different cultures. It is perhaps precisely through this friction at the border, in the jostling of bodies, ideas, and cultural values, that Russia's declaration of a "pivot to the East" (*povorot na vostok*) is gaining weight and momentum.

CODA

Bridging the Gap?

Given the fluidity and rapidity with which current events are evolving, the explosive nature of social movements, the changes under way as a result of climate warming, the unpredictability of the trajectory of the current coronavirus pandemic, and the increasingly authoritarian quality of many world governments, we would be hard put to make even short-term predictions about the relationship between Russia and China.[1] It will continue to evolve in line with geopolitical developments, and notably with Russia's and China's own relationships with Washington, and these can change rapidly.[2]

It is unlikely, however, that a future rapprochement with Washington will cause either China or Russia to jettison their partnership. China's diplomatic support of Russia's domestic system is an existential issue for the Putin regime, and "as long as China treats Russia as an equal, never criticizes it publicly, and is careful about not challenging it directly in their shared neighborhood, the partnership will continue to meet both sides' interests."[3] But as Bobo Lo has argued, this remains a marriage of convenience: privately, Chinese experts do not share Putin's belief that Russia is a global power equal to the United States or China.[4] For its part, Russia is careful to avoid taking a clear position in the dispute between China and the United States.[5] Anxious about being suffocated in China's embrace and reluctant to be seen as overly dependent on its southern neighbor, Russia has also been eager to diversify its relationships and has been actively courting other partners, in particular India.[6] In its development specifically of the Far East region, Moscow has recently sought investments from states other than China—for example, looking to attract Japan and South Korea—a move that bears "testimony to its uneasiness about China's rise and the Kremlin's hedging strategies against the possible negative consequences of Beijing's increase in power."[7] China, meanwhile, is seeking to restructure its production away from a reliance on Western markets and to use its financial, technological, and consumption drivers to promote regional Asia-sited manufacturing and services—all of which would draw a penumbra of countries into China's orbit.

Political predictions are always a difficult endeavor. Fortunately, this is not what this book is about. As anthropologists and border specialists, we are less concerned about the policies and "turns" announced from the capitals than about what happens on the ground. We speak of Russians and Chinese in all their variegated complexities, not about disembodied "Moscow" and "Beijing." Our focus on the border and the people who reside there offers a useful distance from officialdom, and indeed, the dynamics we encountered at the border were frequently at odds with the narratives dominating national news. Social relations between Russians and Chinese, while they do evolve, change at a much slower pace than the political situation. As a result, the diversified picture that emerges in this book provides cultural context crucial to triangulate the significance, reverberations, and limitations of larger geopolitical shifts.

Perhaps the most revealing story the border has to tell about how the two countries actually function is that of the continuing absence of fully working bridges across the Amur. This is where China's Belt and Road Initiative peters out upon meeting the reality of Russia. The two spurs of the BRI crossing the border at Tongjiang and Heihe were intended to be thriving corridors, accelerating transport and shortening journey times from China to Russia and onward to Europe. But a bridge linking two significantly different political entities is always more than just a matter of engineering. When pondering the idea of *res publica* (public matters), Oleg Kharkhordin, a trenchant and original commentator on Russian political thought, argued that the materiality implied by the word *res* (things) should be taken seriously, and he used the bridge as a prime example. Examining the medieval Great Bridge of Novgorod, which linked the Kremlin side of town (governing, mercantile) with the religious side, he wrote, "The bridge is an obvious example of a thing that the whole city shares, an example of *res publica,* common affairs or concerns."[8]

Our book has tried to probe the significant differences between China and Russia and the problem of sharing *res publica* between two sovereign states by examining actual practices. We have shown that a key difference is the Chinese propensity for real (albeit authoritarian) participatory assimilation, in contrast to the Russian predisposition for top-down bureaucratic control and misleading claims. This is illustrated in the way each country has dealt with local volunteering in emergencies such as wildfires, earthquakes, and floods. In both countries, citizens' immediate response was to set up helplines and websites that would match a list of the needs in the disaster area (fire-fighting equipment, transport, food, shelter, etc.) with a list of the volunteers able to provide help. In China, at least in the recent past, the reaction by local authorities has been flexible and participatory. With the idea "we must learn from this," in some places they invited the volunteers to meetings to share their experience and know-how. In 2012 after the floods in Beijing the officials used experimental interactive communication with the media to manage the crisis,[9] and after the 2008 Wenchuan earthquake the provincial government provided accessible new public spaces that enabled volunteers to organize popular disaster relief.[10] In Russia, the government forbade citizens' spontaneous efforts, even though they had been effective after wildfires in 2010. Instead, a state-affiliated organization set up its own platform for which all potential volunteers had to register, but without specifying what help they could provide or what crisis was at issue. The façade presented to the public was official support for local response in emergencies, but what was created was a registry that controlled potential volunteers and rendered independent self-regulated crowdsourcing illegitimate.[11]

With these differences between China and Russia in mind, let us return to the question of bridges. Kharkhordin noted that the bridge that linked the two halves of Novgorod involved a host of further relations: an entire surrounding economy to pay for its periodic replacement, repair, and functioning; social institutions to ensure peace (for battles were fought on this bridge and sinners and enemies were thrown off it); and even God (for this bridge was where God revealed the Word by occasionally sending floods that swept away the structure or fires that destroyed it). Furthermore, the very existence of a bridge bringing together two communities was a sign of the political idea Novgorod stood for, a form of consultative democracy.[12] And one historical fact about the Great Bridge of Novgorod makes it a distant forerunner of our case: for centuries it was the only bridge over a great river in Russia that operated all year round. Everywhere else people made do with crossing the ice in winter and floating pontoon bridges in summer—just like the situation in Blagoveshchensk-Heihe when we visited. True, a bridge between those two towns has now been built. But it is closed—"due to coronavirus," they say—with no date for opening.

However, it is the Tongjiang bridge linking China with Nizhneleninskoe, a hamlet in the wilds of the Jewish Autonomous Region, that best epitomizes the structural differences and the quagmire of actual relations. This long railway bridge stretches 7,200 feet, of which 6,200 feet traverse shallows and sandbanks on the Chinese side, leaving only 1,000 feet to be built over the thalweg by the Russians. After twenty years of delay, an agreement to proceed was signed in 2013. Officials of the Heilongjiang regional government sourced the funding and liaised smoothly with the

China Railway Major Bridge Engineering Company. The Chinese then immediately built their stretch of the bridge. Years passed while the incomplete bridge loomed over the water, posted with what Russians saw as a mysterious and slightly threatening sign in Chinese.[13] After complaints from China and fears for the interstate friendship, President Putin took an interest, and suddenly the Russians started construction. Eventually it was announced that the bridge was complete. But in summer 2020, it turned out that this was not the case. Each side then produced its own statement, at curious cross-purposes. Rostislav Goldshteyn, head of the Jewish Autonomous Region administration, still spoke in fantasy future mode, concerned that his own bridge should outperform the one at Blagoveshchensk. When it opened, he said, the Jewish Autonomous Region would have the best prospects in the entire Russian Far East. But although he also extolled (absurdly) the project's "pivotal positional in the global construction" of the Chinese, Goldshteyn gave little impression of closeness to his neighbors over the river when he called them "Asian dragons."[14] Meanwhile, Chan Di, a Chinese economic advisor, commented diplomatically that he did not want to blame the delay on the laziness of Russian workers: "On the contrary, they are hardworking. But sometimes bureaucrats get in the way."[15]

Both of these comments miss the point, we would suggest, since what seems to have happened in Russia was a concatenation of multiple effects gathering around the bridge, similar to the ones mentioned in the case of the bridge at Novgorod. One element was the economic underpinning—the bridge on the Russian side was to be financed by an unreliable Kazakh magnate, whose investments were to be repaid by a toll collection company appropriately called Rubicon. The Kazakh dropped out and Rubicon never got to work. Then, in the absence of an overall arbiter, fears arose that one side would prevail at the expense of the other: the Chinese would monopolize not only the bridge but also the Russian iron ore mining complex that was due to be its main user. And there was even an "act of God," since the Amur suddenly wreaked havoc by changing and deepening its course at just the place where the Russians were finishing their construction. There were gloomy predictions that the bridge might collapse. The result of all this was the same as before: delay and confusion. Moscow took over and Yury Trutnev, presidential envoy to the Russian Far East, halted the construction, saying that fresh funding would have to be found and a new contract would have to be negotiated.

In 2021, as we were completing this book, the two countries were proceeding in their accustomed ways. China, with its propensity to flexible participatory activity, had developed Tongjiang in anticipation: they had built a logistics center for the expected iron ore imports, another for agricultural produce, and even a passenger station. On the Russian side, Trutnev flew in to Nizhneleninskoe by helicopter (the only convenient means of transport to such a spot) for a meeting with the stakeholders in March 2021. While the construction company said the bridge was only 80 percent ready and would take until late 2022 to finish, Trutnev told the media that he had the companies and investors "under control" and that trains would be crossing by August 2021. Goldshteyn offered his point of view: the bridge should not just take iron ore to China; the trains should travel both ways and benefit the whole district. A passenger station would be a good idea, and should be discussed, as "quite a flow of tourists could be expected."[16]

The reactions of ordinary folk to all this are also revealing. The locals among the hard-working Chinese farmers in the Jewish Autonomous Oblast mentioned in Chapter 3 are now getting on well with the twelve Russian neighbors remaining in the village of Dimitrovka, having laid a new road, fixed the electricity, and organized the only bus stop in the district. They are actively planning for the bridge to open so they can expand their soybean fields and pig farms. Meanwhile, they even have anticipated good neighborly relations and have proposed to build a high fence to shield the village from the noise and dirt of the rushing trains.[17]

By contrast, Russian comments tend to be more disbelieving and mocking. As one person observed, Goldshteyn's plea that the trains should go both ways across the bridge was a thought of "sheer genius."[18]

The unfinished bridge is still the subject of glowing promises. In both countries the officials look more to their own hinterlands than they do over the water. Three decades after the reopening of the border, and despite countless declarations of friendship, the sharing of this important and symbolic *res publica* has not yet quite come about, and the border rivers of the Amur, Argun, and Ussuri remain just as difficult to cross.

NOTES

INTRODUCTION

1. Milanovic (2019).

2. The border is currently the sixth longest in the world. However, prior to Mongolia's and Central Asian nations' independence, it stretched 7,500 miles, from the Central Asian mountain ranges to the Sea of Japan.

3. Headed by Caroline, the project at Cambridge included twenty scholars from China, Russia, Mongolia, the United Kingdom, France, Denmark, Hungary, Germany, Poland, South Korea, and the United States. For details, see the project's website at https://www.miasu.socanth .cam.ac.uk/projects/where-rising-powers-meet-china-and-russia-their -north-asian-border.

4. Rippa (2020: 25).

5. See Saxer and Zhang (2016) and Rippa (2020) for discussion of such large marketplaces in Kazakhstan, Kyrgyzstan, and Xinjiang.

6. Dungans, known as Hui in China, are Muslims who fled China in many waves during the nineteenth century. Today, up to 80,000 Dungans live in Kazakhstan and Kyrgyzstan.

7. For travel accounts, see Iwashita (2004); Legerton and Rawson (2009); Pulford (2019); Ziegler (2015).

8. Nationalism: Bulag (2010). "Agonistic intimacies": Saxer and Zhang (2016). "Border work": Reeves (2014). Trust and mistrust: Humphrey (2018). Territorial imagination: Billé (2020). Gender: Lacaze (2017). Migrations: Dyatlov (2010). Political loyalty: Humphrey (2017).

9. While the Soviet Union's political and economic influence over China is well known, what is often overlooked is the level of Russification that took place in the 1950s. Along with reforms in school education, new architectural and artistic styles emerged, transforming people's

tastes in everything from music, dance, and fine arts to food, clothes, and hobbies, while new concepts of gender, youth, family, and social relations gained traction. As Yan Li (2018) explains, this cultural shift reverberated well beyond the 1950s, into the Sino-Soviet split. The Russian language also served as an important bridge, providing access to a wide range of literary works from the Eastern bloc (Volland 2017).

10. Dyatlov, Guzey, and Sorokina (2020).

11. Damansky Island (Ch: Zhenbao dao, 珍宝岛) was originally connected to the Chinese bank, but water erosion separated it to form an independent island in 1915. It currently lies about 650 feet from the Chinese side and 1,000 feet from the Russian side.

12. According to Chinese sources, loss of life amounted to 58 Russians and 29 Chinese. According to Russian sources, 248 Chinese soldiers died and 32 Soviet border guards were killed.

13. China gained full control of Zhenbao / Damansky Island in 1991 when a new border settlement was agreed upon. Even though the island is regularly flooded and of very little use, the Russian military continues to regret the loss and assiduously maintains honor lists of the soldiers who took part in the fighting.

14. See Iwashita (2004) for an assessment of the Sino-Russian relations in the decade 1990–2000.

15. Writing about the significance, but also limitations, of geography, Chris Miller concedes that geography does create enduring realities, yet insists that it may not be the best guide to understanding Russian engagement with Asia (Miller 2021, 11–12). As he explains in his recent book, Russia's level of interest in foreign policy in Asia has been episodic and erratic (12).

16. Somini Sengupta and Steven Lee Myers, "Latest Arena for China's Growing Global Ambitions: The Arctic," *New York Times,* May 24, 2019.

17. See Abrahm Lustgarten, "How Russia Wins the Climate Crisis," *New York Times,* December 16, 2020.

18. A number of Chinese, Russian, and Western scholars have argued this convincingly. See, for instance, Radchenko (2014); Kaczmarski (2015); Grigas (2017); Pieper (2018); Yu (2018); and Markey (2020). Ironically, in a book where he insists on the genuine and potent nature of the relationship between Russia and China, Alexander Lukin (2018) devotes an inordinate amount of space to the fraught relations of both Russia and China with the United States. As Marcin Kaczmarski (2015: 45) writes, the United States remains for Russia the "most important point of reference for Russia's identity—its major 'other.'"

19. Rozman (2014).

20. This rejection of Western "values" as a Trojan horse for cultural and political hegemony has been witnessed in Russia's anti-gay legislation, where the "gay agenda" is declared incompatible with traditional Russian values.

21. Radchenko (2014: 11).

22. Radchenko (2014: 305).

23. Examining Russia's numerous Asian pivots throughout its history, from Peter the Great to Putin, historian Chris Miller concludes that "diplomatic energy, military power, and economic leverage in Asia has been deployed in spasms," driven largely by subjective factors: hopes and dreams of what might be accomplished in Asia; perceptions of opportunities, some real, many imagined. When these overoptimistic expectations are dashed, claims that Russia has a unique Asian role are promptly rolled back or abandoned. The only enduring feature that unites Russia's various Asian pivots is the role of the excessive optimism in launching them (Miller 2021, 15).

24. Lo (2008).

25. Yu (2018: 12–13).

26. Lukin (2018: 51), citing a 2007 interview with Liu Guchang, Chinese ambassador to Russia.

27. Kaczmarski (2015: 46).

28. Lilya Palveleva and Robert Coalson, "Echoes of War and Collapse: Russia's Demographic Decline as Small 1990s Generation Comes of Age," Radio Free Europe/Radio Liberty: Russia, January 12, 2020, https://www.rferl.org/a/russia-demographic-data-dip-as-small-1990s-generation-comes-of-age/30373049.html.

29. Markey (2020: 111).

30. "Putin Pivots to the East," The Economist, May 24, 2014; Grigas (2017: 343).

31. Quotation: Lukin (2018: x). Technological advantages: Markey (2020: 111). On reverse engineering, see Lee (2018).

32. Grigas (2017: 24, 27).

33. Grigas (2017: 337–338).

34. Ferris and Connolly (2020).

35. Toal (2017: 3).

36. Cited in Lukin (2018: 57).

37. Markey (2020: 89).

38. Raffaello Pantucci, "Is China Prepared for a New Mantle in Central Asia amid the Roll-out of Its Belt and Road?," South China Morning Post, March 19, 2017.

39. Andrei Lankov, "Russia's Waning Influence on North Korea," commentary, Carnegie Moscow Center, December 21, 2020, https://carnegie.ru/commentary/83506.

40. Russia and China also have a short mountainous and mostly snow-covered 62-mile border to the west between the Altai Republic (Russia) and Xinjiang (China). This section is not discussed in the book.

41. Ministers in both countries often reiterate the aim to jettison US- and EU-based payment systems and avoid sanctions by trading directly through new direct cross-border arrangements. Vladimir Soldatkin, "Russia Eyes Unified Payment Systems with China," November 4, 2016, https://www.reuters.com/article/uk-russia-china-payments-sanctions-idUKKBN12Z1RV. But the idea has been moot for several years without much in the way of implementation. Russians are aware of the far greater global clout of Chinese payment systems and want to retain freedom of maneuver.

42. "Kitaitsy ukhodyat s rossiiskogo Dal'nego Vostoka," Vzglyad, August 9, 2017, https://vz.ru/society/2017/8/7/881774.html; Ivan Zuenko, "Aihui za rekoi. Krai surovyi tishinoi ob'yat. Kak kitaiskaya ekspansiya spotknulas' o rossiiskoe prigranich'e," CentrAsia, February 16, 2016, https://centrasia.org/newsA.php?st=1455616020.

43. Chatham House (2015).

44. Andrew Higgins, "An Unfinished Bridge, and Partnership, between Russia and China," *New York Times*, July 16, 2016.

45. Markey (2020: 115).

46. Dyatlov (2008); Billé and Urbansky (2018).

47. Balzer and Repnikova (2010: 4, 22).

48. Hayton (2014).

49. The primary ambition of China, as well as other coastal states in the region, is to define areas in which they have sovereign rights, with the view to exploit natural resources (Billé 2020). In some cases, such as at its border with India, China is specifically seeking to extend its territory—though largely for strategic reasons of connectivity than for the land itself, which is not suitable for human habitation.

50. Kaczmarski (2017: 1359).

51. The BRI was formerly known in English in its direct translation from the Chinese as One Belt One Road (一带一路).

52. Winter (2019: 10).

53. A number of analysts have argued that China's BRI is less a new policy than the "elevation of existing policy goals and practice to the national level" (Summers 2016). Many of what are considered BRI projects in fact precede the launch of BRI.

54. Winter (2019: 16). "Century of humiliation": Callahan (2010).

55. Winter (2019: 34, 182).

56. Kaczmarski (2017: 1374).

57. Pieper (2018: 222).

58. Jon Henley, "A Brief Primer on Vladimir Putin's Eurasian Dream," *The Guardian*, February 18, 2014.

59. That the motivation is political rather than purely economic is suggested by the inclusion of cash-strapped Belarus.

60. Radchenko (2014: 312, 304).

61. Mongolia, only belatedly identified as a partner state, has also felt sidelined. Anxious it might be excluded from the new Eurasian connectivity plans, "Mongolia began to work on ways to be included in the Silk Road Economic Belt, as this was seen as a way to update its generally poor rail and road infrastructure and mitigate disadvantages of its landlocked status" (Pieper 2020, 6).

62. Some in Russia have also embraced local deployments of remoteness. Villagers living along the Baikal–Amur railway line have thus willfully opted out of having a bridge built to their village in order to avoid unwanted connections and outsiders flowing in (Schweitzer and Povoroznyuk 2019). Some Russian residents of closed cities and zones of restricted access have demonstrated similar attitudes (see Chapter 1).

63. At the border between China and Kazakhstan, for instance, hermetically closed for more than two decades, commercial exchange was brisk when it resumed in the late 1980s. It was short-lived, however. Trade turnover in consumer goods between the two countries is now conducted primarily via the hub bazaars of Urumqi, in China, and Almaty, in Kazakhstan, several hundred miles inland from the border. As a result, the borderland community has found itself peripheralized, largely bypassed by commodity flows (Alff 2016).

64. Saxer and Andersson (2019: 141).

65. Pantucci, "Is China Prepared for a New Mantle?"

66. Rippa (2018).

67. Go Yamada and Stefania Palma, "Is China's Belt and Road Working? A Progress Report from Eight Countries," *Nikkei Asia*, March 28, 2018, https://asia.nikkei.com/Spotlight/Cover-Story/Is-China-s-Belt-and-Road-working-A-progress-report-from-eight-countries.

68. Maria Abi-Habib, "How China Got Sri Lanka to Cough Up a Port," *New York Times*, June 25, 2018.

69. See Billé (2015).

70. The rise in authoritarian populism has not been limited to "typical" undemocratic states such as China and Russia. The election

of Donald Trump in the United States, of Boris Johnson in the UK, and of populist governments in Turkey, Israel, India, Hungary, Poland, and elsewhere speaks to a broader political shift. It is increasingly clear that the very notion of "authoritarianism" is labile and slippery, and that it is no longer evident where to draw the line between "authoritarian" and "nonauthoritarian." See Billé, Min, and Makley (in preparation).

71. See Byler (2018); Zenz (2020).

72. See, for instance, Alice Su, "Threats of Arrest, Job Loss and Surveillance: China Targets Its 'Model Minority,'" *Los Angeles Times,* September 23, 2020.

73. Grigas (2016).

74. Maria Repnikova, "Why China's Xi Is Not 'Putin-Plus,'" *Al Jazeera,* March 9, 2018.

75. Kaczmarski (2015). Quotation: Repnikova, "Why China's Xi Is Not 'Putin-Plus.'"

76. Higgins, "An Unfinished Bridge."

77. Lee (2018); Kaczmarski (2015).

78. Repnikova (2017b).

79. Repnikova, "Why China's Xi Is Not 'Putin-Plus.'"

80. A survey conducted during Putin's first year in office ostensibly found that 3,500 out of 5,000 Russian women thought Putin was "the sexiest man in Russia" (Sperling 2015: 44–45).

81. Repnikova, "Why China's Xi Is Not 'Putin-Plus.'"

82. Thus Kazakhs are generally uninterested in keeping up social and kinship links with coethnics in Xinjiang, even though they do trade with Xinjiang. For a study of the Kazakh population of Mongolia and their largely unsuccessful attempts to emigrate to Kazakhstan, see Diener (2009). On the lasting rupture between Georgia and Turkey, see Pelkmans (2006).

83. Zuenko, "Aihui za rekoi."

84. Lustgarten, "How Russia Wins the Climate Crisis."

85. Thus the new trash cans in the shape of Russian matryoshka dolls introduced in the Chinese border city of Heihe did not lead to the desired feeling of closeness and friendship the Chinese municipality was hoping for. On the contrary, Russians were offended by what they saw as an equivalence made between Russian culture and trash (see Chapter 7). A productive comparison can be made here with the evolving Sino-Mozambican relations in which the materiality of Chinese projects has led to the production of mutual incomprehension across the social and cultural terrain (see Nielsen and Bunkenborg 2020).

1. BORDER SPACES

1. Struve (2004: 42); Millward (2004: 113).

2. The major land crossings are at Zabaikal'sk–Manzhouli, Zarubino–Hunchun, and Pogranichny–Suifenhe. See Map 1.

3. Urbansky (2020: 318).

4. Luo, Oakes, and Schein (2019).

5. Boris Rodoman, "Rossiya—administrativno-territorial'nyi monstr," lecture published on Polit.ru website, November 4, 2004, http://polit.ru/article/2004/11/04/rodoman/.

6. Rodoman thus anticipated the argument recently explored by anthropologists that remoteness is a politically created process and not simply a primordial geographical condition (Saxer and Andersson 2019).

7. Rodoman, "Rossiya."

8. Kruglova (2019: 463).

9. For a discussion of the Soviet neglect of Siberia and the question of whether Russia can free itself from the economic habits and structures it inherited from the USSR, see Hill and Gaddy (2003).

10. Ziegler (2015: 227).

11. For an overall analysis of the problems of Russia's current infrastructure, see Ferris and Connelly (2020).

12. Beumers (2016: 25–39).

13. See Brown (2003) for an insightful study of this policy in Russia's Ukrainian-Polish borderlands.

14. Ryzhova (2019).

15. "Pogranichnaya zona," Wikimedia.ru, https://dic.academic.ru/dic.nsf/ruwiki/320416/Пограничная_зона, accessed May 2021.

16. Guy Plopsky, "Why Is Russia Aiming Missiles at China?," *Diplomat,* July 12, 2017, https://thediplomat.com/2017/07/why-is-russia-aiming-missiles-at-china.

17. Billé (2012).

18. Pallot and Piacentini (2012: 50–54).

19. Some bases are maintained in outdated premises with no clear defense purpose beyond training. Plans to close them were reversed after local protests that their removal would have a disastrous effect on local economies.

20. The Power of Siberia gas pipeline travels under the Amur near Blagoveshchensk and began to supply gas to China in December 2019; https://www.gazprom.com/projects/power-of-siberia/, accessed May 15, 2021.

21. Panoptic surveillance: Agnieszka Joniak-Lüthi, "Orbital," Society + Space, July 9, 2019, https://societyandspace.org/2019/04/09/orbital. "Hyperspace": Ong (2011a).

22. The Soviet town, founded in 1961, was given the name Uglegorsk ("coal town") to mislead enemies, when in fact its mining-like facilities were designed to mask the production of rockets. From 1969 to 1994, the closed territory was called Svobodnyi-18 according to the usual system of designating ZATO locations by a number.

23. Alexey Eremenko and Alexander Smith, "Vostnochny Cosmodrome: Russian Space Project Isn't Going to Plan," NBC News, July 31, 2016, http://www.nbcnews.com/science/space/vostochny-cosmodrome-russian-space-project-isn-t-going-plan-n618846.

24. Russia also has an active spaceport and missile launch site at Plesetsk, only 500 miles from Moscow.

25. For a history and atmospheric photographs of Svobodny, see Mikhail Alekseevsky, "Svobodny," trans. Maxwell Koopsen, *Strelka Mag,* December 6, 2017, https://svobodniy.strelka.com/en.

26. Vasilii Orlov, "Delat' vse chtoby lyudi ostavalis,'" *Vzglyad Delovaya Gazeta,* August 30, 2018, https://vz.ru/politics/2018/8/30/939687.html.

27. The Far Eastern Federal District extends northward to the Arctic and includes vast areas that are almost uninhabited. Most of the population is concentrated near the border in the south, but even these regions have been losing population, especially from rural areas. The population in 2018 was around 8.2 million.

28. Globally the accepted source is an anonymous stream that trickles into the Onon River in northeast Mongolia. The Onon joins the Shilka in Russia.

29. Hamashita (2003). We should add that Chinese geographical visions have varied over history and in some periods were more limited and land-based than the account given here; see Mosca (2019).

30. Hamashita (2003: 17).

31. Billé (2016: 102). During the Ming Dynasty (1368–1644) a town called Yongmingcheng ("city of light") existed at this spot, inhabited by predecessors of the Manchus.

32. Billé (2016c: 96).

33. "Manchuria" is a disputed name, not used in contemporary China because it suggests a separate realm and is uncomfortably close to "Manchukuo," the name used by the Japanese when they occupied the region in the 1930s to 1940s and set up a colonial state there. The Willow Palisade was a ditch and earth wall topped with willows. Its aim was not only to preserve a Manchu sense of identity tied to a homeland but also to

prevent an alliance between the Han and indigenous nomadic peoples who might pose the same threat to imperial rule that they themselves had done (Duara 2003: 42). The Willow Palisade has now virtually entirely disappeared as a physical structure, and Chinese farmers plowing the fields where it lay are hardly aware of its former existence (Meyer 2015). See also Bulag (2012).

34. Elliott (2001: 357).

35. Hamashita (2003: 24). By the nineteenth century global political relations had come to be based on the Westphalian concept of sovereignty (that is, territorially defined nation-states), but in Hamashita's view the result in East Asia up to the beginning of the twentieth century was a "mere correspondence of forms." "The concepts of East and West did not spatially overwrite one another, but rather it can be said that the tribute concept, that is the concept of a hierarchical order, remained primary, with the treaty relationship subordinated to it" (Hamashita 2003: 24).

36. Lattimore (1934: 3–4).

37. Duara (2003: 49).

38. Wang (2017: 13).

39. Li (2004).

40. Tom Hancock, "China's Shrinking Cities," *Financial Times Magazine*, April 27/28, 2019, 24–29.

41. Guo (2014).

42. Libman and Rochlitz (2019: 2–5).

43. Joniak-Lüthi and Bulag (2016: 2–3).

44. Makarov (2017: 82–83).

45. Hsing (2008: 58).

46. Bulag (2006).

47. Hsing (2010: 12).

48. Urbansky (2020: 298).

49. Yu (2016: 157–158).

50. Humphrey (2020).

51. On negotiating borders: Amilhat Szary (2020: 11).

52. Fishing or public navigation by each country has to take place on its own side of the thalweg line.

53. Bassin (1999).

54. Fraser (1904: 160).

55. Fraser (1904: 168).

56. Delaplace (2012).

57. Zatsepine (2007: 154).

58. "The river does not behave as a fixed border; it moves when not frozen. The Amur changes shape at least twice each year during spring floods and summer drought. Demarcating and monitoring the Amur

became a constant source of confusion for border authorities and for political centres" (Zatsepine 2007: 158).

59. Vezhenovets (2010: 140–141).

60. The Baikal–Amur Mainline (BAM) runs for 2,700 miles from Eastern Siberia to the Pacific some 250–300 miles north of and parallel to the Trans-Siberian.

61. Simonov et al. (2016).

62. Quoted from exhibits at the Hohhot City Museum, Inner Mongolia, 2019.

63. Akshay Narand, "'This Is Our Land,' China Now Claims Russia's Vladivostok as Part of Its Territory," *TFI Post,* July 4, 2020, https://tfipost.com/2020/07/this-is-our-land-china-now-claims-russias-vladivostok-as-part-of-its-territory.

64. Minakir (2006: 741).

65. "Stroitel'stvo mosta mezhdu Blagoveshchenskom i Kheikhe otslezhivaet kvadrokopter," *Amurskaya Pravda,* February 20, 2018, https://www.ampravda.ru/2018/02/20/080298.html.

66. "Kitaiskim turistam khotyat razreshit' ezdit' po Blagoveshchensk na lichnykh avtomobilyakh," *Amurskaya Pravda,* September 27, 2017, https://www.ampravda.ru/2017/09/26/077435.html.

67. Park (2016).

68. Gang Ding, "China-Russia Bridge Will Heal Old Wounds," *Global Times,* September 20, 2017. See also Billé (2014).

69. "Building Bridges: What Does Russia's Slow Progress on a Transport Link to China Reveal?," *Week in China,* September 18, 2015, https://www.weekinchina.com/2015/09/building-bridges-2/.

70. TOR stands for "Territoriya operezhayushchego sotsial'no-ekonomicheskokogo razvitiya."

71. In 2018 the Buryat Republic and Zabaikal Krai, both economically on their knees, were transferred from the Siberia Federal Okrug to the Far East Okrug, thus enabling them also to benefit from the TOR policy.

72. "Territorii operezhayushchego razvitiya: zachem oni nuzhny i komu eto vygodno?," February 3, 2019, https://inance.ru/2019/02/tor/.

73. TORs have been established not only in the Far East but also in poverty-stricken towns across Russian where the former supporting industry has now closed. The total number of TORs in Russia in 2019 was ninety-nine. "Territorii operezhayushchego razvitiya. Spisok 2019," http://fincan.ru/articles/86_territorii-operezhayushchego-razvitiya-spisok-2019/, accessed May 2021.

74. In the 1990s some regions of Russia, such as Kalmykia and Altai, set up "offshore" zones with low or zero tax rates to attract capital.

Though officially to support development, these were the outcome of privileges granted by the federal government to support loyalty in the context of center-periphery bargaining (Libman and Rochlitz 2019: 19–20). Abolished during Putin's centralization project, these early off-shores were widely seen as corrupt. A further series of broader special economic zones were subsequently established to encourage specific industries in certain regions, but with little success (Yankov et al. 2016). These SEZs are different from TORs in that they coincide with, rather than crosscut, the existing administrative boundaries and do not involve the lifting of such a wide range of laws.

75. These newly injected funds pay not only for the agreed-upon "Chinese side" of the bridges but also for the spans that were supposed to have been provided by Russia. "Tri v odnoi: v Amurskoi oblasti sozdana tret'ya TOR," June 5, 2017, https://ampravda.ru/2017/06/06/075196.html.

76. "Krai surovyi tishinoi ob'yat," February 16, 2016, https://lenta.ru/articles/2016/02/16/gde_kitaicy.

77. The fear of a "dictatorship" under the FED Corporation had already been raised in 2012 in relation to an earlier project law, "On the Assimilation of Siberia and the Far East." To some critics in the business world, the FEDC raised the specter of the Stalin-era Gulag organization Dal'stroi, run by the NKVD (security service). Dal'stroi similarly overrode normal civil law and was ruled directly from Moscow. The organization used convict labor to develop vast swaths of the Far East. Within its territory it was supreme master, exempt from the usual party and state controls. See "Novyi dalstroi," April 23, 2012, https://www.forbes.ru/sobytiya-column/vlast/81507-novyi-dalstroi, accessed April 2019 (this article has since been removed from the internet).

78. Quotation from "Kak zhizn' rasshifruet TORy?," December 24, 2015, http://www.sovross.ru/articles/1325/23194.

79. "Territorii operezhayushchego razvitiya: zachem oni nuzhny i komu eto vygodno?," February 3, 2019, https://inance.ru/2019/02/tor/.

80. Stronski and Ng (2018); Ferris and Connolly (2020).

81. Cheng (2015: 224).

82. Ryzhova (2019: 12).

83. Larin (2014: 40).

84. A free port is a type of SEZ akin to a TOR but with a slightly less advantageous tax regime. See Ferris and Connolly (2020: 13).

85. "Zachem Blagoveshchensku nuzhen most s Kitaem?," October 5, 2018, https://vz.ru/society/2018/10/5/944733.html.

86. All quotations are from Ryzhova (2019).

87. Ryzhova (2019: 16).

88. Quotation from Agamben (2004).

89. Libman and Rochlitz (2019: 20).

2. STANDOFF IN THE BORDER RIVER

1. Amilhat Szary (2020).

2. Amilhat Szary (2020: 51).

3. See Widdis (2004) for a fascinating discussion of the culture of Russian national identity in relation to space. The imperative to conquer territory by means of *osvoyenie* ("making one's own") and the denial of limits was seen as intrinsic to Russia's "natural" identity and gave Russia its pride, its freedom, and its power; but this urge was matched by the might of physical nature itself. Siberia, ending only at the Pacific Ocean, was where this antinomy was archetypally played out.

4. Ouyang (2018).

5. Menon (2009) provides a well-rounded analysis in the long term of the multilateral geopolitical interests of both Russia and China.

6. Kumar (2019).

7. Alexander Gabuev, "Why Foreign Investors Steer Clear of Russia's Far East," Carnegie Moscow Center, September 9, 2019, https://carnegie.ru/2019/09/09/why-foreign-investors-steer-clear-of-russia-s-far-east-pub-79802.

8. Ivan Zuenko, "Kak Kitai budet razvivat' Dal'nii Vostok," *Mir Peremen,* October 29, 2018, http://mirperemen.net/2018/10/kak-kitaj-budet-razvivat-dalnij-vostok.

9. See *Russian-China Dialogue: The 2018 Model,* Report no 39 /2018, Russian International Affairs Council, Institute of Far Eastern Studies of the Russian Academy of Sciences, and Fudan University, https://russiancouncil.ru/papers/Russia-China-Report39-En.pdf.

10. Zuenko, "Kak Kitai budet razvivat' Dal'nii Vostok."

11. The eponymous Heixiazi bear, literally "black blind bear," earned its nickname on account of its allegedly poor vision.

12. Taiwan does not recognize border treaties signed by the PRC and continues to assert title to all parts of the Heixiazi islands.

13. Iwashita (2004).

14. Zhang et al. (2020: 3).

15. "Ostrov. Strakh i nenavist' na Bol'shom Ussuriiskom," February 11, 2015, http://blog.dyos.ru/2015/02/ostrov.html.

16. Billé (2014); Richardson (2017: 11).

17. "Irrigatsionnaya voina s Kitaem," July 9, 2001, http://www.vremya.ru/2001/119/4/11645.html; "Reabilitatsiya Rossii. Ili 'Kemska volost' dlya Kitaya," Politforums.net, June 6, 2013, https://www.politforums.net/russkiyvzgliad/1370504171.html.

18. Anna Leonova, "Bol'shoi Ussuriiskii razdor," *Khabarovskii Ekspress* no. 39 (September 26, 2012), http://www.debri-dv.ru/article /5639.

19. Liu et al. (2006: 60–61); Gottschang and Lary (2000).

20. Liu et al. (2006: 65).

21. Fuyuan County is subordinate to the prefecture-level city of Jiamusi.

22. See Billé (2014) for a discussion of the affect associated with lost lands as metaphorically akin to "phantom pains." Both Billé (2014) and Purdue (2010) argue that the possibility of imagining such lost territories depends greatly on the existence of maps. Consequently, maps, as sources of collective imagination, can also become threatening objects (Purdue 2010: 284).

23. "Heixiazi Island," Windwing blog, October 16, 2008, http:// wiudwing.blogspot.co.uk/2008_10_01_archive.html.

24. "Reportazh o kitaiskoi pogranzastave na ostrove Bol'shoi Ussuriiskii," October 26, 2021, https://aleonkin.livejournal.com/293474 .html?page=2#comments.

25. Leonova, "Bol'shoi Ussuriiskii razdor."

26. This tallies with an earlier "State Program of Russian Far East Development," which highlighted three projects for investment: the Eastern Cosmodrome, the Kamchatka tourist complex, and Ussuriisk Island. The last of these is said to have political and socioeconomic significance for both Russia and China.

27. Bruno Maçães, "Signs and Symbols on the Sino-Russian Border," *The Diplomat,* May 5, 2016, http://thediplomat.com/2016/05/signs-and -symbols-on-the-sino-russian-border.

28. "Heixiazi Island in Fuyuan, a Pure Land Bordering China and Russia," China.com, August 8, 2016, http://english.china.com/special /arctic/14168/20160808/726918.html.

29. Liu et al. (2006: 61–62).

30. Liu et al. (2006: 65).

31. Professor Ma remembered, "Nature seemed vast, the snow deep, the trees straight and tall"; when he revisited the north in 1988, he was appalled by the destruction, and he became one of China's most influential environmental advocates (Liu et al. 2006: 60).

32. Liu et al. (2006: 66–68).

33. Zuenko (2017a, 2017b) discusses the internal career politics of Chinese officials based on his own research in northeast China.

34. Liu et al. (2006: 73).

35. Liu et al. (2006: 71).

36. Between 2005 and 2013, the Asian Development Bank gave grants and loans totaling over US $27 million for ecological preservation in the Sanjiang Plain wetlands area. The project included converting farmland to wetland and resettlement of indigenous people. Asian Development Bank, 2017, "China, People's Republic of: Sanjiang Plain Wetland Protection," Project Data Sheet (pdf), https://www.adb.org/projects/35289-013/main#project-pds-collapse.

37. Quoted in Liu et al. (2006: 75).

38. Ekaterina Vasyukova, "Two Countries, One Island," trans. Kevin Rothrock, *Meduza,* November 1, 2018, https://meduza.io/en/feature/2018/11/02/two-countries-one-island. The Chinese bridges give vehicular access, but private cars are forbidden for environmental reasons. Visitors have to walk or use buses supplied by the tourism organization.

39. Li Kun, ed., "Cartoon Commentary on Xi's Heilongjiang Visit: Guiding New Green Development Concepts," Looking China, CCTV, May 25, 2016, http://english.cctv.com/2016/05/25/ARTIPFBzOxSUobglBXPYf8lB160525.shtml.

40. "Ostrov Bol'shoi Ussuriiskii nel'zya prevrashchat' v ploshchadku dlya razvlechenii—predsedatel' KNR," Novosti Khabarovsk, May 26, 2016, http://www.dvnovosti.ru/khab/2016/05/26/50946/.

41. "Today, the 'East,' 'North' They Wear the Badge to Salute the Flag," Fuyuan Wusu town post, April 10, 2019, http://flag.hackworry.com/blogpost/432061.

42. "Bol'shoi Ussuriiskii ostrov. Zachem nash prezident otdal ego kitaitsam?," April 20, 2021, https://zen.yandex.ru/media/varandej/bolshoi-ussuriiskii-ostrov-zachem-nash-prezident-otdal-ego-kitaicam-5e8d95728e13467f02b3707c. Chinese sources on recent developments on the island are scant, and we refer here to reports from Russian visitors.

43. Vasyukova, "Two Countries, One Island"; Whately (2005: 44–46, 95); "In Pics: Bear Park on Heixiazi Island in Heilongjiang," *Global Times* (China), August 8, 2020, https://www.globaltimes.cn/content/1197070.shtml.

44. "G1012 Jiansanjiang-Heixiazi Island Expressway," https://en.wikipedia.org/wiki/G1012_Jiansanjiang–Heixiazi_Island_Expressway, accessed October 2019.

45. From http://www.dvnovosti.ru/khab/2016/05/26/50946/, accessed May 26, 2016 (no longer available).

46. Leonova, "Bol'shoi Ussuriiskii razdor."

47. "Galushka: territoriami operezhayushchego razvitiya stanut Kyrily i Bol'shoi Ussuriiskii Ostrov," December 16, 2014, https://tass.ru/ekonomika/1651424.

48. "Bol'shoi Ussuriiskii ostrov v prigorode Khabarovska snova okazalsya otrezan ot mira," March 21, 2014, http://amurmedia.ru/news/344492/.

49. Vasyukova, "Two Countries, One Island."

50. Vasyukova, "Two Countries, One Island."

51. "Zhiteli zabytogo vsemi Bol'shogo Ussuriiskogo ostrova prosyat pereselit' ikh," October 20, 2016, https://regnum.ru/news/society/2194 864.html.

52. Quoted in "Ostrov Bol'shoi Ussuriiskii spustya god posle potopa: byt' ili ne byt'?," July 17, 2014, https://ria.ru/society/20140717/10163 60445.html.

53. Vasyukova, "Two Countries, One Island."

54. Vasyukova, "Two Countries, One Island."

55. Orlova (2021).

56. Vasyukova, "Two Countries, One Island."

57. "Bol'shoi Ussuriiskii ostrov. Zachem nash prezident otdal ego kitaitsam?"; "Teper' s innovatsami: Bol'shomu Ussuriiskomu opyat' poobeshchali razvitie," November 13, 2020, https://rg.ru/2020/11/13/reg-dfo/bolshomu-ussurijskomu-ostrovu-opiat-poobeshchali-razvitie .html.

58. Leonid Bershidsky, "Kremlin Has Problem in the Far East That It Can't Solve by Its Customary Methods," *Weekly Blitz,* September 25, 2018, https://www.weeklyblitz.net/oped/kremlin-has-problem-in-the-far -east-that-it-cant-solve-by-its-customary-methods/.

3. MAKING A LIVING IN THE CROSS-BORDER ECONOMY

1. On "cultures of capitalism": Laura Bear et al., "Generating Capitalism," *Fieldsights,* Society for Contemporary Anthropology, March 30, 2015, https://culanth.org/fieldsights/series/generating-capitalism.

2. Gates (1996).

3. Bliakher [Blyakher] and Vasil'eva (2010).

4. Bliakher and Vasil'eva (2010: 87).

5. Wang (2020: 18).

6. Rozelle and Hell (2020).

7. Russia's arms exports form a relatively small part of total sales to China. Wary of a Chinese military buildup and China's capacity to copy the latest technology, Russia's defense chiefs have only recently agreed

to sell high-tech weapons and combat aircraft to China. A considerably larger volume is sold to other countries such as India and Vietnam. China's defense industry has learned from Russia, but it is likely that China's current superiority in electronics, advanced materials, and the shipbuilding industries will enable it to surpass Russia in military production. Siemon Wezeman, "China, Russia and the Shifting Landscape of Arms Sales," Stockholm International Peace Research Institute, July 5, 2017, https://sipri.org/commentary/topical-backgrounder/2017/china-russia-and-shifting-landscape-arms-sales.

8. Sergei Kapitonov, "Zapusk 'Sila Sibirii.' Chto oznachaet dlya Rossii vykhod na gazovyi rynok Kitaya," Carnegie Moscow Center, May 12, 2019, https://carnegie.ru/commentary/80477.

9. China is Russia's major coal buyer, purchasing 3.38 million tons in 2018, rising 32 percent year on year. "Russia June Coal Exports Increase 23.37%, Top China," Shanghai Katalor Enterprises, November 30, 2018, http://www.ice-steels.com/News/Russia-June-Coal-Exports-Increase-2337-a-Top-China.html.

10. China and India are Russia's main destinations for high-tech arms and military aircraft. Both countries are moving toward self-sufficiency or also seeking new suppliers, and Russia is therefore also looking for new world markets; its defense industries remain big employers and produce over 16 percent of Russia's exports (2015 data). Amelia Heathman, "What You Need to Know about Russia's Arms Exports," *Verdict,* GlobalData PLC, London, March 20, 2017, https://www.verdict.co.uk/need-know-russias-arms-exports/.

11. Kapitonov, "Zapusk 'Sila Sibirii.'"

12. "Russia to Double Global Food Exports, Ready to Replace US Agricultural Products in China," RT, June 7, 2019, https://www.rt.com/business/461297-russia-food-exports-china/.

13. In Jason Moore's (2015) ambitious Marxist work on the subordination of nonhuman nature to capital accumulation, he distinguishes between resource-rich "external frontiers," where appropriation of uncommodified nature yields short-term profits, and "internal frontiers," sites where greater income can be extracted by eliminating inefficiencies and restructuring production. The Sino-Russian borderlands could be seen as an arena of competition between these two, the former more prevalent among Russian economic actors and the latter among Chinese. Tsing argues for the need to investigate the edges of capitalism, where noncapitalist forms of values are constantly being converted into capitalist value. "Salvage accumulation" refers to the conversion of material with other histories of social relations, human and nonhuman, into capitalist wealth. Anna Lowenhaupt Tsing, "Salvage Accumula-

tion, or the Structural Effects of Capital Generativity," *Fieldsights,* Society for Cultural Anthropology, March 30, 2015, https://culanth.org/fieldsights/salvage-accumulation-or-the-structural-effects-of-capitalist-generativity.

14. Blyakher (2015). "Stationary bandit" is a term invented by economist Mancur Olson. He argued that unlike "roving bandits," who take 100 percent of the victim's wealth and move on, "stationary bandits" have an interest in repeated grabs; they therefore reduce the percentage levied and start to provide certain public goods that benefit the economy, which in the long run enhances their take. In this way, they become local autocrats. Russia, according to Olson, was a country ruled by roving bandits (the oligarchs) until Putin reined them in and replaced them with stationary bandits close to, or part of, state power. Branko Milanovic, "Oligarchs and Oligarchs," *Global Policy* opinion, July 4, 2019, https://www.globalpolicyjournal.com/blog/04/07/2019/oligarchs-and-oligarchs.

15. Elena Shulman, "Verkhovenstvo prava: Volki i kormovaya baza," *Vedomosti,* November 8, 2013, https://www.vedomosti.ru/newspaper/articles/2013/11/08/volki-i-kormovaya-baza.

16. Because the criminal bosses were still around, to ensure loyalty the cut had to be less than that taken by the mafias. And the price of the "administrative rent" had to conform to the small businesses' ability to pay. When Sergei Darkin was governor of Primorye and sharply raised this price, almost a quarter of businesses in the region moved out and registered themselves elsewhere (Blyakher 2015: 10).

17. Blyakher (2015: 13–14).

18. Blyakher (2015: 14).

19. Ryzhova (2014b).

20. Ryzhova (2018).

21. Andrei Lankov, "The Golden Age of Korean-Russian Shuttle Trading," Russia Beyond, October 26, 2015, https://www.rbth.com/blogs/2015/10/24/the_golden_age_of_korean-russian_shuttle_trading_50171.html.

22. Another consequence of Russia's tightening of customs controls and lengthy delays on the Siberian border is that Chinese firms prefer to export via Kazakhstan or Kyrgyzstan, where border checks are much lighter. From large marts in these countries, merchants take the goods to markets throughout Siberia.

23. Humphrey (2018a).

24. Ryzhova and Zhuravskaya (2015). See also discussion in Chapter 7.

25. Aleksandr Rokhlin and Aleksandr Gronskii, "Na vysokikh beregakh Amura," part 1, Travel.ru, September 1, 2006, http://guide.travel.ru/russia/124107.html.

26. Quotations from Rokhlin and Gronskii, "Na vysokikh beregakh Amura."

27. "Sdelano v SSSR: mertvyi kolkhoz 'Pogranichnik,'" July 5, 2012, https://www.chita.ru/articles/40864/#to_marker.

28. Schiffauer (2018).

29. "Sdelano v Zabaikal'e: fermer kotoromu nekodga rugat' vlast,'" February 15, 2016, https://www.chita.ru/articles/83323/#to_marker.

30. "Sdelano v Zabaikal'e."

31. Kordonskii et al. (2011: 15).

32. Khabarovsk is a good example of this process. Its population grew from 577,400 in 2010 to 629,600 in 2019. Meanwhile, every other town in the Khabarovsk Krai saw a sharp fall in population. "Russia: Khabarovsk Krai," CityPopulation.de, Thomas Brinkoff, https://city population.de/en/russia/chabarovsk/, accessed December 2019.

33. According to OECD data for 2016, 47.7 percent of Russians have completed a full secondary education (eleven years), 26.5 percent have completed nine years, and 8.1 percent have only an elementary education (four years). This contrasts with China, where, according to the 2015 census, only three in ten members of the workforce have attended senior high school, meaning that some 500 million people, almost all of them from rural communities, have only attended elementary school. This creates a large gap between the well-educated youth of China's cities and the rural inhabitants (Rozelle and Hell 2020).

34. Plyusnin et al. (2013: 8).

35. Kordonskii et al. (2011: 14).

36. Zhidkevich (2016); Plyusnin et al. (2013). After Chinese traders were excluded by government policy from 2006 onward, their place in local markets was taken by incomers from the Central Asian republics. Highly visible, the Kyrgyz and other Central Asian merchants, being former Soviet subjects "like us," have been less resented than the Chinese were, however, not everywhere. By contrast, the teams of construction workers brought in by developers from China and North Korea tend to be secluded in fenced-off building sites and dormitories to avoid the prying eyes of officialdom and xenophobic locals alike.

37. Looney and Rithmire (2017: 204).

38. The *hukou* system was established in 1958. It registers households (not individuals, as in Russia) to a given place, which is where they must access rights to land, education, or social insurance. Until recently, the rights were far greater in cities than in rural areas; for example, urban citizens were guaranteed housing, whereas rural dwellers had to build their own houses. Today, schools and hospitals are absent in many rural areas. To access them, villagers need a relative with a town *hukou*.

39. Loyalka (2012).
40. Looney and Rithmire (2017: 206).
41. Zakharov (2015).
42. This video is no longer available online.
43. The "Far Eastern Hectare" scheme, set up in 2016 to offer free land to people who guaranteed to make economic use of it, has had few takers; this was because the property rights were limited, and because—absurdly—the plots had to be located far from any town and consequently were usually lacking roads, electricity, and so on (Ryzhova et al. 2017).
44. The five regions are Amur Oblast, the Jewish Autonomous Region, Primorskii Krai, Khabarovskii Krai, and Zabaikal'skii Krai.
45. This is only 3 percent of the land *officially* designated as "agricultural," but as the report states, much of this land is actually unusable (abandoned, waterlogged, overgrown with bushes and trees, etc.). In Russia as a whole, only 64 percent of such "agricultural land" is actually used. Andrei Zakharov and Anastasiya Napalkova, "'Uyedut Kitaitsy—vse zarastet' kak fermery in KNR osvaivayut rossiiskii Dal'nyi Vostok," BBC News, October 21, 2019, https://www.bbc.com/russian/features-49978027. A Chinese study, based on data supplied by the China and Russia Agricultural Cooperative Association of farmers, gives higher figures. It states that in 2013 Chinese members were already cultivating around 500,000 hectares (1.2 million acres) in Russia, and the total would be even higher (well over one-sixth of useable agricultural land) if informal arrangements were counted (Zhou 2017: 619). However, the chaotic management of cadastral registers in Russia makes it impossible to understand who rents which land, and all of these figures should be taken as highly approximate.
46. The Farm Land Bill of 2002 allowed foreigners to lease Russian agricultural land for up to forty-nine years. Companies where the majority of shareholders are Russian are allowed to purchase land.
47. Ivan Tselichtchev, "Chinese in the Russian Far East: A Geopolitical Time Bomb?," *South China Morning Post,* July 8, 2017. See also Carlsson et al. (2015: 53).
48. In the first half year of 2019, 863,000 Chinese citizens entered Russia and 805,000 departed, with most of those remaining holding short-term visas. In 2018, only 477 arrived intending to stay for a long period. The number of Chinese applying for Russian citizenship was even smaller: 196 people between 2017 and mid-2019. "Masshtab kitaiskoi migratsii v rossiyu yavno preuvelichen," October 8, 2019, https://365info.kz/2019/10/masshtab-kitajskoj-migratsii-v-rossiyu-yavno-preuvelichen.

49. "Masshtab kitaiskoi migratsii v rossiyu yavno preuvelichen."

50. "Farming the World: China's Epic Race to Avoid a Food Crisis," Bloomberg News, May 22, 2017, https://www.bloomberg.com/graphics /2017-feeding-china/. For comparison, the Russian "subsidiary plot" is limited by law to 0.5 hectares (1.2 acres).

51. Meyer (2015: 208).

52. Zhou (2017: 615).

53. Zakharov and Napalkova, "Uyedut Kitaitsy."

54. Zhou (2017: 620).

55. Zakharov and Napalkova, "Uyedut Kitaitsy."

56. The Russian technology company Yandex began to use WeChat for its own payment system in 2019; the service is useful to Russian businesses such as hotels, duty free shops, and travel companies working with Chinese customers. "Yandex Checkout Launches Online Payments via WeChat Pay in Russia," Finextra, June 25, 2019, https://www.finextra .com/pressarticle/78917/yandexcheckout-launches-online-payments -via-wechat-pay-in-russia. See also Kuzmina (2018).

57. Rokhlin and Gronskii, "Na vysokikh beregakh Amura."

58. Zhou (2017: 620).

59. A Chinese manager of a sawmill in Buryatia commented that she was amazed that Russian and Buryat villagers "did not understand money." They had not been brought up from childhood to figure out savings, running costs, interest rates, and profit margins. This was why they were left with the toilsome labor of cutting the wood in the forest, whereas she was able to garner the value added from the saw-mill and also provide local employment. Olga Shaglanova, personal communication.

60. Rokhlin and Gronskii, "Na vysokikh beregakh Amura."

61. Donahoe et al. (2008); Schweitzer and Povoroznyuk (2019: 243).

62. Safonova, Sántha, and Sulyandziga (2018).

63. Makhachkeev (2018: 208).

64. For more information, see "Kammennyi gost': zachem Vitalii Mashchitskii pomogaet Rostekhu osvaivat' dobychu," May 31, 2016, https://www.forbes.ru/kompanii/resursy/321435-kamennyi-gost-zachem -vitalii-mashchitskii-pomogaet-rostekhu-osvaivat-dobychu.

65. "Istoriya zashchitnika korennykh narodov, kotoryi sbezhal v SShA ot rossiiskikh spetssluzhb," December 27, 2019, https://snob.ru /entry/186908/.

66. Safonova, Sántha, and Sulyandziga (2018).

67. Prospective interstate cooperation has focused on the construc-tion of "transport corridors" for Chinese cargo, including the building

of a new port at Bolshoe Zarubino, south of Vladivostok. During the 2014 APEC summit an agreement of intent was signed by Russia's Summa Group and the Chinese state-owned China Merchants Group; but, having failed to receive government funding, Summa froze construction of the port. The problem was one of trust: the investors wanted guarantees from the Chinese exporters, and the exporters wanted to see an actual port and the road to it. Chinese hesitation more broadly is caused by Russia's lack of modern border posts, cumbersome procedures, and underdeveloped infrastructure. "It is easy to understand the Chinese perspective," writes Ivan Zuenko. "A container sent from Mudanjiang to Shanghai via Dalian completes the journey in 85 hours at a cost of $1,200. Though the distance through Vladivostok is three times shorter, the travel time grows to 220 hours, mostly because of customs procedures. The cost is 5–15% higher." Ivan Zuenko, "The Chimera of Chinese Investment in Russia's Far East Ports," commentary, Carnegie Moscow Center, July 5, 2017, https://carnegie.ru/commentary/71427. For Chinese businesses, the attractiveness of Vladivostok is also compromised by the fact that their own Dalian too is a free port; they bear in mind that Russian law allows the status of TOR and free port to be canceled at any time and hence does not provide stability for investors. Indeed, some unsuccessful TORs in the far north of the RFE were annulled in 2019.

68. Ferris and Connolly (2020: 13).

69. Ryzhova (2019).

70. Dominic Martin, personal communication.

71. "Rezidenty TOR i svobodnogo porta Vladivostok investirovali 440 mlrd rublei v proekty," September 2, 2019, https://tass.ru/ekonomika /6834659. The free port comprises the city of Vladivostok as well as fifteen surrounding, mostly depressed municipalities, but it does not include Big Stone, which is a separate TOR. "The Free Port of Vladivostok: Special Investment Regime," Deloitte, January 2016, https://www2 .deloitte.com/content/dam/Deloitte/ru/Documents/tax/free-port-of -vladivostok-special-investment-regime-en.pdf.

72. Mega-companies such as Zvezda can bulldoze through the bureaucracy of the Far East Development Corporation (FEDC) set up to manage the TORs, but Moscow takes a large slice in administrative rent. Meanwhile, smaller potential investors trying to obtain plots in a TOR lose out through inexplicable delays mainly caused by the fact that the municipality and the army challenge the FEDC in claiming rights to the land.

73. Ryzhova (2019).

74. Quoted in Ryzhova (2019: 17–18).

75. Holzlehner (2018). Bliakher and Vasil'eva (2010) discuss the mass protests in Vladivostok, when the authorities raised the customs tax on imported cars.

76. See Ryzhova (2012) for a detailed example.

77. Maryana Rimskaya, "Like 'Lepers': Big Plans in Russia's Far East Leave Locals on Wrong Side of the Tracks," RadioFreeEurope/Radio-Liberty, December 8, 2018, https://www.rferl.org/a/big-plans-in-russian-far-east-leave-locals-on-wrong-side-of-the-tracks/29645054.html.

78. Throughout the Far East, thousands of the rural *otkhodniki* are employed in industrial fishing companies like Dobroflot. Even as regular inhabitants of coastal towns and remote places like Kamchatka seek to emigrate to "the mainland," as they call central Russia, people are streaming in the other direction to take up precarious temporary contracts filleting, salting, canning, and transporting fish; they come from even more deprived corners of the vast country and from Central Asia.

79. As the Dobroflot chair commented: "We are buying back much of our exported fish as ready products. On our side, the whole chain of fish production is strongly monopolized, from access to the bio-resources to the infrastructure to retailing. The result is that the goods go to a foreign buyer, even if Russian consumers would be prepared to pay a good price for wild fish. . . . And when it is imported back, you are interacting with Rossel'khoznadzor, Rospotrebnadzor, Rosryblovstvo, and the border and customs services. While you are filling in all the paperwork, the fish may become unsellable." "Pryamoi navodkoi," July 24, 2018, https://rg.ru/2018/07/24/reg-szfo/pomogut-li-investicionnye-kvoty-rossijskim-rybopromyshlennikam.html.

80. "Pererabotchika ostavili bez ryby," November 25, 2019, https://www.kommersant.ru/doc/4170686.

81. In the 2010s, Chinese fishers in Russian waters were regularly arrested by Russian guards and occasionally shot at and killed. The Chinese media adopted an affronted stance: the action was violent, unacceptable, and contrary to international law. The *People's Daily* observed, "Generally, Chinese society is friendly toward Russia and supports the two countries' strategic cooperation. The aggressive behavior by some Russians at the grass-roots level not only harms Chinese confidence in fostering a long-term friendship with Russia, but also provides excuses for forces seeking to undermine China-Russia ties." "Russian Fire at Civilian Ship Unacceptable," *People's Daily* (China), July 18, 2012, http://en.people.cn/90883/7879005.html.

82. In December 2019, the Russia media reported the reappearance in Irkutsk of Il'ya Simoniya, a "criminal king" known as Makho. He had

been "dethroned" twenty-six years before by Grandfather Khasan and Yaponchik, another crime boss, in part because he was held not to merit the title of *vor* (thief), having been a member of Komsomol in his youth. He became a fugitive and a prisoner. But by 2018 Makho's enemies had been either assassinated or arrested. At a great criminal meeting held that year in Italy, his crown as *vor* was given back to him, and soon he returned to hold sway in Irkutsk. "Neproshchennyi," December 16, 2019, https://lenta.ru/articles/2019/12/16/vvz/.

83. Makhachkeev (2018).

84. Cannabis grows wild in Buryatia in abundance, and occasionally is also cultivated in areas further along the border. Village women gather it at night, often selling it to prisons and labor camps, saying they are ashamed but have no other way of supporting their children. Gangs of young men make a more determined business of this, and some of the drugs then find their way to China. Nadezhda Tsoi, "Anasha," *Ard*, June 11, 2014, http://asiarussia.ru/blogs/3125/; "V Buryatii detei vse chashche lovyat s konoplei," October 26, 2019, https://gazeta-n1.ru/news /incidents/79697/.

85. Frozen fish figure for 2016: "China and Russia Food Trade: What's on the Menu?," ITE Group, Food and Drink, October 19, 2017, http://www.food-exhibitions.com/Market-Insights/Russia/China -Russia-food-trade.

86. "Kvoty v obmen na investitsii," http://tyum-pravda.ru/sport-main /20-newspaper-articles/press-obzor/24857-kvotyi-v-obmen-na-investitsii, accessed December 2019.

87. Ryzhova (2012).

88. "Brakonery protiv predstavitelei pravoporyadka," http://vladmama .ru/forum/viewtopic.php?f=1258&t=236788, accessed December 2019.

89. All quotations from "Brakonery protiv predstavitelei pravopory-adka."

90. Quotation from Kordonskii et al. (2011: 15–16).

91. Abrahm Lustgarten, "How Russia Wins the Climate Crisis," *New York Times*, December 16, 2020. A different global crisis, the COVID-19 pandemic, saw Chinese agricultural workers in Russia retreat home. To the surprise of many, the soybean farms in the RFE were able to keep up decent, if reduced, production by employing Russian workers in the 2020 season. The main problem was their lack of training with high-tech machinery, but companies set up rapid training courses, determined not to lose the great profits to be made. So far, Russia has not succeeded in get-ting companies to invest in processing plants, so soy and corn reinforce Russia's role as a raw materials supplier. Possibly as a consequence of

climate change, corn and even rice are becoming other key agricultural exports to China. Ivan Zuenko, "Pandemic Changes Face of Farming in Russian Far East," commentary, Carnegie Moscow Center, December 18, 2020, https://carnegie.ru/commentary/83484?utm.

4. INDIGENOUS PEOPLES OF THE BORDERLANDS

1. The Daur (Ch: Dawoer) and the Khamnigan speak languages that are grammatically Mongolic but with admixtures of Tungusic vocabulary. The Manchus, having established the Qing Dynasty, spread out over northwest China and became widely Sinicized. At the end of the dynasty only some 100,000 were able to speak Manchu more or less fluently. By the 1980s, self-recognized Manchus were reduced to a few villages with a few hundred speakers of the language (Janhunen 1996: 48). Communist excoriation of the Manchus as exploiters kept self-identification as Manchu to a minimum. However, preferential policies for minorities in recent years have encouraged large numbers to register as Manchu. There are now 10.4 million in China, ranking as the fourth-largest ethnic group after the Han (1.2 billion), Zhuang (16.9 million), and Hui (10.5 million).

It often seems arbitrary whether people alike in language, economy, and way of life were or were not categorized as the same group. The Evenki, for example, today numbering around 38,500 in Russia, 31,000 in China, and 600 in Mongolia, are known as one people, although they live scattered over vast distances from west and north Siberia to Manchuria, have different economies, and speak diverse Tungusic languages (Balajieyi 2016). Meanwhile, the Oroqen in China are held to be distinct from the approximately 600 Oroch (or Orochon) living across the Amur in Russia and on Sakhalin Island. The Ulch group (population 2,765 in 2010), living near Khabarovsk in Russia, call themselves Nani and speak practically the same language as the Nanai (with a population of about 12,000), so it seems strange that they have been granted separate status and their own subdistrict. By far the largest of the non-Russian, non-Chinese peoples of the border are the Buryats and the Koreans. The Buryats, total population around 500,000, are an amalgam of Mongolic-language groups that formed inside Russia from the eighteenth century onward, incorporating sundry western and southern Mongols, Daurs, and Tungus over time. Large numbers of Buryats fled in waves to live in Mongolia (currently around 45,000) and China (currently around 10,000). The Khamnigan have been described as "Mongolized Tungus" in Wikipedia, but historical investigation has shown them to be an ancient Mongolian people (as they themselves claim), later joined by

Tungus migrating from the north (Janhunen 1996). According to unofficial figures, around 5,000 Khamnigan live in Russia, 3,500 in Mongolia, and 2,000 in China, where they are known as Tungus Evenki (Lavrillier et al. 2018: 38).

2. We do not discuss Koreans in this chapter since, although they are historically ancient inhabitants of the Pacific Far East, they are not "indigenous" to these borderlands in the sense in which we use the term. Korean farmers only began moving from the peninsula to Russian and Chinese territories in the nineteenth century, often to escape famine. Now some 1.8 million live in China, where they are called Joseonjok, and have their own autonomous prefecture, Yanbian, adjacent to the North Korean and Russian borders. In Russia, the Koreans go by a different name, Koryo-saram. Suspected of disloyalty by Stalin, they were deported away from the border en masse to Central Asia in the 1930s. The majority of Russian Koreans still live in Kazakhstan and Uzbekistan, but some 170,000 have returned to the border area on the Russian side (Park 2017; Pulford 2019).

3. Reeves (2014).

4. See Donahoe et al. (2008) for a detailed analysis of the politics of indigeneity in Russia and the factor of population size.

5. We adopt the shorthand neologism "Nanai-Hezhe" following Pulford (2017; 2019).

6. On links with Mongolia and Tibet: Bernstein (2013: 34); Zhanaev (2019: 19).

7. Urbansky (2020: 39–122); Pulford (2019: 35–36).

8. Blyakher (2018).

9. On the deportations: Humphrey (2019).

10. Sneath (2008).

11. OMON is a branch of the Russian National Guard that is used to put down disturbances.

12. Andrew Roth, "Siberian Shaman Arrested on Trek to Exorcise Vladimir Putin," *Guardian*, September 19, 2019; Maria Chernova, "A Warrior Shaman and a Disputed Mayor: Russia's Buryatia Is on Edge," Radio Free Europe/Radio Liberty, September 19, 2019, https://www.rferl.org/a/tensions-russia-buryatia-shaman/30173368.html. For an illuminating analysis, see Jonutytė (2020).

13. Peshkov (2014).

14. Scott (1998); Humphrey (2015).

15. Jonutytė (2020).

16. Under the Qing, the term Solon referred to a military formation, whose members, as with the Cossacks in Tsarist Russia, included people

of various indigenous groups. During the twentieth century, Solon became an ethnic identity.

17. Shan (2006: 188).

18. Lavrillier et al. (2018: 7).

19. Nikolai Tsyrempilov, "Samdan Tsydenov and His Buddhist Theocratic Project in Siberia," December 13, 2014, Tibetan Buddhist Encyclopedia, http://www.tibetanbuddhistencyclopedia.com/en/index.php?title =Samdan_Tsydenov_And_His_Buddhist_Theocratic_Project_In_Siberia _by_Nikolay_Tsyrempilov; Damdin Shulunov, "Narod odinnadtsai rodov. Pochemu u khori-buryat net klanovosti?," *Ard,* August 13, 2017, http://asiarussia.ru/articles/17286.

20. Urbansky (2020: 167).

21. A few of these displaced indigenous people may indeed have been forced to become double agents (Namsaraeva 2017).

22. Zhanaev (2019).

23. This experience was to be depicted later in the bestselling semi-autobiographical novel *Lang Tuteng* (Wolf totem, 2004), by Jiang Rong. Jiang, whose real name is Lu Jiamin, used the episode to make a rhetorical contrast between the Mongols, caricatured admiringly as courageous, cruel, and determined (wolf-like, close to nature) and the Han Chinese, who are disparaged as meek (sheep-like, overly urbanized).

24. As in Russia, in China cellphones and satellite television spread in Evenki and Daur villages before houses were supplied with running water (Legerton and Rawson 2009: 29).

25. Ruget and Usmanalieva (2008).

26. Kadare (1998).

27. Kadare (1998: 119).

28. Fromm (2010: 2–3).

29. The politicized concept of indigeneity arose in 1970s debates on Western colonialism and racism. It is not native to either Russia or China, and its spread to those countries can be seen as an aspect of cultural globalization.

30. Janhunen (1996); Lavrillier et al. (2018).

31. The ancestors of the indigenous peoples had been incorporated in successive empires: the Liao dynasty (916–1125), ruled by the proto-Mongol Khitan (Qidan) people; the Jurchen Jin empire (1115–1234), from whose Tungusic rulers the Manchus claimed descent; and the Mongol Yuan empire (1271–1368). From the mid-seventeenth century they paid tribute to or served as auxiliary soldiers in either the tsarist or the Manchu Qing empires.

32. In tsarist Russia, the native peoples of Siberia were subject to classification on non-ethnic principles (Slezkine 1994: 81). Seen as too primitive to qualify as "nations," the natives were classified as "aliens" (*inorodtsy*, literally "people of other birth") and grouped into three subcategories according to their way of life: "settled," "nomadic," and "wandering." The categories had different rights and obligations to the state and, more broadly, were part of the tsarist system of estates (*soslovie*), which lasted until 1917. For discussion of Chinese principles of classification in different periods, see Purdue (2009). Under the Qing, neither language nor ethnicity were decisive. For example, the Solon was a military formation of reserve troops (Banners) consisting of Tungus/Evenki, Orochen, and Daurs living adjacently in northwest Manchuria. Considered uncivilized in Chinese eyes because they were nomadic, lived in the wilderness, and did not have their own writing systems, "the Solon" were reconceptualized in the twentieth century as a "people" (*minzu*). In 1957, they were divided up and moved to scattered new locales; at this point they were reclassified along ethnic lines that took into account differences in language and economy. Many of the former Solon (with a present population of about 25,000) were merged with Reindeer Evenki and Khamnigan under the umbrella Evenki label. As with the Daur (population about 132,000), another territorially divided people, the majority of Solon now live in the interior of Manchuria, not in the borderlands (Shan 2006; Dumont 2017; Lavrillier et al. 2018).

33. Guldin (1994).

34. Dumont (2017).

35. Donahoe et al. (2008: 998–999).

36. These policies change from time to time in accordance with international relations. In recent years, the good relations with China have meant that Buryats living in China can claim "ancestral right of return" to Russia, whereas those descended from the refugees to Mongolia cannot. In 2020, hoping to reverse falling population, Moscow proposed removing its former demand that incomers renounce the citizenship of their country of birth in order to get a Russian passport. See Marc Bennetts, "Putin Relaxes Citizenship Laws to Reverse Falling Population," *The Times*, April 20, 2020, 28; Ksenia Zubacheva, "Does Russia Allow Dual Citizenship?," *Russia Beyond* [Russian state-owned publication], September 18, 2018, https://www.rbth.com/lifestyle/329151-dual-citizenship; and "Dual Citizenship China," dualcitizenship.com, n.d., https://www.dualcitizenship.com/countries/china.html, accessed March 2020.

37. Bashkuev (2015).

38. In the Russian Federation, forty-six peoples have the status of "indigenous small-numbered peoples of the North, Siberia and the Far East." The criteria are that they must not number over 50,000, should maintain a traditional way of life, should live in areas traditionally inhabited by their ancestors, and should self-identify as a distinct ethnic group (Koch and Tomaselli 2015: 7).

39. Donahoe et al. (2008: 993).

40. The "small peoples" have the right to use "territories of traditional use of nature" (TTP) free of charge. However, Federal Law 118-FS of 2007 made use of TTP subject to the Land and Forest Codes and thus subject to payment of licenses. The "small peoples" now must compete with far richer enterprises for licenses (Koch and Tomaselli 2015).

41. The Russian Association of the Indigenous Peoples of the North (RAIPON) provides information to the small peoples about their rights, organizes courses on legal changes, and so forth. When indigenous groups are in conflict with large companies over rights to resources, such as fish or timber, the courts usually decide in favor of the companies, and rights to compensation tend to be blocked. After several failed cases brought by indigenous groups, RAIPON sent a critical report to the UN, but RAIPON was then pursued by the Russian authorities and closed down for a period. It was only allowed to reopen after an international outcry in 2013. For a description of several examples, see Koch and Tomaselli (2015).

42. Available datasets go back to 2002, when life expectancy for males had dropped to 49.1 years when the national average was 59.6 years, with females at 60.5 years, significantly less than the national average of 72.4 years. The unemployment rate reached 50 percent in some communities, according to 2010 data. Around 48 percent of the "small people" population have only elementary education, and 17 percent are illiterate. Many of the smallest groups face extinction of their languages, as very few schools teach in the native languages. Koch and Tomaselli (2015).

43. Dumont (2017).

44. The recognition of an administrative unit as an ethnic autonomy depends on having sufficient Chinese population as well as that of the titular minority. Given that the ruling Communist Party is held to have transcended ethnicity and that minority representation is supposed to be proportional to the percentage of population and is always a minority, the balance of power is always in Chinese hands.

45. A representative of China made the latest statement repeating this standing point at the UN General Assembly (Third Committee, Seventy-

fourth Session) on October 11, 2019, while responding to the accusations made by the representative of the United States on the human rights of Uyghur people in Xinjiang.

46. On rehabilitation aim: Nakawo, Konagaya, and Shinjilt (2010); Fraser (2010); Xie (2018).

47. Dumont (2017).

48. Jonathan Watts, "Inner Mongolia Protests Prompt Crackdown," *Guardian*, May 30, 2011.

49. Chinese scholars have pointed out the lack of a clarity in the legal grounds for intangible cultural heritage (ICH) suits brought by indigenous people. They hail, however, a landmark case in which Sipai, a Hezhe ethnic village, won copyright damages from CCTV for the commercialization of one of their folksongs (Lin and Lian 2018). In contrast to the legal path pursued in China, in Russia, where ICH rights of indigenous people are even more neglected, specialists point to the need for government officials to "take responsibility" (Koptseva and Kirko 2014).

50. Dumont (2017).

51. Fraser (2020).

52. Paula Haas, personal communication based on fieldwork in 2011–2012.

53. Detailed figures are hard to come by. But let us cite one case for which there is information, which, although dated, shows how multiethnic remote border settlements can be. Shibazhan is an "Oroqen township" located near the Amur consisting of several villages. Not including the government forestry company and a military unit nearby, the township in 1994 had 1,357 households, with a total population of 4,458, including 546 Oroqen, 194 Manchu, 21 Mongol, 17 Daur, 13 Korean, 6 Evenki, 6 Hui Muslim, 2 Sibe, and 1 Russian. The remainder, the majority, were Han Chinese (Noll and Shi 2009: 126, quoting Guan and Wang 1998: 24).

54. "Nanaiskaya derevnya Chzhuatszi," http://fuyuan.ru/attractions /chzhuatszi/, accessed April 2020.

55. "Nanaiskaya derevnya 抓吉镇 naprotiv Rossii," May 19, 2021, https://aleonkin.livejournal.com/283333.html.

56. "Nanaiskaya derevnya Zhuatszy," November 21, 2012, https:// aleonkin.livejournal.com/297924.html.

57. In the late nineteenth century, the Nanai-Hezhe were prosperous and firmly attached to the Manchu Qing, both economically and socially. They received imperial rewards of horses, cattle, servants, and clothing in return for their valuable tribute in furs. Tribute gave the right to trade. As well as their plentiful fish, they sold furs, ginseng, and deer horns to

Chinese and Manchu merchants. Classified into four ranks, each rewarded with appropriate symbols of status, the highest were clan chiefs (*hala i da*), who were given judicial rights and entitled to wear silk coats with embroidered dragons and buttons of rank on their hats. The wealthy could pay to have marriages arranged for them with daughters of Manchu aristocrats. With such close and relatively profitable integration, it is not surprising that many Nanai-Hezhe continued to pay tax to the Manchus into the late nineteenth century, long after most of the land they lived on was ceded to Russia (Sasaki 2016: 170–178).

58. See revealing documentary photographs in "Selo Sikachi-Alyan, Khabarovskii Krai," https://golovko.livejournal.com/202225.html, accessed March 2020.

59. See http://trip-dv.ru/object/84. This website, accessed in March 2020, can no longer be located, but a similar tourist's view can be seen at "Sikachi-Ayan," February 21, 2021, https://ku-ku-lena.livejournal.com /37770.html.

60. Pulford (2019: 138–139).

61. Humphrey (2017); Park (2017).

62. Donahoe et al. (2008: 999). National-minded Buryats have bitter memories of the division and reduction of the Buryat-Mongol ASSR in 1937, the removal of "Mongolian" from its name in 1958, the loss of the republic's autonomy in 2002, and the absorption of the two split-off Buryat enclaves into Russian provinces in 2006.

63. Sem (2017: 217–226).

64. Bulgakova (2013: 220).

65. Neo-shamanism is contested by some Nanai leaders, who say it is a dangerous smattering of knowledge picked up from everywhere, and "we are atheists" (Bulgakova 2013: 222).

66. Chi (2005).

67. Pulford (2019: 176–177).

68. Pulford (2017; 2019: 140).

69. Smolyak (2001) and Sasaki (2016) concur that Nanai clans (*hala*), which were divided into exogamous patrilineal subgroups (*mokon*), were not territorial or residential units. The *hala* was used by the Qing as the administrative unit for tax collection among all border populations and it was not a strictly genealogical body (Sasaki 2016: 171–172). Smolyak argues that villages, which always contained members of several clans, were more socially important. They regulated hunting and fishing grounds, whereas the clans, after their political-administrative function ended in 1911, kept a role only in marriage arrangements and certain religious traditions. By the 1960s–1970s the main role of clans was to regulate exogamy (Smolyak 2001: 178–181).

70. However, some enthusiasts and folklorists have resurrected or perhaps invented clan symbols that are painted on shields displayed in the Sikachi-Alyan museum.

71. We are grateful to Professor Sasaki for supplying this information from his field notes.

72. Historically such networks extended to Sakhalin, Hokkaido, and even Alaska (Pulford 2019: 137).

73. Safonova and Sántha (2013).

74. Schweitzer and Povoroznyuk (2019).

75. Pulford (2019: 136).

76. Sungorkin sees the Sinified Hezhe as worse off than the Russian-dominated Nanai, because "the Chinese have not forgiven the Manchus for ruling over them as the Qing dynasty and so they punish all Tungusic people. Us and the Manchus—we used to be known as the Jurchen and we harassed and ruled over the Chinese for centuries!" (quoted in Pulford 2019: 138).

77. Ol'ga Appolonova, "Leonid Sungorkin: ne ryboi edinoi zhiv nanaets," June 5, 2015, https://hab.aif.ru/society/leonid_sungorkin_ne _ryboy_edinoy_zhiv_nanaec.

78. "Nanaitsy idut v sekty: pochemy pravitel'stvo Furgala ignoriruet korennye narody," October 18, 2019, https://www.dvnovosti.ru/khab /2019/10/18/105852/#comments. An interesting insight into Russian minority politics is revealed by Sungorkin's protest staged in 2014 in support of the rights of "indigenous Russians" in Crimea. Part of the motive may have been to curry favor with the authorities. But Sungorkin was too much of a troublemaker in official eyes for this to be an effective move. Paul Goble, "Citing Defense of Ethnic Russians in Crimea, Small Nationality in Russian Far East Demands Moscow Intervene," *Interpreter,* March 21, 2014, https://www.interpretermag.com/citing -defense-of-ethnic-russians-in-crimea-small-nationality-in-russian-far -east-demands-moscow-intervene/.

79. Newell (2004: 134–135).

80. "New Report Highlights Indigenous Rights Violations in Russia," *Cultural Survival,* July 11, 2019, https://www.culturalsurvival.org/news /new-report-highlights-indigenous-rights-violations-russia; "Istoriya zashchitnika korennykh narodov, kotoryi sbezhal v SShA ot russkikh spetssluzhb," December 27, 2019, https://snob.ru/entry/186908/.

81. For the period prior to Xi's tightening of control, Johan Lagerkvist (2015) argued that "staggering numbers" of unnoticed social protests took place in China every year. Although they mostly concerned general problems such as corruption or socioeconomic inequality, they did not spread, in part because the institutions of government still scored high

on legitimacy, despite intrusive surveillance. Lagerkvist's examples come from south China, not the minorities of the far northeast. It is interesting nevertheless, given the concerns of this chapter, that he shows how unofficial social groupings, such a clans, figured strongly as the organizers of protest.

82. Brandtstädter (2020: 8).

83. Approximately 440,000 Buryats live in Russia, 46,000 in Mongolia, and 70,000 in China; 86,000 Bargas live in China (Inner Mongolia) and 2,600 live in eastern Mongolia.

84. The mythical ancestress (mother) of Chinggis's clan, Alan Goa (Alun Gua), is claimed to have been the daughter of Khoridai, the prime ancestor of the Khoris.

85. The chart is in the Cyrillic script used in Buryatia (Russia) and Mongolia but not in China, where the vertical Mongol script is still employed. The restaurant therefore used it to attract transborder customers rather than locals, who would find it difficult to read.

86. Lattimore (1934: 159–161).

87. Around one-third of all Buryats count themselves as Khoris. Most live in a cluster of districts to the east of Lake Baikal, but subgroups are found all over Buryat lands, as well as in Mongolia and China. Shulunov argues that Khoris think of themselves as a "great people" spread through Inner Asia and like to position themselves as standing for the Buryats as a whole. In regional politics they are therefore not narrowly "clannish" in a genealogical sense. They are challenged by the Tsongol-Sartuul groups living in the south of Buryatia, whose ancestors migrated to the Baikal area more recently and speak a different dialect. Political life in Buryatia is based on alliances between such ethno-territorial amalgams. Their leaders are mostly preoccupied with their standing vis-à-vis the Russian majority in the Republic. Sometimes they line up with, and at other times they attempt to oppose, the *varyagi* (imperious placemen delegated from Moscow), so called after the Viking warrior leaders (*varyagi*) who ruled the early Slavs. Shulunov, "Narod odinnadtsai rodov." See also Zhanaev (2019).

88. On weddings: Humphrey (2017). On *oboo* rituals: Dumont (2017); also Charleux and Smith (2021).

89. A traditional male feat is the ability to break a big livestock femur with a chop of the hand.

90. The festival is named after the *altargana* plant (goldenrod) because it is hardy and has strong, deep roots that spread far underground.

91. Zhanaev (2019: 26).

92. Bernstein (2008: 25).

93. Metzo (2002) describes similar dynamics in the festivals of the Khongodory, another ethnic group akin to the Khori that sprawls across the Buryat, Mongolian, and Tyvan borders.

94. The Khamnigan are among the most genuinely autochthonous of the indigenous peoples, and they claim ancient, pre-Chinggisid Mongolian ancestry. The twentieth century treated them harshly. Splintered into three countries, discriminated against by the Buryats for their alleged Tungusic character, they became a kind of satellite ethnicity: poor, marginalized, often ending up as laborers for others. However, of late, Khamnigan activists have crept out of the shadows. Now they too extoll their ancient clans, fashion emblems and flags, and attempt to organize their own cross-border festival.

95. Bernstein (2013).

96. Tibetan monks have become prominent teachers in Russian and Mongolian Buddhist regions, which they tend to see as steeped in superstition (Bernstein 2013: 95). Ayusheev counteracts their influence as best he can and speaks scornfully of the Dalai Lama in comparison to President Putin. Exclaiming that Putin is a deity, the White Tara, in his eyes, he said: "Listen, dear comrades, who feeds me, who gives money to my old people—a foreign big lama or the president of the country?" Ol'ga Andreeva, "Tak govorit Khambo Lama," *Russian Reporter*, May 13, 2013, https://expert.ru/russian_reporter/2013/19/tak-govorit-hambo-lama/.

97. Bernstein (2013: 103).

98. The people of the Barguzin Valley are not Bargas by the usual reckoning. Their ancestors migrated from west of Lake Baikal three centuries ago and belong to different clans from the Khori-Barga. Their Barga identity could not be claimed through ancestry but only by residence in the spirit-domain of the "grandfather" (*baabai*) of Baragkhan mountain.

99. For a detailed description of this event, see Namsaraeva (2020).

100. The history and relative geographical remoteness of the Chinese Bargas and Buryats give them a different perspective on the central state from that adopted by most of the Southern (Inner) Mongols. See Han (2011) for an insightful discussion of the quiescence of the latter and the cooling of their cross-border relations with the Mongols of Mongolia.

101. Abida (1985).

102. For example, Abida's text painted the Shenehen fugitives as victims of "White Terror," when in fact elders remembered well that their parents had fled from the Bolsheviks (Namsaraeva 2012: 235).

5. FRIENDS, FOES, AND KIN ACROSS THE BORDER

1. An eccentric who claims she has extrasensory powers, Nino is well known at the Confucius Institute. Her fame now also extends beyond the institute thanks to local newspapers publishing her story. "'Ya iskala ee vsyu zhizn': Blagoveshchenskaya ekstrasens nashla kitaiskuyu podrugu po perepiske spustya polveka," *Amurskaya Pravda*, April 4, 2013, http://www.ampravda.ru/2013/04/04/038129.html.

2. Patricia Shishmanova, "Bereg Byvshikh Russkikh," *Vokrug Sveta*, February 28, 2011, http://www.vokrugsveta.ru/vs/article/7374.

3. Tianyu Fang, "Who's Chinese? The Farmer-Turned-Livestreaming Star Who's Challenging China's Ideas of Racial Identity," *Radii*, April 4, 2019, https://radiichina.com/farmer-livestreaming-star-china-identity.

4. Beginning in August 1985, this reopening was gradual, with only a few border posts open to travelers. Manzhouli was one such land port (Peshkov 2018: 128). For people living in Blagoveshchensk, which did not reopen until 1991, this involved traveling about 1,000 miles west to be able to cross the border, despite living in a town located merely 500 yards from China.

5. The closure was such that from 1970, China would appear only sporadically in the local newspapers. For twenty-six years the Soviet regional press would refrain from mentioning Chinese cities just across the border. As a result, Russian border dwellers learned surprisingly little about China during the period of conflict (Urbansky 2020: 243–244).

6. A recent Russian-language tourism advertisement prepared by the municipality of Heihe branded the town as a bridge between China and Russia, with the slogan "One City Two Countries. Enchanting Heihe" (一城两国, 魅力黑河).

7. For a full account of the events, see Dyatlov (2003), Qi (2009), and Zatsepine (2011).

8. A visa is required, however, for visits further inland. In 2014, the city of Vladivostok launched a visa-free travel regime with South Korea for stays of up to sixty days. This has led to a rapid rise in the number of South Korean visitors, thus transforming Vladivostok's cityscape and helping local businesses develop. There are now more daily flights between Vladivostok and Seoul than with Moscow, and nine airlines currently operate flights to South Korea. Suggestions of extending this regime to Chinese citizens have not been well received: "Alarmists say an inflow of Chinese could lead to 'ethnic crime,' environmental catastrophes, and even the Far East's secession from Russia." Ivan Zuenko, "The Vladivostok Phenomenon: Should Russia Eliminate Visa Requirements for Chinese Tourists?," Carnegie Moscow Center, September 1, 2019, https://carnegie.ru/commentary/78084.

9. For more details on Sino-Russian trade in the early 1990s, see Kuhrt (2007).

10. In other parts of the Russian Far East, notably in the Primorskii krai, *kirpichi* are referred to as "camels" (*verblyudy*).

11. Anthropologist Vera Skvirskaja notes that for Russians the idea of friendship implies a selfless emotional relationship of trust, but in their eyes the Chinese do not share this cultural understanding. For the Chinese, "friendship is said to be a façade that disguises calculations of benefits" (Skvirskaja 2018).

12. On the question of trust and mistrust in the China-Russia borderlands, see Humphrey (2018c) and Peshkov (2018).

13. Humphrey (2018b).

14. See also Pulford (2019).

15. Ed Pulford (2019: 133) notes that new trends such as bikes and in-line skates originated in China, and that vegetables coming from China have made vegetarianism possible in the Russian borderlands.

16. While, as we discuss later, there is a greater number of intimate exchanges than is publicly acknowledged or imagined, research carried out on HIV genetic variants in the Russian Far East does indicate closer links with other regions of Russia and former USSR countries. Despite close cultural and commercial relationships with China and Japan, researchers confirmed the relationship of subtype A viruses with the IDU-A variant predominating in Ukraine, Russia, and other former Soviet Union countries, and only one sample possibly related to Chinese variants. See Kazennova et al. (2014).

17. Barabantseva and Grillot (2019).

18. Peshkov (2018: 133–134).

19. Barabantseva and Grillot (2019: 296). By "raising population quality" (人口素质, *renkou suzhi*) is meant "improving the general civility of the Chinese population as a whole, including education, manners, and habits" (Barabantseva and Grillot 2019: 293).

20. Barabantseva and Grillot (2019: 293).

21. Barabantseva (2021: 5).

22. Russian women living in China with their Chinese husbands also have to face challenges with regard to parental rights. According to Chinese law, children born of such unions automatically have Chinese citizenship. As China does not allow for dual citizenship, this bestows far more rights on the father and thus increases feelings of precariousness for the foreign wife, particularly in cases of divorce (Barabantseva 2021).

23. Yan (2003).

24. Billé (2015).

25. Gamsa (2018: 48).

26. On the stereotype of the docility of Asian women, see Billé (2018a).

27. Representations of Russian women in the Chinese media are consistently positive. Modern and civilized, they tend to be placed at the top of a hierarchy of "foreign brides" (Barabantseva and Grillot 2019: 296).

28. "Krepkaya kitaiskaya druzhba. Chto kitaitsy dumayut o Rossii," *Varlamov,* January 29, 2015, http://varlamov.ru/1264197.html.

29. The increased flow of migration and trade across northeast Asia, especially from North Korea to China and South Korea, and between China, Mongolia, and Russia, has had repercussions for the spread of HIV in the region. Little is known about infection rates among migrants since studies in Asian countries are "rarely carried out among migrant communities and, if they are, the risk of stigmatization is high" (Iredale, Zheng, and Ko n.d.).

30. Casinos nonetheless remain attractive propositions to lure gamblers from China and other Asian countries. Russia's biggest gambling complex was recently built in Artëm, 25 miles from Vladivostok, financed largely by a Hong Kong company. Andrew Higgins, "In Russia's Far East, a Fledgling Las Vegas for Asia's Gamblers," *New York Times,* July 1, 2017.

31. For an analysis of similar trends at the border between Mongolia and China, see Lacaze (2012).

32. This is not limited to the Russian-Chinese interface. Russian women, and indeed women from the former Soviet Union generally, are also widely perceived as hypersexualized in Turkey where, referred to as "Natashas," they are frequently equated to prostitutes (Bloch 2017: 6–8, 125–126).

33. Pulford (2019: 81). See also Chapter 7.

34. Needless to say, these preconceptions were not borne out by the drawings made by the students.

35. "Wise elder sister": Andrei Piontkovskii, "Mudraya starshaya sestra," Radio Svoboda, May 28, 2014, http://www.svoboda.org/content/article/25399746.html.

36. In recent years, some tourist signs bearing Chinese script have appeared in a few spots in central Blagoveshchensk, but locals are resistant to seeing too much of a Chinese cultural imprint in Russian public spaces, feeling that it looks like China is going to take over.

37. Étienne Bouche, "Fleuve Amour: le jeu en eau rouble de Pékin," *Libération,* April 21, 2017.

38. Close to half of the total number of Confucius Institutes in Russia (seven out of eighteen) are found in the Russian Far East, a region that accounts for only 4.6 percent of Russia's population.

39. In his personal blog, Russian Sinologist Ivan Zuenko notes that the majority of graduates find the cultural differences too big and end up returning from China. Ivan Zuenko, "Pro Kitai i proforientatsiu," Radio Gvadalkvivir: Zametki praktikuyushchego kitayeveda i prochaya *labuda*, July 19, 2019, https://ivan-zuenko.livejournal.com/206202.html.

40. Some Chinese do speak excellent Russian, but they tend to be those working as *pomogaiki*. In many cases, these intermediaries began their careers as traders, learning to speak fluent Russian through interaction with their clients.

41. The most common examples given were *chifanit'* ("to eat," from *chifan,* 吃饭) and *chifan'ka* (restaurant), but other terms such as *fanzi* ("apartment," usually of poor quality, from *fangzi,* 房子) and *laovaiskii* ("foreign," from *laowai,* 老外) were also mentioned. Other expressions such as *mne mafanno* ("it's inconvenient to me," from *mafan,* 麻烦), *khaovarit'sya* ("fun" or "to have fun," from *haowanr,* 好玩儿), and *tinbudun* ("cannot understand" or "someone a little dumb," from *tingbudong,* 听不懂), while less common, were also known to some respondents.

42. Oglezneva (2007); Perekhval'skaya (2008); Fedorova (2018).

43. For an interesting comparison with emerging forms of Sino-African pidgins, see Driessen (2020).

44. See Billé (2016a).

45. See Fedorova (2017).

46. See Li (2018).

47. Callahan (2010).

48. *Ty* is the informal form of "you," equivalent to the French *tu,* and normally used with family members, close friends, and children. A similar observation was also made by Russian linguist Kapitolina Fedorova (2018).

49. Ivan Zuenko, "Aihui za rekoi. Krai surovyi tishinoi ob'yat. Kak kitaiskaya ekspansiya spotknulas' o rossiiskoe prigranich'e," *Centrasia,* February 16, 2016, https://centrasia.org/newsA.php?st=1455616020. Zuenko gives the example of Hunchun, a Chinese city on the border with Russia where not a single one of the ten richest business owners carries out any business with Russia.

50. See also Adda and Lin (forthcoming).

51. Zatsepine (2011: 111–112). In his book, historian Victor Zatsepine argues that the massacre was not an accident "but rather a calculated display of imperial power that Russian colonial authorities on the frontier allowed to happen" (2011: 108). Indeed, the choice of a quiet place on the river, in the village of Verkhne-Blagoveshchensk,

seven miles up the Amur River from Blagoveshchensk, was certainly made in order to avoid accidental witnesses (2011: 111).

52. The Sixty-Four Villages East of the River were a group of Manchu- and Han Chinese–inhabited villages located on the north bank of the Amur River opposite Heihe and on the east bank of the Zeya River opposite Blagoveshchensk. Recognized as Chinese enclaves in Russia according to the Aigun Treaty, they were annexed by Russia during the Boxer Rebellion. Their inhabitants were expelled and suffered the same fate as the Chinese living in Blagoveshchensk. The town of Aihui itself was destroyed during the events, making the location of the museum symbolically potent.

53. Dyatlov (2012: 16).

54. Balzer and Repnikova (2010: 2).

55. Viktor Dyatlov, personal communication.

56. Leonid Yuzefovich, "Zheltorossia: dalnevostochnaya utopia Rossii," *Russkii Zhurnal,* June 15, 2009, http://www.russ.ru/Mirovaya -povestka/ZHeltorossiya-dal-nevostochnaya-utopiya-Rossii. Stringent visa and work quota restrictions have contributed to reducing numbers of Chinese in the region.

57. There has been a resurgence of nationalism and xenophobia in western Russia, and the presence of skinheads in Moscow and elsewhere has negatively impacted the flow of students from China. On the virulence of anti-Chinese sentiments in Mongolia specifically, see Billé (2015).

58. There are other small museum spaces in the city, such as a display of prehistoric artifacts at the Pedagogical Institute and another small display at Amur State University, in both cases a single room with objects found in the region.

59. Alexseev (2006: 111).

60. "The Ussuri River tributaries Iman, Waku, and Li Fuzin became Bolshaya Ussurka, Malinovka, and Rudny respectively. Suchan became Partizansk, Iman Dalnerechensk, and Tetyukhe Dalnegorsk" (Stephan 1994: 19). As Elizabeth Wishnick elaborates, this 1973 decree was followed by a second one that renamed some 250 rivers and mountains that had Chinese names (Wishnick 2011: 55).

61. "Cryptic footnotes": Stephan (1994: 18). Teaching in 1980s: Ziegler (2015: 297–298).

62. For an interview with a couple of Russian settlers, see Qi Yue, "Mixed Blood on the Black Dragon," *Sixth Tone,* Shanghai United Media Group, October 12, 2016, http://www.sixthtone.com/news/1268 /mixed-blood-on-the-black-dragon.

63. Ziegler (2015: 332). See also the recent collection edited by Caroline Humphrey (2018c).

64. Billé (2018b).

65. Baldano (2012).

66. Mongolia and China: Billé (2015); Bulag (1998). Georgia and Turkey: Pelkmans (2006).

67. A similar situation is described by Guzel Sabirova (2016, 61) in the context of a Kyrgyz town on the border with China, where local people often use the term *tupik* (dead end) when speaking of their town.

6. RESOURCES AND ENVIRONMENT

1. "Man'chzhuriya, kotoruyu my ne znali," *ZabKrai,* July 18, 2016, http://zabkrai.ru/articles?path=%2Frfguidecontent-950%2Fman chguriya-kotoruyu-my-ne-znali.

2. Shaglanova (2011).

3. Reardon-Anderson (2005: 80). Much of the migration to Manchuria, as Diana Lary (2017: 35) has noted, was in fact seasonal, and this fluctuation has also been characteristic of Chinese presence in the Russian Far East. Open-cast mines and construction work shut down as the winter comes on; logging, on the other hand, is largely a winter occupation, since it is difficult to move cut timber when the ground is not frozen.

4. Liz Chee (2021, 4) dates the widespread use of animal parts in Chinese pharmacopeia to the early communist era. Many of the new animal-based medicinals or therapies were "new innovations, some were locally specific practices suddenly promoted on a national scale, and some represented new powers and efficacies suddenly bestowed on old and familiar substances." On traditional medicine in Russia, and in particular in Buddhist Siberia, see Chudakova (2021).

5. Although Chinese law makes it illegal to hunt and buy any of the country's 420 protected endangered species (which include Asiatic black bears, South China tigers, golden monkeys, and giant pandas), the statutory language is highly ambiguous. "An IFAW report on the illegal wildlife trade says that it's the fourth most profitable criminal activity in the world, after drug smuggling, financial counterfeiting, and human trafficking. China is the world's largest consumer of illegal wildlife products, which include rhino horn, bear bile, and tiger bone." Kayla Ruble, "China Outlaws the Eating of Tiger Penis, Rhino Horn, and Other Endangered Animal Products," *Vice,* May 2, 2014, https://www.vice.com /en_us/article/nem9ez/china-outlaws-the-eating-of-tiger-penis-rhino -horn-and-other-endangered-animal-products.

6. On *blat,* see Ledeneva (1998, 2006); on *guanxi,* see Kipnis (1997).

7. Forsyth (1992: 28).

8. Forsyth (1992: 41).

9. Forsyth (1992: 40).

10. Forsyth (1992: 40).

11. Fisher (1943: 122).

12. Forsyth (1992: 203).

13. On Mongolia, see Schlesinger (2017). The Chosŏn dynasty was a Korean dynastic kingdom that lasted for approximately five centuries. It was founded in 1392 and was replaced by the Korean Empire in October 1897. For a study of its environmental relations with Qing China, see S. Kim (2017).

14. Jonathan Schlesinger (2017: 67) warns against the assumption that Manchuria was ethnically coherent: the environmental history of Manchuria, he writes, "is illegible without taking seriously categories like [ethnic groups] Solon, *hojihon*, and *butha*." This is also true of the category of "Russian" hunters and Cossacks, who were a mixture of Russians and native populations.

15. Schlesinger (2017: 11).

16. The Jurchens combined with their neighbors as the Manchu and went on to rule China as the Qing Dynasty (1644–1912). Not all symbols were translatable across cultures. As discussed in Chapter 3, while jade has traditionally been culturally valuable in China, this was never the case in Russia.

17. S. Kim (2017: 5–6). As Ning (2018) has recently argued with respect to the Solon (索伦), the largest sable-hunting group of the Qing dynasty in Heilongjiang, the political use of fur tribute items at the Qing center reveals how the privilege of wearing fur defined the boundaries of the ruling hierarchy. Sable tribute, therefore, functioned throughout the dynasty as a mechanism for maintaining relations between the Manchu court and the hunting population.

18. S. Kim (2017: 43).

19. S. Kim (2017: 78). See also Ning (2018).

20. Bello (2015: 39).

21. Bello (2015: 48).

22. Border-making in East Asia has involved complex political, social, cultural, and ethnic interactions. For a detailed history of the border between Korea and China, see Song (2018). See also Kim (2019) for the lasting role played by minorities such as the Oroqen in the establishment of the border between Russia and China. On the understanding of "borders" from a Manchu perspective, see Elliott (2014).

23. S. Kim (2017: 157).

24. Billé (2015: 18).

25. Bello (2015: 74).

26. S. Kim (2017: 135).

27. Guandong is an older name for Manchuria. As historian David Bello notes, thousands of inhabitants in the Amur basin found themselves undergoing a not entirely voluntary removal southward under Qing auspices. "Like the ginseng, river pearls, and sable pelts enriching their forest habitat along the . . . tributary of the Sungari River, thousands of indigenous peoples were being hunted and gathered by both the multiethnic Romanov and Qing empires" (Bello 2015: 74). On the Russian side, the removal of indigenous populations was occasionally genocidal (see Forsyth 1992).

28. Gottschang and Lary (2000).

29. These deportations occurred from western Russia to the Gulags of Siberia and the Russian Far East, but also from the eastern borderlands to more "central" areas. The deportation of Koreans, forcibly moved in the 1930s from the Soviet-Korean border to Central Asia, is one of the better-known cases (see Park 2017).

30. Schlesinger (2017: 161).

31. Schlesinger (2017: 53).

32. Gamsa (2003: 257–258). See also Zatsepine (2018: 64–65); Kurto (2011).

33. These quotas have made it difficult for Chinese restaurants as well, often unable to bring Chinese cooks and having to rely on a local workforce with a lesser knowledge of Chinese culinary traditions and practices.

34. Billé (2015).

35. Urbansky (2020).

36. Ryzhova (2012).

37. For a visual representation of this complex network, see Ryzhova (2012: 106).

38. The region boasts an unusual profusion of hardwood species, including varieties of ash, maple, elm, and oak. The World Wildlife Fund believes the annual total is closer to at least 1 million a year. Sebastian Strangio, "Russia's Far East Forest Mafia," *Diplomat*, April 21, 2011, https://thediplomat.com/2011/04/russias-far-east-forest-mafia.

39. Newell and Lebedev (2000: 23).

40. Strangio, "Russia's Far East Forest Mafia."

41. *Tëmnyi Les* (Dark forest), https://www.youtube.com/watch?v=zM CLC52xSH4.

42. The 2006 Forest Code of the Russian Federation came into force on January 1, 2007, and is the basic law regulating forest management, control, and protection in Russia (Hitchcock 2011).

43. Similar practices are also employed by Russian car dealers importing vehicles from Japan. "One specific form is the practice of cutting the purchased cars in half, thus creating a hybrid commodity that can be declared as spare parts for customs purposes, a trick which substantially reduces the import tax. Back in Russia, the parts are reassembled and the cars refitted with new titles thus legally re-entering the market" (Holzlehner 2014: 25).

44. Strangio, "Russia's Far East Forest Mafia."

45. The view from China about Russian accusations has been met with incomprehension. According to an article published on the Chinese web and published in Russian translation at Inosmi.ru, this trade was carried out legally and honestly, and criticisms are therefore undeserved. "Kak vyshlo, chto Kitay okazalsya vinovatym? Pochemu na 'kitayskoy territorii' 250 tysyach chelovek sobrali podpisi s tsel'yu boykotirovat' Kitay?," *Inosmi,* September 5, 2018, https://inosmi.ru/politic/20180905/243154870.html. The original Chinese link no longer works, but another copy is available at the news aggregator Meiri Toutiao, "Zhongguo zenme dezui ta le? Weihe 'zhongguo tudi' shang 25 wan ren, lianming 'dizhi' zhongguo," August 31, 2018, https://kknews.cc/news/3orrglg.html.

46. Newell and Lebedev (2000: 13).

47. Newell and Lebedev (2000: 7).

48. Newell and Lebedev (2000: 15).

49. A Chinese bottling factory at Lake Baikal has attracted negative media coverage as well, even though other similar enterprises already operate there. Netalya Telegina, "Xenophobia Masquerading as Environmentalism," trans. Kevin Rothrock, May 17, 2019, *Meduza,* https://meduza.io/en/feature/2019/05/17/xenophobia-masquerading-as-environmentalism.

50. See "Huge Wildfires in Russia's Siberian Province Continue," National Aeronautics and Space Administration, August 16, 2019, https://www.nasa.gov/image-feature/goddard/2019/huge-wildfires-in-russias-siberian-province-continue

51. Sergei Vilkov, Viktoria Nemis, and Irina Kapitanova, "'Eto byla porokhovaya bochka': kakiye resheniya priveli k pozharam v Sibiri," *news.ru,* August 7, 2019, https://news.ru/incidents/eto-byla-porohovaya-bochka-kakie-resheniya-priveli-k-pozharam-v-sibiri.

52. Rachael Kennedy, "'Low Chance' Siberia Wildfires Will Be Brought under Control: Greenpeace Fire Expert," *Euronews* August 11, 2019, https://www.euronews.com/2019/08/06/siberian-wildfires-engulf-area-almost-the-size-belgium-as-states-of-emergency-are-declared; Vilkov, Nemis, and Kapitanova, "Eto byla porokhovaya bochka."

53. Shaglanova (2011: 298).

54. Shaglanova (2011: 298).

55. Safonova, Sántha, and Sulyandziga (2018: 209).

56. There are also of course significant cultural differences between the majority groups (Russians and Chinese) and their respective minorities. See, for instance, Ssorin-Chaikov (2000).

57. Humphrey (2018c).

58. Holzlehner (2014: 14).

59. Tom Phillips, "'Parched' Chinese City Plans to Pump Water from Russian Lake via 1,000km Pipeline," *Guardian*, March 7, 2017.

60. Part of a high-modernist imaginary, Natalie Koch writes, "the image of the Soviet man conquering nature figured centrally in the USSR's nationalist tropes. Spectacular projects to control landscapes and natural forces were seen as advertisements for the glories of the communist system over that of capitalism" (Koch 2018: 80).

61. Maria Repnikova and Alexander Gabuev, "Why Forecasts of a Chinese Takeover of the Russian Far East Are Just Dramatic Myth," *South China Morning Post*, July 14, 2017. The use of aggressive fertilizers by Chinese farmers in the Russian Far East is also indirectly encouraged by the short-term nature of lease agreements. Étienne Bouche, "Fleuve Amour: le jeu en eau rouble de Pékin," *Libération*, April 21, 2017.

62. In 2008, milk produced by the Sanlu Group was found to be contaminated with melamine, as a result of which six babies died and thousands were hospitalized. The general lack of trust in Chinese food products has led to a number of fake stories being disseminated on the internet, such as the case of fake eggs made from plastic. In countries neighboring China in particular, such as Mongolia, rumors of food-related Chinese malfeasance abound (Billé 2015).

63. See Lauren Bonilla, "Voluminous," *Fieldsights*, Society for Cultural Anthropology, October 24, 2017, https://culanth.org/fieldsights/1243-voluminous; Zee (2017, 2020).

64. Sergei Blagov, "Khabarovsk Voices China Chem Pollution Concerns," Independent Commodity Intelligence Services, November 10, 2006, https://www.icis.com/explore/resources/news/2006/11/10/1104943/khabarovsk-voices-china-chem-pollution-concerns.

65. Jen (2003).

66. Russian and Chinese majority groups also frequently differ from minority groups with respect to their relation to the environment. In China, minorities in Xinjiang, Tibet, and Inner Mongolia have addressed ecological collapse through popular songs (Baranovitch 2016). In the current context however, most particularly in Xinjiang, such critiques of China's central government are more difficult (and dangerous) to voice.

67. See "Norilsk, Siberia," Terra Satellite, National Aeronautics and Space Administration, July 8, 2008,https://www.nasa.gov/multimedia /imagegallery/image_feature_1124.html.

68. Catherine Belton, "For Russia, Dependence on 'A Man-Made Disaster,'" *New York Times*, January 12, 2006; Katarzyna Wysocka, "Russia: Radiation Contamination Facts Shrouded in Controversy," Radio Free Europe/Radio Liberty, October 9, 1996, https://www.rferl .org/a/1081934.html.

69. Michael Greenstone, "Four Years after Declaring War on Pollution, China Is Winning," *New York Times,* March 12, 2018.

70. Patrick Caughill, "China Is the New World Leader in Renewable Energy," *Futurism,* New York, January 16, 2018, https://futurism.com /china-new-world-leader-renewable-energy.

71. Stern (2013: 2).

72. Stern (2013: 8).

73. See Repnikova (2017b). "Speakability" is borrowed here from Judith Butler's (1997) work on publicly acceptable speech.

74. This of course must be taken in a context where speech censorship is very extensive. As Xinyuan Wang writes: "Generally speaking, censorship in China is implemented in a 'three-layer-filtering' system that includes at least three types of approaches simultaneously: Great Firewall, keyword blocking and manual censoring. The first filter is so-called the 'Great Firewall,' which blocks off certain websites and social media services (such as Facebook, Twitter and YouTube) from mainland China. The second filter is 'keyword blocking,' which automatically prevents people from publishing content containing banned keywords or phrases online. Given the nature of the Chinese language, however (different characters can have the same pronunciation, and many characters look similar), people can easily replace those banned characters with alternatives, either possessing similar sound (homophones) or similar shape (homographs). The third filter is thus the last line of defence, in which 'improper' information that slipped through the cracks of the previous two filters will be censored manually. Given the huge amount of information online, the labour invested in 'manual censoring' is remarkable: it includes 20,000–50,000 internet police (*wang jing*) and internet monitors (*wang guan*) nationwide, around 250,000–300,000 '50-cent party members' (*wu mao dang*), and up to 1,000 in-house censors hired by each individual website for the sake of 'self-censorship'" (Wang 2016: 127).

75. Repnikova (2017b: x). See also Sorace (2017).

76. Repnikova (2017b: 125).

77. Sun and Tysiachniouk (2008: 187–188).

78. Sun and Tysiachniouk (2008).

79. Emily Yeh, "The Cultural Politics of New Tibetan Entrepreneurship in Contemporary China: Valorization and the Question of Neoliberalism," lecture given at the Mongolia and Inner Asia Studies Unit, Cambridge, UK, on June 1, 2021.

80. Telegina, "Xenophobia Masquerading as Environmentalism."

81. Lily Hartzell, "Land of the Big Cats: China and Russia Collaborate in Comeback," *China Dialogue,* London, November 27, 2019, https://www.chinadialogue.net/article/show/single/en/11693-Land-of-the-Big-Cats-China-and-Russia-collaborate-in-comeback. The park, "Land of the Big Cats," would combine China's Northeast Tiger and Leopard National Park with Russia's Land of the Leopard National Park and Kedrovaya Pad Nature Reserve.

82. Positive protection of megafauna can, however, obscure a progressive and incremental climatic damage that is more difficult to track (see Cons 2020). See also Mathur (2021) on tigers in the context of contemporary India.

83. Sperling (2015). A few years ago, state media reported he had personally immobilized one with a tranquilizer dart as it charged toward a nearby camera crew.

84. Laura Dattaro, "Vladimir Putin Really Loves Tigers—And It's Actually Making a Difference in the World," *Vice,* June 3, 2015, https://www.vice.com/en_us/article/59eznn/vladimir-putin-really-loves-tigers-and-its-actually-making-a-difference-in-the-world.

85. Andrew Jacobs, "'Putin's Tiger,' in a Territory Grab All His Own, Swims to China," *New York Times,* October 10, 2014.

86. Describing the reintroduction of a type of vulture called the lammergeyer in a natural reserve located on the mountains between France and Italy, geographer Julie Fall shows that fauna tend to be conceptualized in terms of national belonging: "One bird was released each year, in alternate countries. French managers repeatedly noted that the 'French' birds, bearing French names, inevitably went to live in Italy. . . . For the French managers, this implied that the neighbours had 'stolen' the French birds; for the Italians this meant that the birds preferred to live in Italy because 'nature was more natural' there" (Fall 2005: 251).

7. BRIGHT LIGHTS ACROSS THE AMUR

1. Manzhouli and Heihe are approximately the same size, with 250,000 inhabitants each, while Suifenhe is a little smaller, with 100,000.

2. Originally known as Railroad Siding 86, Zabaikalsk was dubbed Otpor (Repulse) in 1929 during an early Sino-Soviet conflict. In 1953,

provincial authorities tried to persuade Moscow to rename the little settlement to better reflect the friendly relations between the two states. As late as 1958, historian Sören Urbansky writes, it was rumored that it would soon be renamed Druzhba (Friendship). But perhaps nervous that the relations might sour later and require another renaming, "the principal decision makers opted for the neutral geographical choice" of Zabaikalsk (Transbaikalia) in 1958 (Urbansky 2020: 199).

3. Wade Shepard, "China's Largest Ghost City Is Now Almost Completely Full—But There's a Twist," *Forbes,* April 23, 2016. See also Hsing (2010).

4. Kirill Il'in, "Ogni obmana: Eksperty o spornom kosmicheskom snimke Blagoveshchenska i Heihe," *Amurskaya Pravda,* February 16, 2017, https://www.ampravda.ru/2017/02/16/072838.html.

5. However, many of them grew out of earlier settlements, often established by indigenous populations.

6. Widdis (2004: 33).

7. Hill and Gaddy (2003: 15). Some cities, however, are sited remotely because they emerged in relation to the extraction of specific resources and materials, others because they were connected to military industries.

8. As Ed Pulford writes, "ghost villages," numbering possibly as many as 20,000, are found all over Russia's horizonless taiga and tundra, and especially in the Russian Far East (2019: 125).

9. On propaganda, see, for instance, Shulman (2007).

10. Kotkin (1995).

11. Weinberg (1998).

12. Zatsepine (2011: 107).

13. As discussed in earlier parts of the book, during the Qing Dynasty (1644–1912) Manchuria was largely off-limits to Han Chinese settlers. See also Schlesinger (2017).

14. See Gottschang and Lary (2000).

15. Significant population movements were actively encouraged in the early part of the twentieth century to counter territorial encroachments by Russia, Japan, and Western powers, and the Sino-Japanese War of 1894–1895 and the Russo-Japanese War of 1904–1905 both intensified the drive to colonize Manchuria (Li 1989: 511). Spontaneous migration from central China into Manchuria continued into the 1950s, supplemented by planned relocations to Xinjiang and Inner Mongolia, as well as to other border regions. During that decade, the main flows of internal migration were toward the northeast provinces and the major cities, and some 13,000 people from Beijing, Tianjin, and Shenyang were relocated to Inner Mongolia and Manchuria (Li 1989: 512).

16. This is of course not specific to Heihe, or even to border towns. On Chinese urbanization, see Campanella (2008) and Hsing (2010).

17. As Mikhailova, Wu, and Chubarov (2019: 289) note, the use of the twin-city label on the two riverbanks has been asynchronous and asymmetrical: "while the term made its debut in official political discourse in Heihe over a decade ago, the Russian side incorporated it only five years later." If the two sides participate in joint tourism promotion events and trade fairs, they continue nonetheless to promote projects independently or even in competition with each other (297).

18. Bruno Maçães writes that the "border between Russia and China comes closer to our ideal concept of a border than any other contrasting case. The simple act of crossing an arbitrary line is here equivalent to entering a separate cultural world, with no gradients or transition, and the fact that the border has neither an eventful nor a rich history is surely a result of the fact that both countries have so far lived with their backs turned to it" (Maçães 2018: 157).

19. Saxer and Zhang (2016).

20. Fedorova (2017: 99). Another parallel with Las Vegas is the theme park quality of cities such as Manzhouli. Pulford writes that central sections of the town "resemble an effort to reproduce the streets of Paris with only Disney's cartoon *Hunchback of Notre Dame* as a source" (Pulford 2019: 75).

21. The architects use the term "duck" to denote buildings that explicitly represent their function through their shape and construction. By contrast, "decorated sheds" are generic structures with added signs and decor that indicate their purpose (Venturi, Brown, and Izenour 1977).

22. Victor Larin, a leading Russian expert on China at the Far East branch of the Russian Academy of Sciences in Vladivostok, discussing how efforts in building a bridge have stalled for decades, writes that finance officials in Moscow regularly complain about the cost, and military officers ask, "Why build a bridge over which Chinese tanks can come?" Andrew Higgins, "An Unfinished Bridge, and Partnership, between Russia and China," *New York Times,* July 16, 2016. Given that the river is frozen solid for several months every year and that it would therefore be relatively easy for troops to move across it, it seems that the main issue is primarily symbolic rather than pragmatic.

23. In fact, not only do they not travel in the same vessels, but Chinese and Russian travelers are funneled through wholly different immigration channels and do not encounter one another at any point of the crossing.

24. Mikhailova, Wu, and Chubarov (2019: 288).

25. This road bridge will allow both freight and passenger transport, but not the passage of private vehicles, whose traffic is regulated by bilateral agreement. At present, no such agreement exists between Russia and China.

26. David Nye writes that electricity was, from the very beginning, associated with ideas of modernity and spectacle (Nye 2010: 66). While the use of electricity has become commonplace, it continues to track elusive notions of modernity. Thus nighttime photos of the Korean Peninsula, with a bright South Korea and virtually invisible North Korea, position the two halves on a spectrum of modernity and development,

27. These criticisms are not without validity. One of the very first large buildings in Heihe, while the rest of the town was still undeveloped, was the tall Heihe International Hotel. Describing Astana, Kazakhstan, Natalie Koch notes that "many of the colorful new façades are literally just façades: one can walk around to the back of a building and see the old Soviet structure. Behind massive metal barricades along the city's broad new avenues, one can find neighborhoods of decrepit shacks just like those found in the country's provinces" (Koch 2010: 774).

28. There is much truth to this assessment, and the contrast between what is visible to tourists and the residential areas farther away is indeed often dramatic. However, the visible parts of Heihe, Manzhouli, and other border towns do not necessarily have a Russian audience in mind; they are also, indeed increasingly, part of the cities' branding for a domestic audience. In recent years, the residential areas beyond the tourist centers have also developed rapidly, thereby attenuating this contrast.

29. Such Russian assessments echo global associations of China with fake products (see Yu 2011). In the early 1990s fake Adidas trainers were sold in Blagoveshchensk as "Abibas." The name has stuck as shorthand for fake goods. Acknowledging that "China fakes" stories operate as a kind of framing device for Euro-America to cope with the perceived threat of China, Fan Yang (2016) writes that the cultural context from which they emerge is decidedly more complex, and that "real" and "fake" are enmeshed in larger concepts of branding, counterfeiting, and questions of property rights.

30. Peshkov (2018: 133).

31. Natalie Koch writes that "the spectacular and the unspectacular are contextually co-produced. . . . The spectacle of the center can only be intelligible when contrasted with something markedly different beyond its spatial and temporal confines" (Koch 2018: 136).

32. Peshkov (2018: 134).

33. Tuan (1974: 28).

34. Tuan (1974: 29).

35. Humphrey (2002).

36. Pachenkov (2011: 191). See also Spector (2017).

37. "Foreigner" is often a code word for Chinese; the term generally excludes Central Asians, who, although formally "foreigners," are former Soviet citizens and thus have a more ambivalent status.

38. Ashwin (2000).

39. Mandel and Humphrey (2002).

40. See Humphrey (2000: 260); Spector (2008: 47).

41. Humphrey (2000: 260).

42. Paradoxically, the word *yarmarka,* derived from the German words for "year" and "market," originally meant an annual open-air trade fair where foreigners would come to sell their goods and rowdy entertainments were put on as attractions. Recently, trading establishments of various kinds have adopted the word for its popular folk connotations.

43. In various cities such as Vladivostok, Ussuriisk, and Ulan-Ude, the Chinese were compelled to relocate to trade centers, which they disliked because of high rents and stricter regulations. In Vladivostok and Ussuriisk this virtually ended Chinese small trade in the town.

44. Pachenkov (2011: 198).

45. Pachenkov (2011: 182).

46. Oushakine (2009: 20).

47. Oushakine (2009: 17).

48. Chakrabarty (2002: xix).

49. See Ferguson (1999); Hosagrahar (2005).

50. Geographer Natalie Koch notes that this was especially clear in Central Asian cities, such as Tashkent, which "were imagined by early Russian settlers as dangerous and unhealthy because of their labyrinthine nature, allegedly fostering 'fanaticism, disease, and rebellion.' Soviet planners . . . often spoke derogatorily about the non-gridded urban patterns, which were cast as a symbol of an outdated social order" (Koch 2018: 53).

51. Early in Blagoveshchensk's history, travelers paid compliments to the city's wide streets and orthogonal layout (Mikhailova, Wu, and Chubarov 2019: 290). Ed Pulford reports that Blagoveshchensk's appeal for contemporary Chinese visitors continues to lie in its perpendicular streets that "offer 'European' vistas that would not look out of place in Berlin, Prague or Budapest" (Pulford 2019: 121).

52. Chita's central section also "follows a strict grid pattern reflective of the notional order and civility that an influx of Decembrists, more

numerous here than in Nerchinsk, reputedly brought when they arrived in 1827" (Pulford 2019: 64). However, the grid is not a feature of all Russian cities. Older cities such as Moscow or Irkutsk, having evolved organically over time, are not built on such a regular pattern. Moscow's layout is organized on a radial-concentric road pattern. See discussion in Campanella (2008: 100). Despite having been founded in the 1850s, Blagoveshchensk developed into its current form largely in the 1940s and 1950s, when, as mentioned previously, industries were established and many people were relocated there from western Russia.

53. Tuan (1977: 56). This Russian reluctance to embrace the vastness of Siberian geography was analyzed with great humor by Richard Stites in a wonderful article entitled "Crowded on the Edge of Vastness" (Stites 1999).

54. In *The Soviet City,* James Bater (1980: 10) notes that, unlike in western Europe or North America, the development of cities in Russia was very much under the thumb of officialdom from the middle of the seventeenth century until well into the nineteenth. Saint Petersburg was developed on a grid, and its "obvious rectilinearity . . . was further emphasized by regulations pertaining to street widths and building heights. Canals and fountains were liberally incorporated, both as safeguards against flooding and fires and as aesthetic features" (11).

55. Denison and Ren (2016: 12).

56. Denison and Ren (2016: 21–22). On Harbin, see Koga (2016) and Gamsa (2020).

57. Kapitolina Fedorova reports that near Manzhouli's city center, at a distance from usual touristic routes, "there are residential areas with apartment houses, markets, schools, hospitals and other typical city infrastructure. Costs of living are considerably lower than in the center, and most of the resident population lives there. But this 'real Manzhouli,' with its much more traditional way of life for China, is almost invisible to Russian tourists; it does not exist for them. On every Russian map of Manzhouli both published and circulating on the web, street names are given only for the central part of the city, while other areas are either left blank or not represented at all" (Fedorova 2017: 97).

58. Koolhaas (2004). In a study of the geographic imagery of Asia portrayed in James Bond movies, Lisa Funnell and Klaus Dodds note that while "East Asian cities like Tokyo, Hong Kong and Shanghai are depicted as highly developed, modernized, and cosmopolitan spaces, which are defined vertically . . . South, Southeast, and Southwest Asian cities Bangkok, Udaipur, Istanbul, and Ho Chi Minh City are presented as being lesser developed, pre-modern, and unsophisticated; they are

defined horizontally and primarily on the street level, more chaotic in feel, and through more natural materials and lighting" (Funnell and Dodds 2016: 110).

59. Ong (2011a: 207).

60. See discussion of *druga* in Chapter 5.

61. See also discussion in Chapter 3.

62. Sociologists Natalia Ryzhova and Tatiana Zhuravskaya (2015: 212) note that owners of Russian luxury-goods stores continue to assume that their Chinese customers are intermediaries buying for others and cannot reconcile themselves to the fact that the Chinese have gained the necessary wealth and social status to acquire these goods.

63. The precedence given to horizontal functionality did not always dominate Soviet-era architecture. As Vladimir Paperny (2002) has argued in a seminal study of socialist architecture, trends in fact oscillated between horizontality and verticality—the former indexing the values of equality and homogeneity while the latter accompanied the rise of personality cults.

64. Sneath (2009: 87).

65. Oushakine (2009: 21).

66. Gu and Sun (1999). These ambitions are clearly visible in the recent Russian-language tourism advertisement prepared by the municipality of Heihe. "Iz nebolshogo poselka v simvol epohi—Chto kitaitsy rasskazyvayut o Kheikhe," Amur.life, December 22, 2020.

67. See Lam (2013); Boym (2002).

68. Ssorin-Chaikov (2003: 207).

69. On the glorious past, see Gaidar (2007).

70. Woodworth and Wallace (2017: 1271–1272).

71. See, for instance, https://www.instagram.com/kaicaemmerer. In an interview with the *Independent* newspaper, photographer Kai Caemmerer points out that unlike cities in Europe or America, "new Chinese cities are built to the point of near completion before introducing people. Because of this, there is an interim period between the final phases of development and when the areas become noticeably populated, during which many of the buildings stand empty." Sarah Jacobs, "12 Eerie Photos of Enormous Chinese Cities Completely Empty of People," *Independent*, October 4, 2017, https://www.independent.co.uk/travel/empty-china-cities-12-eerie -photos-enormous-chinese-completely-empty-people-ghost-towns -abandoned-a7982646.html.

72. Wade Shepard, "Ghost Towns or Boomtowns? What New Cities Really Become," *Forbes,* March 19, 2018.

73. Looney and Rithmire (2017).

74. Denison and Ren (2016: 23).

75. Writing about Manzhouli, Fedorova writes that for most dwellers of the border zone, "Manzhouli is the only Chinese (and foreign as well) city they can visit, so it functions as a significant other, as a foreign space, different from home but known from personal experience. In a sense Manzhouli belongs to them, it is treated as their own." Frequent visitors to Manzhouli tend to call it by its familiar names: Man'zhurka or Man'ka (Fedorova 2017: 107).

76. On the entanglement of tourism and modernity, see Oakes (1998).

77. Manzhouli has also used prehistory as branding strategy. Previously the site of one of the largest coal mines in the country, Manzhouli has sought to capitalize on archaeological finds, including the bones of a giant mammoth ("the king of Asian mammoths") discovered in 1984. "Man'chzhuriya, kotoruyu my ne znali," *ZabKrai,* July 18, 2016, http:// zabkrai.ru/articles?path=%2Frfguidecontent-950%2Fmanchguriya -kotoruyu-my-ne-znali. A tourist park, complete with giant statues of mammoths, is now one of the prime tourist sites in the city. See also Chapter 1.

78. Matryoshka dolls are produced locally, out of the unused pieces of timber imported from Siberian forests.

79. Peshkov (2018: 129).

80. Pulford (2019: 81); Fedorova (2017: 108).

81. The presence of a cathedral is noteworthy given the significance of religion in the Russian Far East both for Russian (Christian) and Buryat (Buddhist) identity. As discussed in Chapter 2, the one new building erected on Bolshoi Ussuriiskii Island is a chapel.

82. As discussed in Chapter 5, and also perceptively analyzed by Iacopo Adda (2020), these positive representations of Sino-Russian relations are the public side of the actually ambiguous views of state ideologues, which are represented in certain limited access museum displays. The museum in Aihui is a pertinent example of this. In both Russia and China, one finds a tension between, on the one hand, an official promotion of friendship and trust-building and, on the other, also official but concealed entrenched antagonisms.

83. Rykwert (2000: 150).

84. The idea of the miniature has been explicitly mobilized by some heads of state, notably in Central Asia. In 2010, Kazakh president Nursultan Nazarbayev described the newly founded capital, Astana, as Kazakhstan in miniature (Koch 2018: 25).

85. Bosker (2013).

86. Similarly, Kai-Fu Lee writes, Chinese copying practices in the technological realm have often been "derided as cheap knockoffs, embarrass-

ments to their creators and unworthy of the attention of true innovators." However this Western reluctance to copy has also led to complacency in that the first mover is ceded a new market because others don't want to be seen as unoriginal. "Chinese entrepreneurs have no such luxury. If they succeed in building a product that people want, they don't get to declare victory. They have to declare war" (Lee 2018: 28, 45).

87. See the recent photo essay by Karolina Koziol (2020).

88. The largest matryoshka, 100 feet tall, contains a church, a Russian restaurant, and a music hall.

89. On mimetic rivalry, see Kenzari (2011).

90. The opening of the new embankment was staggered, in three sections, over the space of six months.

91. Ong (2011b: 4).

92. In recent years, the number of large stores selling gold, fur, or electronics displaying signs in Chinese has become significant in Blagoveshchensk (Ryzhova and Zhuravskaya 2015: 210).

93. Other examples of this are the roofing material and tiles used in many buildings.

94. Such hyperprojects are, in journalist Peter Pomerantsev's analysis, perfect vehicles for siphoning off the budget. He gives as examples the Russian Winter Olympics in Sochi, which, costing £30 billion, was £18 billion more expensive than the previous summer games in London, as well as the brand-new bridge connecting Vladivostok to Russkii Island (Pomerantsev 2015: 241–242).

95. Humphrey (2020).

96. Harrison (2006: 46).

97. Tsing (2005).

CODA: BRIDGING THE GAP?

1. Various Western analysts see Russia's rapprochement with China as a temporary aberration, a result of Western (and primarily American) policies. However, as Marcin Kaczmarski notes, "the idea that China and Russia are strategically aligned against the West often obscures relevant details and exaggerates negative implications of Sino-Russian ties for the West" (Kaczmarski 2020: 208). In the context of the COVID-19 pandemic, China's decisive action has convinced Russia that its future lies in strengthening the relationship with China. In the opinion of Alexei Maslov, director of the Institute of Far East Studies at the Russian Academy of Sciences, it demonstrated to Russia not only that China had defeated the virus but that it was able to overcome the resulting economic hardships as well. "Hal takun Rusia al-khāsir

al-faᶜli fil-ḥarb al-bārida al-jadīda bayna ʿAmirka wa as-Ṣiin?," Al-Jazeera, May 4, 2020, https://www.aljazeera.net/news/politics/2020/5/4/ حرب-باردة-فيروس-كورنا-صين-روسيا-أميركا. In parallel to this, COVID-19 has also reinforced anti-Chinese fears of disease and epidemics that long preceded the recent coronavirus pandemic, such as the severe acute respiratory syndrome (SARS) outbreak of 2002. As a recent collection shows, these fears are global, even though they play out differently in the Americas, Europe, Africa, and Asia (Billé and Urbansky 2018).

2. Even before the November 2020 US elections, China had already considerably softened its criticisms of the United States, sensing that presidential candidate Joe Biden would emerge the winner and that it would be important to rebuild bridges. Maria Repnikova, "Otnoshenia SShA i Kitaya," interview with Russiantown Atlanta, August 24, 2020, https://www.facebook.com/russiantown.atlanta/videos/77771980 6345611.

3. Stent (2020).

4. Stent (2020).

5. "Hal takun Rusia."

6. Ferris and Connolly (2020: 20).

7. Kaczmarski (2015: 53).

8. Kharkhordin (2005: 282). See also Kharkhordin (2009).

9. Repnikova (2017a: 716).

10. Gao (2020). See also Sorace (2017). This flexibility may be disappearing in the more authoritarian era of President Xi. In 2020, as critics in China have deplored, the COVID-19 outbreak was managed very high-handedly, with stern bans on the reporting of accurate information about the virus, and bureaucrats shrugging off responsibility for the unfolding crisis (Xu 2020: 7).

11. Gregory Asmolov "Vertical Crowdsourcing," Global Informality Project, 2014, https://in-formality.com/wiki/index.php?title=Vertical _Crowdsourcing_(Russia).

12. Novgorod's nascent democracy was bitterly opposed by its eventual conqueror, the tyrannical government of Moscow. Kharkhordin (2005: 286–289).

13. The sign merely reads "China Railway Major Bridge Engineering Company."

14. "Vrio glavy YEAO rasskazal o perspektivakh stroyashchegosya mosta v Kitai," *RIA Novosti*, June 20, 2020, https://ria.ru/20200620 /1573219410.html.

15. Vladimir Vorsobin, "My za tsenoy ne postoyali: Rossiya vse-taki dostroila pervy v istorii avtomost v Kitai," *Komsomolskaya Pravda*, May 15, 2020, https://www.kp.ru/daily/27131.5/4218012/.

16. "Zh-D most iz Yevreiskoi AO v KNR namereny vvesti v ekspluatatsiyu v avgusta," March 19, 2021, RAI Novosti, https://ria.ru/20210319/most-1602011214.html.

17. "Vsegda s perepravoi: chto dast Kitayu most cherez Amur," March 19, 2019, https://iz.ru/856946/ignat-shestakov/vsegda-s-perepravoi-chto-dast-kitaiu-most-cherez-amur.

18. "Gotovnost' mosta Nizhneleninskoe—Tuntszyan sostavlyaet menee 80%," *Vremya Birobizhan*, February 11, 2021, https://vremya-bir.ru/2021/02/11/gotovnost-mosta-nizhneleninskoe-tuntszyan-sostavlyaet-menee-80/.

REFERENCES

Abida, Baodungude. 1985. *Buliatemenggu jianshi*. Hailaer: Hulunbeier men lishi yanjiuhui.

Adda, Iacopo. 2020. "Sino-Russian Relations through the Lens of Russian Border History Museums: The Nerchinsk Treaty and Its Problematic Representations." *Eurasian Geography and Economics,* DOI: 10.1080/15387216.2020.1831938.

Adda, Iacopo, and Yuexin Rachel Lin. Forthcoming. "Geopolitics in Glass Cases: Nationalist Memory-Making versus the (Re-) construction of Sino-Russian Rapprochement in Chinese Border History Museums." *Europe-Asia Studies.*

Agamben, Giorgio. 2004. *State of Exception.* Chicago: University of Chicago Press.

Alexseev, Mikhail A. 2006. *Immigration Phobia and the Security Dilemma: Russia, Europe, and the United States.* Cambridge: Cambridge University Press.

Alff, Henryk. 2016. "Getting Stuck within Flows: Limited Interaction and Peripheralization at the Kazakhstan–China Border." *Central Asian Survey* 35 (3): 369–386.

Amilhat Szary, Anne-Laure. 2020. *Géopolitique des Frontières: Découper la terre, imposer une vision du monde.* Paris: Le Cavalier Bleu.

Ashwin, Sarah. 2000. *Gender, State and Society in Soviet and Post-Soviet Russia.* London: Routledge.

Balajieyi Keladanmu [芭拉杰侬· 柯拉丹木]. 2016. *Xunlu jiao shang de caidai.* Beijing: Zuojia Chubanshe.

Baldano, Marina. 2012. "People of the Border: The Destiny of the Shenehen Buryats." In Billé, Delaplace, and Humphrey 2012: 183–198.

Balzer, Harley, and Maria Repnikova. 2010. "Migration between China and Russia." *Post-Soviet Affairs* 26 (1): 1–37.

Barabantseva, Elena. 2021. "Losing Self to Discover National Citizenship: Contestations over Parental Rights among the Post-Soviet Foreign Wives in China." *Geopolitics* 26 (2): 444–463.

Barabantseva, Elena, and Caroline Grillot. 2019. "Representations and Regulations of Marriage Migration from Russia and Vietnam in the People's Republic of China." *Journal of Asian Studies* 78 (2): 285–308.

Baranovitch, Nimrod. 2016. "Ecological Degradation and Endangered Ethnicities: China's Minority Environmental Discourses as Manifested in Popular Songs." *Journal of Asian Studies* 75 (1): 181–205.

Bashkuev, Vsevolod. 2015. "An Outpost of Socialism in the Buddhist Orient: Geopolitical and Eugenic Implications of Medical and Anthropological Research on Buryat Mongols in the 1920s." *Études mongoles et sibériennes, centralasiatiques et tibétaines* 46.

Bassin, Mark. 1999. *Imperial Visions: Nationalist Imagination and Geographical Expansion in the Russian Far East, 1840–1865.* Cambridge: Cambridge University Press.

Bater, James H. 1980. *The Soviet City: Ideal and Reality.* London: Edward Arnold.

Bello, David A. 2015. *Across Forest, Steppe, and Mountain: Environment, Identity, and Empire in Qing China's Borderlands.* New York: Cambridge University Press.

Bernstein, Anya. 2008. "Remapping Sacred Landscapes: Shamanic Tourism and Cultural Production on the Olkhon Island." *Sibirica* 7 (2): 23–46.

Bernstein, Anya. 2013. *Religious Bodies Politic: Rituals of Sovereignty in Buryat Buddhism.* Chicago: University of Chicago Press.

Beumers, Birgit. 2016. "Crossing Borders / Road Movies in Russia: The Road to Nowhere? Destinations in Recent Russian Cinema." In *Eurasia 2.0: Russian Geopolitics in the Age of the New Media,* ed. Mikhail Suslov and Mark Bassin, 25–40. Lanham, MD: Rowman and Littlefield.

Billé, Franck. 2012. "Concepts of the Border in the Russian and Chinese Social Imaginaries." In Billé, Delaplace, and Humphrey 2012: 19–32.

Billé, Franck. 2014. "Territorial Phantom Pains (and Other Cartographic Anxieties)." *Environment and Planning D: Society and Space* 31: 163–178.

Billé, Franck. 2015. *Sinophobia: Anxiety, Violence, and the Making of Mongolian Identity.* Honolulu: University of Hawai'i Press.

Billé, Franck. 2016a. "Bright Lights across the River: Competing Modernities at China's Edge." In *The Art of Neighbouring:*

Making Relations across China's Borders, ed. Martin Saxer and Juan Zhang, 33–56. Amsterdam: Amsterdam University Press.

Billé, Franck. 2016b. "Futurs non linéaires: Modernité et imaginaires géopolitiques à la frontière sino-russe." *Études mongoles et sibériennes, centralasiatiques et tibétaines* 47.

Billé, Franck. 2016c. "On China's Cartographic Embrace: A View from Its Northern Rim." *Cross-Currents: East Asian History and Culture Review* 21 (December): 88–110.

Billé, Franck. 2018a. "Introduction." In *Yellow Perils: China Narratives in the Contemporary World*, ed. Franck Billé and Sören Urbansky. Honolulu: University of Hawai'i Press.

Billé, Franck. 2018b. "Skinworlds: Borders, Haptics, Topologies." *Environment and Planning D: Society and Space* 36 (1): 60–77.

Billé, Franck. 2020. "Voluminous: An Introduction." In *Voluminous States: Sovereignty, Materiality, and the Territorial Imagination*, ed. Franck Billé. Durham, NC: Duke University Press.

Billé, Franck, Grégory Delaplace, and Caroline Humphrey, eds. 2012. *Frontier Encounters: Knowledge and Practice at the Russian, Chinese and Mongolian Borders*. Cambridge: Open Book.

Billé, Franck, Lisa Sang-Mi Min, and Charlene Makley. In preparation. *Redacted: Ethnography in the Negative Space of Political Power*.

Billé, Franck, and Sören Urbansky, eds. 2018. *Yellow Perils: China Narratives in the Contemporary World*. Honolulu: University of Hawai'i Press.

Bliakher [Blyakher], L. E., and L. A. Vasil'eva. 2010. "The Russian Far East in a State of Suspension: Between the 'Global Economy' and 'State Tutelage.'" *Russian Politics and Law* 48 (1): 80–95.

Bloch, Alexia. 2017. *Sex, Love, and Migration: Postsocialism, Modernity, and Intimacy from Istanbul to the Arctic*. Ithaca, NY: Cornell University Press.

Blyakher, Leonid E. 2015. "Ochen' malen'kii biznes v ochen' bol'shom gosudarstve, ili na chto nadeyat'sya, kogda nadeyat'sya ne na chto." *Politeia* 4 (79): 5–24.

Blyakher, Leonid E. 2018. "Kto takie 'Yevreitsy,' ili opyt kul'turnogo sinteza na Amure." *Idei i Idealy* 4/38 (1): 172–186.

Bosker, Bianca. 2013. *Original Copies: Architectural Mimicry in Contemporary China*. Honolulu: University of Hawai'i Press.

Boym, Svetlana. 2001. *The Future of Nostalgia*. New York: Basic Books.

Brandtstädter, Susanne. 2020. "Rising from the Ordinary: Virtue, the Justice Motif and Moral Change." *Anthropological Theory* 21 (2): 180–205.

Brown, Kate. 2003. *A Biography of No Place: From Ethnic Borderland to Soviet Heartland*. Cambridge, MA: Harvard University Press.

Bulag, Uradyn E. 1998. *Nationalism and Hybridity in Mongolia*. New York: Clarendon Press.

Bulag, Uradyn E. 2006. "Municipalization and Ethnopolitics in Inner Mongolia." In *Mongols from Country to City*, ed. Ole Bruun and Li Narangoa. Richmond: NIAS and Curzon Press.

Bulag, Uradyn E. 2010. *Collaborative Nationalism: The Politics of Friendship on China's Mongolian Frontier*. London: Rowman and Littlefield.

Bulag, Uradyn E. 2012. "Rethinking Borders in Empire and Nation at the Foot of the Willow Palisade." In Billé, Delaplace, and Humphrey 2012: 33–54.

Bulgakova, Tatiana. 2013. *Nanai Shamanic Culture in Indigenous Discourse*. Fürstenberg/Havel: Verlag der Kulturstiftung Sibirien.

Butler, Judith. 1997. *Excitable Speech*. New York: Routledge.

Byler, Darren. 2018. "Violent Paternalism: On the Banality of Uyghur Unfreedom." *Asia-Pacific Journal* 16 (4): 1–15.

Callahan, William A. 2010. *China: The Pessoptimist Nation*. Oxford: Oxford University Press.

Campanella, Thomas J. 2008. *The Concrete Dragon: China's Urban Revolution and What It Means for the World*. New York: Princeton Architectural Press.

Carlsson, Marta, Susanne Oxenstierna, and Mikael Weissmann. 2015. *China and Russia—A Study on Cooperation, Competition and Distrust*. Report FOI-R-4087-SE, Ministry of Defence, Sweden.

Chakrabarty, Dipesh. 2002. *Habitations of Modernity: Essays in the Wake of Subaltern Studies*. Chicago: University of Chicago Press.

Charleux, Isabelle, and Marissa Smith, eds. 2021. "Points of Transition: Ovoo and the Ritual Remaking of Religious, Ecological, and Historical Politics in Inner Asia." Special issue, *Études mongoles et sibériennes, centrasiatiques et tibétaines* 52.

Chatham House. 2015. "Russia and China: Entanglements and Points of Tension." Russia and Eurasia Programme Roundtable Summary, Chatham House, London, October 23, www.chathamhouse.org. https://www.chathamhouse.org/sites/default/files/events/2015-10 -23-russia-and-china-event-summary.pdf.

Chee, Liz P. Y. 2021. *Mao's Bestiary: Medicinal Animals and Modern China*. Durham, NC: Duke University Press.

Cheng, Yang. 2015. "Do National Policies Contribute to Regional Cross-Border Integration? The Case of the Program of Cooperation between Northeast China and Russia's Far East and Eastern

Siberia (2009–2018)." In *International Cooperation in the Development of Russia's Far East and Siberia*, ed. Jing Huang and Alexander Korelev, 202–228. Basingstoke: Palgrave-Macmillan.

Chi Zijian. [迟子建]. 2005. *E'erguna He you'an*. Beijing: Beijing Chubanshe.

Chudakova, Tatiana. 2021. *Mixing Medicines: Ecologies of Care in Buddhist Siberia*. New York: Fordham University Press.

Cons, Jason. 2020. "Seepage: That Which Oozes." In *Voluminous States: Sovereignty, Materiality, and the Territorial Imagination*, ed. Franck Billé. Durham, NC: Duke University Press.

Delaplace, Grégory. 2012. "A Slightly Complicated Door: The Ethnography and Conceptualization of North Asian Borders." In Billé, Delaplace, and Humphrey 2012: 1–18.

Denison, Edward, and Guangyu Ren. 2016. *Ultra-Modernism: Architecture and Modernity in Manchuria*. Hong Kong: Hong Kong University Press.

Diener, Alexander C. 2009. *One Homeland or Two? The Nationalization and Transnationalization of Mongolia's Kazakhs*. Stanford, CA: Stanford University Press.

Donahoe, Brian, Joachim Otto Habeck, Agnieszka Halemba, and István Sántha. 2008. "Size and Place in the Construction of Indigeneity in the Russian Federation." *Current Anthropology* 49 (6): 993–1009.

Driessen, Miriam. 2020. "Pidgin Play: Linguistic Subversion on Chinese-Run Construction Sites in Ethiopia." *African Affairs* 119 (476): 432–451.

Duara, Prasenjit. 2003. *Sovereignty and Authenticity: Manchukuo and the East Asian Modern*. Lanham, MD: Rowman and Littlefield.

Dumont, Aurore. 2017. "*Oboo* Sacred Monuments in Hulun Buir: Their Narratives and Contemporary Worship." *Cross-Currents: East Asian History and Culture Review*, e-journal no. 24, September. http://cross-currents.berkeley.edu/e-journal/issue-24.

Dyatlov, Viktor. 2003. "Blagoveshchenskaya 'Utopia': Iz Istorii Materializatsii Fobii." In *Evrazia: Lyudi i mify*, ed. S. A. Panarin, 123–141. Moscow: Natalis.

Dyatlov, Viktor. 2008. *Rossiya: v predchuvstvii chainataunov*. Irkutsk: Irkutskii gosudarstvennyi universitet.

Dyatlov, Viktor. 2010. *Migratsii i diaspory v sotsiokul'turnom, politicheskom i ekonomicheskom prostrantsve Sibirii: Rubezhy XIX–XX I XX–XXI vekov*. Irkutsk: Ottisk.

Dyatlov, Viktor. 2012. "Chinese Migrants and Anti-Chinese Sentiments in Russian Society." In Billé, Delaplace, and Humphrey 2012: 71–88.

Dyatlov, Viktor, Yana Guzey, and Tatiana Sorokina. 2020. *Kitaiskii pogrom: Blagoveshchenskaya "Utopia" 1900 goda v otsenke sovremennikov i potomkov.* Saint Petersburg: Nestor-Istoria.

Elliott, Mark C. 2001. *The Manchu Way: The Eight Banners and Ethnic Identity in Late Imperial China.* Stanford, CA: Stanford University Press.

Elliott, Mark. 2014. "Frontier Stories: Periphery as Center in Qing History." *Frontiers of History in China* 9 (3): 336–360.

Fall, Juliet. 2005. *Drawing the Line: Nature, Hybridity and Politics in Transboundary Spaces.* Aldershot, UK: Ashgate.

Fedorova, Kapitolina. 2017. "Manzhouli or Manchzhuriya? Linguistic and Cultural Hybridization in the Border City." In *Intercultural Communication with China: Beyond (Reverse) Essentialism and Culturalism?*, ed. Fred Dervin and Regis Machart, 91–110. Singapore: Springer.

Fedorova, Kapitolina. 2018. "The Russian-Chinese Pidgin: An Attempt at the Sociology of Grammar." *Language Ecology* 2 (1/2): 112–127.

Ferguson, James. 1999. *Expectations of Modernity: Myths and Meanings of Urban Life on the Zambian Copperbelt.* Berkeley: University of California Press.

Ferris, Emily, and Richard Connolly. 2020. "Networks and Links: Why Russia's Infrastructure Is Holding Back Its Pivot to Asia." Research Paper, Russia and Eurasia Program, Chatham House, London, July. https://www.chathamhouse.org/sites/default/files/2020-07-27 -networks-links-russias-infrastructure-ferris-connolly.pdf.

Fisher, Raymond H. 1943. *The Russian Fur Trade, 1550–1700.* Berkeley: University of California Press.

Forsyth, J. 1992. *A History of the Peoples of Siberia: Russia's North Asian Colony 1581–1990.* Cambridge: Cambridge University Press.

Fraser, John Foster. 1904. *The Real Siberia.* London: Cassel.

Fraser, Richard. 2010. "Forced Relocation amongst the Reindeer-Evenki of Inner Mongolia." *Inner Asia* 12 (2): 317–346.

Fraser, Richard. 2020. "Cultural Heritage, Ethnic Tourism, and Minority-State Relations amongst the Orochen in North-East China." *International Journal of Heritage Studies* 26 (2): 178–200.

Fromm, Martin. 2010. "Producing History through 'Wenshi Ziliao': Personal Memory, Post-Mao Ideology, and Migration to Manchuria." PhD diss., Columbia University.

Funnell, Lisa, and Klaus Dodds. 2017. *Geographies, Genders and Geopolitics of James Bond.* London: Palgrave Macmillan.

Gaidar, Yegor. 2007. *Collapse of an Empire: Lessons for Modern Russia*. Washington, DC: Brookings Institution Press.

Gamsa, Mark. 2003. "California on the Amur, or the 'Zheltuga Republic' in Manchuria (1883–86)." *Slavonic and East European Review* 81 (2): 236–266.

Gamsa, Mark. 2018. "Mixed Marriages in Russian-Chinese Manchuria." In *Entangled Histories: The Transcultural Past of Northeast China,* ed. Dan Ben-Canaan, Frank Grüner, and Ines Prodöhl, 47–58. Heidelberg: Springer.

Gamsa, Mark. 2020. *Harbin: A Cross-Cultural Biography*. Toronto: University of Toronto Press.

Gao, Huan. 2020. "The Power of the Square: Public Spaces and Popular Mobilization after the Wenchuan Earthquake." *Journal of Chinese Political Science* 25 (1): 89–111.

Gates, Hill. 1996. *China's Motor: A Thousand Years of Petty Capitalism*. Ithaca, NY: Cornell University Press.

Gel'man, V. Ya. 2010. *"Podryvnye" instituty i neformal'noe upravlenie v sovremennoi Rossii*. Preprint M-13/10. Saint Petersburg: Izdatel'stvo Evropeiskogo universiteta v Sankt-Peterburge.

Gottschang, Thomas R., and Diana Lary. 2000. *Swallows and Settlers: The Great Migration from North China to Manchuria*. Ann Arbor: Center for Chinese Studies, University of Michigan.

Grigas, Agnia. 2016. *Beyond Crimea: The New Russian Empire*. New Haven, CT: Yale University Press.

Grigas, Agnia. 2017. *The New Geopolitics of Natural Gas*. Cambridge, MA: Harvard University Press.

Gu, Chaolin, and Ying Sun. 1999. "Jingji quanqiuhua yu zhongguo guoji xing chengshi jianshe." *Urban Planning Forum* 3: 1–6.

Guan Xiaoyun and Wang Honggang. 1998. *Elunchunzu saman jiao diaocha*. Shenyang: Liaoning People's Publishing House.

Guldin, G. E. 1994. *The Saga of Anthropology in China: From Malinowski to Moscow to Mao*. Armonk, NY: M. E. Sharpe.

Guo, Baogang. 2014. "New Trends in China's Administrative Reform." *China Currents* (China Research Center), October 16. http://www.chinacenter.net/2014/china_currents/13-2/new-trends-in-chinas-administrative-reform/.

Hamashita, Takeshi. 2003. "Tribute and Treaties: Maritime Asia and Treaty Port Networks in the Era of Negotiation, 1800–1900." In *The Resurgence of East Asia: 500, 150 and 50 Year Perspectives,* ed. Giovanni Arrighi, Takeshi Hamashita, and Mark Selden, 17–50. London: Routledge Curzon.

Han, Enze. 2011. "The Dog That Hasn't Barked: Assimilation and Resistance in Inner Mongolia, China." *Asian Ethnicity* 12 (1): 55–75.

Harrison, Simon. 2006. *Fracturing Resemblances: Identity and Mimetic Conflict in Melanesia and the West.* New York: Berghahn Books.

Hayton, Bill. 2014. *The South China Sea: The Struggle for Power in Asia.* New Haven, CT: Yale University Press.

Hill, Fiona, and Clifford Gaddy. 2003. *The Siberian Curse: How Communist Planners Left Russia Out in the Cold.* Washington, DC: Brookings Institution Press.

Hitchcock, Ellen. 2010. "The 2006 Forest Code of the Russian Federation: An Evaluation of Environmental Legislation in Russia." *Australian Slavonic and East European Studies* 24 (1–2): 19–39.

Holzlehner, Tobias. 2014. "Trading against the State: Il/legal Cross-Border Networks in the Russian Far East." *Etnofoor* 26 (1): 13–38.

Holzlehner, Tobias. 2018. "Economies of Trust: Informality and the State in the Russian-Chinese Borderland." In *Trust and Mistrust in the Economies of the China-Russia Borderlands,* ed. Caroline Humphrey, 65–86. Amsterdam: Amsterdam University Press.

Hosagrahar, J. 2005. *Indigenous Modernities: Negotiating Architecture and Urbanism.* London: Routledge.

Hsing, You-tien. 2008. "Socialist Land Masters: The Territorial Politics of Accumulation." In *Privatizing China: Socialism from Afar,* ed. Li Zhang and Aihwa Ong, 57–70. Ithaca, NY: Cornell University Press.

Hsing, You-tien. 2010. *The Great Urban Transformation: Politics and Land and Property in China.* Oxford: Oxford University Press.

Humphrey, Caroline. 2000. "An Anthropological View of Barter in Russia." In *The Vanishing Rouble: Barter Networks and Non-Monetary Transactions in Post-Soviet Societies,* ed. P. Seabright. Cambridge: Cambridge University Press.

Humphrey, Caroline. 2002. *The Unmaking of Soviet Life: Everyday Economies after Socialism.* Ithaca, NY: Cornell University Press.

Humphrey, Caroline. 2015. "Is Zomia a Useful Idea for Inner Asia?" *Mongolian Journal of Anthropology, Archaeology and Ethnology* 18 (1): 92–107.

Humphrey, Caroline. 2017. "Loyalty and Disloyalty along the Russian-Chinese Border." *History and Anthropology* 28 (4): 399–405.

Humphrey, Caroline. 2018a. "Introduction: Trusting and Mistrusting across Borders." In *Trust and Mistrust in the Economies of the China-Russia Borderlands,* ed. Caroline Humphrey. Amsterdam: Amsterdam University Press.

Humphrey, Caroline. 2018b. "To Smile and Not to Smile: Mythic Gesture at the Russia-China Border." *Social Analysis* 62 (1): 31–54.

Humphrey, Caroline, ed. 2018c. *Trust and Mistrust in the Economies of the China-Russia Borderlands.* Amsterdam: Amsterdam University Press.

Humphrey, Caroline. 2019. "Deportees in Society: *ssyl'ka* and *spetsposelenie* in Soviet Buryatia." *Inner Asia* 21 (1): 38–60.

Humphrey, Caroline. 2020. "Real Estate Speculation: Volatile Social Forms at a Global Frontier of Capitalism." *Economy and Society* 49 (1): 116–140.

Iredale, Robyn, Zheng Zhenzhen, and Sung Ho Ko. n.d. "The Vulnerability of Migrants to HIV/AIDS in China and Mongolia." https://www.hivpolicy.org/Library/HPP001248.pdf.

Iwashita, Akihiro. 2004. *A 4,000 Kilometer Journey along the Sino-Russian Border.* Sapporo: Slavic Research Center, Hokkaido University.

Janhunen, Juha. 1996. *Manchuria: An Ethnic History.* Helsinki: Finno-Ugrian Society.

Jen, Khak Mun. 2003. "Pollution of the Amur River Attains Crisis Proportions." Erina Report vol. 55. Economic Research Institute for Northeast Asia. https://www.erina.or.jp/wp-content/uploads/2003/01/pp5521_tssc.pdf.

Jiang Rong [姜戎]. 2004. *Lang tuteng.* Wuhan: Changjiang Wenyi Chubanshe.

Joniak-Lüthi, Agnieszka, and Uradyn Bulag. 2016. "Introduction: Spatial Transformations in China's Northwestern Borderlands." *Inner Asia* 18 (1): 1–14.

Jonutytė, Kristina. 2020. "Shamanism, Sanity, and Remoteness in Russia." *Anthropology Today* 36 (2): 3–7.

Kaczmarski, Marcin. 2015. *Russia-China Relations in the Post-Crisis International Order.* London: Routledge.

Kaczmarski, Marcin. 2017. "Non-Western Visions of Regionalism: China's New Silk Road and Russia's Eurasian Economic Union." *International Affairs* 93 (6): 1357–1376.

Kaczmarski, Marcin. 2020. "The Sino-Russian Relationship and the West." *Survival* 62 (6): 199–212.

Kadare, Ismail. 1998. *The Concert.* Trans. Barbara Bray. New York: Arcade.

Kazennova, Elena, Vita Laga, Ilya Lapovok, Nataliya Glushchenko, Dmitry Neshumaev, Alexander Vasilyev, and Marina Bobkova.

2014. "HIV-1 Genetic Variants in the Russian Far East." *AIDS Research and Human Retroviruses* 30 (8): 742–752.

Kenzari, Bechir. 2011. "Construction Rites, Mimetic Rivalry, Violence." In *Architecture and Violence,* ed. Bechir Kenzari. Barcelona: Actar.

Kharkhordin, Oleg. 2005. "Things as Res Publicae: Making Things Public." In *Making Things Public: Atmospheres of Democracy,* ed. Bruno Latour and Peter Weibel, 280–289. Karlsruhe: ZKM Center for Art and Media; Cambridge, MA: MIT Press.

Kharkhordin, Oleg. 2009. "Introduction." In *The Materiality of Res Publica: How to Do Things with Publics,* ed. Dominique Colas and Oleg Kharkhordin, 1–7. Newcastle: Cambridge Scholars Publishing.

Kim, Loretta E. 2019. *Ethnic Chrysalis: China's Orochen People and the Legacy of Qing Borderland Administration.* Cambridge, MA: Harvard University Asia Center.

Kim, Seonmin. 2017. *Ginseng and Borderland: Territorial Boundaries and Political Relations between Qing China and Chosŏn Korea, 1636–1912.* Oakland: University of California Press.

Kipnis, Andrew. 1997. *Producing Guanxi: Sentiment, Self, and Subculture in a North China Village.* Durham, NC: Duke University Press.

Koch, Anna, and Alexandra Tomaselli. 2015. "Indigenous Peoples' Rights and Their (New) Mobilizations in Russia." European Diversity and Autonomy Paper (EDAP), EURAC Research, Bozen, Italy, February. http://www.eurac.edu/en/research/autonomies /minrig/publications/Documents/Tomaselli_FINAL.pdf

Koch, Natalie. 2010. "The Monumental and the Miniature: Imagining 'Modernity' in Astana." *Social and Cultural Geography* 11 (8): 769–787.

Koch, Natalie. 2018. *The Geopolitics of Spectacle: Space, Synecdoche, and the New Capitals of Asia.* Ithaca, NY: Cornell University Press.

Koga, Yukiko. 2016. *Inheritance of Loss: China, Japan, and the Political Economy of Redemption after Empire.* Chicago: University of Chicago Press

Koolhaas, R. 2004. "Beijing Manifesto." *Wired,* August 1, 120–129.

Koptseva, Natalia, and Vladimir Kirko. 2014. "Modern Specificity of Legal Regulation of Cultural Development of the Indigenous Peoples of the Arctic Siberia (the Altay Region, the Zabaikailsky Region, Republic of Buryatia, Russia)." *Life Sciences Journal* 11 (9): 114–119.

Kordonskii, S. G., Yu. M. Plyusnin, Yu. A. Krashennikova, A. R. Tukaeva, O. M. Morguniova, D. E. Akhunov, and D. V. Boikov. 2011. "Sotsial'nyye real'nosti i sotsial'nyye mirazhi." *Mir Rossii* 1: 3–33.

Kotkin, Stephen. 1995. *Magnetic Mountain: Stalinism as a Civilization.* Berkeley: University of California Press.

Koziol, Karolina. 2020. "Representing 'Russianness' in the Chinese-Russian Borderland." *Eurasian Geography and Economics* 61 (1): 100–108.

Kruglova, Anna. 2019. "Driving in Terrain: Automobility, Modernity, and the Politics of Statelessness in Russia." *American Ethnologist* 46 (4): 457–469.

Kuhrt, Natasha. 2007. *Russian Policy towards China and Japan: The El'tsin and Putin Periods.* London: Routledge.

Kurto, Olga I. 2011. "Zheltuga Republic: The Case of Social Development at the Chinese-Russian Border." *Archaeology, Ethnology and Anthropology of Eurasia* 39 (3): 135–142.

Kuzmina, Anna. 2018. "WeChat Pay in Russia." https://medium.com /what-the-money/wechat-pay-and-its-russian-adventure-de24c 98197e7.

Lacaze, Gaëlle. 2012. "Prostitution and the Transformation of the Chinese Trading Town of Ereen." In Billé, Delaplace, and Humphrey: 111–136.

Lacaze, Gaëlle. 2017. *Femmes en quête d'identité(s).* Paris: Editions Pétra.

Lagerkvist, Johan. 2015. "The Unknown Terrain of Social Protests in China: 'Exit,' 'Voice,' 'Loyalty,' and 'Shadow.'" *Journal of Civil Society* 11 (2): 137–153.

Lam, Tong. 2013. *Abandoned Futures: A Journey to the Posthuman World.* London: Carpet Bombing Culture.

Larin, V. L. 2014. "Tikhookeanskaya Aziya v rossiisko-kitaiskikh otnosheniyakh: zatyanuvsheeyesya ozhidanie propryva." *Rossiya i ATP* 2014 (3): 5–21.

Larin, Victor. 2015. "Pacific Russia's Energy Resources in the Geopolitics of Northeast Asia in the Early 21st Century." In *International Cooperation in the Development of Russia's Far East and Siberia,* ed. Jing Huang and Alexander Korelev, 38–60. Basingstoke, UK: Palgrave-Macmillan.

Lary, Diana. 2017. "Manchuria: History and Environment." In *Empire and Environment in the Making of Manchuria,* ed. Norman Smith, 28–52. Vancouver: UBC Press.

Lattimore, Owen. 1934. *The Mongols of Manchuria.* New York: John Day.

Lavrillier, Alexandra, Aurore Dumont, and Donatas Brandišauskas. 2018. "Human-Nature Relationships in the Tungus Societies of Siberia and Northeast China." *Études mongoles et sibériennes, centrasiatiques et tibétaines* 49, http://journals.openedition.org /emscat/3088.

Ledeneva, Alena V. 1998. *Russia's Economy of Favours: Blat, Networking, and Informal Exchange.* Cambridge: Cambridge University Press.

Ledeneva, Alena V. 2006. *How Russia Really Works: The Informal Practices That Shaped Post-Soviet Politics and Business.* Ithaca, NY: Cornell University Press.

Lee, Kai-Fu. 2018. *AI Superpowers: China, Silicon Valley, and the New World Order.* Boston: Houghton Mifflin Harcourt.

Legerton, Colin, and Jacob Rawson. 2009. *Invisible China: A Journey through Ethnic Borderlands.* Chicago: Chicago Review Press.

Li, Cheng. 2004. "China's Northeast: From Largest Rust-Belt to Fourth Economic Engine." *China Leadership Monitor* 9: 1–15.

Li, Rose Maria. 1989. "Migration to China's Northern Frontier, 1953–82." *Population and Development Review* 15 (3): 503–538.

Li, Yan. 2018. *China's Soviet Dream: Propaganda, Culture, and Popular Imagination.* London: Routledge.

Libman, Alexander, and Michael Rochlitz. 2019. *Federalism in China and Russia: Story of Success and Story of Failure?* Cheltenham, UK: Edward Elgar.

Lin, Qing, and Lian Zheng. 2018. "On Protection of Intangible Cultural Heritage in China from the Intellectual Property Rights Perspective." *Sustainability* 10 (12): 4369.

Liu, Yu, Pan Wei, Shen Mingming, Song Guojun, Vivian Bertrand, Mary Child, and Judith Shapiro. 2006. "The Politics and Ethics of Going Green in China: Air Pollution Control in Benxi City and Wetland Preservation in the Sanjiang Plain." In *Forging Environmentalism: Justice, Livelihood and Contested Environments,* ed. Joanne Bauer, 25–102. London: M. E. Sharpe.

Lo, Bobo. 2008. *Axis of Convenience: Moscow, Beijing, and the New Geopolitics.* Washington, DC: Brookings Institution Press.

Looney, Kristen, and Meg Rithmire. 2017. "China Gambles on Modernizing through Urbanization." *Current History* 116 (791): 203–209.

Loyalka, M. D. 2012. *Eating Bitterness: Stories from the Front Lines of China's Great Urban Migration.* Berkeley: University of California Press.

Lukin, Alexander. 2018. *China and Russia: The New Rapprochement.* Cambridge: Polity.

Luo, Yu, Tim Oakes, and Louisa Schein. 2019. "Resourcing Remoteness and the 'Post-Alteric' Imaginary in China." *Social Anthropology/Anthropologie Sociale* 27 (2): 270–285.

Maçães, Bruno. 2018. *The Dawn of Eurasia: On the Trail of the New World Order.* New Haven: Yale University Press.

Makarov, Igor A. 2017. "Transformation of the Economic Model in Asia-Pacific Region: Implications for Russia's Far East and Siberia." In *The Political Economy of Pacific Russia: Regional Developments in East Asia,* ed. Jing Huang and Alexander Korolev, 77–102. London: Palgrave Macmillan.

Makhachkeev, Aleksandr. 2018. *Kriminal'naya Istoriya Buryatii.* Ulan-Ude: NovaPrint.

Mandel, Ruth, and Caroline Humphrey, eds. 2002. *Markets and Moralities: Ethnographies of Postsocialism.* Oxford: Berg.

Markey, Daniel S. 2020. *China's Western Horizon: Beijing and the New Geopolitics of Eurasia.* Oxford: Oxford University Press.

Mathur, Nayanika. 2021. *Crooked Cats: Human-Big Cat Entanglements in the Anthropocene.* Chicago: University of Chicago Press.

Menon, Rajan. 2009. "The Limits of Chinese-Russian Partnership." *Survival* 51 (3): 99–130.

Metzo, Katherine. 2002. "Xongodory and Homeland: Manipulating Identity in a Multi-Ethnic Region." *Kroeber Anthropological Society Papers* 88: 61–76.

Meyer, Michael. 2015. *In Manchuria: A Village Called Wasteland and the Transformation of Rural China.* London: Bloomsbury Press.

Mikhailova, Ekaterina, Chung-Tong Wu, and Ilya Chubarov. 2019. "Blagoveshchensk and Heihe: (Un)contested Twin Cities on the Sino-Russian Border?" In *Twin Cities: Urban Communities, Borders and Relationships over Time,* ed. John Garrard and Ekaterina Mikhailova, 288–300. Abingdon, UK: Routledge.

Milanovic, Branko. 2019. *Capitalism, Alone: The Future of the System That Rules the World.* Cambridge, MA: Harvard University Press.

Miller, Chris. 2021. *We Shall Be Masters: Russian Pivots to East Asia from Peter the Great to Putin.* Cambridge, MA: Harvard University Press.

Millward, James. 2004. "The Qing Formation, the Mongol Legacy, and the 'End of History' in Early Modern Central Eurasia." In *The Qing Formation in World Historical Time,* ed. Lynn Struve, 92–120. Cambridge, MA: Harvard University Asia Center.

Minakir, Pavel A. 2006. *Ekonomika regionov. Dal'niy Vostok.* Moscow: Economica.

Moore, Jason W. 2015. *Capitalism in the Web of Life: Ecology and the Accumulation of Capital.* London: Verso.

Mosca, Matthew. 2019. "Introduction: Empire and Information in Late Imperial Chinese History." *Frontiers of History in China* 14 (1): 2–18.

Nakawo, Masayoshi, Yuki Konagaya, and Shinjilt Chimedyn. 2010. *Ecological Migration: Environmental Policy in China.* New York: Peter Lang.

Namsaraeva, Sayana. 2012. "Saddling Up the Border: A Buriad Community within the Russian-Chinese Border Space." In *Frontiers and Boundaries: Encounters of China's Margins,* ed. Ildikó Bellér-Hann and Zsombor Rajkai, 223–246. Wiesbaden: Harrassowitz.

Namsaraeva, Sayana. 2017. "Caught between States: Urjin Garmaev and the Conflicting Loyalties of Trans-border Buryats." *History and Anthropology* 28 (4): 406–428.

Namsaraeva, Sayana. 2020. "Rhythms of *Nutag:* Slowness and Deceleration in Inner Asian Mobilities." *Inner Asia* 22 (1): 87–110.

Newell, Josh. 2004. *The Russian Far East: A Reference Guide to Conservation and Development.* McKinleyville, CA: Daniel and Daniel.

Newell, Josh, and Anotoly Lebedev. 2000. "Plundering Russia's Far Eastern Taiga: Illegal Corruption and Trade." Report, Bureau for Regional Oriental Campaigns, Vladivostok, Friends of the Earth–Japan, Tokyo, and Pacific Environment Resources Center, Oakland, CA. https://www.yumpu.com/en/document/read /36663127/bureau-for-regional-oriental-campaigns-vladivostok -russia-.

Nielsen, Morten, and Mikkel Bunkenborg. 2020. "Monumental Misunderstandings: The Material Entextualization of Mutual Incomprehension in Sino-Mozambican Relations." *Social Analysis* 64 (3): 1–25.

Ning, Chia. 2018. "The Solon Sable Tribute, Hunters of Inner Asia and Dynastic Elites at the Imperial Centre." *Inner Asia* 20: 26–63.

Noll, Richard, and Shi Kun. 2009. "The Last Shaman of the Oroqen People of Northeast China." *Shaman* 17 (1–2): 117–140.

Nye, David E. 2010. *When the Lights Went Out: A History of Blackouts in America.* Cambridge, MA: MIT Press.

Oakes, Tim. 1998. *Tourism and Modernity in China*. London: Routledge.

Oglezneva, Elena. 2007. *Russko-kitaiskii pidzhin*. Blagoveshchensk: Amur State University Press.

Ong, Aihwa. 2011a. "Hyperbuilding: Spectacle, Speculation, and the Hyperspace of Sovereignty." In *Worlding Cities: Asian Experiments and the Art of Being Global*, ed. Ananya Roy and Aihwa Ong, 205–226. Chichester: Blackwell.

Ong, Aihwa. 2011b. "Introduction: Worlding Cities, or the Art of Being Global." In *Worlding Cities: Asian Experiments and the Art of Being Global*, ed. Ananya Roy and Aihwa Ong, 1–26. Chichester: Blackwell.

Orlova, Vasilina. 2021. "Malfunctioning Affective Infrastructures: How the 'Broken Road' Becomes a Site of Belonging in Post-Industrial Eastern Siberia." *Sibirica* 20 (1): 28–57.

Oushakine, Sergei A. 2009. *The Patriotism of Despair: Nation, War, and Loss in Russia*. Ithaca, NY: Cornell University Press.

Ouyang, Zhiyun. 2018. "Mainstreaming Ecosystem Service Accounting onto Conservation Policy in China." Natural Capital Policy Forum, Paris, November 26–27. https://seea.un.org/sites/seea.un.org/files/03-session_5-ouyang_zhiyun_nca_and_mainstreaming_ecoservice_in_china_paris_2018_11_26g0.pdf.

Pachenkov, Oleg. 2011. "Every City Has the Flea Market It Deserves: The Phenomenon of Urban Flea Markets in St. Petersburg." In *Urban Spaces after Socialism: Ethnographies of Public Places in Eurasian Cities*, ed. T. Darieva, W. Kaschuba, and M. Krebs, 181–206. Frankfurt am Main: Campus Verlag.

Pallot, Judith, and Laura Piacentini. 2012. *Gender, Geography and Punishment: The Experiences of Women in Carceral Russia*. Oxford: Oxford University Press.

Paperny, Vladimir. 2002. *Architecture in the Age of Stalin: Culture Two*. Cambridge: Cambridge University Press.

Park, Hyun-Gwi. 2016. "One River and Three States: The Tumen River Triangle and the Legacy of Postsocialist Transition." *Asian Perspective* 40 (3): 369–392.

Park, Hyun-Gwi. 2017. *The Displacement of Borders among Russian Koreans in Northeast Asia*. Amsterdam: Amsterdam University Press.

Pelkmans, Mathijs. 2006. *Defending the Border: Identity, Religion, and Modernity in the Republic of Georgia*. Ithaca, NY: Cornell University Press.

Perekhval'skaya, E. 2008. *Russkie Pidzhiny*. Saint Petersburg: Aleteiya.

Peshkov, Ivan. 2014. "Useable Past for a Transbaikalian Borderline Town: 'Disarmament' of Memory and Geographical Imagination in Priargunsk." *Inner Asia* 16 (1): 94–115.

Peshkov, Ivan. 2018. "The Trade Town of Manzhouli: Trust Created and Undermined." In *Trust and Mistrust in the Economies of the China-Russia Borderlands*, ed. Caroline Humphrey, 121–142. Amsterdam: Amsterdam University Press.

Pieper, Moritz. 2018. "Mapping Eurasia: Contrasting the Public Diplomacies of Russia's 'Greater Eurasia' and China's 'Belt and Road' Initiative." *Rising Powers Quarterly* 3 (3): 217–237.

Pieper, Moritz. 2020. "The New Silk Road Heads North: Implications of the China-Mongolia-Russia Economic Corridor for Mongolian Agency within Eurasian Power Shifts." *Eurasian Geography and Economics,* DOI: 10.1080/15387216.2020.1836985.

Plyusnin, Yu. M., Ya. D. Zausaeva, N. N. Zhidkevich, and A. A. Pozanenko. 2013. *Otkhodniki*. Moscow: Novyi Khronograf.

Pomerantsev, Peter. 2015. *Nothing Is True and Everything Is Possible: Adventures in Modern Russia*. London: Faber and Faber.

Pulford, Ed. 2017. "The Nanai, Hezhe and Mobilized Loyalties along the Amur." *History and Anthropology* 28 (4): 531–552.

Pulford, Ed. 2019. *Mirrorlands: Russia, China, and Journeys in Between*. London: Hurst.

Purdue, Peter C. 2009. "Nature and Nurture on Imperial China's Frontiers." *Modern Asian Studies* 43 (1): 245–267.

Purdue, Peter. 2010. "Boundaries, Maps and Movement: Chinese, Russian and Mongolian Empires in Early Modern Eurasia." *International History Review* 20 (2): 263–286.

Qi, Xuejun. 2009. *Heihe shihua*. Harbin: Heilongjiang People's Publishing House.

Radchenko, Sergey. 2014. *Unwanted Visionaries: The Soviet Failure in Asia at the End of the Cold War*. Oxford: Oxford University Press.

Reardon-Anderson, James. 2005. *Reluctant Pioneers: China's Expansion Northward, 1644–1937*. Stanford, CA: Stanford University Press.

Reeves, Madeleine. 2014. *Border Work: Spatial Lives of the State in Rural Central Asia*. Ithaca, NY: Cornell University Press.

Repnikova, Maria. 2017a. "Information Management during Crisis Events: A Case Study of Beijing Floods of 2012." *Journal of Contemporary China* 26 (107): 711–725.

Repnikova, Maria. 2017b. *Media Politics in China: Improvising Power under Authoritarianism*. Cambridge: Cambridge University Press.

Richardson, Paul. 2017. "Geopolitical Cultures, Pragmatic Patriotism, and Russia's Disputed Islands." *Eurasian Geography and Economics* 59 (1): 7–27.

Rippa, Alessandro. 2018. "Old Routes, New Roads: Proximity across the China-Pakistan Border." In *Routledge Handbook of Asian Borderlands*, ed. Alexander Horstmann, Martin Saxer, and Alessandro Rippa, 114–126. Abingdon, UK: Routledge.

Rippa, Alessandro. 2020. *Where China Ends: Trade, Infrastructure Development and Control in the Borderlands of Xinjiang and Yunnan.* Amsterdam: Amsterdam University Press.

Rozelle, Scott, and Natalie Hell. 2020. *Invisible China: How the Rural-Urban Divide Threatens China's Rise.* Chicago: University of Chicago Press.

Rozman, Gilbert. 2014. *The Sino-Russian Challenge to World Order: National Identities, Bilateral Relations and East versus West in the 2010s.* Stanford, CA: Stanford University Press.

Ruget, Vanessa, and Burul Usmanalieva. 2008. "Citizenship, Migration, and Loyalty towards the State: A Case Study of the Kyrgyz Migrants Working in Russia and Kazakhstan." *Central Asian Survey* 27 (2): 129–141.

Rykwert, Joseph. 2000. *The Seduction of Place: The History and Future of the City.* Oxford: Oxford University Press.

Ryzhova, Natalia. 2012. "The Case of the Amur as a Cross-border Zone of Illegality." In Billé, Delaplace, and Humphrey 2012: 89–110.

Ryzhova, Natalia. 2014a. "Freedoms, the State and Security: Border Exclusion Zones in Post-Soviet Russia." Master's thesis, University of Cambridge.

Ryzhova, Natalia. 2014b. "National Border, Administrative Rent and Informality: Market Entrance for Chinese Traders and Farmers." *Eurasia Border Review* 5 (1): 77–94.

Ryzhova, Natalia. 2018. "The Emergence of Cross-Border Electronic Commerce: Creativity and Declining Trust." In *Trust and Mistrust in the Economies of the China-Russia Borderlands,* ed. Caroline Humphrey, 229–249. Amsterdam: Amsterdam University Press.

Ryzhova, Natalia. 2019. "Development/Security Dilemma of the Russian Far East: How Experiments become Agents of Degradation." Unpublished manuscript.

Ryzhova, Natalia, and Tatiana Zhuravskaya. 2015. "Transgranichniy shoping na rossiisko-kitaiskoi granitse: Krizis, performativnost' i vospriyatiye 'sebya.'" In *Etnicheskie rynki v Rossii: Prostranstvo torga i mesto vstrechi*, ed. Viktor I. Dyatlov and Konstantin V. Grigorichev, 202–213. Irkutsk: Izdatel'stvo IGU.

Ryzhova, Natalia P., T. N. Zhuravskaya, and K. I. Feoktistova. 2017. "'Dal'nevostochnyi gektar': eksperiment po formirovaniyu instituta prav sobstvennosti na zemliu?" *Oikumena* (4): 40–54.

Sabirova, Guzel. 2016. "'Dead End': A Spatial History of a Border Town in Post-Soviet Kyrgyzstan." In *Eurasian Borderlands: Spatializing Borders in the Aftermath of State Collapse*, ed. Tone Bringa and Hege Toje, 59–86. New York: Palgrave Macmillan

Safonova, Tatiana, and István Sántha. 2013. *Culture Contact in Evenki Land: A Cybernetic Anthropology of the Baikal Region.* Leiden: Global Oriental.

Safonova, Tatiana, István Sántha, and Pavel Sulyandziga. 2018. "Searching for Trust: Indigenous People in the Jade Business." In *Trust and Mistrust in the Economies of the China-Russia Border-lands*, ed. Caroline Humphrey. Amsterdam: Amsterdam University Press.

Sasaki, Shiro. 2016. "A History of the Far East Indigenous Peoples' Transborder Activities between the Russian and Chinese Empires." In *Northeast Asian Borders: History, Politics, and Local Societies*, ed. Yuki Konayaga and Olga Shaglanova, 161–193. Osaka: National Museum of Ethnology.

Saxer, Martin, and Ruben Andersson. 2019. "The Return of Remoteness: Insecurity, Isolation and Connectivity in the New World Disorder." *Social Anthropology / Anthropologie Sociale* 27 (2): 140–155.

Saxer, Martin, and Juan Zhang. 2016. *The Art of Neighbouring: Making Relations across China's Borders.* Amsterdam: Amsterdam University Press.

Schiffauer, Leonie. 2018. "Dangerous Speculation: The Appeal of Pyramid Schemes in Rural Siberia." *Focaal: Journal of Global and Historical Anthropology* 81: 58–71.

Schlesinger, Jonathan. 2017. *A World Trimmed with Fur: Wild Things, Pristine Places, and the Natural Fringes of Qing.* Stanford, CA: Stanford University Press.

Schweitzer, Peter, and Olga Povoroznyuk. 2019. "A Right to Remoteness? A Missing Bridge and Articulations of Indigeneity along an East Siberian Railroad." *Social Anthropology / Anthropologie Sociale* 27 (2): 236–252.

Scott, James C. 1998. *Seeing like a State: How Certain Schemes to Improve the Human Condition Have Failed.* New Haven, CT: Yale University Press.

Sem, T. Yu. 2017. *Shamanizm Evenkov: Po materialam Rossiiskogo etnograficheskogo muzeya.* Saint Petersburg: Humanitarian Academy Publishing Centre.

Shaglanova, Olga. 2011. "Chinese Labour Migration in the Context of a Buryat Village." *Inner Asia* 13: 297–313.

Shan, Patrick Fuliang. 2006. "Ethnicity, Nationalism and Race Relations: The Chinese Treatment of the Solon Tribes in Heilongjiang Frontier Society: 1900–1931." *Asian Ethnicity* 7 (2): 183–193.

Shulman, Elena. 2007. "'Those Who Hurry to the Far East': Readers, Dreamers, and Volunteers." In *Peopling the Russian Periphery: Borderland Colonization in Eurasian History,* ed. Nicholas Breyfogle, Abby Schrader, and Willard Sunderland, 213–237. London: Routledge.

Simonov, Eugene, Oxana Nikitina, Peter Osipov, Evgeny Egidarev, and Andrey Shalikovsky. 2016. "We and the Amur Floods: Lessons (Un)Learned." Report sponsored by WWF and others. Summary (English) and full version (Russian) at https://amurinfocenter.org /en/directions/water/we-and-the-amur-floods-lesson-un-learned/.

Skvirskaja, Vera. 2018. "'Russian Merchant' Legacies in Post-Soviet Trade with China: Moral Economy, Economic Success and Business Innovation in Yiwu." *History and Anthropology* 29 (supp. 1): S48–S66.

Slezkine, Yuri. 1994. *Arctic Mirrors: Russia and the Small Peoples of the North.* Ithaca, NY: Cornell University Press.

Smolyak, A. V. 2001. "Traditional Principles of Natural Resource Use among Indigenous Peoples of the Lower Amur River." *Journal of Legal Pluralism and Unofficial Law* 46: 176–184.

Sneath, David. 2008. "Competing Factions and Elite Power: Political Conflict in Inner Mongolia." In *Conflict and Social Order in Tibet and Inner Asia,* ed. Fernanda Pirie and Tony Huber, 85–112. Leiden: Brill.

Sneath, David. 2009. "Reading the Signs by Lenin's Light: Development, Divination and Metonymic Fields in Mongolia." *Ethnos* 74 (1): 72–90.

Song, Nianshen. 2018. *Making Borders in Modern East Asia: The Tumen River Demarcation, 1881–1919.* Cambridge: Cambridge University Press.

Sorace, Christian P. 2017. *Shaken Authority: China's Communist Party and the 2008 Sichuan Earthquake.* Ithaca, NY: Cornell University Press.

Spector, Regine A. 2008. "Bazaar Politics: The Fate of Marketplaces in Kazakhstan." *Problems of Post-Communism* 55 (6): 42–53.

Spector, Regine A. 2017. *Order at the Bazaar: Power and Trade in Central Asia.* Ithaca, NY: Cornell University Press.

Sperling, Valerie. 2015. *Sex, Politics and Putin: Political Legitimacy in Russia.* New York: Oxford University Press.

Ssorin-Chaikov, Nikolai. 2000. "Bear Skins and Macaroni: The Social Life of Things at the Margins of a Siberian State Collective." In *The Vanishing Rouble: Barter Networks and Non-Monetary Transactions in Post-Soviet Societies,* ed. Paul Seabright, 345–361. Cambridge: Cambridge University Press.

Ssorin-Chaikov, Nikolai V. 2003. *The Social Life of the State in Subarctic Siberia.* Stanford, CA: Stanford University Press.

Stent, Angela. 2020. "Russia and China: Axis of Revisionists?" Washington, DC: Brookings Institution, February. https://www.brookings.edu/wp-content/uploads/2020/02/FP_202002_russia_china_stent.pdf.

Stephan, John J. 1994. *The Russian Far East: A History.* Stanford, CA: Stanford University Press.

Stern, Rachel E. 2013. *Environmental Litigation in China: A Study in Political Ambivalence.* Cambridge: Cambridge University Press.

Stites, Richard. 1999. "Crowded on the Edge of Vastness: Observations on Russian Space and Place." In *Beyond the Limits: The Concept of Space in Russian History and Culture,* ed. Jeremy Smith, 259–270. Helsinki: Finnish Literature Society.

Stronski, Paul, and Nicole Ng. 2018. "Cooperation and Competition: Russia and China in Central Asia, the Russian Far East, and the Arctic." Carnegie Endowment for International Peace, February. https://carnegieendowment.org/files/CP_331_Stronski_Ng_Final1.pdf.

Struve, Lynn. 2004. "Introduction." In *The Qing Formation in World Historical Time,* ed. Lynn Struve, 1–56. Cambridge, MA: Harvard University Asia Center.

Summers, Tim. 2016. "China's 'New Silk Roads': Sub-National Regions and Networks of Global Political Economy." *Third World Quarterly* 37 (9): 1628–1643.

Sun, Yanfei, and Maria Tysiachniouk. 2008. "Caged by Boundaries? NGO Cooperation at the Sino-Russian Border." In *China's Embedded Activism: Opportunities and Constraints of a Social Movement,* ed. Peter Ho and Louis Edmonds, 171–194. Abingdon, UK: Routledge.

Toal, Gerard. 2017. *Near Abroad: Putin, the West, and the Contest over Ukraine and the Caucasus.* Oxford: Oxford University Press.

Tsing, Anna Lowenhaupt. 2005. *Friction: An Ethnography of Global Connection.* Princeton, NJ: Princeton University Press.

Tuan, Yi-Fu. 1974. *Topophilia: A Study of Environmental Perception Attitudes and Values.* Englewood Cliffs, NJ: Prentice-Hall.

Tuan, Yi-Fu. 1977. *Space and Place: The Perspective of Experience.* Minneapolis: University of Minnesota Press.

Urbansky, Sören. 2020. *Beyond the Steppe Frontier: A History of the Sino-Russian Border.* Princeton, NJ: Princeton University Press.

Venturi, Robert, Denise Scott Brown, and Steven Izenour. 1977. *Learning from Las Vegas: The Forgotten Symbolism of Architectural Form.* Cambridge, MA: MIT Press.

Vezhenovets, A. F. 2010. "Chelovek i Amur." *Dal'nevostochnyi Kraeved* 48 (3): 140–146.

Volland, Nicolai. 2017. *Socialist Cosmopolitanism: The Chinese Literary Universe, 1945–1965.* New York: Columbia University Press.

Wang, Ning. 2017. *Banished to the Great Northern Wilderness: Political Exile and Re-education in Mao's China.* Ithaca, NY: Cornell University Press.

Wang, Xiaowei. 2020. *Blockchain Chicken Farm and Other Stories of Tech in China's Countryside.* New York: Farrar, Straus and Giroux.

Wang, Xinyuan. 2016. *Social Media in Industrial China.* London: UCL Press.

Weinberg, Robert. 1998. *Stalin's Forgotten Zion: Birobidzhan and the Making of a Soviet Jewish Homeland.* Berkeley: University of California Press.

Whately, Ben. 2005. *Black Dragon River.* Milton Keynes, UK: Lightning Source.

Widdis, E. 2004. "Russia as Space." In *National Identity in Russian Culture,* ed. S. Franklin and E. Widdis, 30–50. Cambridge: Cambridge University Press.

Winter, Tim. 2019. *Geocultural Power: China's Quest to Revive the Silk Roads for the Twenty-First Century.* Chicago: University of Chicago Press.

Wishnick, Elizabeth. 2011. *Mending Fences: The Evolution of Moscow's China Policy from Brezhnev to Yeltsin.* Seattle: University of Washington Press.

Woodworth, Max D., and Jeremy L. Wallace. 2017. "Seeing Ghosts: Parsing China's 'Ghost City' Controversy." *Urban Geography* 38 (8): 1270–1281.

Xie, Yuanyuan. 2018. "From Hunters to Herders: Reflections on the 'Ecological Migration' of the Chinese Evenki Reindeer-Herders." *Études mongoles et sibériennes, centrasiatiques et tibétaines* 49.

Xu Zhangrun. 2020. "Viral Alarm: When Fury Overcomes Fear," *Journal of Democracy* 31 (2): 5–23.

Yan, Yunxiang. 2003. *Private Life under Socialism: Love, Intimacy, and Family Change in a Chinese Village, 1949–1999*. Stanford, CA: Stanford University Press.

Yang, Fan. 2016. *Faked in China: Nation Branding, Counterfeit Culture, and Globalization*. Bloomington: Indiana University Press.

Yankov, K. V., A. K. Moiseev, and D. A. Efgrafov. 2016. "Problems and Prospects of Economic Zones in Russia." *Studies on Russian Economic Development* 27 (3): 311–317.

Yu Bin. 2018. "Between Past and Future: Implications of Sino-Russian Relations for the United States." *Asia Policy* 13 (1): 12–18.

Yu, Hong. 2016. "Urbanization and Its Impact in China." In *Understanding Chinese Society*, ed. Xiaowei Zhang, 2nd ed., 149–164. Abingdon, UK: Routledge.

Yu Hua. 2011. "山寨 Copycat." In *China in Ten Words*. London: Duckworth Overlook.

Zatsepine, Victor. 2007. "The Amur: As River, as Border." In *The Chinese State at the Borders*, ed. Diana Lary. Vancouver: University of British Columbia Press.

Zatsepine, Victor. 2011. "The Blagoveshchensk Massacre of 1900: The Sino-Russian War and Global Imperialism." In *Beyond Suffering: Recounting War in Modern China*, ed. James Flath and Norman Smith, 107–129. Vancouver: University of British Columbia Press.

Zatsepine, Victor. 2018. *Beyond the Amur: Frontier Encounters between China and Russia, 1850–1930*. Vancouver: UBC Press.

Zee, Jerry. 2017. "Holding Patterns: Sand and Political Time at China's Desert Shores." *Cultural Anthropology* 32 (2): 215–241.

Zee, Jerry. 2020. "Downwind: Three Phases of an Aerosol Form." In *Voluminous States: Sovereignty, Materiality, and the Territorial Imagination*, ed. Franck Billé, 119–130. Durham, NC: Duke University Press.

Zenz, Adrian. 2020. "Sterilizations, Forced Abortions, and Mandatory Birth Control: The CCP's Campaign to Suppress Uyghur Birthrates in Xinjiang." Jamestown Foundation, Washington, DC. https:// jamestown.org/wp-content/uploads/2020/06/Zenz-Sterilizations -IUDs-and-Mandatory-Birth-Control-FINAL-27June.pdf?x71937.

Zhanaev, Ayur. 2019. *The Human Being in Social and Cosmic Orders: Categories of Traditional Culture and the Problems of Contemporary Buryat Identity.* Warsaw: Wydawnictwa Uniwersytetu Warszawskiego.

Zhang, Zhenqing, Thomas Bianchette, Meng Caihong, Qinghai Xu, and Ming Jiang. 2020. "Holocene Vegetation-Hydrology-Climate Interactions of Wetlands on the Heixiazi Island, China." *Science of the Total Environment* 743: 1–10.

Zhidkevich, N. N. 2016. "Sotsial'nyi portret sovremennogo rossiiskogo otkhodnika." *Zhurnal sotsiologii i sotsial'noi antropologii* 19 (1): 73–89.

Zhou, Jiayi. 2017. "Chinese Agrarian Capitalism in the Russian Far East." *Third World Thematics: A TWQ Journal* 1 (5): 612–632.

Ziegler, Dominic. 2015. *Black Dragon River: A Journey down the Amur River between Russia and China.* New York: Penguin.

Zuenko, Ivan. 2017a. "Byurokraktiya v usloviyakh frontira: Problema effektivnosti regional'nykh vlastei v rossiisko-kitaiskikh otnosheniyakh." *Zhurnal Frontirnykh Issledovanii* 1): 51–64.

Zuenko, Ivan. 2017b. "Ukreplenie 'vertikali vlasti' po-kitaiski: Kadrovaya politika v otnoshenii regional'nogo rukovodstva v sovremennom Kitae." *Outlines of Global Transformations* 10 (3): 30–46.

ACKNOWLEDGMENTS

On the Edge would never have seen the light of day without our many interlocutors in China and Russia who kindly shared their expert views and, in some cases, their experiences and life stories with us. Thank you to Boris V. Bazarov, Bi Aonan, Chen Xiangjun, Yang Cheng, Nikolay and Olga Kukarenko, Nina Namsaraeva, Alina Novopashina, Altan Ochir, Darima Ochirova, Daria Palmer, Igor Putilov, Sargai Sha, Portia Spinks, Nikolai Tsyrempilov, Olga Vasilyeeva, Wang Yisha, Xing Guangcheng, Yi Tang, Tatyana Zhuravskaya, and the many others who for various reasons had to remain anonymous.

We are also extremely grateful to the many colleagues who have generously provided feedback, additional materials, suggestions, and criticisms as we were writing this book, in particular Dominic Martin, Sayana Namsaraeva, Hyun-Gwi Park, Ed Pulford, Natalia Ryzhova, and Sören Urbansky, who have become good friends. Thanks also go to the members of our research project, "Where Rising Powers Meet," which ran at the University of Cambridge between 2012 and 2015: Nasan Bayar, Mikkel Bunkenborg, Grégory Delaplace, Gaëlle Lacaze, Morten Axel Pedersen, Ivan Peshkov, Maria Repnikova, Ivan Sablin, Tatiana Safonova, István Sántha, and Olga Shaglanova. For more information on this project, see https://www.miasu.socanth.cam.ac.uk/projects/where-rising-powers -meet-china-and-russia-their-north-asian-border. Libby Peachey provided unstinting administrative support during both the project and the writing of the manuscript. This book also benefited from valuable insights from our colleagues, both at Cambridge (Uranchimeg Borjigin, Uradyn Bulag, Adam Chau, Elvira Churyumova, Paula Haas, Kun-Chin Lin, Nayanika Mathur, Tim Reilly, David Sneath, Baasanjav Terbish, Hürelbaatar Ujeed, Piers Vitebsky, Tom White, and Ruiyi Zhu) and beyond

(Marina Baldano, Elena Barabantseva, Viktor Dyatlov, Natalie Koch, Adam Levy, Ekaterina Mikhailova, Lisa Sang-Mi Min, Paul Richardson, Aimar Ventsel, Aleksei Yurchak, Victor Zatsepine, and Yong Zhou). We are grateful to Ed Pulford for taking the time to read the manuscript and for offering comments and suggestions.

We thank our editor at Harvard University Press, Ian Malcolm, for his enthusiasm and unwavering support for the project, his many helpful suggestions, and his great patience. Thank you also to John Isom at the University of California, Berkeley, for the maps. We acknowledge with gratitude the grant from Economic and Social Sciences Research Council (UK) that funded the research project, and the Mongolia and Inner Asia Studies Unit at the University of Cambridge for its financial support in the writing of this book.

Franck also wishes to thank his wonderful colleagues at UC Berkeley's Institute of East Asian Studies, particularly Martin Backstrom, Shane Carter, Karen Clancy, Dylan Davies, Sanjyot Mehendale, and Angel Ryono. Special thanks also go to his family—his husband, Valerio, and their son, Milo, his parents, Jean-Pierre and Josiane, and his sister, Lori.

Caroline is, as always, deeply grateful to her husband, Martin Rees, for his unwavering support and loving care.

INDEX